Lecture Notes in Artificial Intelligence 1111

Subseries of Lecture Notes in Computer Science
Edited by J. G. Carbonell and J. Siekmann

Lecture Notes in Computer Science

Edited by G. Goos, J. Hartmanis and J. van Leeuwen

Springer
Berlin
Heidelberg
New York
Barcelona
Budapest
Hong Kong
London
Milan
Paris
Santa Clara
Singapore
Tokyo

José Júlio Alferes   Luís Moniz Pereira

Reasoning with Logic Programming

 Springer

Series Editors
Jaime G. Carbonell, Carnegie Mellon University, Pittsburgh, PA, USA
Jörg Siekmann, University of Saarland, Saarbrücken, Germany

Authors

José Júlio Alferes
Universidade de Evora, Departamento de Matematica
Largo dos Colegiais, 7000 Evora, Portugal

Luís Moniz Pereira
Universidade Nova de Lisboa, Departamento de Informatica
2825 Monte da Caparica, Portugal

Cataloging-in-Publication Data applied for

Die Deutsche Bibliothek - CIP-Einheitsaufnahme

Alferes, José Júlio:
Reasoning with logic programming / José Júlio Alferes ; Luís
Moniz Pereira. - Berlin ; Heidelberg ; New York ; Barcelona ;
Hong Kong ; London ; Milan ; Paris ; Santa Clara ; Singapore ;
Tokyo : Springer, 1996
  (Lecture notes in computer science ; 1111 : Lecture notes in artificial
  intelligence)
  ISBN 3-540-61488-5
NE: Pereira, Luís Moniz:; GT

CR Subject Classification (1991): I.2.3-6, D.1.6,F.3-4, D.3

ISBN 3-540-61488-5 Springer-Verlag Berlin Heidelberg New York

© Springer-Verlag Berlin Heidelberg 1996
Printed in Germany

Typesetting: Camera ready by author
SPIN 10513233   06/3142 – 5 4 3 2 1 0   Printed on acid-free paper

Preface

The book and its readership

The present book[1] provides a rigorous treatment and coherent presentation of the consolidated results of the authors' work, over the past four years, on the employment of logic programming as a representational and reasoning tool. It comes out of a background of a world-wide research effort for at least the past six years on the improvement of the semantical basis, the procedures, and the applications of logic programs, thereby showing how they can be used to enact ever wider forms of reasoning by virtue of their rich knowledge representation ability.

The book is a research monograph intended for a diverse public at the post-graduate level: for AI researchers looking for a representation language and implementation vehicle for carrying out reasoning tasks; for those interested in the relationships between logic programming and non-monotonic reasoning, both from a theoretical and an implementation viewpoint; for those of the logic programming persuasion wishing to use logic programming for non-monotonic reasoning; for the Prolog aficionados looking to overcome some of its limitations.

The book also serves as a good platform for understanding the exciting innovations and ongoing research in this rapidly evolving field. It is suitable as well for a MSc level course, and the material has in fact been used by us for just that purpose.

Because our theoretical developments have been implemented – and an interpreter listing is included here – this book functions as a reference book for a readily usable tool.

The book is self-contained: it includes a brief historical overview with pointers to main references, it reviews and compares the main approaches in the field to our own, and it contains all proofs and basic definitions, though the interest reader will want to consult, e.g., [200, 201, 172, 131, 16], for more extensive overviews of its subject matter and surrounding areas.

It shows a variety of applications that illustrate the use, wide scope, and potential of logic programming for performing various types of reasoning,

---

[1] We are honoured to have been awarded in 1995 for this book "Prémio Boa Esperança", the highest science prize from the Portuguese government.

namely non-monotonic ones such as: dealing with incomplete information; default, hypothetical and counterfactual reasoning; contradiction handling; belief revision; and abduction. And it shows a variety of knowledge representation forms such as: falsity, both via explicit negation and (implicit) default negation (or by failure); constraints (denials); default rules; exceptions to defaults; preferences among defaults; hypothetical possibility rules; etc.

Consequently, the book emphasizes the relationships between logic programming and non-monotonic reasoning formalisms, such as default logic, auto-epistemic logic, and circumscription. Non-monotonic reasoning formalisms provide elegant semantics for logic programming, especially in what regards the meaning of negation as failure (or by default); non-monotonic reasoning formalisms help one understand how logic programming can be used to formalize and solve several problems in AI; non-monotonic reasoning formalisms benefit from the existing procedures of logic programming; and, finally, new problems of non-monotonic reasoning are raised and solved by logic programming.

All the examples have been successfully run using the Prolog interpreter that implements top-down procedures for our language, inserted in the appendix. The application domains include: taxonomies with exceptions and preferences, reasoning about actions, model based diagnosis, and declarative debugging.

The detailed structure and contents of the book are presented further below.

The title explained

For some time now, programming in logic has been shown to be a viable proposition. Since the mid-1950s, the desire to impart the computer with the ability to reason logically has led to the development of automated theorem proving, which took up the promise of giving logic to artificial intelligence. As a result of the effort to find simple and efficient theorem proving strategies, Horn clause programming under SLD resolution was discovered and implemented [106, 44].

However, because Horn clauses admit only positive conclusions or facts, they give rise to a monotonic semantics, i.e. one by which previous conclusions are never questioned in spite of additional information, and thus the number of derived conclusions cannot decrease – hence the monotonicity. Also, nothing can be concluded false, except by assuming that that which is not finitely proven true is false. But this condition prevents, by definition, the appearance of any and all contradictions.

Thus, although Horn clause programming augmented with the NOT operator (i.e. Prolog), under the SLDNF derivation procedure [118], does allow negative conclusions; these are only drawn by default (or implicitly), just in case the corresponding positive conclusion is not forthcoming in a finite number of steps, when taking the program as it stands – hence the specific form of Closed World Assumption (CWA) [187] of the completion semantics given to such programs [42].

This form of negation is capable of dealing with incomplete information, by assuming false exactly what is not true in a finite manner. However, there remains the issue of non-terminating computations, even for finite programs. To deal with this and other problems of the completion semantics, a spate of semantic proposals were set forth from the late 1980s onwards, of which the well-founded semantics of [76] is an outcome. It deals semantically with non-terminating computations by assigning such computations the truth value "false" or "undefined", and thereby giving semantics to every program. Moreover it enjoys a number of desirable structural properties spelled out further below.

The well-founded semantics deals with normal programs, i.e. those with only negation by default, and thus it provides no mechanism for explicitly declaring the falsity of literals. As argued in Chapter 2, this can be a serious limitation. In fact, several authors have recently stressed and shown the importance of including a second kind of negation "¬" in logic programs, for use in deductive databases, knowledge representation, and non-monotonic reasoning [18, 80, 81, 91, 104, 107, 141, 154, 157, 159, 162, 209].

Our own Well-Founded Semantics with eXplicit negation, *WFSX*, incorporates into the language of logic programs an explicit form of negation, in addition to the previous implicit negation, relates the two, and extends to this richer language the well-founded semantics.

Of course, introducing explicit negation now requires dealing in addition with veritable contradiction. Indeed, information is not only normally incomplete but contradictory to boot. Consequently, not all negation by default assumptions can be made, but only those not leading to contradiction. This is tantamount to the ancient and venerable logical principle of "reductio ad absurdum": *if an assumption leads to contradiction withdraw it*. One major contribution of our work is that of tackling this issue within our semantics of extended logic programs.

The two forms of negation, default and explicit, are related: our "coherence principle" stipulates that the latter entails the former. Whereas default negation, and the revision of believed assumptions in the face of contradiction, are the two non-monotonic reasoning mechanisms available in logic programming, their use in combination with explicit negation adds on a qualitative representational expressivity that can capture a wide variety of logical reasoning forms, and serve as an instrument for programming them. Hence the title of the book.

Furthermore, it should be noted that our explicit negation differs from classical negation. In particular, the principle of the excluded middle is not adopted, and so neither is classical case analysis, whereby given p if q, and given p if *not* q, then p. Indeed, propositions are not just true or false, exclusively. For one, they may be both true and false. Moreover, once contradiction is removed, even so a proposition and its negation may both be undefined. In fact, truth in logic programming should be taken in an auto-epistemic sense: truth is provability from an agent's knowledge, and possibily neither a proposition nor its negation might be provable from its present knowledge – their truth-value status' might be undefined for both. Hence case analysis is not justified: p may rest undefined if q is undefined as well.

This is reasonable because the truth of q is not something that either holds or not, inasmuch as it can refer to the agent's ability to deduce q, or some other agent's view of q. For that matter, the supposition that either q holds or does not hold might be contradictory with the rest of the agent's knowledge in either case.

There's a crucial distinction to be made between ontological, real world truth, and epistemic, internal world truth. If an agent wants to posit that, about some particular propositional symbol q, either q or the negation of q is held by the agent then this should be duly and explicitly expressed by the disjunction $q \lor \neg q$, and not by some general, and implicit, excluded middle principle.

Also, the procedural nature of logic programming requires that each conclusion be supported by some identifiable rule with a true body whose conclusion it is, not simply by alternatively applicable rules, as in case analysis. Conclusions must be procedurally grounded on known facts. This requirement is conducive to a sceptical view of derived knowledge, which disallows jumping to conclusions when that is not called for.

A formal analysis and clarification of the auto-epistemic nature of logic programming is an important contribution of this book.

Innovations

The main original contributions of the present work are:

- The *WFSX*, a new semantics for logic programs with explicit negation (i.e. extended logic programs), which compares favorably in its properties with other extant semantics.
- A generic characterization schema that facilitates comparisons among a diversity of semantics of extended logic programs, including *WFSX*.
- An autoepistemic and a default logic corresponding to *WFSX*, which solve existing problems of the classical approaches to autoepistemic and default logics, and clarify the meaning of explicit negation in logic programs.
- A framework for defining a spectrum of semantics of extended logic programs based on the abduction of negative hypotheses. This framework allows for the characterization of different levels of scepticism/credulity, consensuality, and argumentation. One of the semantics of abduction coincides with *WFSX*. The techniques used for doing so are applicable as well to the well-founded semantics of normal logic programs.

- By introducing explicit negation into logic programs contradiction may appear. We present two approaches for dealing with contradiction, and prove their equivalence. One of the approaches consists in avoiding contradiction, and is based on restrictions in the adoption of abductive hypotheses. The other approach consists in removing contradiction, and is based on a transformation of contradictory programs into noncontradictory ones, guided by the reasons for contradiction.
- Finally, we proffer an innovative top-down derivation procedure for *WFSX*, of which those for well-founded semantics are a special case, and prove its correctness. Based on it, a query evaluation procedure and an optimized contradiction removal method are defined. [2] For generality, and because contradiction checking and removal is available, the implementation deals with the paraconsistent case too.

Over our semantics several approaches to disjunction might be constructed. We have not adopted any one approach because the ongoing research on disjunction for logic programs is still stabilizing, though we favor one similar to that of [184, 31, 33, 32]. One problem is that none of the proposals to date include explicit negation as we define it. Another is that contradiction removal methods when disjunction is involved have yet to be devised and given a semantics. We are working towards a satisfactory solution to these issues. Until one is found it would premature to incorporate fully fledged disjunction. For the moment though, denials can capture the intended effect of some uses of disjunction.

Main advantages of our approach

We've developed an evolved semantical tool for logic programs (*WFSX*) that we feel constitutes a qualitative leap for expressing knowledge in logic programming, that handles loops, and that characterizes and propitiates a variety of reasoning forms.

Because of its properties, which other approaches do not fully enjoy, it is a natural candidate to be the semantics of choice for logic programs extended with explicit negation (as opposed to having just an implicit default negation).

Namely, *WFSX* exhibits the structural properties of simplicity, cumulativity, rationality, relevance, and partial evaluation. By simplicity we mean that it can be simply characterized by two iterative fixpoint operators, without recourse to three-valued logic. By cumulativity [108, 53, 57] we refer to the efficiency related ability of using lemmas, i.e. the addition of lemmas does not change the semantics of a program. By rationality [108, 53, 57] we refer to the ability to add the negation of a non-provable conclusion without

---

[2] Very special thanks go to our colleague Carlos Viegas Damásio, who co-authors the procedural and implementational work.

changing the semantics, this being important for efficient default reasoning. By relevance [54, 58] we mean that the top-down evaluation of a literal's truth-value requires only the call-graph below it. By partial evaluation we mean that the semantics of a partially evaluated program keeps to that of the original[3].

Also, it has the implementational properties of amenability to both top-down and bottom-up procedures, and the complexity for finite DATALOG programs is polynomial[4].

It is adequate for these forms of reasoning: incomplete information, contradiction handling, belief revision, default, abductive, counterfactual, and hypothetical.

It is adequate for these knowledge representation forms: rules, default rules, constraints (denials), exceptions to defaults, preferences among defaults, hypothetical possibilities, and falsity (whether via explicit or default negation).

It is the only well-founded based semantics with explicit negation which has been given default theory and auto-epistemic logic readings.

Structure of the book

This work is divided into three quite distinct parts: the first gives a brief historical overview of the field of logic programming semantics; the second presents a new semantics for extended logic programming; and the third illustrates the usefulness of the semantics in several examples from distinct domains.

For the sake of completeness we present, in Appendix A, a Prolog top-down interpreter for our semantics *WFSX*, and in Appendix B a Prolog pre-processor for removing contradictions: Appendix C contains the proofs of theorems that, for the sake of continuity, were not inserted along the way in the text.

The aim of the first part is to sensitize the reader to the issue of logic programming semantics, provide background and notation, and make clear the state of the art in the area at the inception of the work reported in this book.

In Chapter 1, we begin by defining the language of normal logic programs. Then we briefly describe several approaches to the semantics of normal programs, and their treatment of negation as failure. Special attention is given

---

[3] Stable model based approaches, such as answer-sets, enjoy neither cumulativity, nor rationality.

[4] Not so for stable model based approaches: there are no iterative top-down or bottom-up operators, and the complexity for computing the stable models of a program is NP-complete, even for DATALOG.

to the stable models and well-founded semantics, for which the formal definitions are presented.

In Chapter 2, we start by providing some motivation for extended logic programs, i.e. normal logic programs extended with explicit negation, and define their language. Next, we present several extant semantics for such programs.

The structure of the second part is as follows:

We begin, in Chapter 3, with the motivation for a new semantics of extended logic programs. There, we point out why we are not completely satisfied with other present-day semantics, and proffer some intuitively appealing properties a semantics should comply with.

In Chapter 4, we expound *WFSX*, a semantics for extended logic programs that subsumes the well founded semantics of normal programs. We begin by providing definitions of interpretation and model, for programs extended with explicit negation. Next we introduce the notion of stability in models, and use it to define the *WFSX*. Finally, some of its properties are examined, with a special focus on those concerning its existence.

The first part of Chapter 5 is devoted to contrasting and characterizing a variety of semantics for extended logic programs, including *WFSX*, in what concerns their use of a second kind of negation and the meaning ascribed it, and how the latter negation is related to both classical negation and default negation (or negation as failure). For this purpose we define a parametrizeable schema to characterize and encompass a diversity of proposed semantics for extended logic programs. In the second part of that chapter, and based on the similarities between the parametrizable schema and the definitions of autoepistemic logics, we proceed to examine the relationship between the latter and extended logic programs. By doing so, an epistemic meaning of the second kind of negation is extracted. The relationship results clarify the use of logic programs for representing knowledge and belief.

Chapter 6 presents a semantics for default theories, and shows its rapport with *WFSX*. First we point out some issues faced by semantics for default theories, and identify some basic principles a default theory semantics should enjoy. Second, we present a default semantics that resolves the issues whilst respecting the principles (which other semantics don't). Afterwards we prove the close correspondence between default theories under such a semantics and *WFSX*. Based on this correspondence result, in Section 6.7 we supply an important alternative definition of *WFSX* not relying on 3-valued logic but instead on 2-valued logic alone, by means of a variation of Gelfond and Lifschitz's Γ operator. The reader interested in this Γ-like formulation may skip other sections of Chapter 6 and go directly to Section 6.7.

Subsequently, in Chapter 7, we characterize a spectrum of more or less sceptical and credulous semantics for extended logic programs, and determine the position of *WFSX* in this respect. We do so by means of a coherent, flexible, unifying, and intuitive appealing framework for the study of explicit negation in logic programs, based on the notion of admissible scenarios. The main idea of the framework is to consider default literals as abducibles, i.e. they can be hypothesized. In the same chapter we also bring out the intimate relationship between this approach and argumentation systems.

With the introduction of explicit negation into logic programs contradiction may arise. In Chapter 8, we put forth two approaches for dealing with contradiction: one persists in avoiding it, based on a generalization of the framework of Chapter 7, whereby additional restrictions on the adoption of abductive hypotheses are imposed; the other approach consists in removing contradiction, and relies on a transformation of contradictory programs into noncontradictory ones, guided by the reasons for contradiction. Moreover we show that the contradiction avoidance semantics of a program P is equivalent to the $WFSX$ of the program resulting from P by transforming it according to the contradiction removal methods.

In Chapter 9, we produce additional properties of $WFSX$, including complexity, and make further comparisons with other semantics on the basis of those properties (which are essentially structural in nature).

Lastly in this part, in Chapter 10 we provide a top-down derivation procedure for $WFSX$.

The aim of the third part is to employ the theoretical results of the second part in several illustrative examples from distinct domains. Its structure is as follows:

We begin, in Chapter 11, by showing how to cast in the language of extended logic programs different forms of nonmonotonic reasoning such as defeasible reasoning, abductive reasoning and hypothetical reasoning, and apply it to several classical problems in diverse domains of knowledge representation such as hierarchies and reasoning about actions and counterfactuals.

In Chapter 12, and with the help of examples, we illustrate the usefulness of extended logic programming and our semantics in diagnosis, in declarative debugging, and in knowledge base updates. To do so we begin by generalizing the contradiction removal methods of Chapter 8 to 2-valued revision, i.e. revision whereby when unassuming some hypothesis its complement is assumed instead.

The best way to read this book is by going through the chapters in the sequence they appear. However, if the reader is not interested in the whole work, or is more keen on some issues than others, alternative reading paths are possible; they are shown in Figure 0.1.

If you are familiar with the issue of extended logic programs semantics you might skip the first part, i.e. Chapters 1 and 2.

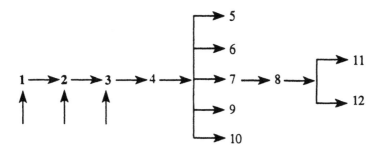

Fig. 0.1. Reading paths, and three possible entry points.

If you are familiar with the issue of normal logic programs semantics, but not with explicit negation, you might skip Chapter 1 and start with Chapter 2. Otherwise, you should start by reading the first part.

The table below indicates, for different possible interests, the corresponding reading paths of Figure 0.1:

Definition of *WFSX*	$3 \rightarrow 4 \rightarrow 6.7$
Extended logic programs and autoepistemic logics	$3 \rightarrow 4 \rightarrow 5$
Extended logic programs and default logic	$3 \rightarrow 4 \rightarrow 6$
ELPs abduction, and argumentation	$3 \rightarrow 4 \rightarrow 7$
Extended logic programs and belief revision	$3 \rightarrow 4 \rightarrow 7 \rightarrow 8$
WFSX, its structural properties, and complexity	$3 \rightarrow 4 \rightarrow 9$
Top-down derivation procedures for *WFSX*	$3 \rightarrow 4 \rightarrow 10$
Application to classical NMR problems	$3 \rightarrow 4 \rightarrow 7 \rightarrow 8 \rightarrow 11$
Application to diagnosis	$3 \rightarrow 4 \rightarrow 7 \rightarrow 8 \rightarrow 12$
Application to Prolog debugging	$3 \rightarrow 4 \rightarrow 7 \rightarrow 8 \rightarrow 12$

June 1996   José Júlio Alferes and Luís Moniz Pereira

Acknowledgements

This book has grown out of part of one author's PhD thesis [12], supervised by the other author. The thesis itself was based on joint work over three years and more than twenty papers published together in conferences and journals. Some of the papers whose material was used in the thesis, as well as additional ones, were co-authored either by Joaquim Nunes Aparício or Carlos Viegas Damásio, both at the time PhD students of Luís Moniz Pereira at Universidade Nova de Lisboa, and under the support of the European ESPRIT basic research projects COMPULOG and COMPULOG 2. To both our colleagues we express our gratitude, for all their stimulus and effort put in the work done together, and for their permission to use our joint results in this book.

We thank too all our colleagues in the two COMPULOG projects who, with their opinions, ideas and publications over the years, have helped us to better forge and shape our own. Special thanks are due to Tony Kakas, Bob Kowalski, and Paolo Mancarella, for such reasons.

We thank Phan Minh Dung, from the Asian Institute of Technology in Bangkok, for permission to use important material from a joint paper, [4], for his influential pioneering opinions, and for his camaraderie.

We thank also our colleagues in the USA, Michael Gelfond, Vladimir Lifschitz, Halina Przymusinska, and Teodor Przymusinski, for all their ground breaking work in this field, and for their helpful discussions with us.

Finally, we wish to acknowledge the organizational and financial support of the AI Centre of UNINOVA, of the Department of Computer Science of Universidade Nova de Lisboa, and of the Junta Nacional de Investigação Científica e Tecnológica, in Portugal.

Table of Contents

Preface V
  The book and its readership V
  The title explained VI
  Innovations VIII
  Main advantages of our approach IX
  Structure of the book... X

Acknowledgements XV

Part I. Semantics of Logic Programs: A brief overview

1. **Normal logic programs** 5
   1.1 Language... 5
        1.1.1 Interpretations and models 6
   1.2 Semantics 8
        1.2.1 Stable model semantics 11
        1.2.2 Well-founded semantics 14

2. **Extended logic programs** 17
   2.1 Language... 20
   2.2 Semantics 21
        2.2.1 Stable Models based semantics 21
        2.2.2 Well-founded based semantics 26
        2.2.3 Other approaches 27

Part II. A New Semantics for Extended Logic Programs

3. **Why a new semantics for extended programs?** 31

4. *WFSX* – **A well founded semantics for extended logic programs** 37
   4.1 Interpretations and models 37

4.2   The definition of *WFSX* 39
4.3   Existence of the semantics 45

5.   *WFSX*, **LP semantics with two negations, and autoepistemic**
     logics 49
     5.1   Generic semantics for programs with two kinds of negation .. 50
           5.1.1   Preliminaries 51
           5.1.2   Stationary and stable semantics for programs with two
                   kinds of negation 51
                   The parametrizeable schema 57
           5.1.3   Properties required of ¬ 58
           5.1.4   Fixing the set $AX_\neg$ and the condition $not_{cond}(L)$ 60
                   WFSX and strong negation 63
           5.1.5   Logic programs with ¬-negation and disjunction...... 65
     5.2   Autoepistemic logics for *WFSX* 67
           5.2.1   Moore's and Przymusinski's autoepistemic logics 68
           5.2.2   A logic of belief and provability 72
                   Provability in extended definite programs........... 72
                   Belief and provability 74
                   Relation to extended logic programs 78
           5.2.3   Provability versus knowledge..................... 79
           5.2.4   Further developments 80

6.   *WFSX* **and default logic** 83
     6.1   The language of defaults 84
           6.1.1   Reiter's default semantics 85
           6.1.2   Well-founded and stationary default semantics for nor-
                   mal logic programs 86
     6.2   Some principles required of default theories 87
     6.3 Ω-default theory 90
     6.4   Comparison with Reiter's semantics...................... 97
     6.5   Comparison with stationary default semantics.............. 99
     6.6   Relation between the semantics of default theories and logic
           programs with explicit negation 99
     6.7   A definition of *WFSX* based on Γ 101

7.   *WFSX* **and hypotheses abduction**........................ 107
     7.1   Admissible scenaria for extended logic programs........... 110
     7.2   A sceptical semantics for extended programs 117
     7.3   The semantics of complete scenaria 120
     7.4   Properties of complete scenaria......................... 123
           7.4.1   Complete scenaria and *WFSX* 125
     7.5   More credulous semantics............................... 125
           7.5.1   Comparisons among the semantics................. 127

8.   **Dealing with contradiction** 129
     8.1 Logic programming with denials 132
     8.2 Contradiction avoidance 133
          8.2.1 Primacy in optative reasoning 139
     8.3 Contradiction removal 142
          8.3.1 Paraconsistent *WFSX* 144
          8.3.2 Declarative revisions 149
          8.3.3 Contradiction support and removal 157
     8.4 Equivalence between avoidance and removal 164

9.   **Further properties and comparisons** 167
     9.1 Properties of *WFSX* 167
          9.1.1 Cumulativity and rationality 168
          9.1.2 Partial evaluation and relevance 173
          9.1.3 Complexity results 181
     9.2 Comparisons 182

10. **Top-down derivation procedures for *WFSX*** 187
     10.1 Semantic tree characterization of *WFSX* 188
     10.2 SLX – a derivation procedure for *WFSX* 193
          10.2.1 Correctness of SLX 195
     10.3 On guaranteeing termination of SLX 200
     10.4 Comparisons 203
     10.5 Further developments 205

Part III. Illustrative Examples of Application

11. **Application to classical nonmonotonic reasoning problems** 209
     11.1 Summary of our representation method 209
     11.2 Defeasible Reasoning 211
          11.2.1 Exceptions 213
                 Exceptions to predicates 213
                 Exceptions to rules 214
                 Exceptions to exceptions 214
          11.2.2 Preferences among rules 214
     11.3 Hierarchical taxonomies 215
     11.4 Hypothetical reasoning 218
          11.4.1 The birds world 218
          11.4.2 Hypothetical facts and rules 219
                 Hypothetical facts 220
                 Hypothetical rules 221
     11.5 Reasoning about actions 223
          11.5.1 The Yale shooting problem 224
          11.5.2 Multiple extensions 225

11.5.3 The Stolen car problem 226

11.5.4 Other reasoning about action problems............. 226

11.6 Counterfactual reasoning 227

11.6.1 Lewis's counterfactuals........................... 228

11.6.2 Counterfactual reasoning by revising assumptions 229

11.6.3 Lewis's similarity precepts obeyed 232

12. Application to diagnosis and debugging................... 235

12.1 Two-valued contradiction removal 237

12.1.1 Computing minimal two-valued revisions 239

12.2 Application to diagnosis 242

12.3 Application to debugging 253

12.3.1 Declarative error diagnosis........................ 255

12.3.2 What is diagnostic debugging? 257

12.3.3 Diagnosis as revision of program assumptions 261

12.4 Updating Knowledge Bases 266

References 271

Part IV. Appendices

A. Prolog top-down interpreter for *WFSX*.................... 285

B. A Prolog pre-processor for contradiction removal 287

C. Proofs of theorems 305

List of Figures

0.1 Possible reading paths XIII

8.1 Submodels lattice with indissociables......................... 152
8.2 Submodels lattice example................................. 153
8.3 Revisions of a program 155
8.4 Sceptical submodels and MNSs............................ 156

11.1 A hierarchical taxonomy 216
11.2 Model of the hierarchy 218
11.3 The birds example submodels lattice 219
11.4 The Nixon diamond 222
11.5 Submodels of the nixon-diamond problem using hypothetical rules 222
11.6 Counterfactuals example 231

12.1 Simple circuit 235
12.2 Two valued revisions................................... 241
12.3 The three or problem 245
12.4 A simple logic circuit 246
12.5 Diagnosis of the circuit 248
12.6 Two inverters circuit 248
12.7 Three bulbs circuit 250
12.8 Causal model in a mechanical domain 251
12.9 One inverter circuit 265

List of Figures

Part I

Semantics of Logic Programs: A brief overview

Computational Logic arose from the work, begun by logicians in the 1950's, on the automation of logical deduction, and was fostered in the 1970's by Colmerauer et al. [44] and Kowalski [101, 102] as Logic Programming. It introduced to computer science the important concept of *declarative* – as opposed to *procedural* – programming. Ideally, a programmer should only be concerned with the declarative meaning of his program, while the procedural aspects of program's execution are handled automatically. The Prolog language [44] became the privileged vehicle approximating this ideal. The first Prolog compiler [214] showed that it could be a practical language and disseminated it worldwide.

The developments of the formal foundations of logic programming began in the late 1970's, especially with the works [69, 42, 187]. Further progress in this direction was achieved in the early 1980's, leading to the appearance of the first book on the foundations of logic programming [118]. The selection of logic programming as the underlying paradigm for the Japanese Fifth Generation Computer Systems Project led to the rapid proliferation of various logic programming languages.

Due to logic programming's declarative nature, it quickly became a candidate for knowledge representation. Its adequateness became more apparent after the relationships established in the mid 1980's between logic programs and deductive databases [189, 73, 120, 121, 130].

The use of both logic programming and deductive databases for knowledge representation is based on the so called *"logical approach to knowledge representation"*. This approach rests on the idea of providing machines with a logical specification of the knowledge that they possess, thus making it independent of any particular implementation, context-free, and easy to manipulate and reason about.

Consequently, a precise meaning (or semantics) must be associated with any logic program in order to provide its declarative specification. The performance of any computational mechanism is then evaluated by comparing its behaviour to the specification provided by the declarative semantics. Finding a suitable declarative semantics for logic programs has been acknowledged as one of the most important and difficult research areas of logic programming.

In this part we make a quick historical overview of the results in the last 15 years in the area of logic program's declarative semantics. This overview is divided into two chapters. In the first we review some of the most important semantics of normal logic programs. In the second we motivate the need for extending logic programming with a second kind of negation, and overview recent semantics for such extended programs.

1. Normal logic programs

Several recent overviews of normal logic programming semantics can be found in the literature (e.g. [200, 201, 172, 131, 16, 59]). Here, for the sake of this monograph's self-sufficiency and to introduce some motivation, we distill a brief overview of the subject. In some parts we follow closely the overview of [172].

The structure of the chapter is as follows: first we present the language of normal logic programs and give some definitions needed in the sequel. Then we briefly recapitulate the first approaches to the semantics of normal programs and point out their problems. Finally, we expound in greater detail two of the more recent and important proposed semantical basis, namely stable models and well-founded semantics.

1.1 Language

By an alphabet $\mathcal{A}$ of a language $\mathcal{L}$ we mean a (finite or countably infinite) disjoint set of constants, predicate symbols, and function symbols. In addition, any alphabet is assumed to contain a countably infinite set of distinguished variable symbols. A term over $\mathcal{A}$ is defined recursively as either a variable, a constant or an expression of the form $f(t_1, \ldots, t_n)$, where f is a function symbol of $\mathcal{A}$, and the t_is are terms. An atom over $\mathcal{A}$ is an expression of the form $p(t_1, \ldots, t_n)$, where p is a predicate symbol of $\mathcal{A}$, and the t_is are terms. A literal is either an atom A or its negation $not\ A$. We dub default literals those of the form $not\ A$.

A term (resp. atom, literal) is called ground if it does not contain variables. The set of all ground terms (resp. atoms) of $\mathcal{A}$ is called the Herbrand universe (resp. base) of $\mathcal{A}$. For short we use $\mathcal{H}$ to denote the Herbrand base of $\mathcal{A}$.

A normal logic program is a finite set of rules of the form:

$$H \leftarrow L_1, \ldots, L_n \qquad (n \geq 0)$$

where H is an atom and each of the L_is is a literal. The comma operator is understood as conjunction. In conformity with the standard convention we write rules of the form $H \leftarrow$ also simply as H.

A normal logic program P is called definite if none of its rules contains default literals.

We assume that the alphabet $\mathcal{A}$ used to write a program P consists precisely of all the constants, and predicate and function symbols that explicitly appear in P. By Herbrand universe (resp. base) of P we mean the Herbrand universe (resp. base) of $\mathcal{A}$.

By grounded version of a normal logic program P we mean the (possibly infinite) set of ground rules obtained from P by substituting in all possible ways each of the variables in P by elements of its Herbrand universe.

In this work we restrict ourselves to Herbrand interpretations and models[1]. Thus, without loss of generality (cf. [172]), we coalesce a normal logic program P with its grounded version.

1.1.1 Interpretations and models

Next we define 2 and 3-valued Herbrand interpretations and models of normal logic programs. Since non-Herbrand interpretations are beyond the scope of this work, in the sequel we sometimes drop the qualification Herbrand.

Definition 1.1.1 (2-valued interpretation). *A 2-valued interpretation I of a normal logic program P is any subset of the Herbrand base $\mathcal{H}$ of P.*

Clearly, any 2-valued interpretation I can be equivalently viewed as a set

$$T \cup not\ F\ ^{2}$$

where $T = I$ and is the set of atoms which are true in I, and $F = \mathcal{H} - T$ is the set of atoms which are false in I. These interpretations are called 2-valued because in them each atom is either true or false, i.e. $\mathcal{H} = T \cup F$.

As argued in [172], interpretations of a given program P can be thought of as "possible worlds" representing possible states of our knowledge about the meaning of P. Since that knowledge is likely to be incomplete, we need the ability to describe interpretations in which some atoms are neither true nor false but rather undefined, i.e. we need 3-valued interpretations:

Definition 1.1.2 (3-valued interpretation). *By a 3-valued interpretation I of a program P we mean a set*

$$T \cup not\ F$$

where T and F are disjoint subsets of the Herbrand base $\mathcal{H}$ of P.

The set T (the T-part of I) contains all ground atoms true in I, the set F (the F-part of I) contains all ground atoms false in I, and the truth value of the remaining atoms is unknown (or undefined).

---

[1] For the subject of semantics based on non-Herbrand models, and solutions to the problems resulting from always keeping Herbrand models see e.g. [109, 178, 76].

[2] Where $not\ \{a_1, \ldots, a_n\}$ stands for $\{not\ a_1, \ldots, not\ a_n\}$.

It is clear that 2-valued interpretations are a special case of 3-valued ones, for which $\mathcal{H} = T \cup F$ is additionally imposed.

Proposition 1.1.1. *Any interpretation $I = T \cup not\ F$ can equivalently be viewed as a function $I : \mathcal{H} \to V$ where $V = \{0, \frac{1}{2}, 1\}$, defined by:*

$$I(A) = \begin{cases} 0 & if & not\ A \in I \\ 1 & if & A \in I \\ \frac{1}{2} & & otherwise \end{cases}$$

Of course, for 2-valued interpretations there is no atom A such that $I(A) = \frac{1}{2}$.

Models are defined as usual, and based on a truth valuation function:

Definition 1.1.3 (Truth valuation). *If I is an interpretation, the truth valuation $\hat{I}$ corresponding to I is a function $\hat{I} : C \to V$ where C is the set of all formulae of the language, recursively defined as follows:*

- *if A is a ground atom then $\hat{I}(A) = I(A)$.*
- *if S is a formula then $\hat{I}(not\ S) = 1 - \hat{I}(S)$.*
- *if S and V are formulae then*
  - *$\hat{I}((S,V)) = min(\hat{I}(S), \hat{I}(V))$.*
  - *$\hat{I}(V \leftarrow S) = 1$ if $\hat{I}(S) \leq \hat{I}(V)$, and 0 otherwise.*

Definition 1.1.4 (3-valued model). *A 3-valued interpretation I is called a 3-valued model of a program P iff for every ground instance of a program rule $H \leftarrow B$ we have $\hat{I}(H \leftarrow B) = 1$.*

The special case of 2-valued models has the following straightforward definition:

Definition 1.1.5 (2-valued model). *A 2-valued interpretation I is called a 2-valued model of a program P iff for every ground instance of a program rule $H \leftarrow B$ we have $\hat{I}(H \leftarrow B) = 1$.*

Some orderings among interpretations and models will be useful:

Definition 1.1.6 (Classical ordering). *If I and J are two interpretations then we say that $I \leq J$ if $I(A) \leq J(A)$ for any ground atom A. If $\mathcal{I}$ is a collection of interpretations, then an interpretation $I \in \mathcal{I}$ is called minimal in $\mathcal{I}$ if there is no interpretation $J \in \mathcal{I}$ such that $J \leq I$ and $I \neq J$. An interpretation I is called least in $\mathcal{I}$ if $I \leq J$ for any other interpretation $J \in \mathcal{I}$. A model M of a program P is called minimal (resp. least) if it is minimal (resp. least) among all models of P.*

Definition 1.1.7 (Fitting ordering). *If I and J are two interpretations then we say that $I \leq_F J$ [72] iff $I \subseteq J$. If $\mathcal{I}$ is a collection of interpretations, then an interpretation $I \in \mathcal{I}$ is called F-minimal in $\mathcal{I}$ if there is no interpretation $J \in \mathcal{I}$ such that $J \leq_F I$ and $I \neq J$. An interpretation I is called*

F-least in $\mathcal{I}$ if $I \leq_F J$ for any interpretation $J \in \mathcal{I}$. A model M of a program P is called F-minimal (resp. F-least) if it is F-minimal (resp. F-least) among all models of P.

Note that the classical ordering is related with the amount of true atoms, whereas the Fitting ordering is related with the amount of information, i.e. nonundefinedness.

1.2 Semantics

As argued above, a precise meaning or semantics must be associated with any logic program, in order to provide a declarative specification of it. Declarative semantics provides a mathematically precise definition of the meaning of a program, which is independent of its procedural executions, and is easy to manipulate and reason about.

In contrast, procedural semantics is usually defined as a procedural mechanism that is capable of providing answers to queries. The correctness of such a mechanism is evaluated by comparing its behaviour with the specification provided by the declarative semantics. Without the latter, the user needs an intimate knowledge of the procedural aspects in order to write correct programs.

The first attempt to provide a declarative semantics for logic programs is due to [69], and the main motivation behind their approach is based on the idea that one should minimize positive information as much as possible, limiting it to facts explicitly implied by a program, making everything else false. In other words, their semantics is based on a natural form of *"closed world assumption"* [187].

Example 1.2.1. Consider program P :

$$able\_mathematician(X) \quad \leftarrow \quad physicist(X)$$
$$physicist(einstein)$$
$$president(soares)$$

This program has several (2-valued) models, the largest of which is the model where both Einstein and Soares are at the same time presidents, physicists and able mathematicians. This model does not correctly describe the intended meaning of P, since there is nothing in P to imply that Soares is a physicist or that Einstein is a president. In fact, the lack of such information should instead indicate that we can assume the contrary.

This knowledge is captured by the least (2-valued) model of P :

$$\{physicist(einstein), able\_mathematician(einstein), president(soares)\}$$

The existence of a unique least model for every definite program (proven in [69]), led to the definition of the so called *"least model semantics"* for definite programs. According to that semantics an atom A is true in a program P iff it belongs to the least model of P; otherwise A is false.

It turns out that this semantics does not apply to programs with default negation. For example, the program $P = \{p \leftarrow not\ q\}$ has two minimal models, namely $\{p\}$ and $\{q\}$. Thus no least model exists.

In order to define a declarative semantics for normal logic programs with negation as failure[3], [42] introduced the so-called *"Clark's predicate completion"*. Informally, the basic idea of completion is that in common discourse we often tend to use "if" statements when we really mean "iff" ones. For instance, we may use the following program P to describe the natural numbers:

$$natural\_number(0)$$
$$natural\_number(succ(X)) \quad \leftarrow \quad natural\_number(X)$$

This program is too weak. It does not imply that nothing but $0, 1, \ldots$ is a natural number. In fact what we have in mind regarding program P is:

$$natural\_number(X) \Leftrightarrow X = 0 \lor$$
$$(\exists Y : X = succ(Y) \land natural\_number(Y))$$

Based on this idea Clark defined the completion of a program P, the semantics of P being determined by the 2-valued models of its completion.

However Clark's completion semantics has some serious drawbacks. One of the most important is that the completion of consistent programs may be inconsistent, thus failing to assign to those programs a meaning. For example the completion of the program $\{p \leftarrow not\ p\}$ is $\{p \Leftrightarrow not\ p\}$, which is inconsistent.

In [72], the author showed that the inconsistency problem for Clark's completion semantics can be elegantly eliminated by considering 3-valued models instead of 2-valued ones. This led to the definition of the so-called *"Fitting semantics"* for normal logic programs. In [109], Kunen showed that that semantics is not recursively enumerable, and proposed a modification.

Unfortunately, the "Fitting semantics" inherits several of the problems of Clark's completion semantics, and in many cases leads to a semantics that appears to be too weak. This issue has been extensively discussed in the literature (see e.g. [200, 178, 76]). Forthwith we illustrate some of these problems with the help of examples:

Example 1.2.2. [4] Consider program P :

---

[3] In this work we adopt the designation of *"negation by default"*. Recently, this designation has been used in the literature instead of the more operational *"negation as failure"*.

[4] This example first appeared in [76].

$$edge(a, b)$$
$$edge(c, d)$$
$$edge(d, c)$$
$$reachable(a)$$
$$reachable(X) \leftarrow reachable(Y), edge(X, Y)$$

that describes which vertices are reachable from a given vertex a in a graph.

Fitting semantics cannot conclude that vertices c and d are not reachable from a. Here the difficulty is caused by the existence of the symmetric rules $edge(c, d)$, and $edge(d, c)$.

Example 1.2.3. Consider P :

$$bird(tweety)$$
$$fly(X) \leftarrow bird(X), not\ abnormal(X)$$
$$abnormal(X) \leftarrow irregular(X)$$
$$irregular(X) \leftarrow abnormal(X)$$

where the last two rules just state that "irregular" and "abnormal" are synonymous.

Based on the fact that nothing leads us to the conclusion that tweety is abnormal, we would expect the program to derive *not abnormal(tweety)*, and consequently that it flies. But Clark's completion of P is:

$$bird(X) \Leftrightarrow X = tweety$$
$$fly(X) \Leftrightarrow bird(X), not\ abnormal(X)$$
$$abnormal(X) \Leftrightarrow irregular(X)$$

from which it does not follow that tweety isn't abnormal.

It is worth noting that without the last two rules both Clark's and Fitting's semantics yield the expected result.

One possible explanation for such a behaviour is that the last two rules lead to a loop. This explanation is procedural in nature. But it was the idea of replacing procedural programming by declarative programming that brought about the concepts of logic programming in first place and so, as argued in [172], it seems that such a procedural explanation should be rejected.

The problems mentioned above are caused by the difficulty in representing transitive closure using completion. In [110] it is formally showed that both Clark's and Fitting's semantics are not sufficiently expressive to represent transitive closure.

In order to solve these problems some model-theoretic approaches to declarative semantics have been defined. In the beginning, such approaches did not attempt to give a meaning to every normal logic program. On the contrary, they were based on syntactic restrictions over programs, and only programs complying with such restrictions were given a semantics. Examples of syntactically restricted program classes are the stratified [15], locally stratified [176] and acyclic [14] ones, and examples of semantics for restricted programs are the perfect model semantics [15, 176, 75], and the weakly perfect model semantics [171]. Here we will not review any of these approaches. For their overview, the reader is referred to e.g. [172].

1.2.1 Stable model semantics

In [78], the authors introduce the so-called *"stable model semantics"*. This model-theoretic declarative semantics for normal programs generalizes the previously referred semantics for restricted classes of programs, in the sense that for such classes the results are the same and, moreover, for some non-restricted programs a meaning is still assigned.

The basic ideas behind the stable model semantics came from the field of nonmonotonic reasoning formalism. There, literals of the form *not A* are viewed as default literals that may or may not be assumed or, alternatively, as epistemic literals $\sim \mathcal{B}A$ expressing that A is not believed.

Informally, when one assumes true some set of (hypothetical) default literals, and false all the others, some consequences follow according to the semantics of definite programs [69]. If the consequences completely corroborate the hypotheses made, then they form a stable model. Formally:

Definition 1.2.1 (Gelfond-Lifschitz operator). *Let P be a normal logic program and I a 2-valued interpretation. The GL-transformation of P modulo I is the program $\frac{P}{I}$ obtained from P by performing the following operations:*

- *remove from P all rules which contain a default literal not A such that $A \in I$;*
- *remove from the remaining rules all default literals.*

Since $\frac{P}{I}$ is a definite program, it has a unique least model J. We define $\Gamma(I) = J$.

It turns out that fixed points of the Gelfond-Lifschitz operator Γ for a program P are always models of P. This result led to the definition of stable model semantics:

Definition 1.2.2 (Stable model semantics). *A 2-valued interpretation I of a logic program P is a stable model of P iff $\Gamma(I) = I$.*

An atom A of P is true under the stable model semantics iff A belong to all stable models of P.

Example 1.2.4. The program P:

$$
\begin{aligned}
a &\leftarrow not\ b \\
b &\leftarrow not\ a \\
c &\leftarrow not\ d \\
d &\leftarrow not\ e \\
p &\leftarrow a \\
p &\leftarrow b
\end{aligned}
$$

has two stable models: $I_1 = \{p, a, d\}$ and $I_2 = \{p, b, d\}$, and so, under to the stable models semantics, both p and d are true.

Note that $\frac{P}{I_1}$ is:

$$
\begin{array}{lll}
a & \leftarrow & \\
d & \leftarrow & \\
p & \leftarrow & a \\
p & \leftarrow & b
\end{array}
$$

and so $\Gamma(I_1) = \{p, a, d\} = I_1$. Similarly for I_2.

One of the main advantages of stable model semantics is its close relationship with known nonmonotonic reasoning formalisms:

As proven in [23], the stable models of a program P are equivalent to Reiter's default extensions [188] of the default theory obtained from P by identifying each program rule:

$$H \leftarrow B_1, \ldots, B_n, not\ C_1, \ldots, not\ C_m$$

with the default rule:

$$\frac{B_1, \ldots, B_n\ :\ \sim C_1, \ldots, \sim C_m}{H}$$

where $\sim$ denotes classical negation.

Moreover, from the results of [77], it follows directly that stable models are equivalent to Moore's autoepistemic expansions [132] of the theory obtained by replacing in P every default literal $not\ A$ by $\sim \mathcal{L}A$ and then reinterpreting the rule connective $\leftarrow$ as material implication. This translation of programs into theories is hereafter refered to as Gelfond's translation.

In spite of the strong relationship between logic programming and nonmonotonic reasoning, in the past these research areas were developing largely independently of one another, and the exact nature of their relationship was not closely investigated or understood.

The situation has changed significantly with the introduction of stable models, and the establishment of formal relationships between these and other nonmonotonic formalisms. In fact, in recent years increasing and productive effort has been devoted to the study of the relationships between logic programming and several nonmonotonic reasoning formalisms. As a result, international workshops have been organized, in whose proceedings [136, 164, 122] many works and references to the theme can be found.

Such relationships turn out to be mutually beneficial. On the one hand, nonmonotonic formalisms provide elegant semantics for logic programming, specially in what regards the meaning of default negation (or negation as failure), and help one understand how logic programs can be used to formalize several types of reasoning in Artificial Intelligence. On the other hand, those formalisms benefit from the existing procedures of logic programming, and some new issues of the former are raised and solved by the latter. Moreover, relations among nonmonotonic formalisms themselves have been facilitated and established via logic programming.

Despite its advantages, including that of being defined for more programs than any of its predecessors, stable model semantics still has some important drawbacks:

- First, some programs have no stable models. For example, the program:

  $$P = \{a \leftarrow not\ a\}$$

  has no stable models. To prove that this is the case, assume such a stable model I exists. Then either $a \in I$ or $a \notin I$. In the first case the rule is delete in $\frac{P}{I}$, and so $a \notin \Gamma(I)$. Thus $I \neq \Gamma(I)$ and I is not a stable model. In the latter case, in $\frac{P}{I}$ $not\ a$ is removed from the body of the rule, and so $a \in \Gamma(I)$. Thus, also in this case $I \neq \Gamma(I)$.
- Even for programs with stable models, their semantics do not always lead to the expected intended results. For example consider program P :

  $$
  \begin{array}{rcl}
  a & \leftarrow & not\ b \\
  b & \leftarrow & not\ a \\
  c & \leftarrow & not\ a \\
  c & \leftarrow & not\ c
  \end{array}
  $$

  Its only stable model is $I = \{c, b\}$.

  In fact $\frac{P}{I}$, obtained by deleting the first and last rules and removing all other default literals from the body of rules, is:

  $$
  \begin{array}{rcl}
  b & \leftarrow & \\
  c & \leftarrow &
  \end{array}
  $$

  whose least model is clearly $\{c, b\}$. Thus b and c are consequences of the stable model semantics of P.

  However, if one adds c to P as a lemma, the semantics changes, and b no longer follows. In fact, the resulting program has two stable models $I_1 = \{c, b\}$ and $I_2 = \{c, a\}$. Note that in $\frac{P \cup \{c\}}{I_2}$ the second, third, and fourth rule of P are deleted. So $\frac{P \cup \{c\}}{I_2} = \{a, c\}$, whose least model equals I_2. Also mark that I_2 is not a stable model of P alone: $\frac{P}{I_2} = \{a\}$, so $\Gamma(I_2) = \{a\} \neq I_2$. This issue is related to the property of cumulativity, and is studied in Chapter 9.

Moreover, it is easy to see that in the above program it is impossible to derive b from P using any derivation procedure based on top-down (SL-like) rewriting techniques. This is because such a procedure, beginning with the goal $\leftarrow b$ would reach only the first two rules of P, from which b cannot be derived.

In fact, the program P_2:

$$a \;\leftarrow\; not\; b$$
$$b \;\leftarrow\; not\; a$$

has two stable models: $\{a\}$, and $\{b\}$. $\frac{P_2}{\{a\}} = \{a \leftarrow\}$ (the second rule is deleted because $a \in \{a\}$, and $not\; b$ is removed from the body of the first rule because $b \notin \{a\}$) and so $\Gamma(\{a\}) = \{a\}$. Similarly for the stable model $\{b\}$.

This issue is related with the property of relevance, and is also studied in Chapter 9.

- The computation of stable models is NP-complete [124] even within simple classes of programs, such as propositional logic programs. This is an important drawback, specially if one is interested in a program for efficiently implementing knowledge representation and reasoning.

- Last but not least, by always insisting on 2-valued interpretations, stable model semantics often lacks expressivity. This issue will be further explored in Section 5.2.

1.2.2 Well-founded semantics

The well-founded semantics was introduced in [76], and overcomes all of the above problems. This semantics is also closely related to some of the major nonmonotonic formalisms (cf. Sections 5.2.1, 6.1.2, and 7.2).

Many different equivalent definitions of the well-founded semantics exist (e.g. [177, 179, 36, 172, 62, 182, 20, 131]). Here we use the definition introduced in [172] because, in our view, it is the one most technically related with the definition of stable models above[5]. Indeed, it consists of a natural generalization for 3-valued interpretations of the stable model semantics. In its definition the authors begin by introducing 3-valued (or partial) stable models, and then show that the F-least of those models coincides with the well-founded model as first defined in [76].

In order to formalize the notion of partial stable models, Przymusinski first expands the language of programs with the additional propositional constant **u** with the property of being undefined in every interpretation. Thus it is assumed that every interpretation I satisfies:

$$\hat{I}(\mathbf{u}) = \hat{I}(not\; \mathbf{u}) = \frac{1}{2}$$

A non-negative program is a program whose premises are either atoms or **u**. In [172], it is proven that every non-negative program has a 3-valued least model. This led to the following generalization of the Gelfond-Lifschitz Γ-operator:

---

[5] For a more practical introduction to the well-founded semantics the reader is referred to [148].

Definition 1.2.3 (Γ^*-operator). *Let P be a normal logic program, and let I be a 3-valued interpretation. The extended GL-transformation of P modulo I is the program $\frac{P}{I}$ obtained from P by performing the operations:*

- *remove from P all rules which contain a default literal not A such that $I(A) = 1$;*
- *replace in the remaining rules of P those default literals not A such that $I(A) = \frac{1}{2}$ by $\mathbf{u}$;*
- *remove from the remaning rules all default literals.*

Since the resulting program is non-negative, it has a unique 3-valued least model J. We define $\Gamma^*(I) = J$.

Definition 1.2.4 (Well-founded semantics). *A 3-valued interpretation I of a logic program P is a partial stable model of P iff $\Gamma^*(I) = I$.*

The well-founded semantics of P is determined by the unique F-least partial stable model of P, and can be obtained by the (bottom-up) iteration of Γ^* starting from the empty interpretation.

Example 1.2.5. Consider again the program P of example1.2.4. Its well-founded model is obtained by iterating Γ^* starting from the empty interpretation.

- $\Gamma^*(\{\})$ is the least 3-valued model of:

$$
\begin{aligned}
a &\leftarrow \mathbf{u} \\
b &\leftarrow \mathbf{u} \\
c &\leftarrow \mathbf{u} \\
d &\leftarrow \mathbf{u} \\
p &\leftarrow a \\
p &\leftarrow b
\end{aligned}
$$

i.e. $\Gamma^*(\{\}) = \{not\ e\}$

- $\Gamma^*(\{not\ e\})$ is the least 3-valued model of:

$$
\begin{aligned}
a &\leftarrow \mathbf{u} \\
b &\leftarrow \mathbf{u} \\
c &\leftarrow \mathbf{u} \\
d &\leftarrow \\
p &\leftarrow a \\
p &\leftarrow b
\end{aligned}
$$

i.e. $\Gamma^*(\{not\ e\}) = \{d, not\ e\}$

- $\Gamma^*(\{d, not\ e\})$ is the least 3-valued model of:

$$
\begin{aligned}
a &\leftarrow \mathbf{u} \\
b &\leftarrow \mathbf{u} \\
\\
d &\leftarrow \\
p &\leftarrow a \\
p &\leftarrow b
\end{aligned}
$$

i.e. $\Gamma^*(\{d, not\ e\}) = \{d, not\ e, not\ c\}$

− $\Gamma^*(\{d, not\ e, not\ c\})$ is the least 3-valued model of:

$$
\begin{array}{rcl}
a & \leftarrow & \mathbf{u} \\
b & \leftarrow & \mathbf{u} \\
\\
d & \leftarrow & \\
p & \leftarrow & a \\
p & \leftarrow & b
\end{array}
$$

i.e. $\Gamma^*(\{d, not\ e, not\ c\}) = \{d, not\ e, not\ c\}$.

Thus, the well-founded model of P is $\{d, not\ e, not\ c\}$. In it d is true, e and c are false, and a, b and p are undefined.

2. Extended logic programs

Recently several authors have stressed and shown the importance of including a second kind of negation ¬ in logic programs, for use in deductive databases, knowledge representation, and non-monotonic reasoning [18, 80, 81, 91, 104, 107, 141, 154, 157, 159, 162, 209].

In this chapter we begin by reviewing the main motivations for introducing a second kind of negation in logic programs. Then we define an extension of the language of programs to two negations, and briefly overview the main proposed semantics for these programs.

In normal logic programs the negative information is implicit, i.e. it is not possible to explicitly state falsity, and propositions are assumed false if there is no reason to believe they are true. This is what is wanted in some cases. For instance, in the classical example of a database that explicitly states flight connections, one wants to implicitly assume that the absence of a connection in the database means that no such connection exists.

However this is a serious limitation in other cases. As argued in [141, 209], explicit negative information plays an important rôle in natural discourse and commonsense reasoning. The representation of some problems in logic programming would be more natural if logic programs had some way of explicitly representing falsity. Consider for example the statement:

"Penguins do not fly"

One way of representing this statement within logic programming could be:

$$no\_fly(X) \leftarrow penguin(X)$$

or equivalently:

$$fly'(X) \leftarrow penguin(X)$$

as suggested in [79].

But these representations do not capture the connection between the predicate $no\_fly(X)$ and the predication of flying. This becomes clearer if, additionally, we want to represent the statement:

"Birds fly"

Clearly this statement can be represented by

$$fly(X) \leftarrow bird(X)$$

But then, no connection whatsoever exists between the predicates $no\_fly(X)$ and $fly(X)$. Intuitively one would like to have such an obvious connection established.

The importance of these connections grows if we think of negative information for representing exceptions to rules [104]. The first statement above can be seen as an exception to the general rule that normally birds fly. In this case we really want to establish the connection between flying and not flying.

Exceptions expressed by sentences with negative conclusions are also common in legislation [103, 105]. For example, consider the provisions for depriving British citizens of their citizenship:

> 40 - (1) Subject to the provisions of this section, the Secretary of State may by order deprive any British citizen to whom this subsection applies of his British citizenship if [...]

> (5) The Secretary of State shall not deprive a person of British citizenship under this section if [...]

Clearly, 40.1 has the logical form "P if Q" whereas 40.5 has the form "¬ P if R". Moreover, it is also clear that 40.5 is an exception to the rule of 40.1.

Above we argued for the need of having explicit negation in the head of rules. But there are also reasons that force us to believe explicit negation is needed also in their bodies. Consider the statement[1]:

> " *A school bus may cross railway tracks under the condition that there is no approaching train*"

It would be wrong to express this statement by the rule:

$$cross \leftarrow not\ train$$

The problem is that this rule allows the bus to cross the tracks when there is no information about either the presence or the absence of a train. The situation is different if explicit negation is used:

$$cross \leftarrow \neg train$$

Then the bus is only allowed to cross the tracks if the bus driver is sure that there is no approaching train. The difference between $not\ p$ and $\neg p$ in a logic program is essential whenever we cannot assume that available positive

---

[1] This example is due to John McCarthy, and was published for the first time in [80].

information about p is complete, i.e. we cannot assume that the absence of information about p clearly denotes its falsity.

Moreover, the introduction of explicit negation in combination with the existing default negation allows for greater expressivity, and so for representing statements like:

" If the driver is not sure that a train is not approaching then he should wait"

in a natural way:

$wait \leftarrow not \ \neg train$

Examples of such combinations also appear in legislation. For example consider the following article from "The British Nationality Act 1981" [88]:

(2) A new-born infant who, after commencement, is found abandoned in the United Kingdom shall acquire british citizenship by section 1.2 if it is not shown that it is not the case that the person is born [...]

Clearly, conditions of the form "it is not shown that it is not the case that P" can be expressed naturally by $not \ \neg P$.

Another motivation for introducing explicit negation in logic programs relates to the symmetry between positive and negative information. This is of special importance when the negative information is easier to represent than the positive one. One can first represent it negatively, and then say that the positive information corresponds to its complement.

In order to make this clearer, take the following example [80]:

Example 2.0.6. Consider a graph description based on the predicate

$arc(X, Y)$

expressing that in the graph there is an arc from vertex X to vertex Y. Now suppose that we want to determine which vertices are terminals. Clearly, this is a case where the complement information is easier to represent, i.e. it is much easier to determine which vertices are not terminal. By using explicit negation in combination with negation by default, one can then easily say that terminal vertices are those which are not nonterminal:

$$\neg terminal(X) \leftarrow arc(X, Y)$$
$$terminal(X) \leftarrow not \ \neg terminal(X)$$

Finally, another important motivation for extending logic programming with explicit negation is to generalize the relationships between logic programs and nonmonotonic reasoning formalisms.

As mentioned in Section 1.2, such relationships, drawn for the most recent semantics of normal logic programs, have proven of extreme importance for both sides, giving them mutual benefits and clarifications. However, normal logic programs just map into narrow classes of the more general nonmonotonic formalisms. For example, simple default rules such as:

$$\frac{\sim a \; : \; \sim b}{c} \qquad\qquad \frac{a \; : \; b}{c} \qquad\qquad \frac{a \; : \; b}{\sim c}$$

cannot be represented by a normal logic program. Note that not even normal nor seminormal defaults rules can be represented using normal logic programs. This is so because these programs cannot represent rules with negative conclusions, and normal rules with positive conclusions have also positive justifications, which is impossible in normal programs.

Since, as shown below, extended logic programs also bear a close relationship with nonmonotonic reasoning formalisms, they improve on those of normal programs as extended programs map into broader classes of theories in nonmonotonic formalisms, and so more general relations between several of those formalisms can now be made via logic programs.

One example of such an improvement is that the introduction of explicit negation into logic programs makes it possible to represent normal and seminormal defaults within logic programming. On the one side, this provides methods for computing consequences of normal default theories. On the other, it allows for the appropriation in logic programming of work done using such theories for representing knowledge.

2.1 Language

As for normal logic programs, an atom over an alphabet $\mathcal{A}$ is an expression of the form $p(t_1, \ldots, t_n)$, where p is a predicate symbol, and the t_is are terms. In order to extend our language with a second kind of negation, we additionally define an objective literal over $\mathcal{A}$ as being an atom A or its explicit negation $\neg A$. We also use the symbol $\neg$ to denote complementary literals in the sense of explicit negation. Thus $\neg\neg A = A$. Here, a literal is either an objective literal L or its default negation $not\ L$. We dub default literals those of the form $not\ L$.

By the extended Herbrand base of $\mathcal{A}$, we mean the set of all ground objective literals of $\mathcal{A}$. Whenever unambiguous we refer to the extended Herbrand base of an alphabet, simply as Herbrand base, and denote it by $\mathcal{H}$.

An extended logic program is a finite set of rules of the form:

$$H \leftarrow L_1, \ldots, L_n \qquad (n \geq 0)$$

where H is an objective literal and each of the L_is is a literal. As for normal programs, if $n = 0$ we omit the arrow symbol.

By the extended Herbrand base $\mathcal{H}$ of P we mean the extended Herbrand base of the alphabet consisting of all the constants, predicate and function symbols that explicitly appear in P.

Interpretation is defined as for normal programs, but using the extended Herbrand base instead.

Whenever unambigous, we refer to extended logic programs simply as logic programs or programs. As in normal programs, a set of rules stands for all its ground instances.

In the sequel we refer to some special forms of programs:

Definition 2.1.1 (Canonical program). *An extended logic program P is a canonical program iff for every rule in P*

$H \leftarrow Body$

if $L \in Body$ then $(not \ \neg L) \in Body$, where L is any objective literal.

Definition 2.1.2 (Semantics kernel). *An extended logic program P is a semantics kernel iff every rule in P is of the form:*

$H \leftarrow not \ L_1, \ldots, not \ L_n \quad (n \geq 0)$

2.2 Semantics

2.2.1 Stable Models based semantics

The first semantics defined for extended logic programs was the so-called *"answer-sets semantics"* [80]. There the authors defined for the first time the language of logic programs with two kinds of negation – default negation *not* and what they called classical negation ¬.

The answer-sets semantics is a generalization of the stable model semantics for the language of extended programs. Roughly, an answer-set of an extended program P is a stable model of the normal program obtained from P by replacing objective literals of the form $\neg L$ by new atoms, say $\neg\_L$. Formally we have:

Definition 2.2.1 (The Γ-operator). *Let P be an extended logic program and I a 2-valued interpretation[2]. The GL-transformation of P modulo I is the program $\frac{P}{I}$ obtained from P by:*

– first denoting every objective literal in $\mathcal{H}$ of the form $\neg A$ by a new atom, say $\neg\_A$;

– replacing in both P and I these objective literals by their new denotations;

---

[2] Recall that by 2-valued, or total, interpretation we mean one that contains *not L* whenever it does not contain L, and vice-versa. In other other the interpretations considered in the definition of answer-sets are 2-valued with respect to the negation *not* . It might happen that an interpretation be not 2-valued with respect to the negation ¬ (i.e. for some atom A, both A and $\neg A$ may be simultaneously absent from the interpretation).

– *then performing the following operations:*
 – *removing from P all rules which contain a default literal not A such that*
   $A \in I$;
 – *removing from the remaning rules all default literals.*
 Since $\frac{P}{I}$ is a definite program it has a unique least model J.

  If J contains a pair of complementary atoms, say A and $\neg\_A$, then $\Gamma(I) = \mathcal{H}$.

  Otherwise, let J' be the interpretation obtained from J by replacing the newly introduced atoms $\neg\_A$ by $\neg A$. We define $\Gamma(I) = J'$.

Definition 2.2.2 (Answer-set semantics). *A 2-valued interpretation I of an extended logic program P is an answer-set of P iff $\Gamma(I) = I$.*

  An objective literal L of P is true under the answer-set semantics iff L belongs to all answer-sets of P; L is false iff $\neg L$ is true; otherwise L is unknown.

Example 2.2.1. Consider the following program (taken from [80]):

$$
\begin{array}{rcl}
eligible(X) & \leftarrow & highGPA(X) \\
eligible(X) & \leftarrow & minority(X), highGPA(X) \\
\neg eligible(X) & \leftarrow & \neg fairGPA(X) \\
interview(X) & \leftarrow & not\ eligible(X), not\ \neg eligible(X) \\
fairGPA(ann) & \leftarrow & \\
highGPA(peter) & \leftarrow & \\
\neg fairGPA(john) & \leftarrow &
\end{array}
$$

stating that:

– every student with a high GPA is eligible for a scholarship;
– every minority student with a fair GPA is also eligible;
– No student with a GPA which is not at least fair is eligible;
– the students whose eligibility is not determined by these rules are interviewed by a scholarship comunity;
– Ann has a fair GPA; Peter has a high GPA; and John has a GPa which is not fair.

Its only answer-set is (where default literals are omitted, for brevity):

$$
I = \left\{
\begin{array}{l}
fairGPA(ann), interview(ann) \\
highGPA(peter), eligible(peter) \\
\neg fairGPA(john), \neg eligible(john)
\end{array}
\right\}
$$

In fact $\frac{P}{I}$ is:

$$
\begin{aligned}
eligible(ann) &\leftarrow highGPA(ann) \\
eligible(ann) &\leftarrow minority(ann), highGPA(ann) \\
\neg\_eligible(ann) &\leftarrow \neg\_fairGPA(ann) \\
interview(ann) &\leftarrow \\
fairGPA(ann) &\leftarrow
\end{aligned}
$$

$$
\begin{aligned}
eligible(peter) &\leftarrow highGPA(peter) \\
eligible(peter) &\leftarrow minority(peter), highGPA(peter) \\
\neg\_eligible(peter) &\leftarrow \neg\_fairGPA(peter) \\
highGPA(peter) &\leftarrow
\end{aligned}
$$

$$
\begin{aligned}
eligible(john) &\leftarrow highGPA(john) \\
eligible(john) &\leftarrow minority(john), highGPA(john) \\
\neg\_eligible(john) &\leftarrow \neg\_fairGPA(john) \\
\neg\_fairGPA(john) &\leftarrow
\end{aligned}
$$

whose least model (after replacing atoms of the form $\neg\_A$ by the corresponding objectives literals $\neg A$) is exactly I.

Thus, according to the answer-sets semantics, Peter is eligible, John is not eligible, and it is unknown whether Ann is eligible though, according to the fourth rule, she should be interviewed. Notice that Ann has a fair GPA, and it is unknown (there is no information about) whether she is a minority student.

Example 2.2.2. The program:

$$
\begin{aligned}
flies(X) &\leftarrow bird(X), not\ \neg flies(X) \\
\neg flies(X) &\leftarrow penguin(X), not\ flies(X)
\end{aligned}
$$

$$
\begin{aligned}
bird(X) &\leftarrow penguin(X) \\
penguin(tweety) &\leftarrow
\end{aligned}
$$

has two answer-sets, namely:

$$
\begin{aligned}
I_1 &= \{flies(tweety), bird(tweety), penguin(tweety)\} \\
I_2 &= \{\neg flies(tweety), bird(tweety), penguin(tweety)\}
\end{aligned}
$$

I_1 is an answer-set: $\frac{P}{I_1}$ deletes the second rule for $X = tweety$ (because $not\ flies(tweety)$ is in its body, and $flies(tweety) \in I_1$), and removes

$$
not\ \neg flies(tweety)
$$

from the body of the first rule (since $\neg flies(tweety) \notin I_1$); it is easy to check that the least model of the resulting definite program coincides with I_1. Similarly for I_2, where the first rule is deleted ($not\ \neg flies(tweety)$ is in its body, and $\neg flies(tweety) \in I_2$), and $not\ flies(tweety)$ is removed from the body of the second rule (since $flies(tweety) \notin I_1$).

From the definitions, it is trivial to verify that for programs without explicit negation, answer-sets coincide with stable models.

An extended program is called *contradictory* with respect to the answer-sets semantics (hereafter dubbed AS-contradictory programs) if it has no consistent answer-sets. For example, the program containing the two facts a and $\neg a$ has a single answer-set $\{a, \neg a\}$ which is inconsistent. So this program is AS-contradictory.

Example 2.2.3. Let P be the program:

$$fly(X) \quad \leftarrow \quad bird(X), not\ abnormal(X).$$

$$bird(tweety) \quad \leftarrow$$
$$\neg fly(tweety) \quad \leftarrow$$

stating that:

– Birds, not shown to be abnormal, fly.
– Tweety is a bird and does not fly.

This program has no consistent answer-sets. In fact, since there are no rules defined for $abnormal(tweety)$ and, by definition, $\frac{P}{I}$ does not add rules to P, independently of I, the least model of $\frac{P}{I}$ can never contain $abnormal(tweety)$. So, every "candidate" S for answer-sets must not contain $abnormal(tweety)$. Thus, $\frac{P}{S}$ always has the rule

$$fly(tweety) \leftarrow bird(tweety)$$

Since $bird(tweety)$ and $\neg fly(tweety)$ are true, a contradiction is reached.

Clearly, normal logic programs (i.e. without explicit negation) can never be AS-contradictory. Moreover, AS-contradictory programs always have a single answer-set.

Proposition 2.2.1. *Every AS-contradictory program has exactly one contradictory answer-set, which coincides with its Herbrand base $\mathcal{H}$.*

As imposed by the definition, any answer-set with a complementary pair of objective literals coincides with $\mathcal{H}$. The fact that no other answer-set exists for contradictory programs follows from:

Lemma 2.2.1. *No extended program can have two answer-sets of which one is a proper subset of the other.*

Being non-AS-contradictory does not guarantee the existence of answer-sets. Note that normal programs can never be AS-contradictory and, as pointed out in Section 1.2.1, some do not have answer-sets (or stable models, since for normal programs these semantics coincide). This is, in our opinion, one of the important shortcomings of the answer-sets semantics (cf. Chapter 3).

Gelfond and Lifshitz [80] showed that the answer-sets of an extended program P are equivalent to Reiter's default extensions of the default theory obtained from P by identifying each program rule:

$$H \quad \leftarrow \quad B_1,\ldots,B_n,\neg C_1,\ldots,\neg C_m,$$
$$not\ D_1,\ldots,not\ D_k, not\ \neg E_1,\ldots,not\ \neg E_j$$

with the default rule:

$$\frac{B_1,\ldots,B_n,\sim C_1,\ldots,\sim C_m \ : \ \sim D_1,\ldots,\sim D_k, E_1,\ldots,E_j}{H'}$$

where $H' = H$ if H is an atom, or $H' =\sim L$ if $H = \neg L$, and $\sim L$ denotes the classical negation of L.

This is the reason why the newly introduced negation was called "classical" – it coincides with classical negation in default theories.

However, the negation used in answer-sets does not exhibit some well known properties of classical negation. For example, the explicit negation of answer-sets does not comply with the "excluded middle" property, i.e. in general $A \lor \neg A$ is not true in an answer-set for every atom A. This can be seen in Example 2.2.1, where neither $eligible(Ann)$ nor $\neg eligible(Ann)$ is true in the only answer-set of the program.

Some authors have argued against ascribing the designation of "classical" to the explicit form of negation used in answer-sets [11, 140, 210]. In [140], Pearce showed that instead of classical negation, answer-sets use in fact Nelson's strong negation [135]. In particular, in [140] it is shown that Nelson's constructive logic with strong negation is a monotonic deductive basis[3] for the answer-sets semantics (where default negation is equated with intuitionistic negation, and explicit negation with Nelson's strong negation). Moreover, the author shows that answer-sets can be completely characterized as particular kinds of minimal models of $N2$ – an extension of Nelson's constructive logic.

Regarding the relationship between answer-sets semantics and autoepistemic logics, [39, 117, 123] noted that Gelfond's translation (cf. page 1.2.1) cannot be generalized to extended programs. A suitable translation between extended logic programs with answer-sets semantics and reflexive autoepistemic theories was proposed independently in [117] and [123]. Reflexive autoepistemic logic, introduced in [198], views the operator $\mathcal{L}$ as "is

---

[3] Roughly, a (monotonic) logic $\mathcal{L}$ is a deductive basis for a (nonmonotonic) semantics $\mathcal{S}$ if for every program P: all consequences of $\mathcal{L}$ are consequences of $\mathcal{S}$; closing the consequences of the semantics under the inference operation $C_{\mathcal{L}}$ of the logic has no effect over the former; and the result of the semantics of P equals that of the closure of P under $C_{\mathcal{L}}$.

known" instead of the "is believed" of Moore's autoepistemic logic [132]. In [117, 123] the authors choose a translation of extended logic programs into theories of reflexive autoepistemic logic, and prove that the answer-sets of an extended logic program correspond to the reflexive expansions of its translation. The translation renders an objective literal A (resp. $\neg A$) as $\mathcal{L}A$ (resp. $\mathcal{L} \sim A$, where $\sim$ denotes classical negation), i.e. "A is known to be true" (resp. "A is known to be false"), and renders $not\ L$ as $\mathcal{L} \sim \mathcal{L}L$, i.e. "it is known that L is not known". The embedding of extended logic programs into reflexive autoepistemic logic can also be defined for (non-reflexive) autoepistemic logic [117, 123], by translating any objective literal L into $L \wedge \mathcal{L}L$. This translation was proposed in [39] too. This issue is further detailed in section 5.2 below.

Another semantics generalizing stable models for the class of extended programs is the e-answer-set semantics of [107]. There, the authors claim that explicitly negated atoms in extended programs play the rôle of exceptions. Thus they impose a preference of negative over positive objective literals.

The e-answer-set semantics is obtainable from the answer-set semantics after a suitable program transformation. For the sake of simplicity, here we do not give the formal definition of e-answer-sets, but instead show its behaviour in an example:

Example 2.2.4. Consider program P :

$$
\begin{aligned}
fly(X) &\leftarrow bird(X) \\
\neg fly(X) &\leftarrow penguin(X) \\
bird(X) &\leftarrow penguin(X) \\
penguin(tweety) &\leftarrow
\end{aligned}
$$

This program allows for both conclusions $fly(tweety)$ and $\neg fly(tweety)$. Thus its only answer-set is $\mathcal{H}$.

In e-answer-set semantics, since conclusions of the form $\neg L$ are preferred over those of the form L, $\neg fly(tweety)$ overrides the conclusion $fly(tweety)$, and thus

$$\{penguin(tweety), bird(tweety), \neg fly(tweety)\}$$

is an e-answer-set of P.

The rationale for this overriding is that the second rule is an exception to the first one.

2.2.2 Well-founded based semantics

In [180], the author argues that the technique used in answer-sets for generalizing stable models is quite general. On the basis of that technique he defines a semantics which generalizes the well-founded semantics for the class of extended programs[4], as follows:

---

[4] In the sequel we refer to this semantics as *"well-founded semantics with pseudo negation"*. The justification for this name can be found in Section 5.1.4.

Definition 2.2.3 (Well-founded semantics with pseudo negation).
A 3-valued interpretation I is a partial stable model of an extended logic program P iff I' is a partial stable model of the normal program P', where I' and P' are obtained respectively from I and P, by replacing every objective literal of the form ¬A by a new atom, say ¬_A.

The well-founded semantics with pseudo negation of P is determined by the unique F-least partial stable model of P.

As in the answer-sets semantics, also in this semantics the meaning of ¬ does not correspond to that of classical negation. In fact, consider the following program P :

$$b \leftarrow a$$
$$b \leftarrow \neg a$$

If *real* classical negation were used then b would be a consequence of P, because for classical negation $a \vee \neg a$ is a tautology. However, it is easy to check that the well-founded model (with pseudo negation) of P is $\{not\ a, not\ \neg a, not\ b, not\ \neg b\}$, and so b is not a consequence of P under that semantics.

In order to introduce *real* classical negation into logic programs, in [183] the author defined the "stationary semantics with classical negation". This semantics is a generalization of the well-founded semantics, and is capable of deriving b in P. For brevity we do not present here its formal definition. However, the definition can be found in Section 5.1, where we compare it with our *WFSX*.

2.2.3 Other approaches

Unlike normal logic programs, none of the semantics of extended programs is defined for every program, i.e. some programs are contradictory. While for some programs this seems reasonable (e.g. a program containing contradictory facts, say $P = \{a \leftarrow,\ \ \neg a \leftarrow\}$), for others this can be too strong:

Example 2.2.5. Let P :

$$\neg p \leftarrow not\ q$$
$$p \leftarrow$$

In all the above semantics this program is not assigned a meaning. Roughly, this is because q has no rules, and thus $not\ q$ must be true. So, by the first rule, $\neg p$ must also be true, and since there is a fact p in P, a contradiction appears.

However, if we see default literals as hypotheses that may or may not be assumed (viz. in [62]), this contradiction seems strange since it relies on the assumption of $not\ q$.

Motivated by this [68] presented a semantics generalizing "well-founded semantics with pseudo negation" which, in order to assign a meaning to more programs, does not assume hypotheses (default literals) that lead to a contradiction[5]. For instance, the semantics of P above does not assume *not q*, and is $\{p\}$.

Another approach to deal with contradictory programs is the one taken by paraconsistent semantics. In these, the contradictory information is accepted into the semantics and reasoning tasks that take it into account are performed. This is not our nor Dung's concern. On the contrary, we wish to remove contradiction whenever it rests on withdrawable assumptions[6].

The ideas for introducing in logic programming paraconsistent reasoning are not all new. Since paraconsistent reasoning seems to be fundamental for understanding human cognitive processes, it has been studied in philosophical logic by several authors [47, 21, 193, 13, 170]. Their intuitions and results have been brought to the logic programming setting mainly by Blair, Pearce, Subrahmanian, and Wagner [26, 142, 138, 139, 212, 213]. With the introduction of (a non-classical) explicit negation in logic programming other researchers addressed this issue for extensions of well-founded and answer sets semantics, e.g Sakama and Inoue [196, 197].

---

[5] At the same conference, we presented a paper [146] exploring similar ideas. The details of that independent work are not presented in this overview but are expounded at length in Chapter 8.

[6] For a more detailed survey on paraconsistent semantics for extended programs see [49].

Part II

A New Semantics for Extended Logic Programs

3. Why a new semantics for extended programs?

The overview above showed that several semantics exist for extended logic programs. In our view none correctly captures the meaning of extended programs. This is why we think a new semantics for extended programs is required. Let's take a look at their shortcomings:

The answer-set semantics [80], being based on the stable model semantics of normal program [78], suffers at least from the same structural and computational problems of the latter. We briefly recall some of those problems (as pointed out in Section 1.2.1):

– Some noncontradictory programs have no answer-sets, e.g.

$$P = \{a \leftarrow not\ a\}.$$

– Even for programs with answer-sets, their semantics does not always render the expected intended results. In particular, the addition of lemmas changes the semantics of the program (this is related with the property of cumulativity mentioned in the preface, and studied in Chapter 9). The problem is illustrated in the example of page 13.
– Derivation procedures for answer-sets cannot be based on top-down (SL-like) rewriting techniques, even for consistent programs (this is related with the property of relevance also mentioned in the preface, and studied in Chapter 9). For example consider the program:

$$
\begin{aligned}
a &\leftarrow not\ b \\
b &\leftarrow not\ a \\
c &\leftarrow not\ a \\
\neg c &
\end{aligned}
$$

whose only answer-set is $\{\neg c, a\}$.

Though a is a consequence of this program, a does not follow from the rules "below"[1] a, which in this case are the first two. Thus, a derivation for a cannot be solely based on top-down (SL-like) rewriting techniques. Indeed, the program containing only the first two rules has two answer-sets: $\{a\}$ and $\{b\}$. Thus neither a nor b are true in this program.

---

[1] For the formalization of what we mean by "below" see Section 9.1.2.

Moreover, as shown in [61, 60], it is not easy to modify answer-sets semantics to incorporate this property[2].

- The computation of answer-sets is NP-complete, even within simple classes of programs such as propositional logic programs. Moreover, for non-propositional programs, in general it is impossible to compute answer-sets by finite approximations (as shown in Section 7.5).
- By always insisting on 2-valued interpretations, answer-set semantics often lacks expressibility. This issue is further explored in Section 5.2.

The e-answer-sets semantics of [107] also inherits the same problems of stable models. Moreover, we think that explicitly negated atoms do not always represent exceptions. For example consider the statements:

- *Animals do not fly.*
- *Birds fly.*
- *Birds are animals.*
- *Ozzy is a bird.*

Here the second statement (with a positive conclusion) is an exception to the first (with a negative conclusion). Of course, in this case we can represent these statements using a predicate $no\_fly(X)$, thereby making the first rule have a positive conclusion and the second a negative one. However this technique cannot be used if, additionally, we want to represent:

- *Penguins do not fly.*
- *Penguins are birds.*
- *Tweety is a penguin.*

If one represents all the statements using predicate $fly(X)$:

$$
\begin{aligned}
\neg fly(X) &\leftarrow animal(X) \\
fly(X) &\leftarrow bird(X) \\
\neg fly(X) &\leftarrow penguin(X)
\end{aligned}
$$

$$
\begin{aligned}
animal(X) &\leftarrow bird(X) \\
bird(X) &\leftarrow penguin(X) \\
bird(ozzy) & \\
penguin(tweety) &
\end{aligned}
$$

then the only e-answer-set contains $\neg fly(ozzy)$ because it is an animal, which is not intuitively correct since $ozzy$ is a bird and so it should fly.

If one represents the statements using predicate $no\_fly(X)$, then the only e-answer-set contains $\neg no\_fly(tweety)$ because it is a bird, which again is not intuitively correct since $tweety$ is a penguin and so it should not fly.

---

[2] Indeed, by redefining answer-sets just focusing on the part of the program below the literals in consideration (i.e. where a literal belongs to the semantics if it belongs to all answer-sets of the program below that literal), it might happen (cf. [61, 60]) that for some rules the body is true and the head isn't. This violates the classical notion of models, and is quite unintuitive.

In our view, a declarative semantics for extended programs should not impose any preference between positive and explicit negative information. Their treatment should be symmetric. It is up to the programmer to, for each specific case, write his program in such a way that the desired preferences are made. The systematization of a representation method for rules and exceptions using extended logic programs is presented in Section 11.1.

The semantics of [180] based on the well-founded semantics does not suffer from the problems of answer-sets. Moreover it does not impose any preference of negative atoms over positive ones.

Unfortunately, because [180] uses the same technique for adding explicit negation to well-founded semantics as answer-sets for stable models semantics, important properties which relate both negations, obeyed by answer-sets, are lost:

Example 3.0.6. Consider program P :

$$
\begin{array}{rcl}
a & \leftarrow & not\ b \\
b & \leftarrow & not\ a \\
\neg a &&
\end{array}
$$

If $\neg a$ were simply to be considered as a new atom symbol, say, $\neg\_a$, and well-founded semantics were used to define the meaning of P (as suggested in [180]), the result would be

$$\{\neg a, not\ \neg b\}$$

so that $\neg a$ is true and a is undefined. This clearly severs the connection between both negations.

In our view, $\neg a$ is an explicit declaration of the falsity of a. Thus, it can always be assumed that a is false by default, i.e. $not\ a$ should also be true.

Example 3.0.7. Consider a program containing the rules:

$$
\begin{array}{rcl}
tryBus & \leftarrow & not\ driversStrike \\
\neg driversStrike &&
\end{array}
$$

advising to plan a trip by bus if it can be assumed the bus drivers are not on strike, and stating bus drivers are not on strike. No matter what the rest of the program is (assuming it is noncontradictory on the whole), it is clear that it should be assumed the bus drivers are not on strike, and of course the trip should be planned by bus.

Intuitively, $\neg driversStrike$ implies $not\ driversStrike$.

In order to relate both negations in extended logic programs, we introduce the *"coherence principle"*:

> *"Let L be an objective literal of an extended logic program P.*
> *If $\neg L$ belongs to the semantics of P then $not\ L$ must also belong to the semantics of P."*

and argue that every semantics should comply with this principle[3].

Answer-set semantics complies with coherence. Simply note that, for non-contradictory programs, if $\neg L$ is in an answer-set then L is not in that answer-set and so, answer-sets being two valued, *not* L is true.

The semantics presented in [68], being a generalization of the semantics of [180], also does not comply with coherence.

The issue, dealtwith by [68], of assigning meaning to more programs by unassuming default literals leading to contradiction is, in our view, an important one. However, we think this should be done on the basis of a coherent semantics, and that its result should also comply with coherence. In Chapter 8, we show how to deal with contradictory programs, when the contradiction is brought about by default literals. There we present a more sceptical semantics (in the spirit of [68]) that avoids contradiction and complies with coherence. Then we show this same semantics can be obtained by using instead a contradiction removal process that transforms programs considered contradictory. The advantages of using the latter instead of the former approach are presented in Section 8.4.

Finally, also the "well-founded semantics with classical negation" of [183] does not capture the intuitive meaning of extended programs. This happens because of its very first motivation, i.e. the introduction of *real* classical negation.

Consider again the program:

$$b \;\leftarrow\; a$$
$$b \;\leftarrow\; \neg a$$

whose well-founded semantics with classical negation entails b.

We recall that the intended meaning of $\neg L$ is that L is explicitly false or, in other words, L is known to be false. With this reading of explicit negation, the rules of the program state that if a is known to be true then b is known to be true, and if a is known to be false then b is known to be true. Given that the knowledge about literals is not always complete, i.e. it might happen that a is neither known to be false nor true, the formula $a \vee \neg a$ is not a tautology. So the law of excluded middle does not apply, and b does not follow from these statements.

Our stance is that if the law of excluded middle is desired of some atom A then so much should be explicitly stated by adding the disjunctive rule $A \vee \neg A$. This expresses that the knowledge about A is complete, i.e. A is known to be either true or false. We have yet to enlarge our language for rules to accomodate such expressiveness.

In Section 5.2 we further explore this view of explicit negation, by comparing extended programs with logics of provability and belief. There, we argue

---

[3] More arguments in favour of the coherence principle can be found spread along this work.

that explicit negation $\neg L$ should have the reading "L is provenly false", and justify that classical negation in extended program corresponds to "it is false that L is provenly true" or "L is not provenly true" or, conflating knowledge with truth, as classical logic does, "L is not true"; whereas *not* L reads "L believed to be false".

Another property not obeyed by classical negation in logic program is supportedness. Roughly, a semantics complies with supportedness if, for every program P, an objective literal L is true only if there is an identifiable rule for L whose body is true[4]. Clearly, this property closely relates to the use of logic as a programming language. One does not expect an objective literal to be true unless some identifiable rule with true body concludes it; in other words, every true objective literal must be solely supported on other definitely true objective literals or on the truth of default literals. Such is the nature of epistemic truth or knowledge. Ontological truth is concerned with truth in the world, not with the epistemically justifiable knowledge an agent may hold. Thus, in the ontological stance $L \vee \sim L$ is true regardless of whether any of the cases is supported.

---

[4] For a formal definition of this property see Section 5.1.3.

4. *WFSX* – A well founded semantics for extended logic programs

In this chapter we present a new semantics for normal logic programs (i.e. with negation by default) extended with explicit negation, that subsumes the well founded semantics [76] of normal programs.

4.1 Interpretations and models

We begin by providing definitions of interpretation and model for programs extended with explicit negation.

Definition 4.1.1 (Interpretation). *An interpretation I of a language $\mathcal{L}$ is any set*

$$T \cup not\ F\ ^1$$

where T and F are disjoint subsets of objective literals over the Herbrand base, and:

$$\textit{if } \neg L \in T \textit{ then } L \in F \textit{ (Coherence Principle)}^2.$$

The set T contains all ground objective literals true *in I, the set F contains all ground objective literals* false *in I. The truth value of the remaining objective literals is* undefined.

Notice how the two types of negation become linked via coherence: for any objective L, if $\neg L \in I$ then $not\ L \in I$. Other semantics introducing a second negation in WFS do not relate the two negation in this way (cf. Chapter 5 on comparisons).

This definition of interpretation not only guarantees that every interpretation complies with coherence but also with noncontradiction.

Proposition 4.1.1 (Noncontradiction condition). *If $I = T \cup not\ F$ is an interpretation of a program P then there is no pair of objective literals A, $\neg A$ of P such that $A \in T$ and $\neg A \in T$.*

---

[1] Where $not\ \{a_1, \ldots, a_n, \ldots\}$ stands for $\{not\ a_1, \ldots, not\ a_n, \ldots\}$.

[2] For any literal L, if L is explicitly false L must be false. Note that the complementary condition "if $L \in T$ then $\neg L \in F$" is implicit.

Proof. (by contradiction) Consider that $I = T \cup not\ F$ is such that $A \in T$ and $\neg A \in T$. By the coherence condition $A \in F$ and $\neg A \in F$. So I is not an interpretation because T and F are not disjoint.

Example 4.1.1. $\{a, \neg a, \neg b\}$ is not an interpretation because a and $\neg a$ belong to it (contradiction) and also because *not b* does not belong to it although $\neg b$ does (incoherence).

An interpretation I can be read intuitively in the following way:

– An atom A is *true* (resp. *explicitly false*) in I iff $A \in I$ (resp. $\neg A \in I$).
– A positive (resp. negative) objective literal A (resp. $\neg A$) is *false* in I iff *not* $A \in I$ (resp. *not* $\neg A \in I$).
– An atom A is *undefined* in I otherwise.

As in [172], an interpretation can be equivalently viewed as a function

$$I : \mathcal{H} \to V$$

where $\mathcal{H}$ is the set of all objective literals in the language and $V = \{0, \frac{1}{2}, 1\}$.

Proposition 4.1.2. *Any interpretation* $I = T \cup not\ F$ *can be equivalently viewed as a function* $I : \mathcal{H} \to V$ *where* $V = \{0, \frac{1}{2}, 1\}$, *defined by:*

$$\begin{array}{lll} I(A) = 0 & if & not\ A \in I; \\ I(A) = 1 & if & A \in I; \\ I(A) = \frac{1}{2} & & otherwise. \end{array}$$

Based on this function we can define a truth valuation of formulae.

Definition 4.1.2 (Truth valuation). *If I is an interpretation, the truth valuation $\hat{I}$ corresponding to I is a function $\hat{I} : C \to V$ where C is the set of all formulae of the language, recursively defined as follows:*

– *if L is an objective literal then $\hat{I}(L) = I(L)$.*
– *if $S = not\ L$ is a default literal then $\hat{I}(not\ L) = 1 - I(L)$.*
– *if S and V are formulae then $\hat{I}((S, V)) = min(\hat{I}(S), \hat{I}(V))$.*
– *if L is an objective literal and S is a formula then:*

$$\hat{I}(L \leftarrow S) = \begin{cases} 1 & if\ \hat{I}(S) \le \hat{I}(L)\ or\ \hat{I}(\neg L) = 1\ and\ \hat{I}(S) \ne 1 \\ 0 & otherwise \end{cases}$$

The only additional condition with respect to WFS (cf. Definition 1.1.3 above), $\hat{I}(\neg L) = 1$ and $\hat{I}(S) \ne 1$, does not affect the valuation of formulae without $\neg$. Its purpose is to allow a conclusion c to be independently false when the premises are undefined for some rule, on condition that $\neg c$ holds. This allows, in particular, explicit negation $\neg$ to override with false the undefinedness of conclusions of rules with undefined bodies.

Definition 4.1.3 (Model). *An interpretation I is called a model of a program P iff for every ground instance of a program rule $H \leftarrow B$ we have $\hat{I}(H \leftarrow B) = 1$.*

Example 4.1.2. The models of the program:

$$\neg b \qquad b \leftarrow a \qquad\qquad c \leftarrow \text{not } \neg c$$
$$a \leftarrow \text{not } a, \text{not } c \qquad \neg c \leftarrow \text{not } c$$

are:

$$
\begin{aligned}
M_1 &= \{\neg b, \text{not } b\} \\
M_2 &= \{\neg b, \text{not } b, c, \text{not } \neg c\} \\
M_3 &= \{\neg b, \text{not } b, c, \text{not } \neg c, \text{not } a\} \\
M_4 &= \{\neg b, \text{not } b, \text{not } c, \neg c\} \\
M_5 &= \{\neg b, \text{not } b, \neg a, \text{not } a\} \\
M_6 &= \{\neg b, \text{not } b, \neg a, \text{not } a, c, \text{not } \neg c\} \\
M_7 &= \{\neg b, \text{not } b, \text{not } \neg a\} \\
M_8 &= \{\neg b, \text{not } b, c, \text{not } \neg c, \text{not } \neg a\} \\
M_9 &= \{\neg b, \text{not } b, c, \text{not } \neg c, \text{not } a, \text{not } \neg a\} \\
M_{10} &= \{\neg b, \text{not } b, \text{not } c, \neg c, \text{not } \cdot a\}
\end{aligned}
$$

Only M_3, M_6, and M_9 are models in the usual sense (i.e. classical models in the sense of Definition 1.1.4).

- M_1, M_2, M_4, M_7, M_8, and M_{10} are not classical models, because in all of them the body of the rule $b \leftarrow a$ is undefined and the head is false, i.e. the truth value of the head is smaller than that of the body.
- M_5 is not a classical model since in it the truth value of the head (false) of rule $a \leftarrow \text{not } a, \text{not } c$ is smaller than that of the body (undefined).

4.2 The definition of *WFSX*

Next we introduce the notion of stability in models, and using it we define the *WFSX* semantics.

As in [172], in order to define the semantics, we expand the language by adding to it the proposition **u** such that every interpretation I satisfies $I(\mathbf{u}) = \frac{1}{2}$. By a non-negative program we also mean a program whose premises are either objective literals or **u**.

We extend with an additional operation the P modulo I transformation of [172], itself an extension of the Gelfond-Lifschitz modulo transformation [78].

Definition 4.2.1 ($\frac{P}{I}$ transformation). *Let P be an extended logic program and let I be an interpretation. $\frac{P}{I}$, P modulo I, is the program obtained from P by performing in the sequence the following four operations:*

- *Remove from P all rules containing a default literal $L = not\ A$ such that $A \in I$.*
- *Remove from P all rules containing in the body an objective literal L such that $\neg L \in I$.*
- *Remove from all remaining rules of P their default literals $L = not\ A$ such that $not\ A \in I$.*
- *Replace all the remaining default literals by proposition* **u**.

Note that the new operation, the second one, is not applicable to non-extended programs, and is only needed by some extended programs. It is required by the coherence principle, as illustrated below in this section.

The resulting program $\frac{P}{I}$ is by definition non-negative.

Definition 4.2.2 (Least operator). *We define $least(P)$, where P is a non-negative program, as the set of literals $T \cup not\ F$ obtained as follows:*

- *Let P' be the non-negative program obtained by replacing in P every negative objective literal $\neg L$ by a new atomic symbol, say $'\neg\_L'$.*
- *Let $T' \cup not\ F'$ be the least 3-valued model of P' (cf. Definition 1.1.6).*
- *$T \cup not\ F$ is obtained from $T' \cup not\ F'$ by reversing the replacements above.*

The least 3-valued model of a non-negative program can be defined as the least fixpoint of the following generalization of the Van Emden-Kowalski least model operator Ψ for definite logic programs:

Definition 4.2.3 (Ψ^* operator). *Suppose that P is a non-negative program, I is an interpretation of P and A and the A_i are all ground atoms. Then $\Psi^*(I)$ is a set of atoms defined as follows:*

- *$\Psi^*(I)(A) = 1$ iff there is a rule $A \leftarrow A_1, \ldots, A_n$ in P such that $I(A_i) = 1$ for all $i \leq n$.*
- *$\Psi^*(I)(A) = 0$ iff for every rule $A \leftarrow A_1, \ldots, A_n$ there is an $i \leq n$ such that $I(A_i) = 0$.*
- *$\Psi^*(I)(A) = 1/2$, otherwise.*

Theorem 4.2.1 (3-valued least model). *The 3-valued least model of a non-negative program is:*

$$\Psi^* \uparrow^\omega (not\ \mathcal{H})$$

The generalization of the Van Emden-Kowalski theorem set forth in [172] is also valid for extended logic of programs.

Theorem 4.2.2. *$least(P)$ uniquely exists for every non-negative program P.*

Proof. Since P' is a non-negative program without explicit negation its least 3-valued model M exists and is unique (by theorem 6.24 of [172] page 357). The theorem follows since $least(P)$ is univocally obtained from M.

Note that $least(P)$ isn't always an interpretation in the sense of Definition 4.1.1. Conditions about noncontradiction and coherence may be violated.

Example 4.2.1. Consider the non-negative program P :

$$
\begin{array}{llll}
a & \leftarrow & \neg a & \leftarrow & \neg b \\
\neg b & \leftarrow & b & \leftarrow & \mathbf{u}
\end{array}
$$

where $least(P) = \{a, \neg a, \neg b\}$. This set is not an interpretation (cf. Example 4.1.1). Noncontradiction and coherence are violated.

Example 4.2.2. Consider the program P :

$$
\begin{array}{lll}
a & \leftarrow & not\ b \\
b & \leftarrow & not\ b \\
\neg a
\end{array}
$$

and the interpretation $I = \{\neg a, not\ a, not\ \neg b\}$.

$$
\frac{P}{I} =
\begin{array}{lll}
a & \leftarrow & \mathbf{u} \\
b & \leftarrow & \mathbf{u} \\
\neg a
\end{array}
$$

So, $least\left(\frac{P}{I}\right) = \{\neg a, not\ \neg b\}$.
Although noncontradictory this set of literals violates coherence.

To impose coherence, when contradiction is not present, we define a partial operator that transforms any noncontradictory set of literals into an interpretation.

Definition 4.2.4 (The Coh operator). *Let $QI = QT \cup not\ QF$ be a set of literals such that QT does not contain any pair of objective literals $A, \neg A$. $Coh(QI)$ is the interpretation $T \cup not\ F$ such that*

$$
T = QT \text{ and } F = QF \cup \{\neg L \mid L \in T\}.
$$

The Coh operator is not defined for contradictory sets of literals.

The result of Coh applied to $least\left(\frac{P}{I}\right)$ is always an interpretation. The noncontradiction and coherence conditions are guaranteed by definition. T and F are disjoint because QT and QF are disjoint and none of the objective literals added to F are in T since T is noncontradictory.

However, it is not enough to simply define the semantics as the result of Coh applied to the WFM as in [180]. This yields quite unintuitive results:

Example 4.2.3. Consider the program of Example 3.0.6.

$$
\begin{array}{lll}
a & \leftarrow & not\ b \\
b & \leftarrow & not\ a \\
\neg a
\end{array}
$$

whose WFM according to [180] is $M = \{\neg a, not\ \neg b\}$. In this case:

$$Coh(M) = \{\neg a, not\ a, not\ \neg b\}$$

Although $Coh(M)$ is coherent, it does not take into account the consequences of literals introduced by Coh. In fact, $not\ a$ is added, but b (a direct consequence of $not\ a$) isn't.

Note that $Coh(M)$ is not a model of the program: it makes the body of the second rule true, and its head undefined.

To take into account the consequences of Coh, we generalize the Γ^* operator of [172].

Definition 4.2.5 (The Φ operator). *Let P be a logic program, I an interpretation, and $J = least\left(\frac{P}{I}\right)$.*
If $Coh(J)$ exists then $\Phi_P(I) = Coh(J)$. Otherwise $\Phi_P(I)$ is not defined.

Definition 4.2.6 (*WFSX*, PSM and WFM). *An interpretation I of an extended logic program P is called an Partial Stable Model (PSM) of P iff*

$$\Phi_P(I) = I.$$

The F-least Partial Stable Model is called the Well Founded Model(WFM). The WFSX *semantics of P is determined by the set of all PSMs of P.*

It is easy to see that some programs may have no *WFSX* semantics.

Example 4.2.4. The program $P = \{a \leftarrow,\ \neg a \leftarrow\}$ has no semantics.

Definition 4.2.7 (Contradictory program). *An extended logic program P is contradictory iff it has no semantics, i.e. there exists no interpretation I such that $\Phi_P(I) = I$.*

Theorem 4.3.3 below expresses an alternative, more illustrative definition of contradictory program. The issue of handling contradictory programs is further discussed in Chapter 8.

Example 4.2.5. Consider again the program of Example 3.0.6. Now

$$\{\neg a, not\ \neg b\}$$

is no longer a PSM as in [180] (where $\neg a$ and $\neg b$ are simply considered new atoms), because it is not an interpretation, and thus Φ does not apply to it.

Its only PSM, and consequently its WFM, is:

$$I = \{\neg a, b, not\ a, not\ \neg b\}.$$

$$\frac{P}{I} = \begin{array}{l} b \leftarrow \\ \neg a \leftarrow \end{array}$$

Indeed, its least model is I, $Coh(I) = I$, and $\Phi_P(I) = I$.

Remark 4.2.1. According to [180], the above program has two PSMs:

$$\{\neg a, not\ \neg b\} \quad \text{and} \quad \{\neg a, b, not\ a, not\ \neg b\}$$

only the second being coherent. It is not enough though to throw out those of his models not complying with coherence. Although that's true for this example, Example 4.2.6 shows that's not the general case.

Example 4.2.6. Consider program P:

$$
\begin{array}{llll}
c & \leftarrow & not\ b & \quad a & \leftarrow & not\ a \\
b & \leftarrow & not\ a & \quad \neg b & \leftarrow
\end{array}
$$

Applying the semantics to P we have the model:

$$PSM = \{\neg b, c, not\ b, not\ \neg c, not\ \neg a\}.$$

Indeed:

$$
\frac{P}{PSM} =
\begin{array}{llll}
c & \leftarrow & & a & \leftarrow & \mathbf{u} \\
b & \leftarrow & \mathbf{u} & \neg b & \leftarrow
\end{array}
$$

its least model is $\{c, \neg b, not\ \neg c, not\ \neg a\}$, and consequently

$$\Phi_P(PSM) = PSM^3.$$

By simply considering $\neg b$ as a new atom (as suggested in [180]) this non-extended program would have a single PSM, $\{\neg b\}$, which is not a coherent interpretation.

It is also interesting to notice in this example that PSM is not a model in the classical sense because for the second rule of P the value of the head $(PSM(b) = 0)$ is smaller than the value of the body $(PSM(not\ a) = \frac{1}{2})$.

The intuitive idea is that the truth of $\neg b$ (or the independent falsity of b) overrides any rule for b with undefined body, so that *not* b becomes true (and b false), rather than undefined. This is important to allow if we consider the existence of the fact $\neg b$ in the program instrumental in specifying the falsity of b in it. In Chapter 5 Section 5.2 this issue is further discussed.

Even though PSMs are not models in the classical sense, they are models as defined above in this chapter (Definition 4.1.3).

Theorem 4.2.3 (PSMs are models). *Every PSM of a program P is a model of P.*

Proof. (by contradiction) Let I be a PSM and not a model of P. By definition of model:

$$\hat{I}(L \leftarrow B) \neq 1$$

only if

$$\hat{I}(L) < \hat{I}(B) \text{ and } \hat{I}(B) = 1, \quad \text{or} \quad \hat{I}(L) < \hat{I}(B) \text{ and } \hat{I}(\neg L) \neq 1.$$

If the first disjunct holds, then since $\hat{I}(B) = 1$ and I is a PSM, $L \in I$ (i.e. $\hat{I}(L) = 1$), so the disjunct cannot hold.

If the second disjunct holds, then

$$\text{either } \hat{I}(B) = 1 \quad \text{or} \quad \hat{I}(B) = \frac{1}{2}.$$

The first case is impossible, as just shown. If $\hat{I}(B) = \frac{1}{2}$ then:

$$least\left(\frac{P}{I}\right)(L) = \frac{1}{2}$$

and since $\hat{I}(\neg L) \neq 1$:

$$Coh\left(least\left(\frac{P}{I}\right)\right)(L) = \frac{1}{2}.$$

As I is a PSM, $\hat{I}(L) = \frac{1}{2} = \hat{I}(B)$, so the disjunct cannot hold.

Example 4.2.7. Consider Example 4.1.2. The only PSMs of that program correspond exactly to models M_7, M_9 and M_{10}.

We now come back to the question of the need for the extra operation introduced in the modulo transformation.

Example 4.2.8. Consider program P :

$$
\begin{array}{llll}
c & \leftarrow & a & \qquad a & \leftarrow & b \\
\neg a & \leftarrow & & \qquad b & \leftarrow & not\ b
\end{array}
$$

Its only PSM is $I = \{\neg a, not\ a, not\ c, not\ \neg b, not\ \neg c\}$. In fact,

$$
\frac{P}{I} = \quad
\begin{array}{llll}
& & a & \leftarrow & b \\
\neg a & \leftarrow & & b & \leftarrow & \mathbf{u}
\end{array}
$$

$$least\left(\frac{P}{I}\right) = \{\neg a, not\ c, not\ \neg b, not\ \neg c\}$$

and consequently $\Phi(I) = I$.

If the new operation for the modulo transformation were absent, $\frac{P}{I}$ would contain the rule $c \leftarrow a$, and c would be undefined rather than false. This would go against the coherence principle, since $\neg a$ entails $not\ a$, and as the only rule for c has a in the body, it should also entail $not\ c$. The rôle of the new operation is to ensure the propagation of false as a consequence of any $not\ L$ implied by a $\neg L$ through coherence.

Consider now a similar program P', in the canonical (cf. Definition 2.1.1) form:

$$
\begin{array}{llll}
c & \leftarrow & a, not\ \neg a & \qquad a & \leftarrow & b, not\ \neg b \\
\neg a & \leftarrow & & \qquad b & \leftarrow & not\ b
\end{array}
$$

Its only PSM is again $I = \{\neg a, not\ a, not\ c, not\ \neg b, not\ \neg c\}$.

$$\frac{P'}{I} = \quad \begin{array}{rcl} a & \leftarrow & b \\ \neg a & \leftarrow & \\ & & b \leftarrow \mathbf{u} \end{array}$$

Because of the canonical form the new operation of the modulo transformation is irrelevant. Even without it the rule $c \leftarrow a, not\ \neg a$ is removed by applying the first operation, given that $\neg a \in I$ and that $not\ \neg a$ is part of its body.

In general, for programs in the canonical form the second operation of the modulo operator is no longer required.

Theorem 4.2.4 (Compact version of $\frac{P}{I}$). *Let P be a canonical extended logic program, and I an interpretation. Then $\frac{P}{I}$ can be equivalently defined as the program obtained from P by performing in sequence the three operations:*

- *Remove from P all rules containing a default literal $L = not\ A$ such that $A \in I$.*
- *Remove from all remaining rules of P their default literals $L = not\ A$ such that $not\ A \in I$.*
- *Replace all the remaining default literals by proposition $\mathbf{u}$.*

Proof. Trivial, given the definitions of canonical program, of interpretation, and of $\frac{P}{I}$.

4.3 Existence of the semantics

In the above definition of the semantics (Definition 4.2.6) we define the WFM as the F-least PSM. This is possible because:

Theorem 4.3.1 (Existence of the semantics). *For   noncontradictory programs there always exists a unique F-least PSM. Moreover a literal L belongs to every PSM of a noncontradictory program P iff L belong to the F-least PSM of P.*

Proof. The proof follows directly from Theorem 4.3.2 below.

Theorem 4.3.2 (Monotonicity of Φ). *Let P be a noncontradictory program. Then the operator Φ_P is monotonic with respect to set inclusion, i.e. $A \subseteq B \Rightarrow \Phi_P(A) \subseteq \Phi_P(B)$ for any interpretations A and B.*

Proof. Since $\Phi_P(I) = Coh(least(\frac{P}{I}))$ we prove this theorem by proving two lemmas, concerning respectively the monotonicity of Coh and that of $least(\frac{P}{I})$.

Lemma 4.3.1. *Consider a program P and let*

$$I = T_I \cup not \ F_I \ and \ J = T_J \cup not \ F_J$$

be two interpretations of P such that $I \subseteq J$. $Coh(I) \subseteq Coh(J)$ *holds.*

Proof. $Coh(I) \subseteq Coh(J)$ is equivalent, by definition of Coh, to

$$T_I \cup not \ (F_I \cup \{\neg L \mid L \in T_I\}) \subseteq T_J \cup not \ (F_J \cup \{\neg L \mid L \in T_J\})$$

since $T_I \subseteq T_J$ by hypothesis, the above is true if:

$$F_I \cup \{\neg L \mid L \in T_I\} \subseteq F_J \cup \{\neg L \mid L \in T_I\} \cup \{\neg L \mid L \in T_J - T_I\}$$

which is equivalent to

$$F_I \subseteq F_J \cup \{\neg L \mid L \in T_J - T_I\}$$

which holds because, by hypothesis, $F_I \subseteq F_J$.

Lemma 4.3.2. *Consider a program P and let*

$$I = T_I \cup not \ F_I \ and \ J = T_J \cup not \ F_J$$

be two interpretations of P such that $I \subseteq J$.

$$least\left(\tfrac{P}{I}\right) \subseteq least\left(\tfrac{P}{J}\right) \ holds.$$

Proof. In [172] this is proven considering the modulo transformation without the second rule. Since this rule does not introduce new undefined literals, it does not affect the monotonicity of the operator.

Now it is easy to complete the proof of the theorem. By lemma 4.3.2:

$$A \subseteq B \ \Rightarrow \ least\left(\frac{P}{A}\right) \subseteq least\left(\frac{P}{B}\right)$$

and by lemma 4.3.1:

$$least\left(\frac{P}{A}\right) \subseteq least\left(\frac{P}{B}\right) \ \Rightarrow \ Coh\left(least\left(\frac{P}{A}\right)\right) \subseteq Coh\left(least\left(\frac{P}{B}\right)\right)$$

for a noncontradictory program P.

Definition 4.3.1 (Iterative construction of the WFM).
In order to obtain a constructive bottom-up definition of the WFM of a given noncontradictory program P, we define the following transfinite sequence $\{I_\alpha\}$ *of interpretations of P:*

$$\begin{aligned}
I_0 &= \{\} \\
I_{\alpha+1} &= \Phi_P(I_\alpha) \\
I_\delta &= \bigcup \{I_\alpha \mid \alpha < \delta\} \quad \text{for a limit ordinal } \delta
\end{aligned}$$

By Theorem 4.3.2, and according to the Knaster-Tarski theorem [204], there must exist a smallest ordinal λ *such that* I_λ *is a fixpoint of* Φ_P, *and* $WFM = I_\lambda$.

Top-down procedures computing this semantics can be easily obtained by adapting existing procedures for WFS of programs without explicit negation, such as [177, 215, 155, 40, 153], as follows: replace every literal of the form $\neg A$ by a new literal, say A'; include two new rules *"not A rewrites to A'"* and *"not A' rewrites to A"*. If A and A' are both derivable then the program is contradictory. A top-down derivation procedure for *WFSX* can be found in Chapter 10.

The constructive bottom-up definition requires one to know *a priori* if the given program is contradictory. This requirement is not needed if we consider the following theorem.

Theorem 4.3.3. *A program P is contradictory iff in the sequence of I_α there exists a λ such that $\Phi_P(I_\lambda)$ is not defined, i.e. $least\left(\frac{P}{I_\lambda}\right)$ has a pair of objective literals A, $\neg A$.*

Proof. The theorem is equivalent to: P is noncontradictory iff in the sequence of I_α there exists no λ such that $\Phi_P(I_\lambda)$ is not defined.

If P is noncontradictory then Φ_P is monotonic, and so no such λ exists. If there is no such λ then there exists an I and a smallest α such that $I = \Phi_P^{\uparrow\alpha}(\{\})$, and I is a fixpoint of Φ_P. Thus, a fixpoint of Φ_P exists, and so P is noncontradictory.

In order to (bottom-up) compute the WFM of a program P start by building the above sequence. If at some step Φ_P is not applicable then end the iteration and conclude that P is contradictory. Otherwise, iterate until the least fixpoint of Φ_P, which is the WFM of P.

Example 4.3.1. Consider program P:

$$a \leftarrow not\ a$$
$$\neg a \leftarrow$$

Let us build the sequence:

$$
\begin{aligned}
I_0 &= \{\} \\
I_1 &= Coh\left(least\left(\tfrac{P}{\{\}}\right)\right) = Coh(least(\{a \leftarrow \mathbf{u}, \quad \neg a \leftarrow\})) \\
&= Coh(\{\neg a\}) = \{\neg a, not\ a\} \\
I_2 &= Coh\left(least\left(\tfrac{P}{\{\neg a, not\ a\}}\right)\right) = Coh(least(\{a \leftarrow, \quad \neg a \leftarrow\})) \\
&= Coh(\{a, \neg a\})
\end{aligned}
$$

which is not defined. So P is contradictory.

Example 4.3.2. Consider program P of Example 4.2.5. The sequence is:

$$I_0 = \{\}$$
$$I_1 = Coh\Big(least\Big(\tfrac{P}{\{\}}\Big)\Big) = Coh(least(\{a \leftarrow \mathbf{u}, \quad b \leftarrow \mathbf{u}, \quad \neg a \leftarrow\}))$$
$$\quad = Coh(\{\neg a, not \ \neg b\}) = \{\neg a, not \ a, not \ \neg b\}$$
$$I_2 = Coh\Big(least\Big(\tfrac{P}{\{\neg a, not \ a, not \ \neg b\}}\Big)\Big)$$
$$\quad = Coh(least(\{a \leftarrow \mathbf{u}, \quad b \leftarrow, \quad \neg a \leftarrow\}))$$
$$\quad = Coh(\{b, \neg a, not \ \neg b\}) = \{b, \neg a, not \ a, not \ \neg b\} = I_3$$

and thus the WFM of P is $\{b, \neg a, not \ a, not \ \neg b\}$.

It is worth noting that this semantics is a generalization of the well-founded semantics to programs with explicit negation.

Theorem 4.3.4 (Generalization of the well-founded semantics). *For programs without explicit negation* WFSX *coincides with well-founded semantics.*

Proof. As noted before, the modulo transformation coincides with the one defined for stationary semantics for the case of non-extended programs. Furthermore, the additional conditions imposed on interpretations are void for those programs and, finally, the Coh operator reduces to identity.

5. *WFSX*, LP semantics with two negations, and autoepistemic logics

In recent years increasing and productive effort has been devoted to the study of the relationships between logic programming and several nonmonotonic reasoning formalisms[1]. Such relationships are mutually beneficial. On the one hand, nonmonotonic formalisms provide elegant semantics for logic programming, specially in what regards the meaning of default negation (or negation as failure), and help one understand how logic programs are used to formalize several types of problems in Artificial Intelligence. On the other hand, those formalisms benefit from the existing procedures of logic programming, and some new issues of the former are raised and solved by the latter. Moreover, relations among nonmonotonic formalisms have been facilitated and established via logic programming.

For normal logic programs, their relationship with default theories [188] was first proposed in [22]. In [70] default negation of normal programs was first formalized as abduction, and in [62] the idea was further explored in order to capture stable models [78] and the well-founded semantics [76] of normal programs.

The idea of viewing logic programs as autoepistemic theories first appeared in [77] where the author proposed to view every negated literal *not L* of logic programs as $\sim \mathcal{B}L$,[2] i.e. *not L* has the epistemic reading: *"there is no reason to believe in L"*. In [28], different transformations between default negation literals and belief literals are studied, in order to show how different logic programming semantics can be obtained from autoepistemic logics.

The establishment of relationships between nonmonotonic formalisms and extended logic programs improve on those for normal programs since extended programs map into broader classes of theories in nonmonotonic formalisms, and so more general relations between several of those formalisms can now be made via logic programs. Moreover, the relationships also provide a clearer meaning of the ¬-negation and its relation to default negation in extended logic programming.

---

[1] As a result, international workshops have been organized, in whose proceedings [136, 164] many additional references can be found.

[2] In the sequel we refer to this transformation, between default negation literals and belief literals, as the Gelfond transformation.

In this and the next chapters we explore the relationship between extended logic programs and several nonmonotonic formalisms: autoepistemic logic, default theory, abduction, and belief revision.

The first part of this chapter is devoted to contrasting and characterizing a variety of semantics for extended logic programs, including *WFSX*, in what concerns their use and meaning of ¬-negation, and its relation to both classical negation and the default negation, *not* , of normal programs.

For this purpose we define a parametrizeable schema to encompass and characterize a diversity of proposed semantics for extended logic programs, where the parameters are two: one the axioms $AX_\neg$ defining ¬-negation; another the minimality conditions not_{cond}, defining *not* -negation.

By adjusting these parameters in the schema we can then specify several semantics involving two kinds of negation [80, 143, 180, 183, 209], including *WFSX*. Other semantics, dealing with contradiction removal [152, 68, 146, 196], are not directly addressed by the schema. The issue of contradiction in extended logic programming is studied in length in Chapter 8.

In the second part of this chapter, and based on the similarities between the parametrizable schema and the definitions of autoepistemic logics, we proceed to examine the relationship between them and extended logic programs.

In the above mentioned comparative study, concerning the use and meaning of ¬-negation in different semantics, no epistemic meaning is assigned to each of the uses of ¬. By relating extended logic programs to autoepistemic logics such a meaning is extracted for some cases. In particular, we show that ¬L in *WFSX* can be read as *"L is provenly false"*. Other semantics give different readings to ¬, e.g. in the stationary semantics with classical negation of [183] ¬L has the epistemic reading: *"L is not provenly true"*.

These results also clarify the use of logic programs for representing knowledge and belief.

5.1 Generic semantics for programs with two kinds of negation

The structure of this section is as follows: we begin with preliminary definitions and subSection 5.1.2 presents the parametrizeable schema; next we present properties important for the study of extended logic program semantics, and show for various $AX_\neg$ whether or not the resulting semantics complies with such properties; afterwards, in subSection 5.1.4, we reconstruct the plurality of semantics for extended logic programs in the schema by specifying, for each, their set $AX_\neg$ and their condition not_{cond}; finally we briefly address the issue of introducing disjunction in extended logic programs.

5.1.1 Preliminaries

In the sequel, we translate every extended logic program P into a set of general clauses $\neg\_P$, which we dub *clausal logic program*. A set of general clauses is, as usual, a set of clauses:

$$L_1 \vee \ldots \vee L_n$$

where each L_i is either an atom A or its *classical negation* $\sim A$. Here, by classical negation we mean the negation of classical logic. Just as it was important to distinguish between classical negation and negation by default in order to develop the relationship between normal logic programming and nonmonotonic reasoning, here it is equally important to distinguish between explicit negation $\neg$ and *real* classical negation $\sim$, specially because our concern is to better characterize the former.

The models and interpretations of clausal logic programs are simply the classical models and interpretations of sets of general clauses.

Propositions of the form not_A (the translation in the clausal logic program $\neg\_P$ for $not\ A$ in P) are called *default* ones, all other propositions being *objective* ones.

5.1.2 Stationary and stable semantics for programs with two kinds of negation

Within this section we present the above mentioned parametrizeable schema. We begin by defining two generic semantics for normal logic programs extended with an extra kind of negation: one extending the stationary semantics [181, 183] for normal programs (itself equivalent to well founded semantics [76]); another extending the stable model semantics [78]. We dub each of these semantics generic because they assume little about the extra kind of negation introduced. The meaning of the negation by default is however completely determined in each of the two generic semantics (both stationary and stable models) that we present.

Subsequently we generalize the schema in order to parametrize it w.r.t. negation by default as well.

Stationary semantics for programs with two kinds of negation. Here we redefine the stationary semantics of [183] in order to parametrize it with a generic second type of negation, in addition to negation by default. We start by defining stationary expansion of normal programs as in [183].

Definition 5.1.1 (Minimal models). *A minimal model of a theory (or set of general clauses) T is a model M of T with the property that there is no smaller model N of T which coincides with M on default propositions.*

If a formula F is true in all minimal models of T then we write:

$$T \models_{CIRC} F$$

and say that F is minimally entailed by T.

This amounts to McCarthy's Parallel Circumscription [125]:

$$CIRC(T; \mathcal{O}; \mathcal{D})$$

of theory T in which objective propositions $\mathcal{O}$ are minimized and default propositions $\mathcal{D}$ are fixed.

Definition 5.1.2 (Stationary expansion of normal programs).

A stationary expansion of a normal program P is any consistent theory P^* which satisfies the fixed point condition:

$$P^* = \neg\_P \cup \left\{ not\_A \mid P^* \models_{CIRC} \sim A \right\} \cup \left\{ \sim not\_A \mid P^* \models_{CIRC} A \right\}$$

where A is any arbitrary atom, $\neg\_P$ is the program obtained from P by replacing every literal of the form not L by not_L.

Note that $\neg\_P$ and P^* are always sets of Horn clauses.

Example 5.1.1. Consider program P :

$$
\begin{array}{lll}
a & \leftarrow & not\ a \\
b & \leftarrow & not\ a, c \\
d & \leftarrow & not\ b
\end{array}
$$

whose clausal program is $\neg\_P$:

$$
\begin{array}{l}
a \vee \sim not\_a \\
b \vee \sim not\_a \vee \sim c \\
d \vee \sim not\_b
\end{array}
$$

The only expansion of P is

$$P^* = \neg\_P \cup \{ not\_b, not\_c, \sim not\_d \}$$

In fact the minimal models of P^* are (for clarity throughout the examples we exhibit all literals, both positive and negative):

$$
\begin{array}{lllllllll}
\{ & not\_a, & not\_b, & not\_c, & \sim not\_d, & a, & \sim b, & \sim c, & d \ \} \\
\{ & \sim not\_a, & not\_b, & not\_c, & \sim not\_d, & \sim a, & \sim b, & \sim c, & d \ \}
\end{array}
$$

As P^* entails $\sim b$, $\sim c$, and d, it must contain $\{ not\_b, not\_c, \sim not\_d \}$ and no more default literals.

As proven in [183], the least stationary expansion of a normal program gives its well-founded semantics (via a definition of meaning similar to Definition 5.1.4), and now we wish to extend WFS with explicit negation to obtain, among others, *WFSX*.

In order to extend this definition to logic programs with a generic second kind of negation $\neg$, we additionally transform any such negated literals into new atoms too:

Definition 5.1.3 (Clausal program $\neg\_P$ of P).
The clausal program $\neg\_P$ of an extended logic program P is the clausal set of Horn clauses obtained by first denoting every literal in $\mathcal{H}$ of the form:

$$
\begin{array}{lll}
\neg A & \textit{by a new atom} & \neg\_A \\
\textit{not } A & \textit{by a new atom} & \textit{not}\_A \\
\textit{not } \neg A & \textit{by a new atom} & \textit{not}\_\neg\_A
\end{array}
$$

then replacing in P such literals by their new denotation and, finally, reinterpreting the rule connective $\leftarrow$ as material implication, expressed by $\Rightarrow$.

Example 5.1.2. Let $P = \{a \leftarrow \neg b\}$. The clausal program $\neg\_P$ is:

$$\neg\_P = \{\neg\_b \Rightarrow a\}$$

or equivalently:

$$\neg\_P = \{a \vee \sim\neg\_b\}.$$

The models of an extended program are determined by the models of its clausal program expansions via an inverse transformation:

Definition 5.1.4 (Meaning of a clausal program P^*). *The meaning of a clausal program expansion P^* is the union of the sets of all atoms:*

$$
\begin{array}{llll}
A & \textit{such that} & P^* \models A \\
\neg A & \textit{such that} & P^* \models \neg\_A \\
\textit{not } A & \textit{such that} & P^* \models \textit{not}\_A \\
\textit{not } \neg A & \textit{such that} & P^* \models \textit{not}\_\neg\_A
\end{array}
$$

where $P^* \models L$ means that literal L belongs to all (classical) models of (the set of general clauses) P^*.

Note that negative literals do not translate over.

In order to specify the second kind of negation one introduces in $\neg\_P$ the axioms $AX_\neg$ defining it. For example, if we want the second negation to be classical negation we must add to $\neg\_P$ the set of clauses

$$\{\neg\_A \Leftrightarrow \sim A \mid A \in \mathcal{H}\}$$

where $\Leftrightarrow$ denotes material equivalence, and is used as shorthand for both clauses $\neg\_A \Rightarrow \sim A$ and $\sim A \Rightarrow \neg\_A$. In this case, the semantics of P is the same whether or not the first part of the transformation to $\neg\_P$ takes place.

We want this generic semantics to be an extension of stationary semantics. So we must guarantee that the semantics of a program without any occurence of $\neg$-negation is the same as for stationary semantics, whatever kind of $\neg$-negation axioms are used and defined in the generic schema. To that end, we must first minimize by circumscription the atoms in the language of P, and only afterwards do we minimize the bar-ed atoms.

Definition 5.1.5 ($M \tilde{\leq} N$). *Let M and N be two models of a program $\neg\_P$ and M_{pos} (resp. N_{pos}) be the subset of M (resp. N) obtained by deleting from it all literals of the form $\neg\_L$.*

We say that $M \tilde{\leq} N$ iff:

$$M_{pos} \subseteq N_{pos} \vee (M_{pos} = N_{pos} \wedge M \subseteq N).$$

This definition is similar to the classical one plus a condition to the effect that, say, model $M_1 = \{\neg\_a\}$ is smaller than model $M_2 = \{a\}$.

Minimal models are now defined as in 5.1.1 but with this new $\tilde{\leq}$ relation. The equivalence between minimality and circumscription is made through the ordered predicate circumscription $CIRC(T; \mathcal{O}; \mathcal{D})$ of the theory T, in which objective propositions $\mathcal{O}$ are minimized, but minimizing first propositions not of the form $\neg\_A$, and only afterwards the latter, and where default propositions $\mathcal{D}$ are fixed parameters.

The definition of stationary expansion of an extended programs is then a generalization of Definition 5.1.2, parametrized by the set of axioms $AX_\neg$ defining $\neg\_A$, plus this new notion of ordered minimality.

Definition 5.1.6 (Stationary $AX_\neg$ expansions). *A stationary expansion of an $AX_\neg$ extended program P is any consistent theory P^* which satisfies the following fixed point condition:*

$$P^* = \neg\_P \cup AX_\neg \cup \left\{ not\_L \mid P^* \models_{\overline{CIRC}} \sim L \right\} \cup \left\{ \sim not\_L \mid P^* \models_{\overline{CIRC}} L \right\}$$

where L is any arbitrary objective proposition, and $AX_\neg$ is the set of axioms for $\neg$-negation in P.

A stationary expansion P^* of a program P is obtained by adding to the corresponding clausal program $\neg\_P$ the axioms defining $\neg$-negation, and the negations by default not_L of those and only those literals L which are false in all minimal models of P^*. The meaning of negation by default is that, in any stationary expansion P^*, not_L holds if and only if P^* minimally entails $\sim L$. Note that the definition of $AX_\neg$ can influence, by reducing the number of models, whether $\sim L$ is in all minimal models of P^*.

It is known (cf. [113, 71, 82]) that for any positive proposition A of any theory T, the above definition of $\models_{\overline{CIRC}}$ implies:

$$T \models_{\overline{CIRC}} A \equiv T \models A$$

Thus, and directly from Definition 5.1.6:

Proposition 5.1.1. *A consistent theory P^* is a stationary expansion of an $AX_\neg$ extended program P iff:*

- *P^* is obtained by augmenting $\neg\_P \cup AX_\neg$ with some default propositions not_A and $\sim not\_A$ where A is an objective proposition;*

- P^* *satisfies the conditions:*

$$P^* \models \quad not\_A \quad \equiv \quad P^* \models_{CIRC} \quad \sim A \qquad and$$
$$P^* \models \sim not\_A \quad \equiv \quad P^* \models \qquad A$$

for any objective proposition A.

Example 5.1.3. Consider program P :

$$p \quad \leftarrow \quad a$$
$$p \quad \leftarrow \quad \neg a$$
$$q \quad \leftarrow \quad not\ p$$

where $\neg$ in P is classical negation, i.e.

$$AX_\neg = \{\neg\_a \Leftrightarrow \sim a,\ \neg\_p \Leftrightarrow \sim p,\ \neg\_q \Leftrightarrow \sim q\}.$$

The clausal program of P is:

$$p \quad \vee \quad \sim a$$
$$p \quad \vee \quad \sim \neg\_a$$
$$q \quad \vee \quad \sim not\_p$$

The only stationary expansion of P is:

$$P_1^* = \neg\_P \cup AX_\neg \cup \{\sim not\_p, not\_\neg\_p, not\_q, \sim not\_\neg\_q, not\_a, \sim not\_\neg\_a\}$$

In fact, the only minimal model of P_1^* is:

$$\{\sim not\_p, not\_\neg\_p, not\_q, \sim not\_\neg\_q, not\_a, \sim not\_\neg\_a,$$
$$p, \sim \neg\_p, \sim q, \neg\_q, \sim a, \neg\_a \qquad \}$$

and the conditions of proposition 5.1.1 hold.

Note how the $\tilde{\leq}$ relation prefers this model to other models that would be minimal if the usual $\leq$ were to be enforced. For example, the classically minimal model:

$$\{\sim not\_p, not\_\neg\_p, not\_q, \sim not\_\neg\_q, not\_a, \sim not\_\neg\_a,$$
$$p, \sim \neg\_p, q, \sim \neg\_q, \sim a, \neg\_a \qquad \}$$

is not minimal when the $\tilde{\leq}$ relation is considered.

If $\neg$ in P is defined by :

$$AX_\neg = \{\neg\_a \Rightarrow \sim a,\ \neg\_p \Rightarrow \sim p,\ \neg\_q \Rightarrow \sim q\}$$

i.e. $\neg$ in P is a *strong* negation in the sense that it implies classical negation in $\neg\_P$, then the only stationary expansion of P is:

$$P_2^* = \neg\_P \cup AX_\neg \cup \{not\_p, not\_\neg\_p, \sim not\_q, not\_\neg\_q, not\_a, not\_\neg\_a\}$$

In fact, the only minimal model of P_2^* is:

$$\{not\_p, not\_\neg\_p, \sim not\_q, not\_\neg\_q, not\_a, not\_\neg\_a,$$
$$\sim p, \sim \neg\_p, q, \sim \neg\_q, \sim a, \sim \neg\_a \qquad \}$$

and the conditions of proposition 5.1.1 hold.

We now define the semantics of a program based on its stationary expansions relative to some $AX_\neg$.

Definition 5.1.7 (Stationary $AX_\neg$ semantics). *A stationary $AX_\neg$ model of a program P is the meaning of P^*, where P^* is a stationary $AX_\neg$ expansion of P.*

The stationary $AX_\neg$ semantics of an extended program P is the set of all stationary $AX_\neg$ models of P.

If $S = \{M_k \mid k \in K\}$ is the semantics of P, then the intended meaning of P is:

$$M = \bigcap_{k \in K} M_k.$$

Example 5.1.4. The meaning of the program of Example 5.1.3 is:

$$\{p, \neg q, \neg a, not\ q, not\ a, not\ \neg p\}$$

if we use classical negation, and:

$$\{q, not\ p, not\ \neg p, not\ \neg q, not\ a, not\ \neg a\}$$

if we use strong negation.

Example 5.1.5. Consider P :

$$
\begin{aligned}
a &\leftarrow not\ b \\
\neg a &
\end{aligned}
$$

where $\neg$ is a weak form of negation determined by:

$$AX_\neg = \{\sim A \Rightarrow \neg\_A \mid A \in \mathcal{H}\}.$$

The only stationary expansion of P is:

$$P^* = \neg\_P \cup AX_\neg \cup \{\sim not\_a, \sim not\_\neg\_a, not\_b, \sim not\_\neg\_b\}$$

determining thus the meaning of P as

$$M = \{a, \neg a, not\ b, \neg b\}.$$

The fact that both a and $\neg a$ belong to M is not a problem since the weak form of negation allows that. Note that $\sim A \Rightarrow \neg\_A$ is equivalent to $A \vee \neg\_A$, and allows models with both A and $\neg\_A$. Literal $\neg b$ also appears in M forced by the weak negation.

Now we state in what sense this semantics is a generalization of stationary semantics:

Proposition 5.1.2 (Generalization of stationary semantics). *Let P be a (non-extended) normal logic program, and let $AX_\neg$ be such that no clause of the form*

$$A_1 \vee \ldots \vee A_n \text{ where } \{A_1, \ldots, A_n\} \subseteq \mathcal{H}$$

is a logical consequence of it.

M is a stationary $AX_\neg$ model of P iff M (modulo the $\neg$-literals) is a stationary model of P.

The reader can check that all sets of axioms $AX_\neg$ used in the sequel satisfy the restriction imposed in the proposition. This restriction on the form of $AX_\neg$ is meant to avoid unusual definitions of $\neg$-negation where positive literals are just a consequence of the axioms independently from the program. For instance:

Example 5.1.6. Let $P = \{a \leftarrow b\}$, and

$$AX_\neg = \{a \vee \sim\neg\_b, \neg\_b\}.$$

P has a stationary $AX_\neg$ model

$$\{a, not\ \neg a, not\ b, \neg b\}$$

which is not a stationary model of P. Note however that a is in the model because it is a logical consequence of $AX_\neg$ irrespective of the program.

The parametrizeable schema. Stable models [78] have a one-to-one correspondence with stable expansions [132], and the latters can be obtained simply by replacing $\models_{\overline{CIRC}}$ by $\models_{\overline{CWA}}$ in the definition of stationary expansion of normal programs, where CWA denotes Reiter's closed world assumption [187], as shown in [183].

As with the stationary semantics of extended programs, a generic definition of stable semantics for extended programs can also be obtained, with $P^* \models_{\overline{CWA}} \sim L$ as the condition for adding negation by default.

So, in general a new parameter in the schema is desirable in order to specify how default negation is to be added to an expansion.

Definition 5.1.8 ($\langle AX_\neg, not_{cond}\rangle$ **expansion**). *A $\langle AX_\neg, not_{cond}\rangle$ expansion of an extended program P is any consistent theory P^* which satisfies the following fixed point condition:*

$$P^* = \neg\_P \cup AX_\neg \cup \{not\_L \mid not_{cond}(L)\} \cup \{\sim not\_L \mid P^* \models L\}$$

where L is any arbitrary objective proposition.

The definition of a generic semantics is similar to that of stationary semantics.

Definition 5.1.9 ($\langle AX_\neg, not_{cond}\rangle$ **semantics**). *A $\langle AX_\neg, not_{cond}\rangle$ model of a program P is the meaning of P^*, where P^* is a $\langle AX_\neg, not_{cond}\rangle$ expansion of P.*

The semantics of a program P is the set of all $\langle AX_\neg, not_{cond}\rangle$ models of P. The intended meaning of P is the intersection of all models of P.

We define Stable $AX_\neg$ Semantics as the generic semantics where:

$$not_{cond}(L) = P^* \models_{\overline{CWA}} \sim L.$$

With this definition, propositions 5.1.1 and 5.1.2 are also valid for stable models.

5.1.3 Properties required of ¬

In this section we present some of the properties of extended logic programs and show for some $AX_\neg$ whether or not the resulting semantics comply with such properties. Here we examine the cases of:

- *classical negation*   i.e. $AX_\neg = \{ \ \neg\_A \Leftrightarrow \sim A \mid A \in \mathcal{H}\}$
- *strong negation*   i.e. $AX_\neg = \{ \ \neg\_A \Rightarrow \sim A \mid A \in \mathcal{H}\}$
- *weak negation*   i.e. $AX_\neg = \{ \ \sim A \Rightarrow \neg\_A \mid A \in \mathcal{H}\}$
- *pseudo negation*   i.e. $AX_\neg = \{\}.$

for both the stationary and stable semantics generic schemes. In Section 5.1.4 we redefine $WFSX$, introducing *explicit negation,* by imposing:

$$AX_\neg = \{\} \quad \text{and} \quad not_{cond}(L) = P^* \models_{\overline{CIRC}} \sim L \vee P^* \models \neg\_L$$

Alternatively, we can define $WFSX$ via stationary $AX_\neg$ semantics with:

- *explicit negation*   i.e. $AX_\neg = \{\neg\_A \Rightarrow not\_A \mid A \in \mathcal{H}\}$

We concentrate next only on properties concerning the ¬-negation. For a comparative study of semantics also concerning negation by default see Section 9.2.

Property 5.1.1 (Intrinsic consistency). A semantics is intrinsically consistent iff, for any program P, if M is a stationary (resp. stable) model of P then for no atom $A \in \mathcal{H}$:

$$\{A, \neg A\} \subseteq M.$$

In other words, a semantics is intrinsically consistent if there is no need for testing for consistency within the final (stationary or stable) models of a program.

Example 5.1.7. Let P be:

$$
\begin{aligned}
a &\leftarrow \quad not\ b \\
\neg a &\leftarrow \quad not\ b
\end{aligned}
$$

where ¬ is weak negation.

The only stationary expansion of P is:

$$P^* = \neg\_P \cup \{\sim A \Rightarrow \neg\_A \mid A \in \mathcal{H}\} \cup \{not\_b, not\_\neg\_b\}.$$

The only minimal model of P^* is:

$$\{a, \sim not\_a, \neg\_a, \sim not\_\neg\_a, \sim b, \sim \neg\_b, not\_b, not\_\neg\_b\}$$

and is consistent.

However the meaning of P^* :

$$\{a, \neg a, not\_b, not\_\neg\_b\}$$

is inconsistent.

As shown with the previous example, semantics with weak negation might not be intrinsically consistent. The same happens with semantics with pseudo negation.

Semantics with classical or strong negation are intrinsically consistent because, by the very definition of $AX_\neg$, for every atom $A \in \mathcal{H}$,

$$\sim A \vee \sim \neg\_A \in P^*,$$

for every expansion P^* of any program P, and thus no model of P^* has A and $\neg\_A$. So the meaning of P^* can never contain both A and $\neg A$.

Property 5.1.2 (Coherence). A semantics is coherent iff, for any program P and objective literal L, whenever M is a stationary (resp. stable) model of P :

- if $\neg L \in M$ then *not* $L \in M^3$.

As argued above, this property plays an important rôle if we consider the second kind of negation instrumental for specifying the falsity of literals. In that case coherence can be read as:

if A is declared false then it must be assumed false by default.

It turns out that, for both stationary and stable semantics, coherence is equivalent to consistency:

Theorem 5.1.1. *A stationary (or stable) semantics is coherent iff it is consistent.*

Proof. In appendix.

Property 5.1.3 (Supportedness). A semantics is necessarily supportive iff, for any program P, whenever M is a stationary (resp. stable) model of P then, for every objective literal L, if $L \in M$ there exists in P at least one identifiable rule of the form:

$$L \leftarrow B_1, \ldots, B_n, not\ C_1, \ldots, not\ C_m$$

such that:

$$\{B_1, \ldots, B_n, not\ C_1, \ldots, not\ C_m\} \subseteq M.$$

---

3 If $L = \neg A$, this reads as $\neg\neg A = A \in M$ then *not* $\neg A \in M$.

Since for any program P :

$$\neg P \cup \left\{ not\_L \mid P^* \models_{CIRC} \sim L \right\}$$

is a Horn clause program, a stationary (or a stable) semantics such that $AX_\neg$ does not contain any clause with positive propositions is necessarily supportive. Thus, semantics with pseudo or strong negation are necessarily supportive.

Semantics that introduce in $AX_\neg$ such clauses might not be necessarily supportive. For example, if $\neg$ is classical negation necessary supportedness does not hold:

Example 5.1.8. Consider program P :

$$
\begin{aligned}
a &\leftarrow b \\
\neg a &
\end{aligned}
$$

The only stationary $\{\neg\_A \Leftrightarrow \sim A\}$ model is:

$M = \{not\ a, \neg a, not\ b, \neg b\}$.

As $\neg b \in M$, and there is no rule for $\neg b$, the semantics is not necessarily supportive.

This property closely relates to the use of logic as a programming language. One does not expect objective literals to be true unless rules stating their truth condition are introduced; in other words, except for default propositions, no implicit information should be expected. We argue that if one wants the result of the previous program one should write:

$$
\begin{aligned}
\neg b &\leftarrow \neg a \\
\neg a &
\end{aligned}
$$

or, if disjunction is introduced:

$$
\begin{aligned}
a &\leftarrow b \\
\neg a & \\
b &\vee \neg b
\end{aligned}
$$

5.1.4 Fixing the set $AX_\neg$ and the condition $not_{cond}(L)$

In this section we reconstruct some semantics for extended programs simply by specifying the set $AX_\neg$ and the condition $not_{cond}(L)$ w.r.t. the generic semantics defined above. We contribute this way for a better understanding of what type of second negation each of those semantics uses, what are the main differences among them, and how they compare to *WFSX*.

We begin by reconstructing answer-sets semantics [80] for programs with consistent answer-sets (equivalent to the semantics of [209]).

Theorem 5.1.2 (Answer-sets semantics). *An interpretation M is   an answer-set of a program P iff M is a stable*

$$AX_\neg = \{\neg\_A \Rightarrow \sim A \mid A \in \mathcal{H}\}$$

model of P (modulo the syntactic representation of models[4]).

Proof. Since:

- stable models correspond to stable expansions for normal logic programs, and
- answer sets are the consistent stable models of the normal program obtained by considering every objective literal of the form $\neg L$ as a new atom $\neg\_L$, i.e. consistent stable $\{\}$ models of P,

for proving this theorem it is enough to prove that:

1. All stable $\{\neg\_A \Rightarrow \sim A \mid A \in \mathcal{H}\}$ expansions are consistent
2. Consistent stable $\{\}$ models are equivalent to stable $\{\neg\_A \Rightarrow \sim A \mid A \in \mathcal{H}\}$ models.

The first point is clear given that, as shown in Section 5.1.3, stable semantics with strong negation are always consistent.

If P^* is a consistent stable $\{\}$ expansion, then for every objective proposition $\neg\_A$:

$$P^* \models \neg\_A \stackrel{\text{by consistency}}{\Rightarrow} P^* \not\models A \stackrel{\text{by CWA}}{\Leftrightarrow} P^* \models_{CWA} \sim A$$

Thus, formulae of the form:

$$\neg\_A \Rightarrow \sim A$$

are theorems in all consistent stable $\{\}$ models.

So, by adding them to expansions the results remain unchanged, i.e. point 2 holds.

This theorem leads to the conclusion that answer-sets semantics extends stable models semantics with strong negation. Thus, from the results of Section 5.1.3, we conclude that answer-sets semantics is consistent, coherent and supportive.

Note that if instead of strong negation one uses pseudo negation and a test for consistency in the final models, the result would be the same. However, we think that the formalization as in Theorem 5.1.2 is more accurate because the consistency there is intrinsic and dealt within the fixpoint condition, with no need for meta-level constraints, and the properties exhibited are those of

---

[4] Recall that in the definition of answer-sets, default literals are not included in models. By "modulo the syntactic representation of models" we mean removing all default literals in models according to this definition.

strong negation and not of pseudo negation. For example, coherence and intrinsic consistency (properties of strong negation but not of pseudo negation) are obeyed by answer-sets semantics.

One semantics extending well founded semantics with $\neg$-negation is presented in [180], and reviewed in Section 2.2 above. It claims that the method used in [80] can be applied to semantics other than stable models, and so that method is used to define the proposed semantics. It happens that the meaning of $\neg$ is not the same as for answer-sets, in the sense that different $AX_{\neg}$s are used:

Theorem 5.1.3 (WFS plus $\neg$ as in [180]). *An interpretation M is an extended stable model of a program P iff M is a consistent stationary $AX_{\neg} = \{\}$ model of P.*

Proof. Trivial, given that for normal logic programs WFS corresponds to stationary models, and WFS plus $\neg$ as in [180] is just the WFS of the normal program obtained by considering literals of the form $\neg L$ simply as new atoms $\neg\_L$.

Note the need for testing consistency in stationary models of the semantics so that L and $\neg L$ are related in the end. As seen in Section 5.1.3, this semantics does not comply with coherence, which imposes a permanent relationship between L and $\neg L$ in the computation of models.

Next we reconstruct the stationary semantics with classical negation presented in [183]. This semantics was originally defined similarly to the generic definition above, but where $AX_{\neg}$ is absent and literals of the form $\neg A$ and $not \ \neg A$ are just transformed into $\sim A$ and $\sim not \ A$, respectively. From this similarity the reconstruction follows easily:

Theorem 5.1.4 (Stationary semantics with classical negation).
An interpretation M is a stationary model (in the sense of [183]) of a program P iff M is a stationary

$$AX_{\neg} = \{\neg\_A \Leftrightarrow \sim A \mid A \in \mathcal{H}\}$$

model of P.

Proof. In appendix.

From the results of Section 5.1.3 we conclude that this semantics does not comply with supportedness. Nevertheless, this semantics is the only one reconstructed here that introduces *real* classical negation into normal logic programs. We argue that, comparing it with other semantics with strong negation, this is not a big advantage since, once disjunction is added to logic programs with strong negation, a programmer can state in the language that the negation is classical rather than strong. This can be done simply by adding rules of the form $A \lor \neg A$ for every atom. Moreover, the programmer has the opportunity of stating which negation, strong or classical, is desired for each of the atoms in the language, by choosing whether to add or not, for each atom, such a disjunctive rule.

WFSX **and strong negation.** Since *WFSX* exhibits all the above mentioned properties of strong negation (cf. Section 9.1) and is defined as an extension of WFS, it seems that it should be closely related to stationary semantics with strong negation. In fact:

Theorem 5.1.5 (*WFSX* and strong negation). *If an interpretation M is a stationary*

$$AX_\neg = \{\neg\_A \Rightarrow \sim A \mid A \in \mathcal{H}\}$$

model of a program P then M is a WFSX *partial stable model of P.*

Proof. Trivial, given the proof of Theorem 5.1.6 below.

Thus *WFSX* gives semantics to more programs and, whenever both semantics give a meaning to a program, the WF model of *WFSX* is a (possibly proper) subset of that of stationary semantics with strong negation. The differences between *WFSX* and stationary semantics with strong negation are best shown with the help of examples.

Example 5.1.9. Consider program P :

$$
\begin{aligned}
shaves(john, X) &\leftarrow not\ shaves(X, X) \\
go\_dine\_out(X) &\leftarrow shaves(Y, X) \\
\neg go\_dine\_out(john)
\end{aligned}
$$

stating that "John shaves everyone not does not shave themselves"; "If x has been shaved (by anyone) then x will go out to dine"; and "John has not gone out to dine".

According to *WFSX* its well founded model (and only partial stable model) is M:

$$\{\neg go\_dine\_out(john), not\ go\_dine\_out(john), not\ \neg shaves(john, john)\}.$$

Note that M is not even a model in the (usual) sense of [172], because for the second rule the truth value of the head (false) is smaller than the truth value of the body (undefined).

Recall that in *WFSX* $\neg$-negation overrides undefinedness (of, in this case, $go\_dine\_out(john)$). The truth of $\neg L$ is an *explicit* declaration that L is false.

Any semantics complying with proposition 5.1.1, and in particular the stationary semantics with strong negation, cannot have M as a model of the program: $not\_go\_dine\_out(john)$ is in an expansion iff $\sim go\_dine\_out(john)$ is in all minimal models of that expansion, but if this is the case then (by the second rule) $\sim shaves(john, john)$ should also be in all minimal models, which would necessarily entail $not\ shaves(john, john)$ in the expansion.

Example 5.1.10. Take the program:

$$
\begin{aligned}
god\_exists &\leftarrow not\ \neg god\_exists \\
\neg god\_exists &\leftarrow not\ god\_exists \\
\neg go\_to\_church &\leftarrow not\ god\_exists \\
go\_to\_church &
\end{aligned}
$$

where the first two rules represent two conflicting default rules about the existence of God, the third rule states that "if I assume God does not exist then I do not go to church", and the last that "I go to church".

According to *WFSX*, the well-founded model of this program is:

$$\{go\_to\_church, not\ \neg go\_to\_church\}$$

whilst according to stationary semantics with strong negation the well-founded model is:

$$\{go\_to\_church, god\_exists, not\ \neg go\_to\_church, not\ \neg god\_exists\}$$

In fact, since go_to_church belongs to all minimal models, by the strong negation axiom, $\sim\neg go\_to\_church$ also belongs to all minimal models. Thus, by the third rule $\sim not\_god\_exists$, must belong to all minimal models. So, $\sim god\_exists$ also belongs to all minimal models (by the second rule), and the result above follows.

This example also shows that the stationary semantics with strong negation does not comply with the property of relevance. In fact god_exists belongs to the semantics of the whole program, but not to the semantics of the program containing only the rules "below" god_exists, i.e. only containing the first two rules.

In order to reconstruct *WFSX* in the generic schema, a new condition for adding default negation is required, forcing a default literal not_L to assuredly belong to an expansion also in the case where the explicit negation $\neg\_L$ is in all models.

Theorem 5.1.6 (*WFSX* semantics). *An interpretation M is a partial stable model of a canonical program[5] P iff M is a stationary*

$$AX_\neg = \{\neg\_A \Rightarrow not\_A \mid A \in \mathcal{H}\}$$

model of P.

Alternatively, M is a partial stable model of P iff M is the meaning of a P^* such that:

$$P^* = \neg\_P \cup \left\{not\_L \mid P^* \models_{CIRC} \sim L \text{ or } P^* \models \neg\_L\right\} \cup \{\sim not\ L \mid P^* \models L\}$$

Proof. In appendix

---

[5] This restriction to canonical programs is done without loss of generality, cf. corollary 9.1.1 which show that for every program P there is a canonical program P' whose *WFSX* semantics is equivalent to that of P.

Example 5.1.11. The program P of Example 5.1.9, abbreviating go_dine_out to gdo, $john$ to j, and $shaves$ to s, has a single expansion:

$$P^* = \neg\_P \cup \{not\_gdo(j), \sim not\_\neg\_gdo(j), not\_\neg\_s(j,j)\}.$$

In fact its minimal models are:

$$\{ \quad not\_s(j,j), \ not\_\neg\_s(j,j), \ not\_gdo(j), \ \sim not\_\neg\_gdo(j),$$
$$s(j,j), \quad \sim\neg\_s(j,j), \qquad gdo(j), \qquad \neg\_gdo(j)\}$$

$$\{\sim not\_s(j,j), \ not\_\neg\_s(j,j), \ not\_gdo(j), \ \sim not\_\neg\_gdo(j),$$
$$\sim s(j,j), \quad \sim\neg\_s(j,j), \quad \sim gdo(j), \qquad \neg\_gdo(j)\}$$

In all these models we have:

- $\sim\neg\_s(j,j)$ so we must introduce $not\_\neg\_s(j,j)$;
- $\neg\_gdo(j)$ so we must introduce $\sim not\_\neg\_gdo(j)$ and, by the second disjunct, $not\_gdo(j)$. Note that there is no need for adding $not\_gdo(j)$ in the first alternative of Theorem 5.1.6 since it follows as a consequence, given the axioms in $AX_\neg$.

The semantics of P is the meaning of P^*, i.e.

$$\{\neg gdo(j), not \ gdo(j), not \ \neg s(j,j)\}.$$

giving its *WFSX* single partial model.

5.1.5 Logic programs with ¬-negation and disjunction

Based on the similarities between the generic definition of stationary semantics for extended programs and that of stationary semantics for normal logic programs, it is easy to extend the former for extended disjunctive logic programs based on the extension of the latter for disjunctive normal programs [183], where the rule syntax is enlarged to include disjunctive conclusions.

First we have to extend the definition of $\neg\_P$ for the case of disjunctive programs. This extension is obtained simply by adjoining to Definition 5.1.3:

> "[...] *reinterpreting the connective* $\vee$ *in logic programs as classical disjunction*".

With this new context we define:

Definition 5.1.10. *A stationary $AX_\neg$ expansion of an extended disjunctive program P is any consistent theory P^* which satisfies the following fixed point condition (where the distributive axiom $not \ (A \wedge B) \equiv not \ A \vee not \ B$ is assumed):*

$$P^* = \neg\_P \cup AX_\neg \cup \left\{not \ F \mid P^* \models_{CIRC} \sim F\right\}$$

where F is an arbitrary conjunction of positive (resp. negative) objective literals.

Given this definition the semantics follows similarly to Section 5.1.2.

Example 5.1.12. Consider program P :

$$p \leftarrow not \ a$$
$$p \leftarrow not \ \neg b$$
$$a \lor \neg b$$

and let $AX_\neg$ be the axioms for strong negation. The only stationary $AX_\neg$ expansion of P is:

$P^* = \neg\_P \cup AX_\neg \cup$
$\{not\_\neg\_a, not\_b, \sim not\_p, not\_\neg\_p, not\_a \lor not\_\neg\_b, \sim not\_a \lor \sim not\_\neg\_b\}$

Thus the only stationary $AX_\neg$ model is $\{p, not \ \neg p, not \ \neg a, not \ b\}$.

Henceforth, the way is open for the study of the interaction between $\neg$ and disjunction in semantics of extended programs, and comparisons among those semantics via disjunction. One such result concerning the latter is the comparison between the use of classical or strong negation mentioned above in page 63.

Example 5.1.13. In Example 5.1.8 it is shown that the program P :

$$a \leftarrow b$$
$$\neg a$$

considering $\neg$ as classical negation, has the single stationary model:

$M = \{not \ a, \neg a, not \ b, \neg b\}$.

This fails to comply with the property of supportedness. There we argue that if one wants the result of M then the program should be written as P_2 :

$$a \leftarrow b$$
$$\neg a$$
$$b \lor \neg b$$

It is easy to see that, with the above definition of stationary expansion of extended disjunctive programs, the only stationary model of P_2, when $\neg$ is strong negation, is M.

It is known [183] that a definition such as 5.1.10 makes program disjunctions exclusive. This is seen in Example 5.1.12. In order to treat disjunctions as inclusive rather than exclusive, in non-extended disjunctive programs, it suffices to replace $\models_{CIRC}$ by $\models_{WECWA}$ in the definition of expansions [183], where $WECWA$ stands for Weak Extended Closed World Assumption [194] or Weak Generalized Closed World Assumption [186].

Further developments on the introduction of disjunction in extended logic programs, including that of inclusive disjunction, are beyond the scope of this work.

5.2 Autoepistemic logics for *WFSX*

In the previous section we identified distinct acceptations of ¬-negation in different semantics for extended logic programs. Some properties of each of those ¬-negations were presented. However no epistemic meaning was given to such ¬-negations.

The main goal of this section is to establish a nonmonotonic epistemic logic with two modalities – provability and belief – capable of expressing the distinct acceptations of ¬-negation described in the previous section.

As noted by [39, 117, 123], Gelfond's translation cannot be generalized to extended programs. A suitable translation between extended logic programs with answer-sets semantics and reflexive autoepistemic theories was proposed independently in [117] and [123]. Reflexive autoepistemic logic, introduced in [198], views the operator $\mathcal{L}$ as "is known" instead of the "is believed" of Moore's autoepistemic logic [132][6]. In [117, 123] the authors choose a translation of extended logic programs into theories of reflexive sutoepistemic logic, and prove that the answer-sets of an extended logic program correspond to the reflexive expansions of its translation. The translation renders an objective literal A (resp. ¬A) as $\mathcal{L}A$ (resp. $\mathcal{L} \sim A$, where $\sim$ denotes classical negation), i.e. "A is known to be true" (resp. "A is known to be false"), and renders *not* L as $\mathcal{L} \sim \mathcal{L}L$, i.e. "it is known that L is not known". The embedding of extended logic programs into reflexive autoepistemic logic can also be defined for (non-reflexive) autoepistemic logic [117, 123], by translating any objective literal L into $L \wedge \mathcal{L}L$. This translation was proposed in [39] too.

The embedding of stable model semantics into autoepistemic logic was generalized to well-founded semantics [182], with Gelfond's translation, but where Generalized Closed World Assumption (GCWA) [129] replaces the Closed World Assumption (CWA) [187] in what regards the adoption of default literals. No study of embeddings of well-founded semantics with ¬-negation exists to date. This is one purpose of this section. Significantly, the embedding proposed in [39, 117, 123] does not generalize to well-founded semantics based extende logic programs semantics. Indeed, that translation is too specific, and can only be applied to semantics based on the stable model semantics (i.e. that are two-valued).

Example 5.2.1. Program $P = \{a \leftarrow not\ a\}$ translates into the non-reflexive autoepistemic theory

$$T = \{\sim\mathcal{L}a \Rightarrow \mathcal{L}a \wedge a\} = \{\mathcal{L}a\}$$

It is easy to see that this theory has no expansion, even when GCWA is taken up instead of CWA.

---

[6] Roughly, this is achieved by adding $F \equiv \mathcal{L}F$, instead of just $\mathcal{L}F$ when F holds.

In contradistinction, our stance is that the second kind of negation introduced in logic programs represents and requires an additional modality to the one necessary for interpreting negation by default. Thus, in order to define a general translation between extended programs and some epistemic logic, the latter must include two modalities[7]. In our view, an objective literal $\neg A$ (resp. A) should be read "A is proven false", denoted by $\mathcal{E} \sim A$ (resp. "A is proven true"); and *not L* should be read "it is believed that L is not proven", denoted by $\mathcal{B} \sim\mathcal{E}L$. $\mathcal{E}$ refers to epistemic knowledge as defined by propositional provability, and relates to the consistency modality $\mathcal{M}$ by $E \equiv \sim\mathcal{M} \sim$. The belief operator of this logic is $\mathcal{B}$, inspired by the one introduced in [184].

The structure of this section is as follows: we begin by reviewing Moore's autoepistemic logic, introduced in [132], and the autoepistemic logic of closed beliefs introduced in [182]. In Section 5.2.2 we define an autoepistemic logic augmented with the modality $\mathcal{E}$, which is capable of expressing and comparing various semantics of extended logic programs. The flexibility and generality of our approach are brought out in Section 5.2.3, by establishing how different notions of provability and knowledge, and different semantics for extended programs are captured by it, providing for a better understanding of the different kinds of negation. The greater generality of the autoepistemic language provides a tool for examining further generalizations of extended logic programming. This is discussed in Section 5.2.4.

5.2.1 Moore's and Przymusinski's autoepistemic logics

A *propositional autoepistemic language* is any propositional language *Lang* with the property that for any proposition A in *Lang*, hereafter called *objective*, its alphabet also contains the corresponding *belief proposition* $\mathcal{L}A$, i.e. the proposition whose name is a string beginning with the symbol $\mathcal{L}$ followed by A. The intended meaning of $\mathcal{L}A$ is "A is believed".

An *autoepistemic theory* is any theory T over an autoepistemic language[8]. The following definition of stable autoepistemic expansion can be easily shown equivalent to Moore's:

Definition 5.2.1 (Stable autoepistemic expansion). *A consistent theory T^* is a stable autoepistemic expansion of the autoepistemic theory T iff:*

- *$T^* = T \cup B$, where B is a (possibly empty) set of belief literals, i.e. literals of the form $\mathcal{L}A$ or $\sim\mathcal{L}A$, where A is an objective proposition, and*

---

[7] In [116] the author also proposes a bi-modal logic (MBNF) for interpreting extended programs. There is a MBNF rendering of answer-sets which, as shown in [39, 117], is equivalent to the AEL-unimodal translations already discussed above that express answer-sets too.

[8] Like in the previous section, we use the symbol $\sim$ to denote classical negation in theories.

$-$ T^* satisfies the following conditions:

$$T^* \models \mathcal{L}A \quad \equiv \quad T^* \models A$$
$$T^* \models \sim\mathcal{L}A \quad \equiv \quad T^* \not\models A$$

This definition expresses positive and negative introspection of a rational agent: an agent believes in some proposition A iff A belongs to all models of its knowledge; and has no reason to believe in A ($\sim\mathcal{L}A$) iff A doesn't belong to all models of its knowledge.

Remark 5.2.1. In the original definition of Moore, the belief operator $\mathcal{L}$ can be applied to any formula, and thus the definition of expansion is modified accordingly. In [182] it is shown the restriction to propositions in the above definition doesn't influence generality. Moreover, as our interest is focused on autoepistemic logic for logic programming, such general formulae do not occur in theories (cf. Gelfond's translation below).

Example 5.2.2. Consider the following autoepistemic theory T, modeling the so called birds fly situation:

$$bird(X) \land \sim\mathcal{L}abnormal(X) \quad \Rightarrow \quad fly(X)$$
$$bird(a)$$
$$bird(b)$$
$$abnormal(b)$$

Its only stable expansion is (with obvious abbreviations):

$$T \cup \{\mathcal{L}b(a), \mathcal{L}b(b), \mathcal{L}ab(b), \mathcal{L}f(a), \sim\mathcal{L}ab(a), \sim\mathcal{L}f(b)\}$$

stating that an agent with knowledge T believes that a and b are birds, b is an abnormal bird and a flies, and has no reason to believe that a is abnormal, and that b flies.

Of course, some autoepistemic theories might have several stable expansions:

Example 5.2.3. The theory T :

$$a \quad \lor \quad \mathcal{L}b$$
$$b \quad \lor \quad \mathcal{L}a$$

has two expansions, namely:

$$T \cup \{\mathcal{L}a, \sim\mathcal{L}b\}$$
$$T \cup \{\mathcal{L}b, \sim\mathcal{L}a\}$$

Each of these can be envisaged as a belief state, i.e. an agent with knowledge T has two possible states of belief: either he believes in a and in that case has no reason to believe in b, or vice-versa. A sceptical agent with these belief states should have no reason to believe nor disbelieve neither a nor b.

In [182] Przymusinski argues, and we concur, that Moore's autoepistemic logic has some important drawbacks:

• First, quite reasonable theories have no stable expansions [133, 179]. For example the theory:

$$broken\_car$$
$$can\_fix\_it \vee \mathcal{L}can\_fix\_it$$

has no stable expansion, because no consistent addition of beliefs to the theory entail believing *can_fix_it*, and disbelieving that it can be fixed leads to an inconsistency[9], the agent should rest agnostic about that, neither believing nor disbelieving it can be fixed. However, one expects a reasoner with this knowledge at least to believe that the car is broken.

• Another important drawback is that, even for theories with stable expansions, Moore's autoepistemic logic does not always lead to the expected intended semantics. For instance consider the example[10]:

Example 5.2.4. A robot is programmed to carry some money from bank 1 to bank 2. There are two possible routes, denoted *a* and *b*; the robot chooses one of them, provided that it has no reason to believe there is trouble along the route. If it can choose any route then it should prefer route *a*. After choosing a route, the robot signals " *I'm leaving*" and tries to reach bank 2. This task can be naturally formalized by the autoepistemic theory:

$$
\begin{aligned}
\mathcal{L}trouble(a) \wedge \sim\mathcal{L}trouble(b) &\Rightarrow choose(b) \\
\mathcal{L}trouble(b) \wedge \sim\mathcal{L}trouble(a) &\Rightarrow choose(a) \\
\sim\mathcal{L}trouble(a) \wedge \sim\mathcal{L}trouble(b) &\Rightarrow choose(a) \\
choose(a) &\Rightarrow signal \\
choose(b) &\Rightarrow signal
\end{aligned}
$$

Given this knowledge, its unique stable expansion captures the intended meaning, i.e. the robot has no reason to believe that there is trouble in any of the routes, and thus chooses route *a* and signals.

Supposed now one adds to the theory the knowledge that there is some trouble in one of the routes, but it is not known which, expressed by:

$$trouble(a) \vee trouble(b)$$

The resulting theory has two stable expansions, both of which contain $\mathcal{L}signal$, and where one contains $\mathcal{L}choose(a)$ and the other contains $\mathcal{L}choose(b)$. According to the stable expansions a sceptical reasoner would believe neither in *choose(a)* nor in *choose(b)*, i.e. the robot wouldn't choose any of the routes, which is reasonable. However such a reasoner would believe

---

[9] Note that by adding $\sim\mathcal{L}can\_fix\_it$ to the theory, *can_fix_it* follows as a consequence, and thus $\mathcal{L}can\_fix\_it$ must be added (inconsistency).

[10] This example first appeared in [29], in the form of a logic program.

in *signal*, i.e. the robot says " *I'm leaving*", which clearly doesn't express the intended meaning.

• Stable expansions cannot be effectively computed even within simple classes of theories, such as propositional logic programs [96]. This is an important drawback, specially if one is interest in a theory for implementing knowledge representation and reasoning.

• Last but not least, by always insisting on completely deciding all of an agent's beliefs, stable expansions often lack expressibility. This issue will be further explored in this section.

In order to overcome these drawbacks Przymusinski introduced in [182] the general notion of autoepistemic logics of closed beliefs, and presented the circumscriptive autoepistemic logics as an important special case.

The notion of autoepistemic logics of closed beliefs arises naturally as a generalization of Moore's autoepistemic logics. First Przymusinski points out that in the definition of stable expansion, $T^* \not\models A$ can be replaced by $T^* \models_{\overline{CWA}} \sim A$, and proceeds to argue that stable expansions are a special case of expansions based on the general notions of positive and negative introspection.

Definition 5.2.2 (Autoepistemic expansion). *A consistent theory T^* is an autoepistemic expansion of a theory T iff*

- $T^* = T \cup B$, *where B is a (possibly empty) set of belief literals, i.e. literals of the form $\mathcal{L}A$ or $\sim\mathcal{L}A$, where A is an objective proposition, and*
- T^* *satisfies the following conditions:*

$$
\begin{array}{ccccc}
T^* & \models & \mathcal{L}A & \equiv & T^* \models_{op} A \\
T^* & \models & \sim\mathcal{L}A & \equiv & T^* \models_{cl} \sim A
\end{array}
$$

where $\models_{op}$ is a general entailment operator of open beliefs (or positive introspection) and $\models_{cl}$ is a general entailment operator of closed beliefs (or negative introspection).

Depending on the chosen positive and negative introspection entailment operators different autoepistemic logics are obtained.

Based on this general definition, Przymusinski defines Circumscriptive Expansions simply by choosing $\models$ as the positive and $\models_{\overline{CIRC}}$ [11] as the negative introspection operators. He also shows that with this definition of expansion, all of the above pointed out drawbacks are overcome, and that, through Gelfond's transformation between normal logic programs and autoepistemic theories (whereby *not L* is construed as $\sim\mathcal{L}L$), the least expansion is equivalent to the well-founded semantics of [76].

---

[11] Here $\models_{\overline{CIRC}}$ is as in the previous section (cf. page 54), but where the fixed propositions are of the form $\mathcal{L}A$ instead of *not_A*.

5.2.2 A logic of belief and provability

In this section we define an epistemic logic, $\mathcal{EB}$, with provability and belief modalities, and show how it captures the *WFSX* semantics.

We begin by analyzing definite extended logic programs (i.e. extended logic programs without negation by default), and by defining a modal logic to interpret such programs. We then extended this logic to deal with belief propositions. Finally, we relate the $\mathcal{EB}$ logic to *WFSX*.

Provability in extended definite programs. To motivate and make clear the meaning of the provability modality, we begin with the simpler problem of how to capture the meaning of extended logic programs without negation by default, i.e. sets of rules of the form:

$$L_0 \leftarrow L_1, \ldots, L_n \quad n \geq 0 \tag{5.1}$$

where each L_i is an atom A or its explicit negation $\neg A$. Without loss of generality, as in [172] we assume that all rules are ground.

The semantics of these programs is desireably monotonic, and must be noncontrapositive, i.e. distinguish between

$$a \leftarrow b$$

and

$$\neg b \leftarrow \neg a$$

so that rules are viewed as (unidirectional) "inference rules"; Gelfond's translation does not capture this distinction: both rules translate to

$$b \Rightarrow a$$

Example 5.2.5. According to Gelfond's translation, P :

$$a \quad \leftarrow \quad b$$
$$\neg a$$

is rendered as the theory T :

$$b \quad \Rightarrow \quad a$$
$$\sim a$$

This theory entails $\{\sim a, \sim b\}$, and the semantics of P (both under *WFSX* and answer-sets) is $\{\neg a\}$. Note how $\sim b$ is derived in T via the contrapositive of the first rule.

The cause of the problem is that $\neg A$ translates into "A is false", and rule connective $\leftarrow$ as material implication. In contrast, the semantics of extended logic programs wants to interpret $\neg A$ as "A is provenly false", in a grounded sense, and $\leftarrow$ as an inference rule. To capture this meaning we introduce the modal operator $\mathcal{E}$, referring to *(propositional)* *"provability"*, or *"epistemic knowledge"*, and translate rule (5.1) into:

$$\mathcal{E}L_1 \wedge \ldots \wedge \mathcal{E}L_n \Rightarrow \mathcal{E}L_0 \qquad (5.2)$$

where any explicitly negated literal $\neg A$ is translated into $\mathcal{E} \sim A$ and reads "A is provenly false", and any atom A is translated into $\mathcal{E}A$ and reads "A is provenly true".

This translation directly captures the intuitive meaning of a rule, "if all $L_1, \ldots, L_n$ are provable then L_0 is provable", and does not conflate contrapositives: $a \leftarrow b$ becomes $\mathcal{E}b \Rightarrow \mathcal{E}a$, whilst $\neg b \leftarrow \neg a$ gives $\mathcal{E} \sim a \Rightarrow \mathcal{E} \sim b$.

Note the similarities to the translation defined in [117, 123] into reflexive AEL, where an atom A is translated into $\mathcal{L}A$, and $\neg A$ into $\mathcal{L} \sim A$, and where $\mathcal{L}$ is the knowledge operator of modal logic **SW5**.

We need to assume little about $\mathcal{E}$, and this guarantees flexibility. $\mathcal{E}$ is defined as the necessity operator of the smallest normal modal system, modal logic **K**. This logic includes only modus ponens, necessitation, distribution over conjunctions, and the axiom[12]:

$$K: \quad \mathcal{E}(F \Rightarrow G) \Rightarrow (\mathcal{E}F \Rightarrow \mathcal{E}G)$$

In logic **K**, $\mathcal{E}$ is the dual of the modal consistency operator $\mathcal{M}$, i.e. $\mathcal{E} \equiv \sim \mathcal{M} \sim$. This weak modal logic, although sufficient for *WFSX* when combined with a belief modality and nonmonotonicity (as shown below), can also express other meanings of $\mathcal{E}$ just by introducing more axioms for it. In Section 5.2.3 in particular, we interpret $\mathcal{E}$ as knowledge by introducing the additional axioms for logic **SW5**.

Since at this stage we are simply interested in the semantics of monotonic (definite) extended logic programs, we do not require a nonmonotonic version of this logic.

Above we said that translation (5.2) can capture the semantics of extended logic programs. The next theorem makes this statement precise for answer-sets and *WFSX* semantics. It generalizes for almost every semantics of extended logic programs, the only exception being, to our knowledge, the "stationary semantics with classical negation" defined in [183], which is contrapositive.

Theorem 5.2.1. *Let P be an extended logic programs, and T the theory obtained from P by means of translation (5.2). If for no atom A, $T \vdash_K$ $\mathcal{E}A \wedge \mathcal{E} \sim A$ then:*

$$T \vdash_K \mathcal{E}A \quad \equiv \quad P \models_{AS} A \quad \equiv \quad P \models_{WFSX} A$$
$$T \vdash_K \mathcal{E} \sim A \quad \equiv \quad P \models_{AS} \neg A \quad \equiv \quad P \models_{WFSX} \neg A$$

where $\vdash_S$ denotes, as usual, the consequence relation in modal logic S, and $P \models_{AS} L$, resp. $P \models_{WFSX} L$, means that L belong to all answer-sets, resp. all WFSX partial stable models, of P.

---

[12] For a precise definition of logic **K** and its properties see [38, 89].

Otherwise, the only answer-set is the set of all objective literals, and P is contradictory with respect to WFSX.

Belief and provability. Besides explicit negation extended logic programs also allow negation by default, which is nonmonotonic and usually understood as a belief proposition. Thus, we need to enlarge modal logic **K** with a nonmonotonic belief operator.

Before tackling the more general problem, we begin by defining what beliefs follow from definite extended logic programs. Such programs are readily translatable into sets of Horn clauses, thereby possessing a unique minimal model. So, as a first approach consider: "the agent believes in every formula belonging to the minimal model of the theory", i.e. if $T \models_{min} F$ then $\mathcal{B}F$ (*introspection*).

Example 5.2.6. The program of Example 5.2.5 translates into T :

$$\mathcal{E}b \quad \Rightarrow \quad \mathcal{E}a$$
$$\mathcal{E} \sim a$$

whose least model is (apart irrelevant literals) $\{\mathcal{E} \sim a\}$.

Thus an agent with knowledge T believes all of $\mathcal{B}\mathcal{E} \sim a$, $\mathcal{B} \sim \mathcal{E}a$, $\mathcal{B} \sim \mathcal{E}b$, and $\mathcal{B} \sim \mathcal{E} \sim b$.

Moreover we insist that, for rational agents, if $T \models \mathcal{E}L$ then $\mathcal{B} \sim \mathcal{E} \sim L$ (*coherence*). In this context, coherence states that whenever L is provenly true then it is mandatory to believe that L is not provenly false[13]. In the above example this rule does not interfere with the result. This is not in general the case:

Example 5.2.7. Consider $T = \{\mathcal{E}a; \ \mathcal{E} \sim a\}$ whose least model is

$$\{\mathcal{E}a, \mathcal{E} \sim a\}$$

$\mathcal{B}\mathcal{E}a$ and $\mathcal{B}\mathcal{E} \sim a$ hold by introspection. Moreover, by coherence, an agent should sustain both $\mathcal{B} \sim \mathcal{E} \sim a$ and $\mathcal{B} \sim \mathcal{E}a$.

This kind of reasoning may seem strange since the agent believes in complementary formulae (e.g. in $\mathcal{E}a$ and in $\sim \mathcal{E}a$.). But, as shown below, when axioms for $\mathcal{B}$ are introduced, they will detect inconsistency out the intuitively inconsistent theory T, i.e. belief cannot be held of proven complements.

As for $\mathcal{E}$, also for $\mathcal{B}$ little is assumed about it, for the sake of flexibility and, we shall show, because it is enough for characterizing *WFSX*. More precisely, we assume the axioms introduced in [184] for the belief operator:

- For any tautologically false formula F: $\sim \mathcal{B}F$.
- For any formulae F and G: $\mathcal{B}(F \wedge G) \equiv \mathcal{B}F \wedge \mathcal{B}G$.

---

[13] Note that $\mathcal{B} \sim \mathcal{E} \sim L \equiv \mathcal{B}\mathcal{M}L$.

As proven in [184], from these axioms it follows for every formula F that

$$\mathcal{B}F \Rightarrow \sim\mathcal{B} \sim F$$

Consequently, from believing two complementary formulae, $\mathcal{B}F$ and $\mathcal{B} \sim F$, inconsistency follows, because $\mathcal{B} \sim F \Rightarrow \sim\mathcal{B}F$.

In summary, for a theory T resulting from a definite extended logic program, the set of beliefs of an agent is the closure under the above axioms of:

$$\{\mathcal{B}F \mid T \models_{min} F\} \cup \{\mathcal{B} \sim\mathcal{E} \sim F \mid T \models \mathcal{E}F\}$$

as required by introspection and coherence, respectively.

In order to enlarge the logic **K** with a nonmonotonic belief operator we proceed as above, but now consider the case where formulae of the form $\mathcal{B}F$ or $\sim\mathcal{B}F$ (hereafter called belief formulae) occur in theories. In this case, it is not adequate to obtain the belief closure as above. To deal with belief formulae in theories we must consider, as usual in AEL, the expansions of a theory.

An expansion of a theory T is a fixpoint of equation $T^* = T \cup Bel$, where Bel is a set of belief formulae depending on T^*. Intuitively, each expansion stands for a belief state of a rational agent. By so doing one new problem arises:

> which nonmonotonicity to introduce in such theories or, in other words, under what conditions is an agent to augment his set of beliefs ?

In this respect two main approaches have been followed in the literature: One, present in Moore's AEL and reflexive AEL, is based on CWA and captures two-valued (or total) semantics of logic programs. The other approach is based on GCWA and captures three-valued (or partial) semantics of LPs. The latter is followed in the AEL of closed beliefs [182], and in the static semantics [184][14]. Here, and based on the reasons presented in Section 5.2.1 above, we adopt the second approach.

In the sequel we formally define our epistemic logic: first we extend the language of propositional logic with modal operators $\mathcal{E}$ and $\mathcal{B}$, standing for "provability" and "belief". Theories are recursively defined as usual. Moreover we assume every theory contains all axioms of logic **K** for $\mathcal{E}$, and the two axioms above for $\mathcal{B}$.

Definition 5.2.3 (Minimal models). *A minimal model of a theory T is a model M of T such that there is no smaller model N of T coinciding with M on belief propositions.*

---

[14] Note that the question of distinguishing between these two approaches is not relevant for definite programs, since in them nonderivability coincides with deriving the complement in the (single) minimal model.

If F is true in all minimal models of T then we write $T \models_{min} F$.

An expansion T^* corresponds to a belief state where the agent believes in F if $T^* \models_{min} F$, and does not believe in F if $T^* \models_{min} \sim F$. Note that, with the axioms introduced for $\mathcal{B}$, the second statement is subsumed by the first. In fact, by the first statement, if $T^* \models_{min} \sim F$ then $\mathcal{B} \sim F$, and from the axioms for $\mathcal{B}$ it follows that $\sim \mathcal{B} F$.

As argued for definite extended programs, when considering theories with provability and belief one new form of obtention of beliefs (coherence) is in order, namely that if $T^* \models \mathcal{E} F$ then $\mathcal{B} \sim \mathcal{E} \sim F$. Thus expansions should formalize the following notion of belief $\mathcal{B}$:

$\mathcal{B} F \equiv$ F is minimally entailed, or $F = \sim \mathcal{E} \sim G$ and $\mathcal{E} G$ is entailed.

Definition 5.2.4 (Expansion). *An expansion of a theory T is a consistent theory T^* satisfying the fixed point condition:*

$$T^* = T \cup \{\mathcal{B} F \mid T^* \models_{min} F\} \cup \{\mathcal{B} \sim \mathcal{E} \sim G \mid T^* \models \mathcal{E} G\}$$

Example 5.2.8. Consider the following autoepistemic theory T, which is a modification of the birds fly situation of Example 5.2.2:

$$\sim \mathcal{B} \mathcal{E} \sim fly(X) \wedge \mathcal{E} bird(X) \Rightarrow \mathcal{E} fly(X)$$
$$\mathcal{E} bird(a)$$
$$\mathcal{E} bird(b)$$
$$\mathcal{E} \sim fly(b)$$

where the last clause expresses that b is proven not to fly.

Its only expansion is (with obvious abbreviations):

$$T \cup \{\mathcal{B} \mathcal{E} b(a), \mathcal{B} \mathcal{E} b(b), \mathcal{B} \mathcal{E} f(a), \mathcal{B} \mathcal{E} \sim f(b), \mathcal{B} \sim \mathcal{E} \sim b(a), \mathcal{B} \sim \mathcal{E} \sim b(b),$$
$$\mathcal{B} \sim \mathcal{E} \sim f(a), \mathcal{B} \sim \mathcal{E} f(b)\}$$

stating that an agent with knowledge T believes that a and b are birds, b doesn't fly, a flies, and disbelieves that a and b are not birds, that a doesn't fly, and that b flies.

Example 5.2.9. [15] Consider an agent with the following knowledge:

- *Peter is a bachelor;*
- *A man is proven not to be married if he is provenly a bachelor;*
- *Susan is proven to be married to Peter, if we do not believe she's married to Tom.*
- *Susan is proven to be married to Tom, if we do not believe she's married to Peter.*
- *It is proven that no one is married to oneself.*

---

[15] This example first appeared in [212], in the form of a logic program.

rendered by the autoepistemic theory T (with obvious abbreviations):

$$\begin{aligned}
\mathcal{E}b(p) & \\
\mathcal{E}b(X) &\Rightarrow \mathcal{E} \sim m(X,Y) \\
\mathcal{B} \sim\mathcal{E}m(t,s) &\Rightarrow \mathcal{E}m(p,s) \\
\mathcal{B} \sim\mathcal{E}m(p,s) &\Rightarrow \mathcal{E}m(t,s) \\
\mathcal{E} \sim m(X,X) &
\end{aligned}$$

The only expansion of T contains, among others, the belief propositions:

$$\{\mathcal{B}\mathcal{E}b(p), \mathcal{B}\mathcal{E} \sim m(p,s), \mathcal{B} \sim\mathcal{E}m(p,s), \mathcal{B}\mathcal{E}m(t,s)\}$$

In both the above examples all of an agent's beliefs are completely decided, in the sense that for any proposition A the agent either believes or disbelieves A. This is not in general the case.

Example 5.2.10. Consider the statements:

- *if it is believed that the car cannot be fixed then it is proven that it can be fixed.*
- *If it is not believed that one can fix the car then it is proven that an expert is called for.*
- *It is proven that an expert is not called for.*

rendered by the autoepistemic theory T :

$$\begin{aligned}
\mathcal{B} \sim\mathcal{E}can\_fix\_car &\Rightarrow \mathcal{E}can\_fix\_car \\
\mathcal{B} \sim\mathcal{E}can\_fix\_car &\Rightarrow \mathcal{E}call\_expert \\
\mathcal{E} \sim call\_expert &
\end{aligned}$$

The only expansion of T is:

$$T \cup \{\mathcal{B}\mathcal{E} \sim call\_expert, \mathcal{B} \sim\mathcal{E}call\_expert\}$$

stating that an agent believes that an expert is not called and that he disbelieves an expert is called.

Like Moore's autoepistemic theories, $\mathcal{E}\mathcal{B}$ theories might have several expansions:

Example 5.2.11. Consider the theory T, describing the so-called Nixon diamond situation:

$$\begin{aligned}
\mathcal{E}republican(nixon) & \\
\mathcal{E}quaker(nixon) & \\
\mathcal{E}republican(X), \mathcal{B} \sim\mathcal{E}pacifist(X) &\Rightarrow \mathcal{E} \sim pacifist(X) \\
\mathcal{E}quaker(X), \mathcal{B} \sim\mathcal{E} \sim pacifist(X) &\Rightarrow \mathcal{E}pacifist(X)
\end{aligned}$$

T has three expansions, namely those resulting from T union with:

$$\begin{aligned}
&\{\mathcal{B}\mathcal{E}r(n), \mathcal{B}\mathcal{E}q(n), \mathcal{B}\mathcal{E}p(n), \quad \mathcal{B} \sim\mathcal{E} \sim r(n), \mathcal{B} \sim\mathcal{E} \sim q(n), \mathcal{B} \sim\mathcal{E} \sim p(n)\} \\
&\{\mathcal{B}\mathcal{E}r(n), \mathcal{B}\mathcal{E}q(n), \mathcal{B}\mathcal{E} \sim p(n), \mathcal{B} \sim\mathcal{E} \sim r(n), \mathcal{B} \sim\mathcal{E} \sim q(n), \mathcal{B} \sim\mathcal{E}p(n)\} \\
&\{\mathcal{B}\mathcal{E}r(n), \mathcal{B}\mathcal{E}q(n), \qquad\qquad\quad \mathcal{B} \sim\mathcal{E} \sim r(n), \mathcal{B} \sim\mathcal{E} \sim q(n)\}
\end{aligned}$$

The first states that it is believed that Nixon is a pacisfist; the second that it is believed that Nixon is not a pacifist; and the third remains undefined in what concerns Nixon being or not a pacisfist.

When confronted with several expansions (i.e. several possible states of beliefs) a sceptical reasoner should only conclude what is common to all. Here that coincides with the third expansion.

Relation to extended logic programs. Recall that an extended program is as set of rules of the form:

$$L_0 \leftarrow L_1, \ldots, L_m, not \ L_{m+1}, \ldots, not \ L_n \tag{5.3}$$

where each L_i is an objective literal, i.e. an atom A or its $\neg$-negation $\neg A$.

As argued above, an atom A is translated into $\mathcal{E} A$, and an explicitly negated atom $\neg A$ into $\mathcal{E} \sim A$. In [117, 123] literals of the form *not L* are translated into $\mathcal{L} \sim \mathcal{L} L$ in reflexive AEL. [123] gives an intuitive reading of this formula:"it is known that L is not known". In our approach we translate *not L* into $\mathcal{B} \sim \mathcal{E} L$, i.e. "it is believed (or can be assumed) that L is not proven". So, each rule of the form (5.3) is translated into:

$$\mathcal{E} L_1, \ldots, \mathcal{E} L_m, \mathcal{B} \sim \mathcal{E} L_{m+1}, \ldots, \mathcal{B} \sim \mathcal{E} L_n \Rightarrow \mathcal{E} L_0 \tag{5.4}$$

Definition 5.2.5 (Models and expansion). *A model M of an extended logic P corresponds to an expansion T^* iff:*

– For an objective literal L : $L \in M$ iff $T^* \models \mathcal{B} \mathcal{E} L$.
– For a literal not L :   not $L \in M$ iff $T^* \models \mathcal{B} \sim \mathcal{E} L$.

Theorem 5.2.2 (*WFSX*, provability and belief). *Let T be the theory obtained from a canonical extended logic program P by means of translation (5.4). Then there is a one-to-one correspondence between the* WFSX *partial stable models of P and the expansions of T.*

This relationship brings mutual benefits to both *WFSX* and the $\mathcal{E} \mathcal{B}$ logic. On the one hand, the logic allows for a more intuitive view of *WFSX*, specially in what concerns its understanding as modeling provability and belief in a rational agent. This allows for a clearer formalation within *WFSX* of some problems of knowledge representation and reasoning, and for a better understanding of *WFSX*'s results. In particular, it shows that explicit negation stands for proving falsity, default negation for believing that the literal is not proven, and undefinedness for believing neither the falsity nor the verity of a literal. The relationship also sheds light on several extensions of *WFSX* (cf. Section 5.2.4).

On the other hand, for the class of theories resulting from some extended programs, the logic can be implemented using the procedures defined for *WFSX* in Chapter 10. Moreover, for this class, the logic enjoys the properties of cumulativity, rationality, relevance [54, 58], and others proven for *WFSX* below. In addition, the relationship also raises new issues in epistemic logics, and points towards their solution via the techniques in use in extended logic programming (cf. Section 5.2.4).

5.2.3 Provability versus Knowledge

Above we claimed logic $\mathcal{EB}$ is flexible and general. Next we express in it different meanings for $\mathcal{E}$, and hence a variety of semantics for extended logic.

The logic **K** introduced for $\mathcal{E}$ is the simplest normal modal system. With additional axioms in our theories we can define other meanings for $\mathcal{E}$. In particular, with the axioms of logic **SW5**[16] $\mathcal{E}$ represents "knowledge" in its sense [198, 123]. Other formalizations of knowledge, such as that of logic **S4.2**[17], are similarly obtainable.

Using the **SW5** meaning of $\mathcal{E}$, but keeping with the same translation, a different semantics for extended programs is obtained:

Theorem 5.2.3 (Knowledge and strong negation). *Let T be the theory obtained from an ELP P by means of translation (5.4), augmented with the* **SW5** *axioms for $\mathcal{E}$. Then there is a one-to-one correspondence between expansions of T and the partial stable models of P according to the WFS with strong negation.*

Example 5.2.12. Program P :

$$\neg a$$
$$a \;\leftarrow\; not\; b$$
$$b \;\leftarrow\; not\; b$$

translates into the theory T :

$$\mathcal{E} \sim a$$
$$\mathcal{B} \sim \mathcal{E} b \;\Rightarrow\; \mathcal{E} a$$
$$\mathcal{B} \sim \mathcal{E} b \;\Rightarrow\; \mathcal{E} b$$

Using logic **K**, there is one expansion

$$T^* = T \cup \{\mathcal{B}\mathcal{E} \sim a, \mathcal{B} \sim \mathcal{E} a, \mathcal{B} \sim \mathcal{E} \sim b\}.$$

If logic **SW5** is used instead there is no expansion. This happens because, by axiom T, $\mathcal{E} \sim a$ entails $\sim \mathcal{E} a$, and by the second clause $\sim \mathcal{E} a$ entails $\sim \mathcal{B} \sim \mathcal{E} b$. Thus, by the third clause, every minimal model of every possible expansion has $\sim \mathcal{E} b$, and so $\mathcal{B} \sim \mathcal{E} b$ must be added. This is inconsistent with having $\sim \mathcal{B} \sim \mathcal{E} b$ in all models, and so no expansion exists. *WFSX* assigns a meaning, namely $\{\neg a, not\; a, not\; \neg b\}$, to P because axiom T is not assumed.

---

[16] I.e. axioms T: $\mathcal{E}F \Rightarrow F$, 4: $\mathcal{E}F \Rightarrow \mathcal{E}\mathcal{E}F$, and W5: $\sim\mathcal{E} \sim F \Rightarrow (F \Rightarrow \mathcal{E}F)$.

[17] [111] uses **S4.2** to formalize knowledge in a logic which also includes belief. We intend to compare this logic with ours when the final version becomes available.

From Theorem 5.2.3 and the results of Section 5.1 regarding classical negation it follows that:

Theorem 5.2.4 (Classical negation). *Let T be the theory obtained from an ELP P by means of translation (5.4), augmented with the* **SW5** *axioms for $\mathcal{E}$, and the axiom $\sim\!\mathcal{E}F \Rightarrow \mathcal{E} \sim\!F$. Then there is a one-to-one correspondence between expansions of T and the partial stable models of P according to the "stationary semantics with classical negation".*

Since answers-sets are the total stable models of WFS with strong negation:

Definition 5.2.6 (Total expansions). *An expansion T^* is total iff for every formula F :*

$$T^* \not\models \mathcal{B}F \quad \Rightarrow \quad T^* \models \mathcal{B} \sim\!F$$

Theorem 5.2.5 (Answer-sets). *Let T be the theory obtained from an ELP P by means of translation (5.4), augmented with the* **SW5** *axioms for $\mathcal{E}$. Then there is a one-to-one correspondence between total expansions of T and the answer-sets of P.*

5.2.4 Further developments

Since the language of $\mathcal{EB}$ is more general than that of extended programs, our logic is a tool for further generalizations of extended logic programming, for for instance disjunction. All is required is to define a translation of disjunctive extended programs into the logic. The study of possible translations, and the relationship between the resulting and extant semantics for disjunctive programs is the subject of ongoing investigations.

Another possible direct generalization of extended logic programming is with the modal operators of the logic, allowing for conjunction and disjunction within their scope. Examples of the use and usefulness of the belief operator for normal disjunctive programs can be found in [184].

With the relationship between $\mathcal{EB}$ logic and extended logic programming now established, some issues already tackled in the latter can also be raised in the former. Furthermore, the former can profit from adapting techniques employed in the latter. One of the issues presented here in more detail is contradiction removal, or belief revision.

Recently, several authors have studied this issue in extended logic programming [10, 68, 92, 144, 146, 152]. The basic idea behind these approaches is that *not L* literals be viewed as assumptions, so that if an assumption partakes in a contradiction then its revision is in order. In epistemic logics this idea translates into:

> "If the results of introspection lead to the inexistence of expansions then revise your beliefs".

Example 5.2.13. The theory T :

$$\mathcal{B} \sim\mathcal{E}\,ab \;\Rightarrow\; \mathcal{E}\,fly$$
$$\mathcal{E} \sim fly$$

is consistent but has no expansion. This is so because $\sim\mathcal{E}\,ab$ is true in all minimal models and thus, by introspection, $\mathcal{B} \sim\mathcal{E}\,ab$ must be added causing a contradiction. In fact, a typical case where the result of introspection leads to contradiction[18].

In order to assign a meaning to consistent theories without expansions two approaches are possible: to define a more sceptical notion of expansion, introducing less belief propositions by introspection; or to minimally revise the theory in order to provide for expansions.

Contradiction avoidance in the $\mathcal{E}\mathcal{B}$ logic amounts to weakening the condition for introspection. This can be accomplished by introducing belief propositions solely for a chosen subset of the formulae minimally entailed by the theory. Of course, not all subsets are allowed. In particular, we are only interested in maximal subsets. The study of additional preference conditions among these subsets is tantamount to the one in extended logic programming. This issue is studied in length in Chapter 8 for logic programs, and is thus not further explored in this section for the corresponding autoepistemic theories.

Contradiction removal in the $\mathcal{E}\mathcal{B}$ logic amounts to minimally adjoining, to a consistent theory without expansions, new clauses that inhibit the addition, by introspection, of belief propositions responsible for contradiction. Again, by the equivalence between this autoepistemic logic and *WFSX*, the study of extra such mechanism is tantamount to contradiction removal in logic programming as studied in Chapter 8.

---

[18] Note this problem is not peculiar to our logic. The same also occurs in e.g. Moore's autoepistemic logic and reflexive autoepistemic logic.

6. *WFSX* and default logic

A relationship between logic programs and default theories was first proposed in [22] and [23]. The idea is to translate every program rule, into a default one and then compare the extensions of the default theory with the semantics of the corresponding program.

The main motivations for such a relationship are, on the one hand, the use of logic programming as a framework for nonmonotonic reasoning and, on the other hand, the computation of default logic extensions by means of logic programming implementations algorithms. Moreover, having already the relationship established for some semantics of logic programs, it is important to keepup with such a relationship, for mutual clarification.

In [23] stable model semantics [78] was shown equivalent to a special case of default theories in the sense of Reiter [188]. This result was generalized in [80] to programs with explicit negation and answer-set semantics, where they make explicit negation correspond to classical negation used in default theories.

Well Founded Semantics for Default Theories [19] extends Reiter's semantics of default theories, resolving some issues of the latter, namely that some theories have no extension and also that some theories have no least extension. Based on the way such issues were resolved in [20], the well founded semantics for programs without explicit negation was shown by them equivalent to a special case of the extension classes of default theories in the sense of [19]. It turns out that in attempting to directly extend this result to extended logic programs with explicit negation one gets some unintuitive results and no semantics of such logic programs relates to known default theories.

To overcome that, here we first identify principles a default theory semantics should enjoy to that effect, and introduce a default theory semantics that extends that of [20] to the larger class of extended logic programs, but still complying with those principles.

Such a relationship to a larger program class improves the cross-fertilization between logic programs and default theories, since we generalize previous results concerning their relationship [19, 20, 22, 23, 80, 173, 174]. Moreover, there is an increasing use of logic programming with explicit negation as a nonmonotonic reasoning tool [18, 80, 154, 156, 157, 162, 163, 209], which can thus be a vehicle for implementing default theories as well. The relationship also further clarifies the meaning of logic programs combining both explicit negation and negation by default. In particular, it shows in what way explicit negation corresponds to classical negation in our default theory, and elucidates the use of rules in extended logic programs. Like defaults, rules are unidirectional, so their contrapositives are not implicit: the rule connective ← is not material implication but has rather the flavour of an inference rule.

Implementationwise, since *WFSX* is definable by a monotonic fixpoint operator, it has desirable computational properties, including top-down and bottom-up procedures. As the default semantics is sound with respect to Reiter's default semantics, whenever an extension exists, we thus provide sound methods for computing the intersection of all extensions for an important subset of Reiter's default theories.

The semantics for default theories presented here is restricted to the language where prerequisites and justifications are finite sets of ground literals, the conclusion is a literal, and all formulas not in default rules are literals as well. Note that when relating defaults to logic programming in the usual way, the language of theories corresponding to programs is already thus restricted. Furthermore, in Section 6.6 we show that default theories with this language restriction are nevertheless as powerful as logic programs with explicit negation.

In this chapter we present a semantics for default theories, and show its relationship with *WFSX*. Based on this relationship, we give an alternative definition of *WFSX* which does not rely on 3-valued logic but on 2-valued logic alone. This is achieved by resorting to a variant of Gelfond and Lifschitz's Γ operator, whose connection to Reiter's defaults is well-known. The reader more interested in this Γ-like definition of *WFSX* than in the default theory may skip directly to Section 6.7.

This definition of *WFSX* is also an important consequence of the established relationship. It allows for viewing *WFSX* as a partial 2-valued semantics, where undefined literals are those that can neither be proven true nor false, i.e. those whose truth in a 3-valued logic is *"unknown"*.

6.1 The language of defaults

First we review the language of propositional defaults, and some known default logics.

Definition 6.1.1 (Default rule). *A propositional default d is a triple*

$$d = \langle p(d),\ j(d),\ c(d) \rangle$$

where $p(d)$ and $c(d)$ are propositional formulas and $j(d)$ is a finite subset of propositional formulas. $p(d)$ (resp. $j(d)$, resp. $c(d)$) is called the prerequisite *(resp.* justification, *resp.* consequence*) of default d. The default d is also denoted by*

$$\frac{p(d) \; : \; j(d)}{c(d)}$$

Definition 6.1.2 (Default theory). *A default theory* Δ *is a pair* (D, W) *where W is a set of propositional formulas and D is a set of default rules.*

As remarked above the definition of the semantics of default theories is herein defined only for a restricted language, though powerful enough to map extended logic programs. Accordingly we define:

Definition 6.1.3 (Restricted default theory). *A restricted default rule is a default rule*

$$\frac{p(d) \; : \; j(d)}{c(d)}$$

where $p(d)$, $j(d)$, *and* $c(d)$ *are literals.*

A restricted default theory Δ *is a pair* (D, W) *where W is a set of literals and D is a set of restricted default rules.*

Next we review, for the case of propositional defaults, some known default theory semantics. We start by reviewing Reiter's classical default logic [188]. Then we review (partly following [20]) the well-founded [20] and stationary [174] default logics, which correspond respectively to the well founded [76] and stationary semantics [180] of (nonextended) logic programs.

6.1.1 Reiter's default semantics

To every default theory Δ Reiter associates the operator Γ_Δ, acting on sets of objective literals called contexts:

Definition 6.1.4 (The Γ_Δ operator). *Let* $\Delta = (D, W)$, *be a propositional default theory and let E be any set of objective literals, called a context.* $\Gamma_\Delta(E)$ *is the smallest context which:*

1. *contains W;*
2. *is closed under all derivation rules of the form* $\frac{p(d)}{c(d)}$, *where* $\frac{p(d) \; : \; j(d)}{c(d)} \in D$ *and* $\neg f \notin E$, *for every* $f \in j(d)$.

Intuitively, $\Gamma_\Delta(E)$ represents all objective literals *derivable* from W plus E, closed under all default rules whose justifications are consistent with E.

Definition 6.1.5 (Reiter's default extensions). *A context E is an extension of a default theory* Δ *iff:*

$$E = \Gamma_\Delta(E)$$

The cautious default semantics of Δ *is the context consisting of all objective literals which belong to all extensions of* Δ.

As argued in [174], default extensions can be viewed as *rational sets of conclusions* deducible from Δ.

One problem of Reiter's default logic is that it may have multiple extensions and in that case the cautious default semantics is not an extension. If one views extensions as the only rational sets of conclusion then, surprisingly, the (cautious) semantics is not itself one such set.

Example 6.1.1. Consider the default theory Δ :

$$\left(\left\{ \frac{c \; : \; \neg a}{b}, \frac{c \; : \; \neg b}{a} \right\}, \{c\} \right)$$

which has two extensions:

$$
\begin{aligned}
E_1 &= \{a, \neg b, c\} \\
E_2 &= \{b, \neg a, c\}
\end{aligned}
$$

The cautious default semantics is $\{c\}$, itself not an extension, and thus, according to Reiter's semantics, is not a rational set of conclusions.

Another problem is that, in cases where a definite meaning is expected, no extensions exist (and thus no meaning is given).

Example 6.1.2. The default theory:

$$\left(\left\{ \frac{: \; \neg q}{q} \right\}, \{p\} \right)$$

has no extensions. However p is a fact, and we would expect it to be true.

6.1.2 Well-founded and stationary default semantics for normal logic programs

Here we review two approaches which relate normal logic programs with default theories, and resolve the above mentioned issues of Reiter's default logic.

Baral and Subrahmanian [20] introduced the well founded semantics for (propositional) default theories giving a meaning to default theories with multiple extensions. Furthermore, the semantics is defined for all theories, identifying a single extension for each.

Let $\Delta = (D, W)$ be a default theory, and let $\Gamma_\Delta(E)$ be as above. Since $\Gamma_\Delta(E)$ is antimonotonic $\Gamma_\Delta^2(E)$ is monotonic [20], and thus has a least fixpoint[1].

Definition 6.1.6 (Well founded semantics).

– A formula F is true in a default theory Δ with respect to the well-founded semantics iff $F \in lfp(\Gamma^2)$.

---

[1] Least with respect to set inclusion in contexts.

- F *is false in* Δ *w.r.t. the well founded semantics iff* $F \notin gfp(\Gamma^2)$.
- *Otherwise* F *is said to be* unknown *(or* undefined*)*.

This semantics is defined for all theories and is equivalent to the Well Founded Model semantics [76] of normal logic programs.

More recently [174], Przymusinska and Przymusinski generalized this work by introducing the notion of stationary default extensions[2].

Definition 6.1.7 (Stationary extension). *Given a default theory* Δ, E *is a stationary default extension iff:*

- $E = \Gamma_\Delta^2(E)$
- $E \subseteq \Gamma_\Delta(E)$

Definition 6.1.8 (Stationary default semantics). *Let* E *be a stationary extension of a default theory* Δ.

- *A formula* L *is true in* E *iff* $L \in E$.
- *A formula* L *is false in* E *iff* $L \notin \Gamma_\Delta(E)$.
- *Otherwise* L *is said to be* undetermined *(or* undefined*)*.

This semantics has been shown equivalent to stationary semantics of normal logic programs.

Remark 6.1.1. Note that every default theory has at least one stationary default extension. The least stationary default extension always exists, and corresponds to the well founded semantics for default theories above. Moreover, the least stationary default extension can be computed by iterating the monotonic operator Γ_Δ^2.

Example 6.1.3. Consider the default theory of Example 6.1.2. We have $\Gamma_\Delta(\{p\}) = \{p, q\}$ and $\Gamma_\Delta^2(\{p\}) = \{p\}$. p is true in the theory Δ.

6.2 Some principles required of default theories

Next we argue about some principles a default theory semantics should enjoy, and relate it to logic programs extended with explicit negation, where the said principles are also considered desirable.

Property 6.2.1 (Uniqueness of minimal extension). We say that a   default theory has the uniqueness of minimal extension property if when it has an extension it has a minimal one.

It is well known that Reiter's default theories do not comply with this principle, which plays an important rôle, specially if we consider the so called *cautious version* of a default semantics [127]:

---

[2] In [174] the work of [20] is also generalized to deal with nonpropositional default theories.

Example 6.2.1. Consider the default theory

$$\left\{ \frac{republican(X) \; : \; \neg pacifist(X)}{\neg pacifist(X)}, \frac{quaker(X) \; : \; pacifist(X)}{pacifist(X)} \right\}$$

$$\{republican(nixon), quaker(nixon)\}$$

where Reiter's semantics identifies two extensions:

$$E_1 = \{ \; pacifist(nixon), \; republican(nixon), \; quaker(nixon) \; \}$$
$$E_2 = \{ \; \neg pacifist(nixon), \; republican(nixon), \; quaker(nixon) \; \}$$

Thus the cautious Reiter's semantics is

$$\{republican(nixon), quaker(nixon)\}$$

As noted in [174], if we view an extension as a rational set of conclusions, it is strange that the cautious semantics itself does not constitute one such set.

By obeying the uniqueness of minimal extension property, a default semantics avoids this problem. Moreover, this property also eases finding iterative algorithms to compute the cautious version of a default semantics.

Definition 6.2.1 (Union of theories). *The union of two default theories*

$$\Delta_1 = (D_1, W_1) \quad and \quad \Delta_2 = (D_2, W_2)$$

with languages $L(\Delta_1)$ and $L(\Delta_2)$ is the theory:

$$\Delta = \Delta_1 \cup \Delta_2 = (D_1 \cup D_2, W_1 \cup W_2)$$

with language $L(\Delta) = L(\Delta_1) \cup L(\Delta_2)$.

Example 6.2.2. Consider the two default theories:

$$\Delta_1 = (\{ \frac{: \; \neg a}{\neg a}, \frac{: \; a}{a} \}, \{\})$$
$$\Delta_2 = (\{ \frac{: \; b}{b} \}, \{\})$$

Classical default theory, well-founded semantics, and stationary semantics all identify $\{b\}$ as the single extension of Δ_2.

Since the languages of the two theories are disjoint, one would expect their union to include b in all its extensions. However, both the well founded semantics as well as the least stationary semantics give the value undefined to b in the union theory; therefore they are not modular[3] . There is an objectionable interaction among the default rules of both theories when put together. In this case, classical default theory is modular but has two extensions: $\{\neg a, b\}$ and $\{a, b\}$, failing to give a unique minimal extension to the union.

---

[3] This shortcoming of least stationary semantics was detected independently in [56].

Property 6.2.2 (Modularity). Let Δ_1, Δ_2 be two default theories with consistent extensions such that $L(\Delta_1) \cap L(\Delta_2) = \{\}$ and let $\Delta = \Delta_1 \cup \Delta_2$, with extensions $E^i_{\Delta_1}$ $E^j_{\Delta_2}$ and E^k_{Δ}. A semantics for default theories is *modular* iff:

$$\forall_A (\forall_i A \in E^i_{\Delta_1} \Rightarrow \forall_k A \in E^k_{\Delta})$$
$$\forall_A (\forall_j A \in E^j_{\Delta_2} \Rightarrow \forall_k A \in E^k_{\Delta})$$

Informally, a default theory semantics is modular if any theory resulting from the union of two consistent theories with disjoint language contains the consequences of each of the theories alone.

Proposition 6.2.1. *Reiter's default logic is modular.*

Proof. Since a modular theory must be consistent by definition, the disjoint alphabets of two theories can never interact.

Consider now the following examples:

Example 6.2.3. The default theory

$$\left(\left\{ d_1 = \frac{: \neg b}{a}, d_2 = \frac{: \neg a}{b} \right\}, \{\} \right).$$

has two classical extensions, $\{a\}$ and $\{b\}$. Stationary default semantics has one more extension, namely $\{\}$.

Example 6.2.4. Let (D, W) be:

$$\left(\left\{ d_1 = \frac{: \neg b}{a}, d_2 = \frac{: \neg a}{b} \right\}, \{\neg a\} \right).$$

The only classical extension is $\{\neg a, b\}$. In the least stationary extension, $E = \Gamma^2_\Delta(E) = \{\neg a\}$, $j(d_2) \in E$ but $c(d_2) \notin E$.

Definition 6.2.2 (Applicability of defaults). *Given an extension E:*

- *a default d is* applicable *in E iff $p(d) \subseteq E$ and $\neg j(d) \cap E = \{\}$*
- *an applicable default d is* applied *in E iff $c(d) \in E$*

In classical default semantics every applicable default is applied. This prevents the uniqueness of a minimal extension. In Example 6.2.3, because one default is always applied, one can never have a single minimal extension. In [20, 173, 174], in order to guarantee a unique minimal extension, it becomes possible to apply or not an applicable default. However, this abandons the notion of maximality of application of defaults of classical default theory. But, in Example 6.2.4, we argue that at least rule d_2 should be applied.

We want to retain the principle of uniqueness of minimal extension coupled with a notion of maximality of application of defaults we call enforcedness.

Property 6.2.3 (Enforcedness). Given a theory Δ with extension E, a default d is *enforceable in E* iff $p(d) \in E$ and $j(d) \subseteq E$. An extension *is enforced* if all enforceable defaults in D are applied.

We argue that, whenever E is an extension, if a default is enforceable then it must be applied. Note that an enforceable default is always applicable.

Another way of viewing enforcedness is that if d is an enforceable default, and E is an extension, then the default rule d must be understood as an inference rule $p(d), j(d) \rightarrow c(d)$ and so $c(d) \in E$ must hold.

The well founded semantics and stationary semantics both sanction minimal extensions where enforceable defaults are not applied, viz. Example 6.2.4. However, in this example they still allow an enforced extension $\{b, \neg a\}$. This is not the case in general:

Example 6.2.5. Let $(D, W) = \left(\left\{ \frac{: \neg b}{c}, \frac{: \neg a}{b}, \frac{: \neg a}{a} \right\}, \{\neg b\} \right)$. The only stationary extension is $\{\neg b\}$, which is not enforced.

Based on this notion of enforcedness (first presented in [150]), in [174], Przymusinska and Przymusinki defined saturated default theories:

Definition 6.2.3 (Saturated default theory). *A default theory*

$$\Delta = (D, W)$$

is saturated iff for every default rule

$$\frac{p(d) \; : \; j(d)}{c(d)} \in D$$

if $p(d) \in W$ and $j(d) \subseteq W$, then $c(d) \in W$.

For this class of default theories they prove that both stationary and well founded default semantics comply with enforcedness. However considering only saturated default theories is a severe restriction since it requires a kind of closure in the theory W.

6.3 Ω-default theory

Next we introduce a default theory semantics which is modular and enforced for every (restricted) default theory. Moreover, when it is defined it has a unique minimal extension.

In the sequel, whenever unambigous, we refer to restricted default rules and theories, simply as default rules and theories.

In order to relate default theories to extended logic programs, we must provide a modular semantics for default theories, except if they are contradictory, as in the example below:

Example 6.3.1. In the default theory:

$$\left(\left\{ \frac{:}{\neg a}, \frac{:}{a} \right\}, \{\} \right)$$

its two default rules with empty prerequesites and justifications should always
be applied, which clearly enforces a contradiction. Note that this would also
be the case if the default theory were to be written as $(\{\}, \{a, \neg a\})$.

Consider now Example 6.2.2, that alerted us about nonmodularity in
stationary default semantics, where $D = \{ \frac{: \neg a}{\neg a}, \frac{: a}{a}, \frac{: b}{b} \}$, and $\{\}$ is the
least stationary extension.

This result is obtained because $\Gamma_\Delta(\{\})$, by having a and $\neg a$ forces, via
the deductive closure, $\neg b$ (and all the other literals) to belong to it. This
implies the non-applicability of the third default in the second iteration. For
that not to happen one should inhibit $\neg b$ from belonging to $\Gamma_\Delta(\{\})$, which
can be done by preventing, in the deductive closure in Γ, the explosion of
conclusions in presence of inconsistency[4]. This is one reason why [20]'s use
of Γ_Δ^2 does not extend to programs with explicit negation.

In our restricted language this is not problematic, because as formulae are
just literals, the inhibition of that principle can simply be made by renaming
negative literals, without side-effects.

Definition 6.3.1 ($\Gamma_\Delta'(E)$). *Let $\Delta = (D, W)$ be a propositional default theory and E a context. Let E' be the smallest set of atoms which:*

1. contains W';

2. is closed under all derivation rules of the form $\frac{p(d)'}{c(d)'}$, such that

$$\frac{p(d) \ : \ j(d)}{c(d)} \in D$$

and $\neg f \notin E$, for every $f \in j(d)'$, and $f \notin E$ for every $\neg\_f \in j(d)'$.

*where W' (resp. $p(d)'$, $j(d)'$, and $c(d)'$) is obtained from W (resp. $p(d)$, $j(d)$,
and $c(d)$) by replacing in it every negative literal $\neg A$ by a new atom $\neg\_A$.*

$\Gamma_\Delta'(E)$ *is obtained from E' by replacing every atom of the form $\neg\_A$ by
$\neg A$.*

Reconsider now Example 6.2.4, that showed that stationary default extensions are not always enforced. The non-enforced extension is (the least
extension) $E = \Gamma^2(E) = \{\neg a\}$, where $\Gamma(E) = \{\neg a, a, b\}$. The semantics
obtained is that $\neg a$ is true and a is undefined.

To avoid this counterintuitive result we want to ensure that, for an extension E :

---

[4] By the explosion of conclusions we mean the principle *"Ex Contradictione Sequitur Quot Libet"* (From a contradiction everything follows), which is a property of the deductive closure in classical logic. Wagner [210] argues against this
principle.

$$\forall d \in D \ \ \neg c(d) \in E \Rightarrow c(d) \notin \Gamma(E),$$

i.e. if $\neg c(d)$ is true then $c(d)$ is false[5].

It is easily recognized that this condition is satisfied by seminormal default theories: if $\neg c(d)$ belongs to an extension then any seminormal rule with conclusion $c(d)$ cannot be applied. This principle is exploited in the default semantics.

Definition 6.3.2 (Seminormal version of a default theory). *Given a default theory Δ, its seminormal version[6] Δ^s is obtained by replacing each default rule $d = \frac{p(d) \ : \ j(d)}{c(d)}$ in Δ by the default rule*

$$d^s = \frac{p(d) \ : \ j(d), c(d)}{c(d)}.$$

Definition 6.3.3 (Ω_Δ operator). *For a theory Δ we define:*

$$\Omega_\Delta(E) = \Gamma'_\Delta(\Gamma'_{\Delta^s}(E)).$$

Definition 6.3.4 (Ω-extension). *Let Δ be a default theory. E is an extension iff:*

- *$E = \Omega_\Delta(E)$*
- *$E \subseteq \Gamma'_{\Delta^s}(E)$*

Based on Ω-extensions we define the semantics of a default theory.

Definition 6.3.5 (Ω-default semantics). *Let Δ be a default theory, E an extension of Δ, and L a literal.*

- *L is true w.r.t. extension E iff $L \in E$*
- *L is false w.r.t. extension E iff $L \notin \Gamma'_{\Delta^s}(E)$*
- *Otherwise L is undefined*

The Ω-default semantics of Δ is determined by the set of all Ω-extensions of Δ.

The cautious Ω-default semantics of Δ is determined by the least Ω-extensions of Δ[7].

---

[5] Note the similarity with the coherence principle.

[6] In Reiter's formalization a default is seminormal if it is of the form

$$\frac{p(d) \ : \ j(d) \wedge c(d)}{c(d)}.$$

The definitions are equivalent because only ground versions of the defaults are considered.

[7] The existence of a least extension is guaranteed by Theorem 6.3.2 below.

Like in [174], we also require that each extension E be a subset of $\Gamma'_{\Delta^s}(E)^8$. By not doing so (i.e. considering as extensions all the fixpoints of Ω), the semantics would allow for an objective literal to be both true and false in some extensions.

Example 6.3.2. For the default theory

$$\Delta = \left(\left\{ \frac{:\neg a}{a}, \frac{:\neg b}{b}, \frac{a:\neg a}{c}, \frac{b:\neg b}{c} \right\}, \{\} \right)$$

there are four fixpoints of Ω_Δ :

$$
\begin{array}{llll}
E_1 & = & \{\} & \Gamma'_{\Delta^s}(E_1) & = & \{a,b,c\} \\
E_2 & = & \{a,c\} & \Gamma'_{\Delta^s}(E_2) & = & \{b,c\} \\
E_3 & = & \{b,c\} & \Gamma'_{\Delta^s}(E_3) & = & \{a,c\} \\
E_4 & = & \{a,b,c\} & \Gamma'_{\Delta^s}(E_4) & = & \{\}
\end{array}
$$

Only E_1 is an extension, and thus it determines the Ω-default semantics of Δ..

Note how, for instance, $a \in E_2$ and $a \notin \Gamma'_{\Delta^s}(E_2)$. Thus, if E_2 were to be considered as an extension a would be both true and false in E_2.

Moreover, intuitively no extension should contain c, since for each rule with conclusion c, the prerequisites are incompatible with the justification. In E_2 c is true because a being true satisfies the prerequisites, and a being false satisfies the justifications.

This definition of extension guarantees that no pair of contradictory literals belongs to E.

Proposition 6.3.1. *If E is a Ω-extension of a default theory Δ then:*

$$\nexists L \mid \{L, \neg L\} \subseteq E.$$

Proof. Assume the contrary, i.e. $\exists L \mid \{L, \neg L\} \subseteq E$ and E is an extension. By seminormality, $L \notin \Gamma'_{\Delta^s}(E)$ and $\neg L \notin \Gamma'_{\Delta^s}(E)$. Thus $E \nsubseteq \Gamma'_{\Delta^s}(E)$, and so is not an extension.

Example 6.3.3. Consider the default theory

$$\Delta = \left(\left\{ \frac{:\neg c}{c}, \frac{:\neg b}{a}, \frac{:\neg a}{b}, \frac{:}{\neg a} \right\}, \{\} \right).$$

Its only extension is $\{\neg a, b\}$.
In fact:

$$
\begin{array}{lll}
\Gamma'_{\Delta^s}(\{\neg a, b\}) & = & \{c, b, \neg a\} \qquad \text{and} \\
\Gamma'_\Delta(\{c, b, \neg a\}) & = & \{\neg a, b\}
\end{array}
$$

Thus $\neg a$ and b are true, c is undefined, and a and $\neg b$ are false.

---

[8] In [174] the requirement is with respect to $\Gamma_\Delta(E)$ instead of with respect to $\Gamma'_{\Delta^s}(E)$.

It is easy to see that some theories may have no Ω-extension.

Example 6.3.4. The theory $\Delta = (\,\{\frac{:}{a}, \frac{:}{\neg a}\}, \{\})$ has no Ω-extension.

Definition 6.3.6 (Contradictory theory). *A default theory Δ is contradictory iff it has no Ω-extension.*

In order to guarantee the existence of a least extension we prove:

Theorem 6.3.1 (Ω is monotonic). *If Δ is a noncontradictory theory then Ω_Δ is monotonic.*

Proof. We begin by stating two lemmas:

Lemma 6.3.1. *Let $\Delta = (D, W)$ be a noncontradictory default theory, and*

$$\Delta' = \left(D \cup \left\{\frac{:}{L} \mid L \in W\right\}, \{\}\right).$$

E is an Ω-extension of Δ iff is an Ω-extension of Δ'.

Proof. It is easy to see that every Ω-extension of Δ and of Δ' contains W. Thus for each Ω-extension of one of the theories the set of rules in D applied is the same as in the other theory.

Lemma 6.3.2. *If Δ is a noncontradictory default theory then Γ'_Δ is antimonotonic.*

Proof. Without loss of generality (cf. lemma 6.3.1 above) we consider

$$\Delta = (D, \{\}).$$

First we define two transformations over sets of objective literals, and one over default theories.

- A^- is a set of atoms obtained from a set of objective literals A by replacing every negative literal $\neg L$ by the new atom $\neg\_L$.
- A^+ is a set of objective literals obtained from a set of atom A by replacing every atom of the form $\neg\_L$ by the objective literal $\neg L$.
- Δ^{--} is the default theory obtained from $\Delta = (D, W)$ by replacing in D every occurence of a negative literal $\neg A$ by the new atom $\neg\_A$.

Clearly, the first two transformations are monotonic, i.e.:

$$A \subseteq B \Rightarrow A^+ \subseteq B^+$$

$$A \subseteq B \Rightarrow A^- \subseteq B^-$$

Directly from the definition of Γ'_Δ, and given that we are assuming $W = \{\}$, and Δ is noncontradictory:

$$\Gamma'_\Delta(A) = (\Gamma_{\Delta^{--}}(A^-))^+ \quad (*)$$

Now we prove that:

$$A \subseteq B \Rightarrow \Gamma'_\Delta(B) \subseteq \Gamma'_\Delta(A)$$

By monotonicity of A^- :

$$A \subseteq B \Rightarrow A^- \subseteq B^-$$

Given that Γ is antimonotonic for any default theory:

$$A^- \subseteq B^- \Rightarrow \Gamma_{\Delta--}(B^-) \subseteq \Gamma_{\Delta--}(A^-)$$

By monotonicity of A^+ :

$$\Gamma_{\Delta--}(B^-) \subseteq \Gamma_{\Delta--}(A^-) \Rightarrow (\Gamma_{\Delta--}(B^-))^+ \subseteq (\Gamma_{\Delta--}(A^-))^+$$

By the result of $(*)$:

$$(\Gamma_{\Delta--}(B^-))^+ \subseteq (\Gamma_{\Delta--}(A^-))^+ \Rightarrow \Gamma'_\Delta(B) \subseteq \Gamma'_\Delta(A)$$

i.e. Γ'_Δ is antimonotonic.

Since Ω_Δ is the composition of two antimonotonic operators, it is monotonic.

Definition 6.3.7 (Iterative construction). *To obtain a constructive definition for the least (in the set inclusion order sense) Ω-extension of a theory we define the following transfinite sequence $\{E_\alpha\}$:*

$$\begin{aligned} E_0 &= \{\} \\ E_{\alpha+1} &= \Omega(E_\alpha) \\ E_\delta &= \bigcup \{E_\alpha \mid \alpha < \delta\} \quad \text{for limit ordinal } \delta \end{aligned}$$

By Theorem 6.3.1, and the Knaster-Tarski theorem [204], there must exist a smallest ordinal λ for the sequence above, such that E_λ is the smallest fixpoint of Ω. If E_λ is a Ω-extension then it is the smallest one. Otherwise, by the proposition below, there are no Ω-extensions for the theory.

Proposition 6.3.2. *If the least fixpoint E of Ω_Δ is not a Ω-extension of Δ then Δ has no Ω-extensions.*

Proof. We prove that if there exists an extension E^* of Ω_Δ, then the least fixpoint of Ω_Δ is an extension.

Assume that such an E^* exists. Given that, by hypothesis, E is the least fixpoint of Ω_Δ, $E \subseteq E^*$.

On the assumption that E^* is an extension, Δ is noncontradictory and, by lemma 6.3.2, Γ'_{Δ^s} is antimonotonic. Thus:

$$E \subseteq E^* \Rightarrow \Gamma'_{\Delta^s}(E^*) \subseteq \Gamma'_{\Delta^s}(E)$$

Since, by hypothesis, E^* is an extension, $E^* \subseteq \Gamma'_{\Delta^s}(E^*)$. Thus:

$$E^* \subseteq \Gamma'_{\Delta^s}(E^*) \subseteq \Gamma'_{\Delta^s}(E)$$

Again using the fact that $E \subseteq E^*$:

$$E \subseteq E^* \subseteq \Gamma'_{\Delta^s}(E^*) \subseteq \Gamma'_{\Delta^s}(E)$$

Thus $E \subseteq \Gamma'_{\Delta^s}(E)$, and so E is an extension of Ω_Δ.

Example 6.3.5. Consider the default theory Δ of Example 6.3.3. In order to obtain the least (and only) extension of Δ we build the sequence:

$$
\begin{aligned}
E_0 &= \{\} \\
E_1 &= \Gamma'_\Delta(\Gamma'_{\Delta^s}(\{\})) &&= \Gamma'_\Delta(\{c, a, b, \neg a\}) &&= \{\neg a\} \\
E_2 &= \Gamma'_\Delta(\Gamma'_{\Delta^s}(\{\neg a\})) &&= \Gamma'_\Delta(\{c, b, \neg a\}) &&= \{\neg a, b\} \\
E_3 &= \Gamma'_\Delta(\Gamma'_{\Delta^s}(\{\neg a, b\})) &&= \Gamma'_\Delta(\{c, b, \neg a\}) &&= \{\neg a, b\} = \\
&= E_2
\end{aligned}
$$

Because $E_2 \subseteq \Gamma'_{\Delta^s}(E_2)$, it is the least Ω-extension of Δ.

Example 6.3.6. Let $\Delta = \left(\; \{ \frac{\cdot}{a}, \frac{\cdot}{\neg a} \}, \{\} \right)$. Let us build the sequence:

$$
\begin{aligned}
E_0 &= \{\} \\
E_1 &= \Gamma'_\Delta(\Gamma'_{\Delta^s}(\{\})) &&= \Gamma'_\Delta(\{a, \neg a\}) &&= \{a, \neg a\} \\
E_2 &= \Gamma'_\Delta(\Gamma'_{\Delta^s}(\{a, \neg a\})) &&= \Gamma'_\Delta(\{\}) &&= \{a, \neg a\} = E_1
\end{aligned}
$$

Since $E_1 \not\subseteq \Gamma'_{\Delta^s}(E_1)$, Δ has no Ω-extensions.

We will now prove that this new default semantics satisfies all the principles required above (Section 6.2).

Theorem 6.3.2 (Uniqueness of minimal extension). *If Δ has an extension then there is one least extension E.*

Proof. Trivial, given that Ω_Δ is monotonic for noncontradictory program. ∎

Theorem 6.3.3 (Enforcedness). *If E is a Ω-extension then E is enforced.*

Proof. Without loss of generality (cf. lemma 6.3.1 above) we consider

$$\Delta = (D, \{\}).$$

We want to prove that for any default rule d :

$$p(d) \in E \text{ and } j(d) \subseteq E \Rightarrow c(d) \in E$$

If $j(d) \subseteq E$ then, by seminormality, no rule with a conclusion $\neg f$, such that $f \in j(d)$, is applicable in $\Gamma'_{\Delta^s}(E)$. So, given that we are assuming $W = \{\}$ for theory Δ :

$$\text{for all literals } f \text{ in } j(d), \; \neg f \notin \Gamma'_{\Delta^s}(E).$$

Thus the default d is applicable in $\Gamma'_\Delta \Gamma'_{\Delta^s}(E)$, i.e., by definition of Γ, $\Gamma'_\Delta \Gamma'_{\Delta^s}(E)$ must be closed under the derivation rule $\frac{p(d)}{c(d)}$.

Given that E is an Ω-extension:

$$p(d) \in E \Rightarrow p(d) \in \Gamma'_\Delta \Gamma'_{\Delta^s}(E)$$

and because $\Gamma'_\Delta \Gamma'_{\Delta^s}(E)$ must be closed under that derivation rule:

$$c(d) \in \Gamma'_\Delta \Gamma'_{\Delta^s}(E)$$

Again because E is an extension, if $c(d) \in \Gamma'_\Delta \Gamma'_{\Delta^s}(E)$ then $c(d) \in E$.

Corollary 6.3.1. *If E is an Ω-extension of Δ then for any $d = \frac{\cdot}{c(d)} \in \Delta$, $c(d) \in E$.*

Proof. Follows directly from enforcedness for true prerequisites and justifications.

Theorem 6.3.4 (Modularity). *Let L_{Δ_1} and L_{Δ_2} be the languages of two default theories. If $L_{\Delta_1} \cap L_{\Delta_2} = \{\}$ then, for any corresponding extensions E_1 and E_2, there always exists an extension E of $\Delta = \Delta_1 \cup \Delta_2$ such that $E = E_1 \cup E_2$.*

Proof. Since the languages are disjoint, the rules of Δ_1 and Δ_2 do not interact on that count. Additionally, since there is no explosion of conclusions in the presence of inconsistency, one can never obtain the whole set of literals as a result of a contradictory Γ'_{Δ^s}, and hence they do not interact on that count either.

6.4 Comparison with Reiter's semantics

Comparing this semantics for defaults theories with Reiter's, we prove that for restricted default theories (cf. Definition 6.1.3) the former is a generalization of the latter, in the sense that whenever Reiter's semantics (Γ-extension) gives a meaning to a theory (i.e. the theory has at least one Γ-extension), Ω semantics provides one too.

Moreover, whenever both semantics give meaning to a theory Ω semantics is sound w.r.t. the intersection of all Γ-extensions. Thus we provide a monotonic fixpoint operator for computing a subset of the intersection of all Γ-extensions. For that purpose we begin by stating and proving:

Theorem 6.4.1. *Consider a theory Δ such that Ω-semantics is defined. Then every Γ-extension is a Ω-extension.*

Proof. First two lemmas:

Lemma 6.4.1. *If E is consistent and $E = \Gamma_\Delta(E)$ then $E = \Gamma'_{\Delta^s}(E)$.*

Proof. By definition of Γ_Δ,

$$E = \Gamma_\Delta(E) \Longrightarrow (\forall_{d \in D} \ p(d) \in E \ \wedge \ \neg j(d) \cap E = \{\} \Rightarrow c(d) \in E).$$

Thus, since E is consistent:

$$\forall_{d \in D} \ p(d) \in E \wedge \neg j(d) \cap E = \{\} \wedge \neg c(d) \cap E = \{\} \Rightarrow c(d) \in E$$

and so, by definition of Γ'_{Δ^s}, it follows easily that $E = \Gamma'_{\Delta^s}(E)$.

Lemma 6.4.2. *If E is consistent and $E = \Gamma_\Delta(E)$ then $E = \Gamma'_\Delta(E)$.*

Proof. Similar to the one of lemma 6.4.1.

Now we prove that for an E such that

$$E = \Gamma_\Delta(E)$$

$E = \Omega_\Delta(E)$ holds.

By definition,

$$\Omega_\Delta(E) = \Gamma'_\Delta(\Gamma'_{\Delta^s}(E)).$$

By lemma 6.4.1,

$$\Omega_\Delta(E) = \Gamma'_\Delta(E).$$

And by lemma 6.4.2,

$$\Gamma'_\Delta(E) = E.$$

For E to be a Ω-extension one more condition must hold:

$$E \subseteq \Gamma'_{\Delta^s}(E).$$

It is easy to recognize given the hypothesis

$$E = \Gamma_\Delta(E).$$

The next two results follow directly from the above theorem.

Theorem 6.4.2 (Generalization of Reiter's semantics). *If a theory Δ has at least one Γ-extension, it has at least one Ω-extension.*

Theorem 6.4.3 (Soundness wrt to Reiter's semantics). *If a theory Δ has a Γ-extension, whenever L belongs to the least Ω-extension it also belongs to the intersection of all Γ-extensions.*

It is interesting to note that any other combination of the Γ-like operators that are used to define Ω (i.e. the operators: $\Gamma'_{\Delta^s}, \Gamma'_\Delta$, $\Gamma'^2_{\Delta^s}$, and Γ'^2_Δ) also give semantics that are sound with respect to Reiter's, but which are not as close to the latter as the semantics defined by Ω. By "not as close" we mean that its least fixpoints are subsets of the intersection of all Reiter's extensions, that are smaller (with respect to set inclusion) than the least fixpoint of Ω. Thus we say that Ω is the best approximation of Reiter's default semantics, when compared to the others.

Proposition 6.4.1. *Let Δ be a noncontradictory default theory. Then:*

1. $lfp(\Gamma'_{\Delta^s}, \Gamma'_\Delta) \subseteq lfp(\Gamma'^2_{\Delta^s})$
2. $lfp(\Gamma'_{\Delta^s}, \Gamma'_\Delta) \subseteq lfp(\Gamma'^2_\Delta)$
3. $lfp(\Gamma'^2_{\Delta^s}) \subseteq lfp(\Omega)$
4. $lfp(\Gamma'^2_\Delta) \subseteq lfp(\Omega)$

Proof. In appendix.

6.5 Comparison with stationary default semantics

We now draw some brief comparisons with stationary extensions [174]. It is not the case that every stationary extension is a Ω-extension since, as noted above, non-modular or non-enforced stationary extensions are not Ω-extensions. As shown in the example below, it is also not the case that every Ω-extension is a stationary extension.

Example 6.5.1. Let Δ be:

$$\left(\left\{ \frac{: \neg b}{c}, \frac{: \neg a}{b}, \frac{: \neg a}{a}, \frac{:}{\neg b} \right\}, \{\} \right)$$

The only Ω-extension of Δ is $\{c, \neg b\}$. This is not a stationary extension.

As stated above, for saturated default theories stationary semantics complies with enforcedness. However, even for this class of theories, the two semantics might not coincide. This is because in general stationary default extensions are not modular.

Example 6.5.2. The default theory of Example 6.2.2 is saturated and has a non-modular stationary extension.

However, in a large class of cases these semantics coincide. In particular:

Proposition 6.5.1. *If for every default $d = \frac{p(d) : j(d)}{c(d)}$ $c(d)$ is a positive literal then Ω coincides with Γ^2_Δ.*

Proof. For such theories $\Gamma'_{\Delta^s} = \Gamma'_\Delta = \Gamma_\Delta$. Thus $\Gamma'_\Delta \Gamma'_{\Delta^s} = \Gamma^2_\Delta$.

6.6 Relation between the semantics of default theories and logic programs with explicit negation

Here we state the equivalence of Ω-extensions and partial stable models of extended logic programs as defined in Chapter 4. For the sake of brevity proofs are in Appendix C.

Definition 6.6.1 (Program corresponding to a default theory).
Let $\Delta = (D, \{\})$ be a default theory. We say an extended logic program P corresponds to Δ iff:

- *For every default of the form:*

$$\frac{\{a_1, \ldots, a_n\} : \{b_1, \ldots, b_m\}}{c} \in \Delta$$

there exists a rule

$$c \leftarrow a_1, \ldots, a_n, not \; \neg b_1, \ldots, not \; \neg b_m \in P$$

where $\neg b_j$ denotes the $\neg$-complement of b_j.

– No rules other than these belong to P.

Definition 6.6.2 (Interpretation corresponding to a context).
An interpretation I of a program P corresponds to a default context E of the corresponding default theory T iff for every objective literal L of P (and literal L of T):

- $I(L) = 1$ iff $L \in E$ and $L \in \Gamma'_\Delta.(E)$.
- $I(L) = \frac{1}{2}$ iff $L \notin E$ and $L \in \Gamma'_\Delta.(E)$.
- $I(L) = 0$ iff $L \notin E$ and $L \notin \Gamma'_\Delta.(E)$.

The main theorem relating both semantics is now presented:

Theorem 6.6.1 (Correspondence). *Let $\Delta = (D, \{\})$ be a default theory corresponding to program P. E is a Ω-extension of Δ iff the interpretation I corresponding to E is a partial stable model of P.*

According to this theorem we can say that explicit negation is nothing but classical negation in (restricted) default theories, and vice-versa. As Ω default semantics is a generalization of Γ default semantics (cf. Theorems 6.4.2 and 6.4.3), and since answer-sets semantics corresponds to Γ default semantics [80], it turns out that answer-sets semantics (and hence the semantics defined in [209]) is a special case of *WFSX*. Other properties of Ω-extensions can also be translated into properties of models of extended logic programs, e.g. modularity, uniqueness of minimal extension, etc.

On the other hand, with this theorem one can rely on the top-down procedures of logic programming to compute default extensions. In particular, in accordance with Theorem 6.4.3, the top-down procedures for *WFSX* (namely those described in Chapter 10) can be used as sound top-down procedures for Reiter's default logic.

Example 6.6.1. Consider program P :

$$
\begin{aligned}
c &\leftarrow not\ c \\
a &\leftarrow not\ b \\
b &\leftarrow not\ a \\
\neg a &\leftarrow
\end{aligned}
$$

The corresponding default theory is

$$
\Delta = \left(\left\{ \frac{:\ \neg c}{c}, \frac{:\ \neg b}{a}, \frac{:\ \neg a}{b}, \frac{:}{\neg a} \right\}, \{\} \right).
$$

As calculated in Example 6.3.3, the only Ω-extension of Δ is $E = \{\neg a, b\}$ and $\Gamma'_\Delta.(E) = \{\neg a, b, c\}$. The PSM corresponding to this extension is

$$
M = \{\neg a, not\ a, b, not\ \neg b, not\ \neg c\}[9].
$$

It is easy to verify that M is the only *PSM* of P.

---

[9] Note that c is undefined in M.

6.7 A definition of *WFSX* based on Γ

In [80], it is proven that, with the above correspondences between programs and default theories, and between interpretations and default contexts, Reiter's Γ operator for defaults is equivalent to the Gelfond-Lifschitz (GL) Γ operator for extended logic programs (cf. Definition 2.2.1). Thus, the above relationship between *WFSX* and Ω extensions directly suggests an alternative definition of *WFSX*.

Based on this relationship, and on the fact that the GL Γ operator is not based on 2-valued logic, in this section we present an alternative definition of *WFSX* not relying in a 3-valued logic, but rather on a partial 2-valued logic.

We begin by defining in logic programs the notion corresponding to seminormality in default theories.

Definition 6.7.1 (Seminormal version of a program).
The seminormal version of a program P is the program P_s obtained from P by adding to the (possibly empty) Body of each rule:

$$L \leftarrow Body$$

the default literal $not \ \neg L$, where $\neg L$ is the complement of L with respect to explicit negation.

For short, when P is understood from context, we use $\Gamma(S)$ to denote $\Gamma_P(S)$, and $\Gamma_s(S)$ to denote $\Gamma_{P_s}(S)$.

Theorem 6.7.1 (Partial stable models). *Let P be an extended logic program.*

$$M = T \cup not \ F$$

is a partial stable model of P iff:

(1) $T = \Gamma\Gamma_s T$
(2) $T \subseteq \Gamma_s T$

Moreover $F = \{L \mid L \notin \Gamma_s T\}$, and members of $\Gamma_s T$ not in T are undefined *in M.*

In the sequel we refer to T as the generator of M.

Proof. Follows directly from Theorem 6.6.1.

Note that in these alternative definitions each PSM is completely determined by the objective literals true in it.

Theorem 6.7.2 (Well-founded model). *Let P be a noncontradictory program.*

$M = T \cup not \ F$ *is the well-founded model of P iff T is the least fixpoint of $\Gamma\Gamma_s$ and generates M.*

Thus the WFM can be obtained by iterating $\Gamma\Gamma_s$ from the empty set[10]. If a fixpoint S is reached, then it contains objective literals true in the WFM. False literals in it are the ones compatible with $\Gamma_s S$, i.e. those literals not in $\Gamma_s S$. It is also possible to define an iterative construction of false literals in the WFM, and determine instead true literal from false ones.

The next proposition helps us build one such iterative construction.

Proposition 6.7.1. *Let P be a noncontradictory program. Then:*

$$\Gamma_s(lfp(\Gamma\Gamma_s)) = gfp(\Gamma_s\Gamma)$$

Proof. First we prove that $\Gamma_s(lfp(\Gamma\Gamma_s))$ is a fixpoint of $\Gamma_s\Gamma$. By definition:

$$lfp(\Gamma\Gamma_s) = \Gamma\Gamma_s(lfp(\Gamma\Gamma_s))$$

Thus:

$$\Gamma_s(lfp(\Gamma\Gamma_s)) = \Gamma_s(\Gamma\Gamma_s(lfp(\Gamma\Gamma_s)))$$

By associativity of function compositions:

$$\Gamma_s(lfp(\Gamma\Gamma_s)) = \Gamma_s\Gamma(\Gamma_s(lfp(\Gamma\Gamma_s)))$$

i.e. $\Gamma_s(lfp(\Gamma\Gamma_s))$ is a fixpoint of $\Gamma_s\Gamma$.

Now let S be a fixpoint of $\Gamma_s\Gamma$. We have to prove that:

$$S \subseteq \Gamma_s(lfp(\Gamma\Gamma_s))$$

To that proof, we begin by showing that $lfp(\Gamma\Gamma_s) \subseteq \Gamma S$

Given that $\Gamma\Gamma_s$ is monotonic, there exists a smallest ordinal λ such that:

$$lfp(\Gamma\Gamma_s) = \Gamma\Gamma_s^{\uparrow\lambda}\{\}$$

We now prove by transfinite induction that for any ordinal α

$$\Gamma\Gamma_s^{\uparrow\alpha}\{\} \subseteq \Gamma S$$

— *For limit ordinal δ:* Suppose that for all $\alpha < \delta$

$$\Gamma\Gamma_s^{\uparrow\alpha}\{\} \subseteq \Gamma S$$

Then clearly

$$\bigcup \{\Gamma\Gamma_s^{\uparrow\alpha}\{\} \mid \alpha < \delta\} \subseteq \Gamma S$$

i.e.

$$\Gamma\Gamma_s^{\uparrow\delta}\{\} \subseteq \Gamma S$$

---

[10] In the case of normal programs $\Gamma\Gamma_s$ reduces to Γ^2. This Γ^2 characterization of the WFM of normal programs was first set forth in [20]. Note that the effect of Γ_s is to ensure the Coherence Principle. Indeed, it is easily seen that one can replace $\Gamma\Gamma_s$ by $\Gamma^2 Coh$, where Coh is a new operator that takes a program P and transforms it with respect to some interpretation I, by deleting from P all rules for any objective literal L such that $\neg L$ is in I. Consequently, *not* L will belong to the semantics of the transformed program. Γ_s achieves the same effect by falsifying the body of such rules in P_s.

– *Induction step:* Assume that for some ordinal i

$$\Gamma\Gamma_s^{\uparrow i}\{\} \subseteq \Gamma S$$

Then, given that $\Gamma\Gamma_s$ is monotonic:

$$\Gamma\Gamma_s(\Gamma\Gamma_s^{\uparrow i})\{\} \subseteq \Gamma\Gamma_s(\Gamma S)$$

By associativity of function compositions, this inequality is equivalent to:

$$\Gamma\Gamma_s^{\uparrow i+1}\{\} \subseteq \Gamma(\Gamma_s\Gamma S)$$

Given that by hypothesis S is a fixpoint of $\Gamma_s\Gamma$:

$$\Gamma\Gamma_s^{\uparrow i+1}\{\} \subseteq \Gamma S$$

At this point we've proven that $lfp(\Gamma\Gamma_s) \subseteq \Gamma S$. From this result, and given that Γ_s is antimonotonic, it follows that:

$$\Gamma_s\Gamma S \subseteq \Gamma_s(lfp(\Gamma\Gamma_s))$$

Again because by hypothesis S is a fixpoint of $\Gamma_s\Gamma$:

$$S \subseteq \Gamma_s(lfp(\Gamma\Gamma_s))$$

We now define two (monotonic) operators: one which given a set of true objective literals, determines additional true objective literals; another which given a set of false objective literals determines additional false objective literals.

Definition 6.7.2. *For a program P define:*

$$\begin{aligned}
\mathcal{T}(S) &= \Gamma\Gamma_s(S) \\
\mathcal{F}(R) &= \mathcal{H} - \Gamma_s\Gamma(\mathcal{H} - R)
\end{aligned}$$

where $\mathcal{H}$ denotes the Herbrand base of P.

Theorem 6.7.3. *For any noncontradictory program, both $\mathcal{T}$ and $\mathcal{F}$ are monotonic.*

Proof. The proof of monotonicity of $\mathcal{T}$ is trivial given that of Ω for defaults (Theorem 6.3.1), and that a program is noncontradictory iff the corresponding default theory is also noncontradictory. This last results follows directly from Theorem 6.6.1.

Similarly to the proof of Theorem 6.3.1, one can prove that $\Gamma_s\Gamma$ is also monotonic. So:

$$\begin{aligned}
A \subseteq B \quad &\Rightarrow & \mathcal{H} - B &\subseteq \mathcal{H} - A & &\Rightarrow \\
&\Rightarrow & \Gamma_s\Gamma(\mathcal{H} - B) &\subseteq \Gamma_s\Gamma(\mathcal{H} - A) & &\Rightarrow \\
&\Rightarrow & \mathcal{H} - \Gamma_s\Gamma(\mathcal{H} - A) &\subseteq \mathcal{H} - \Gamma_s\Gamma(\mathcal{H} - B) & &\Rightarrow \\
&\Rightarrow & \mathcal{F}(A) &\subseteq \mathcal{F}(B)
\end{aligned}$$

i.e. $\mathcal{F}$ is monotonic.

Theorem 6.7.4. *Let P be a noncontradictory program. Then:*

$$WFM(P) = lfp(T) \cup not \; lfp(\mathcal{F})$$

Proof. We begin with the lemma:

Lemma 6.7.1. *For any noncontradictory program:*

$$lfp(\mathcal{F}) = \mathcal{H} - gfp(\Gamma_s\Gamma)$$

Proof. We begin by proving by transfinite induction that:

$$\mathcal{F}^{\uparrow\alpha}\{\} = \mathcal{H} - (\Gamma_s\Gamma)^{\downarrow\alpha}\mathcal{H}$$

- *For limit ordinal δ:* Suppose that for all $\alpha < \delta$:

$$\mathcal{F}^{\uparrow\alpha}\{\} = \mathcal{H} - (\Gamma_s\Gamma)^{\downarrow\alpha}\mathcal{H}$$

Then, clearly:

$$\bigcup\{\mathcal{F}^{\uparrow\alpha}\{\} \mid \alpha < \delta\} = \mathcal{H} - \bigcap\{(\Gamma_s\Gamma)^{\downarrow\alpha}\mathcal{H} \mid \alpha < \delta\}$$

i.e.

$$\mathcal{F}^{\uparrow\delta}\{\} = \mathcal{H} - (\Gamma_s\Gamma)^{\downarrow\delta}\mathcal{H}$$

- *Induction step:* Assume that for some ordinal i

$$\mathcal{F}^{\uparrow i}\{\} = \mathcal{H} - (\Gamma_s\Gamma)^{\downarrow i}\mathcal{H}$$

Then:

$$\mathcal{F}^{\uparrow i+1}\{\} = \mathcal{F}(\mathcal{F}^{\uparrow i}\{\}) = \mathcal{F}(\mathcal{H} - (\Gamma_s\Gamma)^{\downarrow i}\mathcal{H})$$

Applying the definition of $\mathcal{F}$:

$$\mathcal{F}^{\uparrow i+1}\{\} = \mathcal{H} - \Gamma_s\Gamma(\mathcal{H} - (\mathcal{H} - (\Gamma_s\Gamma)^{\downarrow i}\mathcal{H}))$$

Given that for any two sets A and B, $B - (B - A) = B \cap A$:

$$\mathcal{F}^{\uparrow i+1}\{\} = \mathcal{H} - \Gamma_s\Gamma(\mathcal{H} \cap (\Gamma_s\Gamma)^{\downarrow i}\mathcal{H})$$

Since the result of $\Gamma_s\Gamma$ is a subset of the Herbrand base, i.e. for any S, $\mathcal{H} \supseteq \Gamma_s\Gamma S$:

$$\mathcal{F}^{\uparrow i+1}\{\} = \mathcal{H} - \Gamma_s\Gamma((\Gamma_s\Gamma)^{\downarrow i}\mathcal{H}) = \mathcal{H} - (\Gamma_s\Gamma)^{\downarrow i+1}\mathcal{H}$$

Given this result, the proof follows directly from the iterative construction of least and gretaest fixpoints of monotonic operators.

According to this lemma and proposition 6.7.1:

$$lfp(\mathcal{F}) = \mathcal{H} - \Gamma_s(lfp(\Gamma\Gamma_s))$$

From Theorem 6.7.2:

$$WFM(P) = lfp(T) \cup not \; (\mathcal{H} - \Gamma_s(lfp(\Gamma\Gamma_s)))$$

Example 6.7.1. Consider the program P :

$$
\begin{aligned}
c &\leftarrow b, not\ c \\
a &\leftarrow not\ b \\
b &\leftarrow not\ a \\
\neg a &
\end{aligned}
$$

Next we show two alternative ways of computing the WFM.

1. Start from an empty set of true objective literals, and iterate consecutively, in order to get more objective literals true, until a fixpoint is reached:

$$
\begin{aligned}
T_0 &= \{\} \\
T_1 &= \Gamma\Gamma_s\{\} &&= \Gamma\{c, a, b, \neg a\} &&= \{\neg a\} \\
T_2 &= \Gamma\Gamma_s\{\neg a\} &&= \Gamma\{c, b, \neg a\} &&= \{b, \neg a\} \\
T_3 &= \Gamma\Gamma_s\{b, \neg a\} &&= \Gamma\{c, b, \neg a\} &&= \{b, \neg a\}
\end{aligned}
$$

Then:

$$
\begin{aligned}
WFM &= T_3 \quad \cup \quad not\ (\mathcal{H} - \Gamma_s T_3) \\
&= \{b, \neg a\} \quad \cup \quad not\ (\mathcal{H} - \{c, b, \neg a\}) \\
&= \{b, \neg a\} \quad \cup \quad \{not\ a, not\ \neg b, not\ \neg c\}
\end{aligned}
$$

2. Start from an empty set of false objective literals and iterate consecutively, in order to get more objective literals false, until a fixpoint is reached:

$$
\begin{aligned}
F_0 &= \{\} \\
F_1 &= \mathcal{H} - \Gamma_s\Gamma(\mathcal{H} - \{\}) &&= \mathcal{H} - \Gamma_s\{\neg a\} \\
&= \mathcal{H} - \{c, b, \neg a\} &&= \{a, \neg b, \neg c\} \\
F_2 &= \mathcal{H} - \Gamma_s\Gamma\{c, b, \neg a\} &&= \mathcal{H} - \Gamma_s\{b, \neg a\} \\
&= \mathcal{H} - \{c, b, \neg a\} &&= \{a, \neg b, \neg c\}
\end{aligned}
$$

Then:

$$
\begin{aligned}
WFM &= \Gamma(\mathcal{H} - F_2) \quad \cup \quad not\ F_2 \\
&= \Gamma\{c, b, \neg a\} \quad \cup \quad \{not\ a, not\ \neg b, not\ \neg c\} \\
&= \{b, \neg a\} \quad \cup \quad \{not\ a, not\ \neg b, not\ \neg c\}
\end{aligned}
$$

7. *WFSX* and hypotheses abduction

Approaches to nonmonotonic reasoning semantics clash on two major intuitions: scepticism and credulity [207]. In normal logic programming the credulous approach includes semantics such as stable models [78] and preferred extensions [62], while the well-founded semantics [76] is the sole representative of scepticism [62].

In extended logic programming, while generalizations of stable models semantics are clearly credulous in their approach, no semantics whatsoever has attempted to seriously explore the sceptical approach. A closer look at some of the works generalizing well-founded semantics [68, 180, 183, 196] shows these generalizations to be rather technical in nature, where the different techniques introduced to formally characterize the well-founded semantics of normal logic programs are slightly modified in some way to become applicable to the more general case.

In this chapter we characterize a spectrum of more or less sceptical and credulous semantics for extended logic programs, and determine the position of *WFSX* in this respect.

We do so by means of a coherent, flexible, unifying, and intuition appealing framework for the study of explicit negation in logic programs, based on the notion of admissible scenaria. This framework extends the approach originally proposed in [62] for normal logic programs.

The basic idea of the framework is to consider default literals as abducibles, i.e. they must be hypothesized. This idea was first proposed in [70], and in [62] it was further explored in order to capture stable models [78] and the well-founded semantics [76] of normal programs. There, an hypothesis is acceptable iff there is no evidence to the contrary: roughly no set of hypotheses derives its complement[1]. Semantics are then defined by adding to a program sets of acceptable hypotheses, according to additional specific choice criteria. Depending on the chosen criteria, more sceptical or credulous semantics are obtained.

---

[1] In [30] the authors develop an assumption-based argumentation framework for logic programming where a variety of alternative of evidence to the contrary notions are studied. In our approach the notion of evidence to the contrary is kept fixed.

In trying to extend these notions to extended logic programs, a new kind of hypotheses appears – mandatory hypotheses.

Example 7.0.2. Consider a program containing the rules:

$$tryBus \quad \leftarrow \quad not\ driversSrike$$
$$\neg driversStrike$$

advising to plan a trip by bus if it can be assumed the bus drivers are not on strike, and stating bus drivers are not on strike. No matter what the rest of the program is (assuming it is consistent on the whole), it is clear that a rational agent assumes the bus drivers are not on strike, and of course he plans his trip by bus.

In this case it is mandatory to assume the hypothesis *not driversSrike*.

Intuitively, an hypothesis *not L* is mandatory if $\neg L$ is a consequence of the program, i.e. if objective literal L is explicitly stated false then the hypothesis that assumes it false must per force be accepted. This amounts to the coherence principle.

In other words, in extended programs default literals can be view as hypotheses, where an objective literal L inhibits the hypothesis *not L* (as in normal programs), and $\neg L$ makes the assumption of hypothesis *not L* imperative.

Moreover, viewing default literals as hypotheses that may or may not be accepted, helps us provide semantics for contradictory programs where contradiction is brought about by such hypotheses[2]. Indeed, if default literals are just hypotheses, and if some of them cause contradiction, then it seems natural not to accept these in order to assign a meaning to a program. Even though there may be no specific evidence to the contrary of a hypothesis, if its adoption leads to a global contradiction then its acceptance is questionable. This is an instance of the *"reductio ad absurdum"* principle.

In this section to begin we define, in a simple way, an ideal sceptical semantics and its well-founded (or grounded) part; in fact an entirely declarative semantics able to handle programs like:

$$a \quad \leftarrow \quad not\ p \qquad b \quad \leftarrow \quad not\ r$$
$$\neg a \quad \leftarrow \quad not\ q$$

and assigning it the semantics $\{b, not\ r\}$.

WFSX cannot deal with such programs because, as neither p nor q have rules, it assumes both *not p* and *not q* without regard to the ensuing contradiction, except as an after-the-fact filter. In our ideal sceptical semantics this program is not contradictory at all.

---

[2] Note that these are the cases presented above, where *WFSX* provides no meaning and we argue that it might be natural to provide one.

However, the issue of dealing with such contradictory programs within *WFSX*, and assigning to them a semantics is explored in detail in Chapter 8, where we use the framework of this chapter, plus the additional notion of optative hypothesis, as its basis.

One advantage of viewing logic programs as abduction is its close relationship with argumentation system and dialogue games. In [67, 93], the authors have pointed out the similarities between the ideas of acceptability of hypotheses and evidence to the contrary, and the notions of arguments and attacks of argumentation systems. Based on that they sustain that [62] is in fact an argumentational approach to normal logic programs. In the same way, our approach can be viewed as an argumentational approach to extended logic programs.

The problem of understanding the process of argumentation (or dialogue games) has been addressed by many researchers in different fields [206, 25, 128, 87, 43, 166]. The understanding of the structure and acceptability of arguments is essential for a computer system to be able to engage in exchanges of arguments with other systems.

The ability of viewing extended logic programs as argumentation systems opens the way for its use in formalizing communication among reasoning computing agents in a distributed framework [134].

A dialogue game is an exchange of arguments between two players where each alternately presents arguments attacking the arguments of the opponent. The player who fails to present counterarguments looses the game. As shown in [63, 65, 66] a game theoretical semantics for logic programming can be defined by interpreting programs as schemas for forming arguments, where a literal can be concluded if it is supported by acceptable arguments constructed according to the rules of the program:

Example 7.0.3. Consider program P :

$$\begin{array}{llll} \neg fly(X) & \leftarrow & animal(X), not\ ab\_a(X) & \quad animal(tweety) \\ ab\_a(X) & \leftarrow & bird(X), not\ ab\_b(X) & \quad bird(tweety) \\ ab\_b(X) & \leftarrow & penguin(X) & \quad penguin(tweety) \end{array}$$

P can be viewed as the rules for constructing the arguments:

1. Tweety does not fly since it is an animal and animals normally do not fly.
2. Tweety is an abnormal animal since it is a bird and normally birds are abnormal animals with respect to flying.
3. Tweety is an abnormal bird since it is a penguin and penguins are abnormal birds with respect to flying.

A dialogue game to determine whether or not tweety flies proceeds as follows:

- Player 1 presents argument 1 supporting the conclusion that tweety cannot fly. His argument is based on the assumption that animals normally do not fly.
- In the next move player 2 presents argument 2 which *"attacks"* argument 1 by defeating the assumption made by the latter. His argument is based on the assumption that normally birds are abnormal animals.
- Then player 1 presents argument 3 *"counterattacking"* the argument of player 2.
- As player 2 cannot find any argument *counterattacking* the argument of player 1, he looses the game and gives up his claims.

In the framework we present in this chapter, hypotheses can be viewed as arguments, that may or may not be accepted, in the same way arguments may or may not be winning ones. An argument is acceptable if every attack against it can be counterattacked by it. As we point out below, this is tantamount to the acceptance of hypotheses, where an hypothesis is acceptable in the context of other hypotheses if every set of hypotheses that constitutes evidence to its contrary is in turn defeated by the context where it is accepted. To make this clearer we explain, for the program of Example 7.0.3, why *not ab_a(tweety)* is acceptable:

The hypotheses *not ab_a(tweety)* is acceptable because the only evidence to the contrary, i.e. to *ab_a(tweety)*, is the hypothesis *not ab_b(tweety)*, and this evidence is defeated by *not ab_a(tweety)* : in the context where this assumption is made true in the program *ab_b(tweety)* follows as a consequence.

A detailed study of logic programming as dialogue games and argumentation systems is not in the scope of this work. However, the intuitions behind the relationship between the concepts introduced here and those of dialogue games and argumentation systems can be found throughout this chapter.

7.1 Admissible scenaria for extended logic programs

In this section we generalize the notions of scenario and evidence for normal logic programs given in [62], to those extended with explicit negation. They are reminiscent of the notions of scenario and extensions of [167].

In [62, 35, 67] a normal logic program is viewed as an abductive framework where literals of the form *not L* (NAF-hypotheses) are considered as new atoms, say *not_L*, and are abducibles, i.e. they must be hypothesized. The set of all ground NAF-hypotheses is *not H*, where $\mathcal{H}$ denotes the Herbrand base of the program, as usual, and *not* prefixed to a set denotes the set obtained by prefixing *not* to each of its elements[3]. Here we generalize these notions to extended logic programs.

In order to introduce explicit negation we first consider negated objective literals of the form $\neg A$ as new symbols (as in [78]). The Herbrand base is now extended to the set of all such objective literals. Of course, this is not enough to correctly treat explicit negation. Relations among $\neg A$, A, and *not A*, must be established, as per the definitions below.

Definition 7.1.1 (Scenario). *A scenario of an extended logic program P is the Horn theory $P \cup H$, where $H \subseteq not\ \mathcal{H}$.*

For scenaria we define a derivability operator in a straightforward way, given that every scenario is a Horn theory:

Definition 7.1.2 ($\vdash$ operator). *Let P be an extended logic program and H a set of NAF-hypotheses.*

P' is the Horn theory obtained from P by replacing:

— every objective literal of the form $\neg L$ by the atom $\neg\_L$
— every default literal of the form not L by the atom not$\_L$
— every default literal of the form not $\neg L$ by the atom not$\_\neg\_L$

where $\neg\_L$, not$\_L$, and not$\_\neg\_L$ are new atoms not appearing in P.
A set H' is obtained from H using the same replacement rules.

By definition $P' \cup H'$ is a Horn theory, and so it has a least model M. We define $\vdash$ in the following way (where A is any atom of P):

$P \cup H \vdash A$	iff	$A \in M$
$P \cup H \vdash \neg A$	iff	$\neg\_A \in M$
$P \cup H \vdash not\ A$	iff	$not\_A \in M$
$P \cup H \vdash not\ \neg A$	iff	$not\_\neg\_A \in M$

In argumentation systems a scenario can be viewed as a possible set of arguments. In particular the arguments corresponding to a scenario $P \cup H$ are those engendered by the hypotheses in H.

When introducing explicit negation into logic programs one has to reconsider the notion of NAF-hypotheses, or simply hypotheses. As the designation "explicit negation" suggests, when a scenario $P \cup H$ entails $\neg A$ it is *explicitly* stating that A is false in that scenario. Thus the hypothesis *not A* is enforced in the scenario, and cannot optionally be held independently. This is the *"coherence principle"*, which relates both negations.

---

[3] In [35] the authors dub these programs open positive ones. Positive because all negated literals are transformed into new atoms, and open because the program can be completed with additional information, i.e. default literals can be added (or hypothesized) in order to give the program a meaning.

Definition 7.1.3 (Mandatory hypotheses wrt $P \cup H$).
The set of mandatory hypotheses (or mandatories) with respect to a scenario $P \cup H$ is:

$$Mand(H) = \{not\ L \mid P \cup H \cup \{not\ K \leftarrow \neg K \mid K \in \mathcal{H}\} \vdash \neg L\}$$

where L or K is any objective literal, and $\neg K$ (resp. $\neg L$) denotes the complement of K (resp. L) with respect to explicit negation. The extra rules enforce coherence.

Alternatively, the set of mandatory hypotheses with respect to $P \cup H$ is the smallest set $Mand(H)$ such that:

$$Mand(H) = \{not\ L \mid P \cup H \cup Mand(H) \vdash \neg L\}.$$

Example 7.1.1. Consider program P:

$$
\begin{aligned}
q &\leftarrow\ not\ r \\
\neg r &\leftarrow\ not\ p \\
\neg p &
\end{aligned}
$$

Then:

$$Mand(\{\}) = \{not\ p, not\ r, not\ \neg q\}.$$

Indeed, the Horn theory:

q	$\leftarrow$	not_r	$not\_\neg\_q \leftarrow q$	$not\_\neg\_p \leftarrow p$	
$\neg\_r$	$\leftarrow$	not_p	$not\_q \leftarrow \neg\_q$	$not\_p \leftarrow \neg\_p$	
$\neg\_p$			$not\_\neg\_r \leftarrow r$		
			$not\_r \leftarrow \neg\_r$		

derives $\{not\_p, not\_r, not\_\neg\_q\}$ and no more hypotheses.

Example 7.1.2. Consider the program P:

$$
\begin{aligned}
b(p) & \\
\neg m(X,Y) &\leftarrow\ b(X) \\
m(p, s) &\leftarrow\ not\ m(t, s) \\
m(t, s) &\leftarrow\ not\ m(p, s) \\
\neg m(X, X) &
\end{aligned}
$$

obtained from the autoepistemic theory of Example 5.2.9.
 The mandatory hypotheses with respect to $P \cup \{\}$ are:

- from the last rule, all ground instances of literals of the form $not\ m(X, X)$;
- from the first rule, $not\ \neg b(p)$;
- from the first and second rules $P \vdash \neg m(p, Y)$, and thus ground instances of literals of the form $not\ m(p, Y)$ are mandatories;
- from the above points and the third rule it follows that P and its mandatories derive $m(t, s)$, and so $not\ \neg m(t, s)$ is also mandatory.

Mandatory hypotheses correspond in argumentation systems to arguments that cannot be directly attacked because they are sustained by conclusions. For instance, the fact $\neg fly(tweety)$ in a program states that Tweety does not fly. Since no argument can attack this fact, the argument *not* $fly(tweety)$ is unattackable.

Example 7.1.3. Consider a program containing the rules:

$$newsAboutStrike \;\leftarrow\; driversStrike$$
$$\neg driversStrike$$

stating that newspapers publish news about the strike if the drivers are on strike, and that the bus drivers are definitely not on strike.

For a rational reasoner the second rule should not provide a pretext for newspapers to publish news about a strike by possibly assuming it, since indeed the first rule (or some other) may actually state or conclude the contrary of that assumption.

Note how this is accomplished by using always programs in the canonical form (Definition 2.1.1), where any true rule head has the effect of falsifying the body of all rules containing its complement literal with respect to explicit negation.

Recall that, within a program in the canonical form, any objective literal L in the body of a rule is to be considered shorthand for the conjunction L, *not* $\neg L$. This allows for technical simplicity in capturing the relation between $\neg L$ and *not* L (cf. justification in the compact version of the modulo operator in Chapter 4). Thus, without loss of generality (cf. corollary 9.1.1), and for the sake of technical simplicity, whenever refering to a program in this section we always mean its canonical form. In all examples we expressly use the canonical program.

Definition 7.1.4 (Consistent scenario). *A scenario* $P \cup H$ *is consistent iff for all objective literals* L *such that:*

$$P \cup H \cup Mand(H) \vdash L$$

then

$$not\ L \notin H \cup Mand(H)$$

Note that, by the definition of mandatory hypotheses, for every consistent scenario:

if $\;P \cup H \cup Mand(H) \vdash L\;$ then $\;P \cup H \cup Mand(H) \not\vdash \neg L.$

Unlike the case of non-extended logic programs, an extended logic program may in general have no consistent scenaria:

Example 7.1.4. Program

$$P = \left\{ \begin{array}{l} \neg p \\ p \; \leftarrow \; not \; p \end{array} \right\}$$

has no consistent scenario.

Note that $P \cup \{\}$ is not consistent since $Mand(\{\}) = \{not \; p\}$ and $P \cup \{not \; p\} \vdash p$.

A notion of program consistency is needed. Intuitively, a program is consistent iff it has some consistent scenario. Because for a given H, if $P \cup H$ is consistent then $P \cup \{\} \cup Mand(\{\})$ is also consistent, we define:

Definition 7.1.5 (Consistent program). *An extended logic program P is consistent iff*

$$P \cup Mand(\{\})$$

is a consistent scenario.

Inconsistent programs are those that derive a contradiction even without assuming any hypotheses (except, of course, for those for which it is mandatory to do so, i.e. the mandatories). The rôle of the semantics here being to determine sets of hypotheses that can be added to a program without making it inconsistent, and since no set whatsoever is in these conditions for an inconsistent program, no semantics is given it.

By adding to the body of each rule a private default literal $not \; L'$, where L' is a new atom not appearing elsewhere in the program, every program becomes consistent. This operation, similar to the naming device of [167], renders every rule hypothetical because its condition is contingent on the prior acceptance of its private "naming" default literal. Ultimately, inconsistency can thus be always avoided. Semantics that assign meaning to inconsistent programs by considering consistent subsets of its rules can be "simulated" in ours via the naming device.

Thus, from now on, unless otherwise stated, we restrict programs to consistent ones only.

Not every consistent scenario specifies a consensual semantics for a program [167], in the same way that not every set of arguments is a winning set in dialog games. For example [62] the program P :

$$p \leftarrow not \; q$$

has a consistent scenario $P \cup \{not \; p\}$ which fails to give the intuitive meaning of P. It is not consensual to assume $not \; p$ since there is the possibility of p being true (if $not \; q$ is assumed), and $\neg p$ is not explicitly stated (if this were the case then $not \; q$ could not be assumed).

Intuitively, what we wish to express is that a hypothesis can be assumed only if there can be no evidence to the contrary.

Clearly a hypothesis *not L* is only directly contradicted by the objective literal L. Evidence for an objective literal L in a program P is a set of hypotheses which, if assumed in P together with its mandatories, would entail L.

Definition 7.1.6 (Evidence for an objective literal L). *A subset E of not $\mathcal{H}$ is evidence for an objective literal L in a program P iff:*

$$E \supseteq Mand(E) \quad \text{and} \quad P \cup E \vdash L^4$$

If P is understood and E is evidence for L we write $E \rightsquigarrow L$.

Note here the similarities between *evidence to the contrary* of an hypothesis and *attack* to an argument.

As in [62] a hypothesis is acceptable with respect to a scenario iff there is no evidence to the contrary, i.e. iff all evidence to the contrary is itself defeated by the scenario:

Definition 7.1.7 (Acceptable hypothesis). *A hypothesis not L is acceptable with respect to the scenario $P \cup H$ iff:*

$$\forall E : E \rightsquigarrow L \Rightarrow \exists not\ A \in E \mid P \cup H \cup Mand(H) \vdash A,$$

i.e. each evidence for L is defeated by $P \cup H$.
The set of all acceptable hypotheses with respect to $P \cup H$ is denoted by $Acc(H)$.

This is tantamount to the acceptability of arguments in dialogue games. In the latter an argument is acceptable if it can *counterattack* (i.e. defeat) every *attack* made on it (i.e. every evidence to the contrary).

Example 7.1.5. Consider program P :

$$a \leftarrow not\ b, not\ c \qquad \neg c$$
$$b \leftarrow not\ d$$

In the scenario $P \cup \{not\ c, not\ d, not\ a\}$:

- *not c* is mandatory because $P \vdash \neg c$;
- *not d* (resp. *not ¬a, not ¬b*) is acceptable because there is no evidence for d (resp. $\neg a, \neg b$);
- *not a* is acceptable because any evidence for a must contain $\{not\ b, not\ c\}$, and so is defeated by the scenario since

$$P \cup \{not\ c, not\ d, not\ a\} \cup Mand(\{not\ c, not\ d, not\ a\}) \vdash b$$

---

[4] The consistency of $P \cup E$ is not required; e.g. $P \cup \{not\ A\} \vdash A$ is allowed.

For example, *not b* is neither mandatory nor acceptable because, respectively:

$$P \cup \{not\ c, not\ d, not\ a\} \cup Mand(\{not\ c, not\ d, not\ a\}) \not\vdash \neg b$$

and $\{not\ d\}$ is an evidence for b not defeated by the scenario, i.e.:

$$P \cup \{not\ d\} \cup Mand(\{not\ d\}) \vdash b$$

and

$$P \cup \{not\ c, not\ d, not\ a\} \cup Mand(\{not\ c, not\ d, not\ a\}) \not\vdash d$$

In a consensual semantics we are interested only in admitting consistent scenaria whose hypotheses are either acceptable or mandatory. As the designation "mandatory hypotheses" suggests, any scenario to be considered must include all its mandatory hypotheses:

Definition 7.1.8 (Admissible scenario). *A scenario $P \cup H$ is admissible iff it is consistent and:*

$$Mand(H) \subseteq H \subseteq Mand(H) \cup Acc(H)$$

We must guarantee that by considering only admissible scenaria one does not fail to give semantics to consistent programs, i.e.:

Proposition 7.1.1. *Any consistent program P has at least an admissible scenario.*

Proof. By hypothesis P is consistent and so the scenario $P \cup Mand(\{\})$ is also consistent.

By definition $Mand(H)$ is closed under mandatories, i.e.

$$Mand(H) = Mand(Mand(H))$$

So $P \cup H$, where $H = Mand(\{\})$, is an admissible scenario:

$$Mand(Mand(\{\})) = Mand(\{\}) \subseteq Mand(Mand(\{\})) \cup Acc(Mand(\{\}))$$

The notion of admissible scenario discards all hypotheses which are unacceptable, whatever the semantics of extended logic programs to be defined.

One semantics can be defined as the class of all admissible scenaria, where the meaning of a program is determined, as usual, by the intersection of all such scenaria.

However, since $P \cup Mand(\{\})$ is always the least admissible scenario (cf. proof of proposition 7.1.1), this semantics does not include any non-mandatory hypothesis. Consequently this semantics is equivalent to replacing every *not L* by the corresponding objective literal $\neg L$.

Example 7.1.6. Let P :

$$\neg p$$
$$a \quad \leftarrow \quad not\ b$$

Its admissible scenaria are:

$P \cup \{not\ p\}$
$P \cup \{not\ p, not\ \neg a\}$
$P \cup \{not\ p, not\ \neg b\}$
$P \cup \{not\ p, not\ b, not\ \neg a\}$
$P \cup \{not\ p, not\ \neg a, not\ \neg b\}$
$P \cup \{not\ p, not\ b, not\ \neg a, not\ \neg b\}$

the least admissible scenario being the first.

Thus the literals entailed by the semantics of admissible scenaria are

$$\{\neg p, not\ p\}.$$

Note *not b* and *a* are not entailed by this extremely sceptical semantics.

The semantics of admissible scenaria is the most sceptical one for extended logic programs: it contains no hypotheses except for mandatory ones[5]. In order to define more credulous semantics, we define classes of scenaria based on proper subsets of the class of admissible scenaria, as governed by specific choice criteria. Constraining the set of admissible scenaria reduces undefinedness but may restrict the class of programs having a semantics.

In the next sections we define a spectrum of semantics which, by restricting the set of admissible scenaria, are more credulous, but give meaning to narrower classes of programs. *WFSX* turns out to be one of the semantics in that spectrum.

7.2 A sceptical semantics for extended programs

Several proposals, already mentioned above, have been made to generalize well-founded semantics[6] to logic programs with explicit negation, in order to obtain a sceptical semantics for extended logic programs. But a closer look at these works shows these generalizations to be of a rather technical nature, where different techniques introduced to characterize the well-founded semantics of normal logic programs (those without explicit negation) are in someway modified to become applicable to the more general case. So it would not be surprising if tomorrow some new *"sceptical"* semantics for programs with explicit negation were to be presented. So which of them is really

---

[5] This semantics is equivalent to one which only accepts hypotheses if it is explicitly negated in the program that there is evidence to the contrary. Hence it contains only the mandatory literals.

[6] By its nature the representative of scepticism in normal logic programs.

"sceptical"? And what is the essential difference between them? How many "sceptical" semantics are we going to have? After all, what makes a semantics "sceptical"? Certainly not just because it is in some way "technically" similar to one or other presentation of the well-founded semantics of Van Gelder et al. [76][7].

It is natural and important to ask the question of what is an ideally sceptical semantics for explicit negation, *i.e. one which would be part of the semantics of every rational reasoner.*

Suppose that $P \cup H$ is this *"ideal"* sceptical semantics. In the previous section, we have introduced and argued that an admissible scenario represents a scenario which is admissible for a rational reasoner. Let one such admissible scenario be $P \cup K$. It is clear that $P \cup K \cup H$ is again admissible since H must be part of this agent's semantics. This leads to an immediate definition of the *"ideal"* or *"idealized"* sceptical semantics.

Definition 7.2.1 (Ideal sceptical semantics). *A set of hypotheses H is called the ideal sceptical semantics, ISS, if it is the greatest set satisfying the condition:*

For each admissible scenario $P \cup K$, $P \cup K \cup H$ is again admissible.

It is clear that if P is consistent then such a set exists, a consequence of the fact that the union of sets satisfying the above condition satisfies it too.

Example 7.2.1. Consider program P :

$$
\begin{array}{rcl}
a & \leftarrow & not\ p \\
\neg a & \leftarrow & not\ q \\
c & \leftarrow & not\ r
\end{array}
$$

The admissible scenaria are (apart from literals $not\ \neg p$, $not\ \neg q$, and $not\ \neg r$, which are irrelevant to this example and are omitted):

$$
\begin{array}{ll}
P \cup \{\} & \\
P \cup \{not\ \neg c\} & P \cup \{not\ r, not\ \neg c\} \\
P \cup \{not\ \neg c, not\ p, not\ \neg a\} & P \cup \{not\ r, not\ \neg c, not\ p, not\ \neg a\} \\
P \cup \{not\ \neg c, not\ q, not\ a\} & P \cup \{not\ r, not\ \neg c, not\ q, not\ a\}
\end{array}
$$

It is not difficult to see that the greatest admissible scenario whose union with any other is again admissible is $\{not\ r, not\ \neg c\}$, i.e. $ISS = \{not\ r, not\ \neg c\}$. So we are able to conclude c despite the inconsistency potentially caused by the other rules.

Note that according to *WFSX* this program is contradictory.

The most sceptical well-founded semantics, or WFS0, is next construable as the *grounded* part of the ideal sceptical semantics. Indeed, in the case of

---

[7] Dung [64] has shown that stable model semantics can also be viewed as wellfounded semantics, since it can be defined a similar way.

normal programs, the ideal sceptical semantics is determined as the greatest lower bound of all preferred extensions [62], well-founded semantics being the grounded part of this ideal sceptical semantics. This corroborates the intuitions of other related fields, where a distinction is made between restricted and ideal scepticism [202][8].

In this context, in order to define the well-founded sceptical semantics for programs with explicit negation, all we need is introduce the grounded part of ideal scepticism:

Definition 7.2.2 (WFS0). *Let P be an extended logic program whose ideal sceptical semantics is $P \cup H$. First define a transfinite sequence $\{K_\alpha\}$ of sets of hypotheses of P :*

$$
\begin{aligned}
K_0 &= \{\} \\
K_{\alpha+1} &= K_\alpha \cup (H \cap MA(K_\alpha))
\end{aligned}
$$

where

$$MA(K_\alpha) = Mand(K_\alpha) \cup Acc(K_\alpha).$$

The well-founded (sceptical) semantics of P, denoted WFS0, is defined as:

$$P \cup \bigcup_\alpha K_\alpha$$

Hypotheses belonging to WFS0 belong perforce to ISS, because that is imposed at each step of the above iterative process by $MA(K_\alpha)$, and are also grounded in the sense that they are obtained by this bottom-up process starting from $\{\}$.

Example 7.2.2. Consider program P :

$$
\begin{aligned}
a &\leftarrow \quad not\ a \\
a &\leftarrow \quad not\ b \\
b &\leftarrow \quad not\ a
\end{aligned}
$$

Apart from literals $not\ \neg a$, and $not\ \neg b$ which are irrelevant to this example, admissible scenaria are:

$$P \cup \{\} \qquad P \cup \{not\ b\}[9]$$

Thus $ISS = \{not\ b\}$.

In order to calculate the WFS0 let us build the sequence:

– By definition $K_0 = \{\}$.

---

[8] One other example of such restricted scepticism in logic programming is the "well-founded semantics with respect to Opt" presented in Chapter 8, which is even more sceptical then the aforementioned WFS0.

[9] Note that scenario $P \cup \{not\ a\}$ is inconsistent.

- Since the program is normal there are no mandatories with respect to $P \cup \{\}$.
    - *not b* is not acceptable because $\{not\ a\}$ is evidence for b not defeated by $P \cup \{\}$, i.e. $P \cup \{\} \not\vdash a$;
    - Similarly, *not a* is also not acceptable.
  Thus $MA(K_0) = Mand(\{\}) \cup Acc(\{\}) = \{\}$, and

$$K_1 = \{\} \cup (\{not\ b\} \cap \{\}) = \{\} = K_0$$

So $WFS0 = P \cup \{\}$ because *not b* is not grounded.

Theorem 7.2.1. *WFS0 is defined uniquely for every consistent program.*

Proof. Trivial since, as stated above, ISS is defined for every consistent programs and WFS0 is obtained uniquely from ISS.

The next theorem states this definition of well-foundedness is a generalization of the one for non-extended (i.e. normal) programs.

Theorem 7.2.2 (Relation to the WFS of normal programs). *If P is a normal program then the WFS0 and the the well-founded semantics of [76] coincide.*

Proof. Clearly, if a program P has no explicit negation for every scenario $P \cup H$

$$Mand(H) = \{\}$$

Thus the definitions of evidence to the contrary, acceptability, and admissible scenario are equivalent to those for normal programs presented in [62]. So the ideal sceptical semantics corresponds to the intersection of preferred extensions and, as proven in [62], its grounded part coincides with the well-founded semantics of [76].

7.3 The semantics of complete scenaria

In this section we present a semantics less sceptical than WFS0 but failing to give semantics to all consistent programs. We call it *"complete scenaria semantics"* (CSS for short). Then we exhibit and prove some properties of CSS, in particular that it coincides with *WFSX*.

For normal programs every acceptable hypothesis can be accepted. In extended programs an acceptable hypotheses may fail to be accepted, in case a contradiction is verified.

Example 7.3.1. Consider the consistent program P:

$$\neg a$$
$$a \leftarrow not\ b$$

The hypothesis *not b* is acceptable with respect to every scenario of P. However, by accepting *not b* the program becomes inconsistent. Thus *not b* can never be accepted. In a semantics like WFS0 such hypotheses are not accepted.

ISS and WFS0 model a reasoner who assumes the program correct and so, whenever confronted with an acceptable hypothesis leading to an inconsistency he cannot accept such a hypothesis; he prefers to assume the program correct rather than assume that an acceptable hypothesis must be accepted (cf. Example 7.2.1 where both *not p* and *not q* are acceptable, but not accepted). We can also view this reasoner as one who has a more global notion of acceptability. For him, as usual, an hypothesis can only be acceptable if there is no evidence to the contrary, but if by accepting it (along with others) a contradiction arises, then that counts as evidence to the contrary.

It is easy to imagine a less sceptical reasoner who, confronted with an inconsistent scenario, prefers considering the program wrong rather than admitting that an acceptable hypothesis be not accepted. Such a reasoner is more confident in his acceptability criterium: an acceptable hypothesis is accepted once and for all; if an inconsistency arises then there is certainly a problem with the program, not with the acceptance of each acceptable hypothesis. This position is justified by the stance that acceptance be grounded on the absence of specific contrary evidence rather than on the absence of global non-specific evidence to the contrary. We come back to this issue in Chapter 8, where we compare the more sceptical semantics with a revision process acting over the less sceptical one.

In order to define a semantics modeling the latter type of reasoner we begin by defining a subclass of the admissible scenaria, which directly imposes that acceptable hypotheses are indeed accepted.

Definition 7.3.1 (Complete scenario). *A scenario $P \cup H$ is complete iff is consistent, and*

$$H = Mand(H) \cup Acc(H)$$

i.e. $P \cup H$ is complete iff is consistent, and for each not L :

(i)		$not\ L \in H \quad \Rightarrow$	$not\ L \in Acc(H) \vee$
			$not\ L \in Mand(H)$
(ii)	$not\ L \in Mand(H)$	$\Rightarrow$	$not\ L \in H$
(iii)	$not\ L \in Acc(H)$	$\Rightarrow$	$not\ L \in H$

where (i) and (ii) jointly express admissibility.

Example 7.3.2. The only complete scenario of program P :

$$\neg b$$
$$b \; \leftarrow \; not \; c$$
$$c \; \leftarrow \; not \; c$$
$$a \; \leftarrow \; b, not \; \neg b$$

is $P \cup \{not \; a, not \; \neg a, not \; b, not \; \neg c\}$. In fact:

- the mandatory hypotheses of that scenario are $\{not \; b\}$;
- $not \; \neg a$ is acceptable because there is no evidence for $\neg a$;
- $not \; \neg c$ is acceptable because there is no evidence for $\neg c$;
- $not \; a$ is acceptable because $not \; \neg b$ belongs to every evidence for a, and $\neg b$ is entailed by the scenario;
- $not \; c$ is not acceptable because $\{not \; c\}$ is evidence for c.

Since every acceptable or mandatory hypothesis is in the scenario, and every hypothesis in the scenario is either acceptable or mandatory, the scenario is complete.

Mark that if $not \; \neg b$ were not part of the last rule, as required by Definition 2.1.1 of canonical program, then $not \; a$ would not be acceptable.

As expected, and in contradistinction to WFS0, complete scenaria may in general not exist, even when the program is consistent.

Example 7.3.3. Program P :

$$\neg a \; \leftarrow \; not \; b$$
$$a \; \leftarrow \; not \; c$$

has several admissible scenaria:

$$P \; \cup \; \{\} \qquad\qquad P \; \cup \; \{not \; b\} \qquad\qquad P \; \cup \; \{not \; c\}$$
$$P \; \cup \; \{not \; a, not \; b\} \quad P \; \cup \; \{not \; \neg a, not \; c\}$$

None is complete. For example $P \cup \{not \; \neg a, not \; c\}$ is not complete because $not \; b$ is acceptable with respect to that scenario.

Definition 7.3.2 (Contradictory program). *A program is contradictory iff it has no complete scenaria.*

Definition 7.3.3 (Complete scenaria semantics). *Let P be a noncontradictory program.*

The complete scenaria semantics of P is the set of all complete scenaria of P.

As usual, the meaning of P is determined by the intersection of all such scenaria.

The inexistence of semantics for some consistent programs might be seen as showing the inadequacy of CSS in certain cases, specially if compared to WFS0. As we will see in Chapter 8, this is not the case since less sceptical semantics can be captured using CSS[10] and a revision process. The rationale of this view is:

"If an inconsistency arises then there is certainly a problem with the program, not with the acceptance of each acceptable hypothesis. If the problem is with the program then its revision is in order."

By using CSS one can rely on structural properties that, unlikely those of WFS0, make it amenable for devising bottom-up and top-down procedures, and also allow for more favourable computational complexity results (cf. Chapter 9).

7.4 Properties of complete scenaria

In this section we study some properties of this semantics, present a fixpoint operator for it, and show its relationship with *WFSX*.

Theorem 7.4.1. *Let $CS_P \neq \{\}$ be the set of all complete scenaria of non-contradictory program P. Then:*

1. *CS_P is a downward-complete semilattice, i.e. each nonempty subset of CS_P has a greatest lower bound.*
2. *There exists a least complete scenario.*
3. *In general, CS_P is not a complete partial order[11], i.e. maximal elements might not exist.*

For the sake of simplicity the proof of this theorem is in appendix. However we would like to present here an example showing that in general maximal complete scenario might not exist (viz. point 3 above):

Example 7.4.1. Consider the program:

$$
\begin{array}{rcl}
a & \leftarrow & not\ b \\
\neg a & \leftarrow & not\ b \\
b & \leftarrow & not\ p(X) \\
p(X) & \leftarrow & not\ q(X) \\
q(X) & \leftarrow & not\ p(X)
\end{array}
$$

with Herbrand base $\mathcal{H} = \{0, 1, 2, 3, \ldots\}$.

For this program every set of the form

$$S_i = \{not\ q(k) \mid k \leq i\}$$

is a complete scenario, but there exists no complete scenario containing

$$\bigcup_i S_i.$$

---

[10] In Chapter 8 we use *WFSX* instead of CSS. However, as we prove afore, these semantics coincides.

[11] However, for normal programs CS_P is a complete partial order.

Given that a least scenario always exists, we define:

Definition 7.4.1 (Well-founded complete scenario). *Let P be noncontradictory. The well-founded complete scenario $WF(P)$, is the least complete scenario of P.*

For this semantics we define an operator over scenaria such that every fixpoint of it is a complete scenario.

Definition 7.4.2 (V_P operator). *Given a program P and a set of hypotheses H we define:*

$$V_P(H) = H \cup Mand(H) \cup Acc(H)$$

just in case $P \cup V_P(H)$ is a consistent scenario; otherwise $V_P(H)$ is not defined.

The correctness of this operator is shown by the following (trivial) lemma.

Lemma 7.4.1. *$P \cup H$ is a complete scenario iff $H = V_P(H)$.*

Another important result regarding the properties of the V_P operator is:

Lemma 7.4.2. *V_P is monotonic, by construction of its parts.*

From this lemma, and point 2 of Theorem 7.4.1, it follows that:

Theorem 7.4.2. *If P is noncontradictory then the least fixpoint of V_P is the $WF(P)$.*

Theorem 7.4.3 (Construction of the WF complete scenario). *In order to obtain a constructive bottom-up iterative definition of the WF scenario of a noncontradictory program P, we define the following transfinite sequence $\{H_\alpha\}$ of sets of hypotheses of P:*

$$
\begin{aligned}
H_0 &= \{\} \\
H_{\alpha+1} &= V_P(H_\alpha) \\
H_\delta &= \bigcup \{H_\alpha \mid \alpha < \delta\} \quad \text{for a limit ordinal } \delta
\end{aligned}
$$

By lemma 7.4.2 and the Knaster-Tarski theorem [204], there exists a smallest ordinal λ such that H_λ is a fixpoint of V_P. The WF complete scenario is $P \cup H_\lambda$.

This constructive definition obliges one to know *a priori* whether a program is contradictory. This prerequisite is not needed if we employ the following theorem.

Theorem 7.4.4. *A program P is contradictory iff in the sequence of the H_α there exists a λ such that $P \cup V_P(H_\lambda)$ is an inconsistent scenario.*

Thus, in order to compute the $WF(P)$ start building the above sequence. If, at some step i, H_i introduces a pair of complementary objective literals then end the iteration and P is contradictory. Otherwise iterate until the least fixpoint of V_P, which is the $WF(P)$.

Note the similarities between this process and the one described in Section 6.7 for $WFSX$, where the iteration also provides the default literals $not\ F$ (here caled hypotheses) true in the model, other literals T being determined by the former (there $T = \Gamma(\mathcal{H} - F)$, and here $T = \{L \mid P \cup not\ F \vdash L\}$).

7.4.1 Complete scenaria and *WFSX*

Next we present the relationship between the complete scenaria semantics CSS for extended logic programs and *WFSX*, showing they are the same. The significance of this result is underscored in the introduction to this chapter. Proofs of lemmas can be found in Appendix C.

Lemma 7.4.3 (*PSM*s correspond to complete scenaria). *Let*

$$S = T \cup not\ F$$

be a PSM of a program P, where T and F are disjoint sets of objective literals. Then:

$$P \cup not\ F$$

is a complete scenario.

Lemma 7.4.4 (Complete scenaria correspond to *PSM*s). *If*

$$P \cup H$$

is a complete scenario then:

$$\{L \mid P \cup H \vdash L\} \cup H$$

is a PSM of P.

Theorem 7.4.5 (Equivalence). *The complete scenaria semantics CSS is equivalent to* WFSX.

7.5 More credulous semantics

Along the same lines of complete scenaria semantics, we can continue restricting the set of admissible scenaria, thus defining more credulous semantics.

The most immediate semantics more credulous than CSS (or *WFSX*) is the one obtained by considering only maximal (with respect to $\subseteq$) complete scenaria. We call this semantics "preferred extensions" following the tradition for normal programs [62].

Definition 7.5.1 (Preferred extensions semantics). *The preferred extensions semantics of an extended program P is the set of its maximal complete scenaria.*

Example 7.4.1 shows that maximal elements might not exist for a collection of complete scenaria, hence preferred extensions are defined for less programs than *WFSX*. Another straightforward result is that this semantics is in general more credulous than *WFSX*.

Example 7.5.1. Consider the program:

$$
\begin{aligned}
a &\leftarrow not\ p, not\ \neg p \\
p &\leftarrow not\ \neg p \\
\neg p &\leftarrow not\ p
\end{aligned}
$$

Complete scenaria are (where the last two are preferred):

$$
\begin{aligned}
&P \cup \{not\ \neg a\} \\
&P \cup \{not\ \neg a, not\quad p, not\ a\} \\
&P \cup \{not\ \neg a, not\ \neg p, not\ a\}
\end{aligned}
$$

Thus *not a* is a consequence of the preferred extensions semantics but not of complete scenaria semantics.

A reasoner can even be more credulous by considering only preferred extensions that are two valued (or total), i.e. extensions such that whenever L is not a consequence of them *not L* is assumed in them.

Definition 7.5.2 (Total scenario). *A scenario $P \cup H$ is total iff for every objective literal L:*

$$
P \cup H \vdash L \quad \equiv \quad not\ L \notin H
$$

Definition 7.5.3 (Total scenaria semantics). *The total scenaria semantics of an extended program P is the set of its total complete scenaria.*

Given the results of [62], where stable models are total complete scenaria in normal logic programs, it follows easily:

Theorem 7.5.1 (Answer-sets). *The total scenaria semantics   coincides with the answer-sets semantics of [80].*

Clearly answer-sets semantics is defined for less programs than the previous semantics, since such total scenaria may in general not exist. The typical program for which answer-sets semantics is not defined but *WFSX* is defined is $P = \{a \leftarrow not\ a\}$, where assuming *not a* leads to an inconsistency between a and *not a*, and *not a* cannot be left unassumed because a is not a consequence. This program has only one complete scenario, $\{not\ \neg a\}$, and it is not total.

Explicit negation introduces other cases of inexistence of answer-sets appear.

Example 7.5.2. Let P be:

$$
\begin{array}{rcl}
p & \leftarrow & not\ \neg p \\
\neg p & \leftarrow & not\ p \\
b & \leftarrow & not\ \neg p \\
a & \leftarrow & not\ p \\
\neg a & & \\
\neg b & &
\end{array}
$$

The only complete scenario is $P \cup \{not\ a, not\ b\}$, which is not total. Thus no answer-sets exist.

Here the inexistence of answer-sets is due to inconsistency between an objective literal and its explicit negation:

– assuming $not\ p$ leads to an inconsistency between a and $\neg a$;
– the assumption $not\ p$ can be dropped only if p is a consequence. In order to make p a consequence $not\ \neg p$ must be assumed, and then an inconsistency between b and $\neg b$ appears.

Example 7.4.1 shows additional issues regarding the existence of answersets. In particular that example shows that the computation of an answer-set cannot in general be made by finite approximations.

7.5.1 Comparisons among the semantics

From the Definition 7.2.2 of WFS0 and the iterative construction of the WF complete scenario of CSS (Theorem 7.4.3) it follows almost directly that:

Theorem 7.5.2 (WFS0 is more sceptical than $WFSX$). *For any non-contradictory program P*

$$WFS0(P) \subseteq WFSX(P).$$

Example 7.5.3. Consider program P :

$$
\begin{array}{rcl}
p & \leftarrow & not\ q \\
\neg p & \leftarrow & a \\
\neg p & \leftarrow & b \\
a & \leftarrow & not\ b \\
b & \leftarrow & not\ a
\end{array}
$$

whose $WFSX$ is $\{not\ q\}$ (apart from irrelevant literals such as $not\ \neg a$).

Since $P \cup \{not\ q, not\ \neg p\}$, $P \cup \{not\ a, not\ p\}$, and $P \cup \{not\ b, not\ p\}$ are all admissible scenaria (though not them all), and neither $not\ a$ nor $not\ b$ can be added to the first scenario, and also $not\ q$ cannot be added neither to the second nor to the third scenario above, then $ISS = \{\}$. Thus $WFS0 = \{\}$.

Interesting questions are: *When do all these semantics coincide? Can we state sufficient conditions guaranteeing such an equivalence?*

In order to answer the second question we introduce the notion of semantically normal (s-normal for short) programs; i.e. those whose admissible scenaria can all be completed.

Definition 7.5.4 (S-normal program). *An extended program is s-normal iff for each admissible scenario* $P \cup H$:

$$P \cup H \cup Acc(H)$$

is consistent.

Lemma 7.5.1. *Let* P *be a s-normal program,* $P \cup H$ *be an admissible scenario, and let not A, not B be acceptable with respect to* $P \cup H$. *Then:*

1. $P \cup H \cup \{not\ A\}$ *is admissible and*
2. *not B is acceptable with respect to* $P \cup H \cup \{not\ A\}$.

Proof. Trivial, given the definition of s-normal program.

From this lemma it follows immediately that the set of all admissible scenarios (with respect to set inclusion) forms a complete partial order for s-normal programs. Hence each admissible scenario can be extended into a complete scenario. Thus, for s-normal programs, ISS is contained in a complete scenario.

Moreover, it is easy to see that for each admissible scenario $P \cup H$, $P \cup H \cup CSS(P)$ is again admissible. Therefore:

Theorem 7.5.3. *Let* P *be a s-normal program. Then:*

− *The set of complete scenaria of* P *forms a complete semilattice.*
− *ISS coincides with the intersection of preferred extensions.*
− $WFS0(P) = CSS(P) \subseteq ISS(P)$.

To define larger classes of programs also guaranteeing these comparability results is beyond the scope of this work. Of special interest, and subject of future investigation by the authors, is to determine syntatic conditions over programs (e.g. a generalization of the notion of stratified normal programs [15]) guaranteeing the equivalence between answer-sets and *WFSX*, in the vein of the work in [64] regarding well founded and stable models semantics of normal programs.

However, for normal logic programs, since acceptable hypotheses can never lead to an inconsistency, both WFS0 and *WFSX* coincide.

Theorem 7.5.4 (Relation to the WFS of normal programs). *If* P *is a normal (non-extended) program then* WFSX, *WFS0 and the well-founded semantics of [76] coincide.*

Example 7.2.2 shows this equivalence cannot be extended to ISS. There, *WFSX* coincides with WFS0 and with WFS and is $\{\}$. ISS is $\{not\ b\}$.

8. Dealing with contradiction

As we've seen before, *WFSX* is not defined for every program, i.e. some programs are contradictory and are given no meaning[1]. While for some programs this seems reasonable (e.g. Example 4.2.4 in page 42), for others this can be too strong.

Example 8.0.4. Consider the statements:

- *Birds, not shown to be abnormal, fly.*
- *Tweety is a bird and does not fly.*
- *Socrates is a man.*

naturally expressed by the program:

$$fly(X) \quad \leftarrow \quad bird(X), not\ abnormal(X).$$

$$bird(tweety)$$
$$\neg fly(tweety).$$

$$man(socrates).$$

WFSX assigns no semantics to this program. However, intuitively, we should at least be able to say that *Socrates* is a *man* and *tweety* is a *bird*. It would also be reasonable to conclude that *tweety* doesn't *fly*, because the rule stating that it doesn't *fly*, since it is a fact, makes a stronger statement than the one concluding it *flies*. The latter relies on accepting an assumption of non-abnormality, enforced by the closed world assumption treatment of the negation as failure, and involving the abnormality predicate. Indeed, whenever an assumption supports a contradiction it seems logical to be able to take the assumption back in order to prevent it – "*Reductio ad absurdum*", or "*reasoning by contradiction*".

In Chapter 7 we present semantics more sceptical than *WFSX*, that avoid contradiction in many cases where the latter gives no meaning to a program. For example ISS assigns to the above program the meaning (with the obvious abbreviations for constants):

---

[1] Other researchers have defined paraconsistent semantics for even contradictory programs e.g. [47, 26, 99, 196, 212]. This is not our concern. On the contrary, we wish to remove contradiction whenever it rests on withdrawable assumptions.

$$\{man(s), \neg fly(t), bird(t), not\ fly(t)\}$$

which exactly corresponds to the intuition above.

Furthermore, there is motivation to consider even more sceptical semantics, where some of the acceptable assumptions or hypotheses might not in fact be accepted.

For instance, the acceptance of a hypothesis may be conditional upon the equal acceptance of another. This is typical of hypothesizing faults in a device, whenever causally deeper faults are to be preferred over hypothesized faults that are simply a consequence of the former: the latter cannot be hypothesized without the first. Moreover, problem specific and user defined preference criteria affecting acceptance of hypotheses may also come to bear. Another case in point is logic program debugging, where one wants to hypothesize about the primitive cause of a bug, and not about the bugginess of some clause, if there is the possibility that that clause relies in fact on a still buggy predicate [162, 163, 161]. In general, the clauses of a logic program may be seen as providing a causal directionality of inference, similar to physical causality directionality, so that a distinction can sometimes be drawn about the primacy of one hypothesis over another, cf. [100, 34].

Example 8.0.5. Consider this program, describing bycicle behaviour:

$$
\begin{aligned}
\neg wobbly\_wheel &\leftarrow\ not\ flat\_tyre, not\ broken\_spokes \\
flat\_tyre &\leftarrow\ leaky\_valve \\
flat\_tyre &\leftarrow\ punctured\_tube \\
\neg no\_light &\leftarrow\ not\ faulty\_dynamo
\end{aligned}
$$

plus the factual observation:

  $wobbly\_wheel$

The ISS assigns to it the meaning:

$$\{wobbly\_wheel, not\ faulty\_dynamo, \neg no\_light, not\ no\_light,$$
$$not\ leaky\_valve, not\ punctured\_tube\}$$

neither accepting the hypothesis *not flat_tyre* nor *not broken_spokes* because acceptence of any of them, if the other were accepted too, would lead to a contradiction. Being sceptical ISS accepts neither. However, one would like the semantics in this case to delve deeper into the bycicle model and, again being sceptical, accept neither *not leaky_valve* nor *not punctured_tube* as well.

In order to respond to such epistemological requirements as above, we begin by introducing into the complete scenario semantics the more flexible notion of optative acceptance of hypotheses. Optative hypotheses are those that might or might not be accepted if acceptable at all. On the other hand, non-optative hypotheses must be accepted if acceptable.

First we make no restriction on what the optatives are, and consider that they are given by the user along with the program. Then we proceed to consider the issue of infering optative hypotheses from the program, given some specific criteria. In particular we show how to infer optatives when the criteria is to consider as such those hypotheses that do not depend on any other[2].

As claimed before, these very sceptical semantics model rational reasoners who assume the program absolutelly correct and so, whenever confronted with an acceptable hypothesis leading to an inconsistency cannot accept such a hypothesis; i.e. they prefer to assume the program correct rather than assume that an acceptable hypothesis must perforce be accepted.

WFSX models less sceptical reasoners who, confronted with an inconsistent scenario, prefer considering the program wrong rather than admitting that an acceptable hypothesis be not accepted. Such a reasoner is more confident in his acceptability criterium: an acceptable hypothesis is accepted once and for all; if an inconsistency arises then there is certainly a problem with the program, not with the individual acceptance of each acceptable hypothesis. If the problem is with the program its revision is in order.

This view position can be justified if we think of a program as something dynamic, i.e. evolving in time. In this position each program results from the assimilation of knowledge into a previous one. If an inconsistency arises from the knowledge assimilation then a revision process should be considered so as to restore consistency.

In [104], Kowalski presents a detailed exposition of the intended behaviour of this knowledge assimilation processes in various cases. There he claims the notion of integrity constraints is needed in logic programming both for knowledge processing, representation, and assimilation. The problem of inconsistency arises from nonsatisfaction of the integrity constraints. If some new knowledge can be shown incompatible with the existing theory and integrity constrains, a revision process is needed to restore satisfaction of those constraints.

In extended logic programming we can view the requirement of noncontradiction as integrity constraint satisfaction, where constraints are of the form $\leftarrow L, \neg L$. But then there is no reason why we should not allow a more general form of integrity contraints. In this chapter we extend logic programs with integrity constraints in the form of denials.

Example 8.0.6. Suppose we have some program describing political affiliation and don't want to say that non democrats are republicans and viceversa. Thus $\neg republican(X)$ should not correspond to $democrat(X)$ and $\neg democrat(X)$ should not correspond to $republican(X)$. However, no one must be known both as a republican and a democrat. This knowledge can be easily represented by the integrity constraint:

---

[2] Considered above as the preferred criterium for the case of fault finding, and debugging.

$\leftarrow democrat(X),\ republican(X)$

Let's go back now to Example 8.0.4. We can also view that program as the result of knowledge assimilation into a previous knowledge base expressed by a program. For example the program can be thought of as the adding to the previous knowledge the fact that tweety does not fly. According to *WFSX* the resulting program is inconsistent. One way of restoring consistency to the program would be to add a rule stating that $ab(tweety)$ cannot be false, viz. it would lead directly to a contradiction:

$ab(tweety) \leftarrow not\ ab(tweety)$

The resulting program is now noncontradictory and its *WFSX* is:

$\{man(s), \neg fly(t), bird(t), not\ fly(t)\}$

which corresponds to the intuition.

In this chapter we begin by presenting a sceptical semantics for extended logic programs plus integrity contraints in the form of denials, based on the notion of optative hypotheses, which avoids contradiction. We also define a program revision method for removing contradiction from contradictory programs under *WFSX*. Then, we show the equivalence between the (contradiction avoidance) semantics and the *WFSX* of the revised program obtained by the contradiction removal method.

8.1 Logic programming with denials

As argued by Reiter in [191], the basic idea of integrity constraints is that only some program (or database) states are considered acceptable, and those constraints are meant to enforce these acceptable states.

Integrity constraints can be of two types:

Static The enforcement of these constraints depends only on the current state of the program, independently of any prior state. The democrat/republican constraint above is one such example.

Dynamic These depend on two or more program states. In [191], Reiter gives as example the knowledge that employee salaries can never decrease.

It is not a purpose of this work to deal with the evolution of a program in time. Thus dynamic integrity contraints are not addressed. Since we only want to deal with the problem of inconsistency, it is enough that the only static integrity constraints considered be in the form of denials. For a study of different forms of static constraints and their satisfaction see [191].

Next we formally define the language of extended logic programs plus denials, and the notion of integrity contraint satisfaction adopted in this chapter.

A program with integrity rules (or constraints) is a set of rules as defined in Section 2.1, plus a set of denials, or integrity rules, of the form:

$$\perp \leftarrow A_1, \ldots, A_n, not\ B_1, \ldots, not\ B_m$$

where $A_1, \ldots, A_n, B_1, \ldots, B_m$ are objective literals, and $n + m > 0$. The symbol $\perp$ stands for falsity.

A program P with a semantics SEM satisfies the integrity constrains iff:

$$P \not\models_{SEM} \perp$$

8.2 Contradiction avoidance

In this section we present a semantics more sceptical than ISS, based on the notion of scenaria described in Section 7. Thus the attending notions of program transformation (in order to obtain only Horn programs),of consequence given a scenario, etc., all apply here.

To deal with denials we extend the notion of consistent scenario.

Definition 8.2.1 (Consistent scenario wrt ICs). *A scenario* $P \cup H$ *of a program with integrity constraints IC is consistent iff:*

– for all objective literals L *such that:*

$$P \cup H \cup Mand(H) \vdash L,$$

neither

$$not\ L \in H \cup Mand(H) \text{ nor } P \cup H \cup Mand(H) \vdash \neg L,$$

and
– $P \cup H \cup Mand(H) \cup IC \not\vdash \perp^3$.

If one implicitly adds to a program P constraints of the forms:

$$\perp \ \leftarrow \ L, not\ L$$

for every objective literal L of P, then the first condition above is obviously subsumed by the second one, and thus can be withdrawn.

Proposition 8.2.1. *A scenario* $P \cup H$ *of a program with integrity constrains IC is consistent iff:*

$$P \cup H \cup Mand(H) \cup NIC \not\vdash \perp$$

where:

$$NIC = IC \cup \{\perp \leftarrow L, not\ L;\ \perp \leftarrow L, \neg L \mid L \in lang(P)\}$$

---

[3] ICs are treated like any other rule for deriving $\perp$, hence the designation of *"integrity rule"*.

Like for extended logic programs before, an extended logic program with denials may have no consistent scenaria.

Example 8.2.1. Program P :

$$\neg democrat(husband(mary)) \quad \leftarrow$$
$$republican(mary) \quad \leftarrow$$
$$democrat(X) \quad \leftarrow \quad \neg democrat(husband(X))$$

$$\bot \quad \leftarrow \quad democrat(X), republican(X)$$

has no consistent scenario.

Definition 8.2.2 (Consistent program with ICs). *An extended   logic program P with integrity constraints IC is consistent iff it has some consistent scenario.*

N.B. From now on, unless otherwise stated, we restrict programs to consistent ones only.

In *WFSX* every acceptable hypothesis must be accepted. Consequently some programs might have no meaning. In ISS some acceptable hypotheses are not accepted in order to avoid inconsistency. However, as shown in Example 8.0.5, ISS allows no the control over which acceptable hypotheses are not accepted. Conceivably, any acceptable hypothesis may or may not actually be accepted, in some discretionary way.

It is clear from Example 8.0.5 that we wish to express that only the hypotheses *not broken_spokes, not leaky_valve, not faulty_dynamo*, and *not punctured_tube* may be optative, i.e. to be possibly accepted or not, if at all acceptable. The acceptance of hypotheses like *not flat_tyre* is to be determined by the acceptance of other hypotheses, and so we wish them accepted once acceptable.

Thus we should distinguish between *optative hypotheses* (or optatives) and non-optative ones. That distinction made, we can conceive of scenaria that might not be complete with respect to optatives, but are still complete with respect to non-optatives, i.e. scenaria which contain all acceptable hypotheses except for possibly optative ones.

Definition 8.2.3 (Optative hypotheses). *The set of optative hypotheses Opt is any subset of not $\mathcal{H}$.*

In general, when not accepting some optative hypothesis *not L*, i.e. when not assuming the falsity of L, then some otherwise acceptable hypotheses become unacceptable. The sense desired is that program models where the optative is true are not ruled out.

Example 8.2.2. Let P :

$$p \leftarrow not\ a$$
$$a \leftarrow b$$

$$\bot \leftarrow p$$

where $not\ b$ is the only optative, i.e. $Opt = \{not\ b\}$.

In our notion of optative, if $not\ b$ is not accepted then $not\ a$ is unacceptable, i.e. if optative b is not assumed false, the possibility of being true must be considered and so a cannot be assumed false; $P \cup \{b\} \vdash a$ counts as evidence against $not\ a$.

Definition 8.2.4 (Acceptable hypothesis wrt Opt). *A hypothesis $not\ L$ is acceptable with respect to scenario $P \cup H$ and set of optatives Opt iff*

$$not\ L\ is\ acceptable^4\ both\ with\ respect\ to\ P \cup H\ and\ P \cup H \cup F$$

where F is the set of facts

$$not\ ((Opt \cap Acc(H)) - H)$$

i.e. F is the set of complements of acceptable $Opts$ with respect to H which are not in H (that is which were not accepted).

$Acc_{Opt}(H)$ *denotes the set of acceptable hypotheses with respect to $P \cup H$ and Opt.*

Example 8.2.3. In Example 8.2.2 $Acc_{Opt}(\{not\ p\}) = \{\}$.

$not\ b$ is not acceptable because, even though acceptable with respect to $P \cup \{not\ p\}$, it is not acceptable with respect to $P \cup \{not\ p\} \cup \{b\}^5$. The same happens with $not\ a$.

With this new more general notion of acceptability, we can define scenaria that are partially complete, in the sense that they are complete with respect to non-optatives, but might not be complete with respect to optatives (condition (iii) below).

Definition 8.2.5 (Complete scenario wrt Opt). *A scenario $P \cup H$ is a complete scenario with respect to a set of optatives Opt iff it is consistent, and for each $not\ L$:*

(i)	$not\ L \in H \Rightarrow not\ L \in Acc_{Opt}(H) \vee not\ L \in Mand(H)$
(ii)	$not\ L \in Mand(H) \Rightarrow not\ L \in H$
(iii)	$not\ L \in Acc_{Opt}(H)$ and $not\ L \notin Opt \Rightarrow not\ L \in H$

Remark 8.2.1. By making $Opt = \{\}$ the previous definitions of acceptability with respect to Opt and of complete scenaria with respect to Opt correspond exactly to those of acceptability and complete scenaria in Section 7.

By making $Opt = not\ \mathcal{H}$ the definitions of acceptability with respect to Opt and of complete scenaria with respect to Opt correspond exactly to those of acceptability and admissible scenaria in Section 7.

---

[4] Acceptable cf. Definition 7.1.7.

[5] Note that here $not\ ((Opt \cap Acc(H)) - H) = not\ (\{not\ b\} - \{not\ p\}) = \{b\}$.

Note that in complete scenario $S = P \cup H$ with respect to Opt a hypothesis in Opt which is acceptable with respect to $P \cup H$ but leads to an inconsistent scenario, will not be accepted in S to preserve consistency. This amounts to contradiction avoidance.

Example 8.2.4. Recall the wobbly wheel Example 8.0.5. If Opt were $\{\}$ there would be no complete scenaria. If (with the obvious abbreviations):

$$Opt = \{not\ bs, not\ lv, not\ pt, not\ fd\}$$

complete scenaria with respect to Opt are :

$$\{not\ \neg ww\} \qquad \{not\ \neg ww, not\ fd, not\ bs\}$$
$$\{not\ \neg ww, not\ fd\} \qquad \{not\ \neg ww, not\ lv, not\ pt, not\ ft\}$$
$$\{not\ \neg ww, not\ bs\} \qquad \{not\ \neg ww, not\ fd, not\ lv\}$$
$$\{not\ \neg ww, not\ lv\} \quad \{not\ \neg ww, not\ lv, not\ pt, not\ ft, not\ fd\}$$
$$\{not\ \neg ww, not\ pt\} \qquad \qquad \ldots$$

Intuitively, it is clear that some of these scenaria are over-sceptical, in the sense that they fail to accept more optatives than need be to avoid contradiction. For example in the first scenario in order to avoid contradiction none of the optatives where accepted. This occurs because no condition of maximal acceptance of optatives has been enforced.

In order to impose this condition we begin by identifying, for each complete scenario with respect to Opt, those optatives that though acceptable were not accepted.

Definition 8.2.6 (Avoidance set). *Let $P \cup H$ be a complete scenario with respect to Opt. The avoidance set of $P \cup H$ is (the subset of Opt):*

$$(Opt \cap Acc(H)) - H$$

Example 8.2.5. The avoidance set of the first scenario in Example 8.2.4 is:

$$\{not\ lv, not\ pt, not\ fd\}$$

and of the second one is:

$$\{not\ lv, not\ pt\}$$

In keeping with the vocation of scepticism of *WFSX*, we are specially interested in those scenaria which, for some given avoidance set, are minimal.

Definition 8.2.7 (Base scenario wrt Opt). *A complete scenario $P \cup H$ with respect to Opt, is a base scenario if there exists no scenario $P \cup H'$ with the same avoidance, set such that $H' \subset H$.*

Example 8.2.6. Consider the program P :

$$a \leftarrow not\ b$$
$$b \leftarrow not\ a$$
$$c \leftarrow not\ d$$

$$\perp \leftarrow c$$

with $Opt = \{not\ d\}$.

Complete scenaria with respect to Opt are:

$$\{\} \qquad \{a, not\ b\} \qquad \{b, not\ a\}$$

For all the avoidance set is $\{not\ d\}$. The corresponding base scenario with respect to Opt is the first.

Proposition 8.2.2. *The set of all base scenaria with respect to Opt under set inclusion forms a lower semi-lattice.*

Proof. Let $P \cup H_1$ and $P \cup H_2$ be two base scenaria with avoidance sets S_1 and S_2 respectively. We prove that there is a single maximal scenario $P \cup H$ such that $H \subseteq H_1$ and $H \subseteq H_2$.

Such a scenario must have an avoidance set $S \supseteq S_1 \cup S_2$. From the definition of complete scenario with respect to Opt there exists one scenario such that its avoidance set $S = S_1 \cup S_2$. It is clear from lemma 8.4.1 below, that there is a least scenario with S as avoidance set.

Consider now those scenaria comprising as many optatives as possible, i.e. have minimal avoidance sets:

Definition 8.2.8 (Quasi-complete scenario wrt Opt). *A base scenario $P \cup H$ with respect to Opt, with avoidance set S, is quasi-complete if there is no base scenario $P \cup H'$ with respect to Opt with avoidance set S', such that $S' \subset S$.*

Example 8.2.7. In Example 8.2.4 the quasi-complete scenaria with respect to Opt are:

$$\{not\ \neg ww, not\ fd, not\ bs, not\ lv\}$$
$$\{not\ \neg ww, not\ fd, not\ bs, not\ pt\}$$
$$\{not\ \neg ww, not\ fd, not\ lv, not\ pt, not\ ft\}$$

These correspond to minimal faults compatible with the wobbly wheel observation, i.e. the ways of avoiding contradiction (inevitable if Opt were $\{\}$) by minimally not accepting acceptable optatives. In the first $not\ pt$ was not accepted, in the second $not\ lv$, and in the third $not\ bs$.

As the consequences of all these quasi-complete scenaria are pairwise incompatible[6] the well-founded model, being sceptical, is their meet in the semi-lattice of proposition 8.2.2, so that its avoidance set is the union of their avoidance sets.

---

[6] In the sense that neither contains any other.

Definition 8.2.9 (Well-founded semantics wrt *Opt*). *The well-founded model of an extended logic program P with ICs is the meet of all quasi-complete scenaria with respect to Opt in the semi-lattice of all base scenaria.*

For short we use WFS_{Opt} *to denote the well-founded model with respect to Opt.*

Example 8.2.8. In Example 8.2.4 WFS_{Opt} is:

$$P \cup \{not \ \neg ww, not \ fd\}$$

Thus one can conclude:

$$\{ww, \neg nl, not \ \neg ww, not \ fd\}$$

i.e. no other hypothesis can be assumed for certain; everything is sceptically assumed faulty except for fd. This differs from the result of ISS, shown in Example 8.0.5.

Example 8.2.9. Consider the statements:

− *Let's go hiking if it is not known to rain.*
− *Let's go swimming if it is not known to rain.*
− *Let's go swimming if the water is not known to be cold.*
− *We cannot go both swimming and hiking.*

They render the set of rules P:

$$
\begin{aligned}
hiking &\leftarrow not \ rain \\
swimming &\leftarrow not \ rain \\
swimming &\leftarrow not \ cold\_water
\end{aligned}
$$

$$\bot \leftarrow hiking, swimming$$

and let $Opt = \{not \ rain, not \ cold\_water\}$.

Complete scenaria with respect to Opt are:

$$P \cup \{\} \qquad P \cup \{not \ cold\_water\}$$

where the latter is the well founded with respect to Opt. It entails that *swimming* is true. Note that *not rain* is not assumed because it is optative to do so, and by assuming it contradiction would be unavoidable.

To obtain less sceptical complete scenaria with respect to Opt, and in the spirit of the above described partial stable models, we introduce:

Definition 8.2.10 (Partial scenario wrt *Opt*). *Let P be an extended logic program with ICs, and let the well-founded semantics of P with respect to Opt be $P \cup H$.*

$P \cup K$ is a partial scenario of P with respect to Opt iff it is a base scenario with respect to Opt and $H \subseteq K$.

Example 8.2.10. The partial scenaria of P with respect to Opt in Example 8.2.4 are the union of P with each of:

$$\{not \ \neg ww, not \ fd\} \qquad \{not \ \neg ww, not \ fd, not \ bs, not \ lv\}$$
$$\{not \ \neg ww, not \ fd, not \ bs\} \qquad \{not \ \neg ww, not \ fd, not \ bs, not \ pt\}$$
$$\{not \ \neg ww, not \ fd, not \ lv\} \quad \{not \ \neg ww, not \ fd, not \ lv, not \ pt, not \ ft\}$$
$$\{not \ \neg ww, not \ fd, not \ pt\}$$

The first is the WFS_{Opt} (cf. Example 8.2.8), which corresponds to the most sceptical view whereby all possibly relevant faults are assumed. The other partial scenaria represent, in contrast, all other alternative hypothetical presences and absences of faults still compatible with the wobbly wheel observation.

If a program is noncontradictory (i.e. its *WFSX* exists) then no matter which are the optatives, the well-founded semantics with respect to Opt is always equal to the least complete scenario (and so, ipso facto, equivalent to the *WFSX*).

Theorem 8.2.1 (Relation to *WFSX*). *If* WFSX *is defined for a program* P *with empty set of ICs then, for whatever* Opt, WFS_{Opt} *is the least complete scenario of* P.

Proof. If *WFSX* is defined for P then there exists at least one complete scenario of P. Thus there exists at least one complete scenario with respect to Opt, $P \cup H$, such that its avoidance set is empty. So the only quasi-complete scenario, and WFS_{Opt}, is the base scenario with empty avoidance set.

By definition, the set of complete scenaria with respect to Opt with empty avoidance set coincides with the set of complete scenaria, and thus the least complete scenario coincides with the base scenario with respect to Opt.

Since, cf. Theorem 4.3.4, for programs without explicit negation *WFSX* is equivalent to the well-founded semantics of [76] (WFS):

Theorem 8.2.2. *Let* P *be a (non-extended) normal program. Then, for whatever* Opt, *the well-founded semantics with respect to* Opt *is equivalent to its WFS.*

8.2.1 Primacy in optative reasoning

Up to now no restriction whatsoever was enforced regarding the optatives of programs. It is possible for optatives to be identified by the user along with the program, or for the user to rely on criteria for specifying the optatives, and expect the system to infer them from the program.

Next we identify a special class of optatives, governed by an important criterium [100, 34]:

Exactly the hypotheses not depending on any other are optative.

Example 8.2.11. Let P :

$$
\begin{array}{rcl}
a & \leftarrow & not\ b \\
b & \leftarrow & not\ c \\
c & \leftarrow & not\ d
\end{array}
$$

Clearly *not a* depends on *not b*, *not b* on *not c* and *not c* on *not d*. *not d* alone does not depend on any other hypothesis, thus according to this criterium, it should be the only optative.

In diagnosis this criterium means hypothesizing as abnormal first the causally deeper faults.

It is known that in taxonomies with exceptions, this is not the desired preference criterium. To give priority to the most specific default information only a hypothesis on which no other depends should be optatives. This way the relinquishing of default hypotheses to avoid contradiction begins with less specific ones.

The subject of defining preference criteria to automatically determine optative hypotheses is complex. It is closely related to that of preference among defaults [74].

The study of how to infer optatives for criteria different from the one above, is left as an open problem.

Clearly, every hypothesis which is not acceptable in $P \cup \{\}$ depends on the acceptance of some other hypothesis. In other words, if a hypothesis *not L* is acceptable in a scenario $P \cup H$, but is not acceptable in $P \cup \{\}$, this means that in order to make *not L* acceptable some other hypotheses $S \subseteq H$ have to be accepted first. Thus *not L* depends on the hypotheses of S, and the latter are more primal than *not L*. As a first approximation, let me define the set of prime optative hypotheses as $Acc(\{\})$.

Example 8.2.12. In program P of Example 8.2.11 $Acc(\{\}) = \{not\ d\}$. So the only prime optative hypothesis is *not d*. Hypothesis *not b* is not prime optative because it is only acceptable once *not d* is accepted, otherwise *not c* constitutes evidence to the contrary.

In general, not all hypotheses in $Acc(\{\})$ though are independant of one another. Hence we must refine our first approximation to prime optatives.

Example 8.2.13. Consider P :

$$
\begin{array}{rcl}
a & \leftarrow & b \\
b & \leftarrow & c \\
p & \leftarrow & not\ a
\end{array}
$$

$$
\bot \ \leftarrow \ p
$$

$$
Acc(\{\}) = \{not\ a, not\ b, not\ c\}
$$

and the WFS with respect to $Acc(\{\})$ is $P \cup \{not\ b, not\ c\}$.

However, it is clear from the program that only $not\ c$ should be prime optative, since the acceptance of $not\ b$ depends on the absence of conclusion c in P, but not vice-versa, and likewise regarding the acceptance of $not\ a$.

Any definition of a semantics based on the notions of scenaria and evidence alone cannot distinguish the optative primacy of $not\ c$, because it is insensitive to the groundedness of literals, viz. there being no rules for c, and thus its non-dependance on other hypotheses.

An assymmetry must be introduced, based on a separate new notion, to capture the causal directionality of inference implicit in logic program rules, as mentioned in the introduction to this chapter:

Definition 8.2.11 (Sensitive hypotheses). *A hypothesis $not\ A \in Acc(\{\})$ is sensitive to a separate set of hypotheses $not\ S$ in program P iff*

$$not\ A \notin Acc(P \cup S)$$

Note that S is a set of facts.

Definition 8.2.12 (Prime optatives). *A hypothesis $not\ A \in Acc(\{\})$ is prime optative iff for all $not\ S \subseteq Acc(\{\})$:*

if $not\ A$ is sensitive to $not\ S$ then some element of $not\ S$ is sensitive to $not\ A$.

The set of all prime optatives is denoted by $\mathcal{POpt}$.

As shorthand, we refer to the well-founded semantics with respect to the set of prime optatives as the *prime optative semantics*, or $\mathcal{POS}$.

Example 8.2.14. In Example 8.2.13 the only prime optative hypothesis is $not\ c$. For example, $not\ a$ is not prime optative since $not\ a$ is sensitive to $not\ b$ and $not\ b$ is not sensitive to $not\ a$.

Example 8.2.15. In the wobbly wheel example:

$$\mathcal{POpt} = \{not\ bs, not\ pt, not\ lv, not\ fd\}$$

For this example $Acc(\{\}) = \mathcal{POpt} \cup \{not\ ft\}$.

However $not\ ft$ is not prime optative since it is sensitive to both $not\ lv$ and $not\ pt$.

Example 8.2.16. Consider program P :

$$
\begin{array}{llllll}
p & \leftarrow & not\ a & a & \leftarrow & b & c & \leftarrow & not\ d \\
\neg p & \leftarrow & & b & \leftarrow & a, not\ c
\end{array}
$$

where:

$$Acc(\{\}) = \{not\ a, not\ b, not\ d\}$$

All of these are prime optatives:

- *not d* is prime optative because it is insensitive to other hypotheses;
- *not b* is prime optative because it is only sensitive to *not a*, and *not a* is sensitive to *not b*;
- similarly for *not a*.

By insisting on only allowing prime optatives to be possibly accepted, even if acceptable, one may fail to give meaning to some consistent programs, as there are less options for avoiding inconsistency.

Example 8.2.17. Consider program P :

$$
\begin{array}{rcl}
c & \leftarrow & not\ b \\
b & \leftarrow & not\ a \\
\neg a & & \\
\perp & \leftarrow & not\ c
\end{array}
$$

In this case $\mathcal{POpt} = Acc(\{\}) = \{not\ a\}$, and no complete scenario with respect to $\mathcal{POpt}$ exists. Thus neither ISS with respect to $\mathcal{POpt}$ nor $\mathcal{POS}$ are defined.

Note that by making $Opt = \{not\ c\}$, $P \cup \{not\ a\}$ is now complete with respect to Opt. In fact this scenario correspont to the $WFM_{\{not\ c\}}$, expressing that contradiction is avoided by not assuming the optative hypothesis *not c*. It still allows the conclusions $\{\neg a, not\ a, b\}$.

8.3 Contradiction removal

It has argued in the introduction to this chapter that, to deal with the issue of contradiction brought about by closed world assumptions, rather then defining more sceptical semantics one can rely instead on a less sceptical semantics and accompany it with a revision process that restores consistency, whenever violation of integrity contraints occurs.

In this section we define a revision process, that restores consistency for programs contradictory with respect to *WFSX*. This process relies on the allowing to take back assumptions about the truth of negative literals.

The set negative literals on which a revision can be made, i.e. the assumption of their truthfulness can be removed, is the set of *revisable literals*, and can be any subset of *not H*.

In [146] a revision semantics was defined where only base closed world assumption are revisables. There revisables are default literals whose complement has no rules. In [152] the notion of base closed world assumption was improved, in order to deal with the case of loops without interposing *not s*[7]. The notion of revisables presented there is similar to the notion of prime optatives above.

---

[7] If *not a* is considered a base closed world assumption in a program without rules for *a*, then there is no reason for *not a* not being one such assumption in a program where the only rule for *a* is $a \leftarrow a$.

As we show in Section 8.4 the issue of which are the revisables (in contradiction removal) is tantamount to that of which are the optatives (in contradiction avoidance). Thus the discussion on primacy of optatives is applicable to the issue of what literals are to be revisables.

So no restriction is made here on which default literals should be considered revisables. Revisable literal are supposed provided by the user along with the program[8].

For instance, in Example 8.0.5 the revisable literals might be:

$$\{not\ fd, not\ lv, not\ pt, not\ bs\}$$

By not introducing $not\ fd$ in this set, we are declaring that, in order to remove some contradiction, we will not consider directly revising its truth value. However, this does not mean that by revising some other literal the truth value of $not\ fd$ will not change.

We take back revisable assumptions, i.e. assumptions on revisable literals, in a minimal way, and in all alternative ways of removing contradiction. Moreover, we identify a single unique revision that defines a sceptical revision process which includes all alternative contradiction removing revisions, so as not to prefer one over the other. This is akin in spirit to the approach of PSMs in [172, 180], where the WFM is the intersection of all the PSMs.

The notions of minimality and contradiction removal employed are useful for dealing with Belief Revision through *WFSX*. Consider the noncontradictory program P :

$$p \leftarrow not\ q$$
$$\neg p \leftarrow r, not\ t$$

and the additional information: r. Our proposed revision for $P \cup \{r\}$ provides the minimal model $\{r\}$, and two extended additional ones, namely:

$$\{r, p, not\ \neg p, not\ q\} \quad \text{and} \quad \{r, \neg p, not\ p, not\ t\}.$$

These two models can be seen as alternative minimal changes to the WFM of P in order to incorporate the new information: one making t undefined rather than false by CWA, and the other making q undefined instead. Model $\{r\}$ is obtained by making both t and q undefined. It is the one with sufficient and necessary changes compatible with the new information, whenever no preference is enforced about which relevant revisable literals to unassume, in fact by unassuming them all. Revisions can be defined as those programs, obtained from the original one in a unique way, whose *WFSX* are each of the noncontradictory models above. In this example these programs are:

---

[8] The declaration of revisable literals by the user is akin to that of abducible literals. Although some frameworks identify what are the abducible for some particular problems ([70] where abducibles are of the form a^*), theories of abduction, for the sake of generality, make no restriction on which literals are abducibles, and assume them provided by the user.

$$P \quad \cup \quad \{r\} \quad \cup \quad \{t \leftarrow not\ t\}$$
$$P \quad \cup \quad \{r\} \quad \cup \quad \{q \leftarrow not\ q\}$$
$$P \quad \cup \quad \{r\} \quad \cup \quad \{t \leftarrow not\ t;\ \ q \leftarrow not\ q\}$$

Notice how a rule of the form $L \leftarrow not\ L$ changes the assumption $not\ L$ from true to undefined.

The structure of this section is as follows: first we present a paraconsistent extension of *WFSX*. Then we define the intended revisions declaratively. Afterwards we define some useful sets for establishing the causes of and the removal of contradictions within *WFSX*, and prove that the result of their use concurs with the intended revisions defined. Finally some hints for the implementation are given.

8.3.1 Paraconsistent *WFSX*

In order to revise possible contradictions we need first to identify those contradictory sets implied by a program under a paraconsistent *WFSX*. The main idea here is to compute all consequences of the program, even those leading to contradictions, as well as those arising from contradictions. The following example provides an intuitive preview of what we intend to capture:

Example 8.3.1. Consider program P :

$$\begin{array}{llll} a \leftarrow & not\ b & \text{(i)} & \qquad d \leftarrow & not\ a & \text{(iii)} \\ \neg a \leftarrow & not\ c & \text{(ii)} & \qquad e \leftarrow & not\ \neg a & \text{(iv)} \end{array}$$

1. $not\ b$ and $not\ c$ hold since there are no rules for either b or c
2. $\neg a$ and a hold from 1 and rules (i) and (ii)
3. $not\ a$ and $not\ \neg a$ hold from 2 and the coherence principle
4. d and e hold from 3 and rules (iii) and (iv)
5. $not\ d$ and $not\ e$ hold from 2 and rules (iii) and (iv), as they are the only rules for d and e
6. $not\ \neg d$ and $not\ \neg e$ hold from 4 and the coherence principle.

The whole set of literal consequences is then:

$$\{not\ b, not\ c, \neg a, a, not\ a, not\ \neg a, d, e, not\ d, not\ e, not\ \neg d, not\ \neg e\}.$$

Without loss of generality (cf. corollary 9.1.1), and for the sake of simplicity, we consider that programs are always in their canonical form (cf. Definition 2.1.1).

For the purpose of defining a paraconsistent extension of *WFSX*, we begin by defining what an interpretation is in the paraconsistent case.

Definition 8.3.1 (p-interpretation). *A p-interpretation I is any set*

$T \cup not\ F$

such that if $\neg L \in T$ then $L \in F$ (coherence).

The modification of the Coh operator is also straightforward:

Definition 8.3.2 (The Coh^p operator). *Let $QI = QT \cup not\ QF$ be a set of literals. We define $Coh^p(QI)$ as the p-interpretation $T \cup not\ F$ such that*

$$T = QT \text{ and } F = QF \cup \{\neg L \mid L \in T\}.$$

Note that in both definitions the enforcement of disjointness on sets T and F has been withdrawn.

Now we generalize the modulo transformation (Definition 4.2.1 in page 39) to the paraconsistent case. If we assume, without loss of generality, that programs are always in their canonical form, according to Theorem 4.2.4 the generalization can be made in the compact version of the transformation, thereby simplifying the exposition.

In the compact definition of the $\frac{P}{I}$ transformation one can apply the first two operations in any order, because the conditions of their application are disjoint for any interpretation. A potencial conflict would rest on applying both the first and the second operation, but that can never happen because if some $A \in I$ then $not\ A \notin I$, and vice-versa.

This is not the case for p-interpretations pI, where for some objective literal A both A and $not\ A$ might belong to pI. Thus if one applies the transformation to p-interpretations, different results are obtained depending on the order of the application of the first two operations.

Example 8.3.2. Consider program P of Example 8.3.1, and let us compute:

$$\frac{P}{\{a, \neg a, not\ \neg a, not\ a, not\ b, not\ c\}}.$$

If one applies the operations in the order they are presented:

- Rules (iii) and (iv) of P are removed since both a and $\neg a$ belong to the p-interpretation.
- $not\ b$ and $not\ c$ are removed from the bodies of rules since $not\ b$ and $not\ c$ belong to the p-interpretation.

and the resulting program is:

$$
\begin{array}{ll}
a & \leftarrow \\
\neg a & \leftarrow
\end{array}
$$

But if one applies the second operation first:

- $not\ b$, $not\ c$, $not\ a$, and $not\ \neg a$ are removed from the bodies of rules since $not\ b$, $not\ c$, $not\ a$, and $not\ \neg a$ belong to the p-interpretation.
- Since no literals remain in the body of rules no other operation is applicable.

The resulting program in this case is:

$$
\begin{array}{llll}
a & \leftarrow & d & \leftarrow \\
\neg a & \leftarrow & e & \leftarrow
\end{array}
$$

In order make the transformation independent of the order of application of the operations we define the corresponding transformation for the paraconsistent case as being nondeterministic in the order of application of those rules.

Definition 8.3.3 ($\frac{P}{I}p$ transformation). *Let P be a canonical extended logic program and let I be a p-interpretation. By a $\frac{P}{I}p$ program we mean any program obtained from P by first non-deterministically applying the operations until they are no longer applicable:*

– Remove all rules containing a default literal $L = not\ A$ such that $A \in I$.
– Remove from rules their default literals $L = not\ A$ such that $not\ A \in I$.

and by next replacing all remaining default literals by proposition **u**.

In order to get all consequences of the program, even those leading to contradictions, as well as those arising from contradictions, we consider the consequences off all possible such $\frac{P}{I}p$ programs[9].

Definition 8.3.4 (The Φ^p operator). *Let P be a canonical extended logic program, I a p-interpretation, and let P_k such that $k \in K$ be all the possible results of $\frac{P}{I}p$. Then:*

$$\Phi^p{}_P(I) = \bigcup_{k \in K} Coh^p(least(P_k))$$

Theorem 8.3.1 (Monotonicity of Φ^p). *The Φ^p operator is monotonic under set inclusion of p-interpretations.*

Proof. We have to prove that for any two p-interpretation A and B such that $A \subseteq B$, then $\Phi^p(A) \subseteq \Phi^p(B)$.

Let P_{A_k}, $k \in K$, and P_{B_j}, $j \in J$, be the programs obtained from, respectively, $\frac{P}{A}p$ and $\frac{P}{B}p$. Since $A \subseteq B$ then for every P_{A_k} there exists a P_{B_j} such that for every rule

$$H \leftarrow Body \in P_{B_j}$$

there exists a rule

$$H \leftarrow Body \cup Body' \in P_{A_k}.$$

This is necessarily the case because B, having more literals than A, can always remove more rules and default literals in the bodies than A. Thus:

$$\forall P_{A_k} \exists P_{B_j} \mid least(P_{A_k}) \subseteq least(P_{B_j})$$

Now we prove that Coh^p is monotonic, i.e for any two p-interpretations

---

[9] As proven in [50], it is enough to consider only two such $\frac{P}{I}p$ program: the ones obtained by the maximal and by the least (according to the classical ordering) I. Here, for the sake of simplicity, and since it is not essential in the sequel, we consider all divided programs.

$$I = T_I \cup not\ F_I \text{ and } J = T_J \cup not\ F_J$$

such that

$$T_I \subseteq T_J \text{ and } F_I \subseteq F_J,$$

$Coh^p(I) \subseteq Coh^p(J)$ holds.

$Coh^p(I) \subseteq Coh^p(J)$ is equivalent, by definition of Coh^p, to

$$T_I \cup not\ (F_I \cup \{\neg L \mid L \in T_I\}) \subseteq T_J \cup not\ (F_J \cup \{\neg L \mid L \in T_J\})$$

since $T_I \subseteq T_J$ by hypothesis, the above is true if:

$$F_I \cup \{\neg L \mid L \in T_I\} \subseteq F_J \cup \{\neg L \mid L \in T_I\} \cup \{\neg L \mid L \in T_J - T_I\}$$

which is equivalent to

$$F_I \subseteq F_J \cup \{\neg L \mid L \in T_J - T_I\}$$

which holds because, by hypothesis, $F_I \subseteq F_J$.

With this result, and the other one above:

$$\forall P_{A_k} \ \exists P_{B_j} \mid Coh^p(least(P_{A_k})) \subseteq Coh^p(least(P_{B_j}))$$

and consequently:

$$\bigcup_{k \in K} Coh^p(least(P_{A_k})) \subseteq \bigcup_{j \in J} Coh^p(least(P_{B_j}))$$

Given that Φ^p is monotonic, then for every program it always has a least fixpoint, and this fixpoint can be obtained by iterating Φ^p starting from the empty set:

Definition 8.3.5 (Paraconsistent $WFSX$). *The paraconsistent* WFSX *of an (canonical) extended logic program P, denoted by $WFSX_p(P)$, is the least fixpoint of Φ^p applied to P.*

If some literal L belongs to the paraconsistent WFSX *of P we write:*

$$P \models_p L$$

Proposition 8.3.1 (Existence of $WFSX_p$). $WFSX_p(P)$ *is defined   for every program with ICs.*

Proof. Since no restriction whatsoever has been made on the application of Φ^p, and given the proof of monotonicity of this operator, a least fixpoint of it exists for every program.

Example 8.3.3. Let us compute the paraconsistent *WFSX* of the program in Example 8.3.1. *P* is already in canonical form.

We start with the empty set. The only program obtained from $\frac{P}{\{\}}p$ is $P_{0,1}$:

$$
\begin{array}{rcl}
a & \leftarrow & \mathbf{u} \\
\neg a & \leftarrow & \mathbf{u}
\end{array}
\qquad
\begin{array}{rcl}
d & \leftarrow & \mathbf{u} \\
e & \leftarrow & \mathbf{u}
\end{array}
$$

and $I_1 = Coh^p(least(P_{0,1})) = \{not\ b, not\ c\}$

By $\frac{P}{I_1}p$ we only get one program, $P_{1,1}$:

$$
\begin{array}{rcl}
a & \leftarrow & \\
\neg a & \leftarrow &
\end{array}
\qquad
\begin{array}{rcl}
d & \leftarrow & \mathbf{u} \\
e & \leftarrow & \mathbf{u}
\end{array}
$$

and $I_2 = Coh^p(least(P_{1,1})) = \{a, not\ \neg a, \neg a, not\ a, not\ b, not\ c\}$

The result of $\frac{P}{I_2}p$ are the four programs:

$$
\begin{array}{llll}
P_{2,1}: & a \leftarrow & P_{2,2}: & a \leftarrow & P_{2,3}: & a \leftarrow & P_{2,4}: & a \leftarrow \\
& \neg a \leftarrow & & \neg a \leftarrow & & \neg a \leftarrow & & \neg a \leftarrow \\
& d \leftarrow & & d \leftarrow & & e \leftarrow & & \\
& e \leftarrow & & & &
\end{array}
$$

For example, $P_{2,1}$ was obtained by applying the second operation to both rules (iii) and (iv), which is possible because both $not\ a$ and $not\ \neg a$ belong to I_2. $P_{2,4}$ was obtained by applying the first operation to both rules (iii) and (iv), which is possible because both a and $\neg a$ belong to I_2.

It is easy to see that $I_3 = \Phi^p(I_2) =$

$$\{not\ b, not\ c, \neg a, a, not\ a, not\ \neg a, d, e, not\ d, not\ e, not\ \neg d, not\ \neg e\}$$

By applying $\frac{P}{I_3}p$ one gets exactly the same program as in $\frac{P}{I_2}p$ and thus $\Phi^p(I_3) = I_3$. So, I_3 is the least fixpoint of Φ^p and, consequently, the paraconsistent $WFSX$ of P.

Now we can give a definition of a contradictory program with ICs:

Definition 8.3.6 (Contradictory program with ICs). *A program* P *with language Lang where A is an atom, and a set of integrity constraints IC is contradictory iff*

$$P \cup ICs \cup \{\perp \leftarrow A, \neg A \mid A \in Lang\} \models_p \perp$$

In this section we always refer to the paraconsistent $WFSX$ as an extension of $WFSX$ for noncontradictory programs. This is so because:

Proposition 8.3.2. *For a noncontradictory program P the paraconsistent* WFSX *coincides with* WFSX.

Proof. Since interpretations are p-interpretations, and for any noncontradictory set S of literals $Coh(S) = Coh^p(S)$, and for any interpretation I $\frac{P}{I}p$ is deterministic and equal to $\frac{P}{I}$, the result follows trivially.

8.3.2 Declarative revisions

Before tackling the question of which assumptions to revise to abolish contradiction, we begin by showing how to impose in a program a revision that takes back some revisable assumption, identifying rules of a special form, which have the effect of prohibiting the falsity of an objective literal in models of a program. Such rules can prevent an objective literal being false, hence their name:

Definition 8.3.7 (Inhibition rule). *The inhibition rule for a default literal not L is:*

$$L \leftarrow not \ L$$

By $IR(S)$ where S is a set of default literals, we mean:

$$IR(S) = \{L \leftarrow not \ L \mid not \ L \in S\}$$

These rules state that if *not A* is true then *A* is also true, and so a contradiction arises. Intuitively this is quite similar to the effect of integrity constraints of form $\perp \leftarrow not \ A$. Technically the difference is that the removal of such a contradiction in the case of inhibition rules is dealt by *WFSX* itself, where in the case of those integrity constraints isn't.

Proposition 8.3.3. *Let P be any program such that for objective literal L, $P \not\models_p \neg L$. Then:*

$$P \cup \{L \leftarrow not \ L\} \not\models_p not \ L$$

Moreover, if there are no other rules for L, the truth value of L is undefined in $WFSX_p(P)$.

Proof. Let $P' = P \cup \{L \leftarrow not \ L\}$. We prove by transfinite induction that:

$$not \ L \notin I_\alpha, \quad \text{where } I_\alpha = \Phi^{P'\uparrow\alpha}(\{\})$$

– *For limit ordinal δ:* Suppose that for all $\alpha < \delta$

$$not \ L \notin \Phi^{P'\uparrow\alpha}(\{\})$$

Then, clearly:

$$not \ L \notin \bigcup \left\{\Phi^{P'\uparrow\alpha}(\{\}) \mid \alpha < \delta\right\}$$

i.e. $not \ L \notin \Phi^{P'\uparrow\delta}(\{\})$.

– *Induction step* Assume that $not \ L \notin I_i$, for some ordinal i. Then:

– if $L \notin I_i$ then every transformed program $\frac{P'}{I_i}p$ has the rule $L \leftarrow u$. Thus for every transformed program

$$not \ L \notin least\left(\frac{P'}{I_i}p\right)$$

and given that by hypothesis $P \not\models_p \neg L$

$$not \ L \notin Coh^p\left(least\left(\frac{P'}{I_i}p\right)\right).$$

Thus $not \ L \notin I_{i+1}$.

– if $L \in I_i$ then by monotonicity of Φ^p every transformed program has a rule $L \leftarrow$, and thus $not\ L \notin I_{i+1}$.

Since $WFSX_p(P') = \Phi^{p\uparrow\lambda}(\{\})$ for some smallest ordinal λ, then

$$not\ L \notin WFSX_p(P').$$

These rules allows, by adding them to a program, to force default literals in the paraconsistent *WFSX* to become undefined. Note that changing the truth value of revisable literals from true to undefined is less committing than changing it to false. In order to obtain revisions where the truth value of revisable literals is changed from true to false, one has to iterate the process we're about to define. The formal definition of such revisions can be found in [162].

To declaratively define the intended program revisions void of contradiction we start by first considering the resulting *WFSX*s of all possible ways of revising a program P with inhibition rules, by taking back revisable assumptions, even if some revisions are still contradictory programs.

However, it might happen that several different revisions in fact correspond to the same, in the sense that they lead to the same consequences.

Example 8.3.4. Consider program P:

$$\perp \ \leftarrow \ not\ a$$

$$a \ \leftarrow \ b$$
$$b \ \leftarrow \ a$$
$$a \ \leftarrow \ c$$

with revisables $Rev = \{not\ a, not\ b, not\ c\}$.

Note that adding $a \leftarrow not\ a$, $b \leftarrow not\ b$, or both, leads to the same consequences. Intuitively they are the same revision, since undefining a leads to the undefinedness of b and vice-versa. Considering all three as distinct can be misleading because it appear that the program has three different revisions.

Revisables $not\ a$ and $not\ b$ are indissociable, and it is indifferent to introduce inhibition rules for one, the other, or both. Moreover, only one of these hypotheses should be considered as a revision. In the sequel, we coalesce the three revisions into a single standard one, that adds both inhibition rules.

Definition 8.3.8 (Indissociable literals). *Let P be an extended logic program with revisables Rev. The set $Ind(S) \supseteq S$ of indissociable literals of a set S of default literals is the largest subset of Rev such that:*

– $Ind(S) \subseteq WFSX_p(P)$ *and*
– $WFSX_p(P \cup IR(S)) \cap Ind(S) = \{\}$

i.e. Ind(S) is the set of all revisables that change their truth value from true to undefined, once inhibition rules are added for every default literals of S to change their truth value.

It is easy to see that such a largest set always exists (since Ind is monotonic), and that Ind is a closure operator. Moreover:

Proposition 8.3.4. *Let $M = WFSX_p(P \cup IR(S))$ for some subset of S of Rev. Then:*

$$WFSX_p(P \cup IR(Ind(S))) = M$$

Proof. Let $P' = P \cup IR(S)$, and let *not L* be an arbitrary literal such that *not* $L \in Ind(S)$ and *not* $L \notin S$.

Directly from the second point of the definition of indissociables, it follows that *not L* is undefined in P'. Moreover, it is clear that the addition into any program P, of an inhibition rule for some literal undefined in $WFSX_p(P)$ does not change the well-founded model. Thus:

$$WFSX_p(P') = WFSX_p(P' \cup IR(\{not\ L\}))$$

Example 8.3.5. In Example 8.3.4:

$$Ind(\{not\ a\}) = Ind(\{not\ b\}) = \{not\ a, not\ b\}$$

and

$$Ind(\{not\ c\}) = \{not\ a, not\ b, not\ c\}$$

Definition 8.3.9 (Submodels of a program). *A submodel of a (contradictory) program P with ICs, and revisable literals Rev, is any pair $\langle M, R \rangle$ where R is a subset of Rev closed under indissociable literals, i.e:*

$$\forall S \subseteq R,\ Ind(S) \subseteq R$$

and $M = WFSX_p(P \cup \{L \leftarrow not\ L \mid not\ L \in R\})$[10].
    In a submodel $\langle M, R \rangle$ we dub R the submodel revision, and M are the consequences of the submodel revision. A submodel is contradictory iff M is contradictory (i.e. either contains $\perp$ or is not an interpretation)[11].

The existence of $WFSX_p(P)$ for any program P (cf. proposition 8.3.1) grants that M exists for every subset of Rev. Moreover, since Ind is a closure operator:

Proposition 8.3.5 (Submodels lattice). *The set of all submodels $\langle M, R \rangle$ of any program P with revisable literals Rev forms a complete lattice under set inclusion on the submodel revisions.*

The submodels lattice of Example 8.3.4 is presented in figure 8.1.

---

[10] For a study of submodels based on the PSMs instead of on the well-founded model see [147].

[11] Note the one-to-one correspondence between submodels and program revisions.

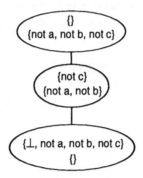

Fig. 8.1. Submodels lattice of Example 8.3.4.

Example 8.3.6. Consider program P :

$$p \leftarrow not\ q$$
$$\neg p \leftarrow not\ r$$
$$a \leftarrow not\ b$$

with revisable literals $Rev = \{not\ q, not\ r, not\ b\}$. Its submodels lattice is depicted in figure 8.2, where shadowed submodels are contradictory ones. For simplicity, contradictory models are not presented in full in the figure.

As we are interested in revising contradiction in a minimal way, we care about those submodels that are noncontradictory and among these, about those that are minimal in the submodels lattice.

Definition 8.3.10 (Minimal noncontradictory submodel).
A submodel $\langle M, R \rangle$ is a minimal noncontradictory submodel (MNS for short) of a program P iff it is noncontradictory and there exists no other noncontradictory submodel $\langle M', R' \rangle$, such that $R' \subset R$.

By definition, each MNS of a program P reflects a revision of P, $P \cup RevRules$[12] that guarantees noncontradiction, and such that for any set of rules $RevRules' \subseteq RevRules$ closed under indissociables, $P \cup RevRules'$ is contradictory. In other words, each MNS reflects a revision of the program that restores consistency, and which adds a minimal set, closed under indissociables, of inhibition rules for revisables.

Example 8.3.7. Consider program P :

$$p(X) \leftarrow p(s(X))$$
$$a \leftarrow not\ p(s(X))$$
$$\neg a$$

where $s(X)$ denotes the successor of X, and let $Rev = \{not\ p(i) \mid i > 0\}$.

---

[12] Where *RevRules* is the set of inhibition rules for some submodel revision.

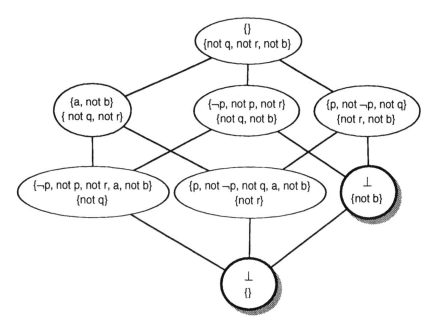

Fig. 8.2. Submodels lattice of Example 8.3.6

The only sets of inhibition rules that remove the contradiction are $IR(S_k)$, such that:

$$S_k = \{not\ p(i) \mid i > k\}.$$

None of them is minimal.

However the closure under indissociable of each of them is:

$$S = \{not\ p(i) \mid i > 0\}$$

Thus the only noncontradictory submodel is $\langle M, S \rangle$, where

$$M = \{\neg a, not\ a, not\ p(0)\}$$

and so it is also the only MNS.

Note that the revision models of each of the revisions above is indeed M (cf. proposition 8.3.4).

It is also clear that literals in the submodel revision indeed change their truth value once the inhibition rules are added:

Proposition 8.3.6. *If $\langle M, R \rangle$ is a MNS of program P then:*

$$R \subseteq WFSX_p(P)$$

Proof. Assume the contrary, i.e. $\langle M, R \rangle$ is a MNS of P and $R \not\subseteq WFSX_p(P)$. Then:

$$\exists not\ L \in R \mid not\ L \notin WFSX_p(P)$$

Thus, the addition of inhibition rule $L \leftarrow not\ L$ has no effect in $WFSX_p(P)$. Consequently, $R - \{not\ L\}$ is a noncontradictory submodel of P, and so $\langle M, R \rangle$ is not minimal.

Definition 8.3.11 (Minimally revised program). *Let P be a program with revisable literals Rev, and $\langle M, R \rangle$ some MNS of P. A minimally revised program MRP of P is:*

$$P \cup IR(R)$$

i.e. P plus one inhibition rule for each element of R.

It is clear that:

Proposition 8.3.7. *If P is noncontradictory its single MNS is*

$$\langle WFSX(P), \{\} \rangle,$$

and P itself is its only minimally revised program

Example 8.3.8. The minimally revised programs of the program in Example 8.3.6 are:

$$\begin{aligned} MRP_1 &= \{p \leftarrow not\ q; \neg p \leftarrow not\ r; a \leftarrow not\ b; q \leftarrow not\ q\} \quad and \\ MRP_2 &= \{p \leftarrow not\ q; \neg p \leftarrow not\ r; a \leftarrow not\ b; r \leftarrow not\ r\}. \end{aligned}$$

Each of these two programs is a transformation of the original one that minimally removes contradiction by taking back the assumption of truth of some revisables via their inhibition rules[13]. In this example, one can remove the contradiction in p either by going back on the closed world assumption of falsity of q (or truth of $not\ q$) or on the falsity of r. The program that has the first effect is MRP_1, the one with the second effect being MRP_2. Having no reason to render q alone, or r alone undefined, it is natural that a sceptical revision should accomplish the effect of undefining them both.

Definition 8.3.12 (Sceptical revision). *The sceptical submodel of a program P is the join $\langle M_J, R_J \rangle$ of all MNSs of P. The sceptical revised program of P is the program obtained from P by adding to it an inhibition rule for each element of R_J.*

It is important to guarantee that the sceptical revision indeed removes contradiction from a program. This is so because:

Proposition 8.3.8. *Let $\langle M_1, R_1 \rangle$ and $\langle M_2, R_2 \rangle$ be any two noncontradictory submodels. Then submodel $\langle M, R_1 \cup R_2 \rangle$ is also noncontradictory.*

---

[13] Non-minimally revised programs can be defined similarly, by considering all non-contradictory submodels instead of minimal ones only. We won't consider them in the sequel however, though they are useful for other purposes: viz. counterfactual reasoning, as defined in [154].

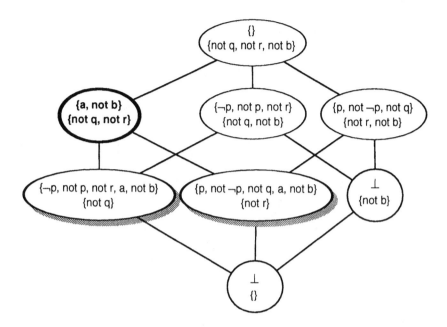

Fig. 8.3. The MNSs of the program from Example 8.3.6 are shadowed. Its sceptical submodel, the join of the MNSs, is in bold. Note that inhibiting b is irrelevant for revising P, and how taking the join of the MNSs captures what's required.

Proof. Since it is clear that $R_1 \cup R_2$ is closed under indissociable, we only have to prove that $\perp \notin M$. Since $\perp \notin M_1$ and $\perp \notin M_2$ it is enough to prove that $M \subseteq M_1 \cap M_2$.

By definition:

$$M = WFSX_p(P \cup \{L \leftarrow not\ L \mid not\ L \in R1 \cup R2\}).$$

As the extra rules only make literals undefined, and undefinedness only results in undefinedness, adding them all leads at most to the same set of literals being true or false, compared to adding them separately for only R_1 or R_2.

Example 8.3.9. Consider contradictory program P :

p	$\leftarrow$	$not\ q$	$\neg p$	$\leftarrow$	$not\ a$
q	$\leftarrow$	$not\ r$	$\neg a$	$\leftarrow$	$not\ b$
r	$\leftarrow$	$not\ s$			

with revisables $Rev = \{not\ q, not\ a, not\ b\}$. Figure 8.4 shows its submodels lattice, where MNSs are shadowed and the sceptical submodels is in bold.

Example 8.3.10. Consider the so-called Nixon diamond:

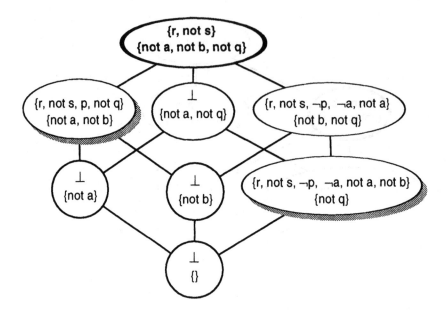

Fig. 8.4. Sceptical submodels and MNSs of Example 8.3.9.

$$
\begin{aligned}
\bot &\leftarrow pacifist(X), hawk(X) \\
pacifist(X) &\leftarrow quaker(X), not\ ab\_quaker(X) \\
hawk(X) &\leftarrow republican(X), not\ ab\_republican(X) \\
quaker(nixon) & \\
republican(nixon) &
\end{aligned}
$$

This contradictory program P has two MRPs:

– one by adding to P $ab\_quaker \leftarrow not\ ab\_quaker$
– another by adding to P $ab\_republican \leftarrow not\ ab\_republican$

Both these programs have noncontradictory *WFSX*s:

$$
\{hawk(nixon), quaker(nixon), republican(nixon), \\
not\ ab\_republican(nixon)\}
$$

$$
\{pacifist(nixon), quaker(nixon), republican(nixon), \\
not\ ab\_quaker(nixon)\}
$$

The sceptical submodel of the program results from adding to it both inhibition rules. Its *WFSX* is $\{quaker(nixon), republican(nixon)\}$.

The importance of having a single sceptical revision can be observed here, since there is no reason for preferring between Nixon being a pacifist or a hawk. Nevertheless, the other revisions also give relevant information[14].

---

[14] Their *WFSX*s correspond to the two usual default extensions.

It is clear that with these intended revisions some programs have no revision. This happens when contradiction has a basis on non-revisable literals.

Example 8.3.11. Consider program P :

$$a \leftarrow not\ b \qquad b \leftarrow not\ c$$
$$\neg a \qquad\qquad\qquad c$$

with revisables $Rev = \{not\ c\}$.

The only submodels of P are:

$$\langle WFSX_p(P), \{\}\rangle \text{ and } \langle WFSX_p(P \cup \{c \leftarrow not\ c\}), \{not\ c\}\rangle.$$

As both these submodels are contradictory P has no MNS, and thus no revisions. Note that if $not\ b$ were revisable, the program would have a revision $P \cup \{b \leftarrow not\ b\}$. If $not\ b$ were absent from the first rule, P would have no revision no matter what revisables.

Definition 8.3.13 (Unrevisable program). *A contradictory program P with revisables Rev is unrevisable iff it has no noncontradictory submodel.*

However it is possible to guarantee that consistent programs have revisions.

Proposition 8.3.9. *Let P be a consistent program with ICs and revisable literals $Rev = not\ \mathcal{H}$. Then, if P is contradictory it is revisable.*

Proof. By definition of consistent program (Definition 8.2.2), if no negative literal is assumed, the program is noncontradictory. Thus, at least the submodel obtained by adding to P an inhibition rule for every objective literal L in $\mathcal{H}$ such that $P \not\models_p \neg L$, is noncontradictory.

8.3.3 Contradiction support and removal

Submodels characterize which are the possible revisions, and the minimality criterium. Of course, a procedure for finding the minimal and the sceptical submodels can hardly be based on their declarative definition: one have to generate all the possible revisions to select these intended ones. In this section we define a revision procedure, and show that it concurs with the declaratively intended revisions.

The procedure relies on the notions of contradiction support, and of contradiction removal sets. Informally, contradiction supports are sets of revisable literals present in the $WFSX_p$ which are sufficient to support $\perp$ (i.e. contradiction)[15]. From their truth the truth of $\perp$ inevitably follows.

Contradiction removal sets are built from the contradiction supports. They are minimal sets of literals chosen from the supports such that any

---

[15] This notion can be seen as a special case of the notion of Suspect Sets introduced in declarative debugging in [160].

support of $\perp$ contains at least one literal in the removal set. Consequently, if all literals in some contradiction removal set were to become undefined in value then no support of $\perp$ would subsist. Thus removal sets are the hitting sets of the supports.

Example 8.3.12. Consider the program of Example 8.3.6. Its only contradiction support is $\{not\ q, not\ r\}$, and its contradiction removal sets are $\{not\ q\}$ and $\{not\ r\}$.

Suppose we had q undefined as a result of rules for q. In that case $\perp$ would also be undefined, the program becoming noncontradictory. The same would happen if r alone were undefined. No other set, not containing one of these two alternatives, has this property.

Definition 8.3.14 (Support of a literal). *The supports[16] of a literal L belonging to $WFSX_p$ of a program P with revisables Rev (each represented as $SS(L)$) are obtained as follows:*

1. *If L is an objective literal:*
   a) *If there is a fact for L then a support of L is $SS(L) = \{\}$.*
   b) *For each rule:*
      $$L \leftarrow B_1, \ldots, B_n \qquad n \geq 1$$
      in P such that $\{B_1, \ldots, B_n\} \subseteq WFSX_p(P)$, there exists a support of L
      $$SS(L) = \bigcup_i SS_{j(i)}(B_i)$$
      for each combination of one $j(i)$ for each i.
2. *If $L = not\ A$ (where A is an objective literal):*
   a) *If $L \in Rev$ then a support of L is $SS(L) = \{L\}$.*
   b) *If $L \notin Rev$ and there are no rules for A then a support of L is $SS(L) = \{\}$.*
   c) *If $L \notin Rev$ and there are rules for A, choose from each rule defined for A, a literal such that its default complement belongs to $WFSX_p(P)$. For each such choice there exists several $SS(L)$; each contains one support of each default complement of the choosen literals.*
   d) *If $\neg A \in WFSX_p(P)$ then there are, additionally, supports*
      $$SS(L) = SS_k(\neg A)$$
      for each k.

Example 8.3.13. Consider program P of Example 8.3.9, whose paraconsistent well-founded consequences are:

$$WFSX_p(P) = \{not\ s, r, not\ q, p, not\ \neg p, not\ b, \neg a, not\ a, \neg p, not\ p\}$$

---

[16] An alternative definition of supports relies on a notion of derivation for a literal in the $WFSX_p$, and doesn't require the previous availability of the WF Model. The derivation procedures for $WFSX_p$ can be obtained by adapting those of $WFSX$ described in Chapter 10, and can be found in [3].

The supports of p are computed as follows:

- From the only rule for p conclude that the supports of p are the supports of $not\ q$.
- Since $not\ q$ is a revisable then one of its supports is $\{not\ q\}$.
- As $\neg q \notin WFSX_p(P)$, there are no other supports of q.

Thus the only support of p is $\{not\ q\}$.

The supports of $\neg p$ are:

- From the only rule for $\neg p$ conclude that the supports of $\neg p$ are the supports of $not\ a$.
- Since $not\ a$ is a revisable then one of its support is $\{not\ a\}$.
- Since $\neg a \in WFSX_p(P)$, then supports of $\neg a$ are also supports of $not\ a$.
- From the only rule for $\neg a$ conclude that the supports of $\neg a$ are the supports of $not\ b$.
- Identically to $not\ q$ above, the only support of $not\ b$ is $\{not\ b\}$.

Thus $\neg p$ has two supports, namely $\{not\ a\}$ and $\{not\ b\}$.

Example 8.3.14. The supports of a in Example 8.3.7 are:

$$SS_1(a) \quad = \quad \{not\ p(1)\}$$
$$\vdots$$
$$SS_i(a) \quad = \quad \{not\ p(i)\}$$
$$\vdots$$

Proposition 8.3.10 (Existence of support). *A literal L belongs to the $WFSX_p$ of a program P iff it has at least one support $SS(L)$.*

Proof. The proof follows directly from the results in [3] regarding derivation procedures for $WFSX_p$.

Definition 8.3.15 (Contradiction support). *A contradiction support of a program P is a support of $\bot$ in the program obtained from P by adding to it constraints of the form $\bot \leftarrow L, \neg L$ for every objective literal L in the language of P.*

N.B. From now on, unless otherwise stated, when we refer to a program we mean the program obtained by adding to it all such constraints.

Example 8.3.15. The contradiction supports of program P from Example 8.3.9 are the union of pairs of supports of p and $\neg p$.

Thus, according to the supports calculated in Example 8.3.13, P has two contradiction supports, namely $\{not\ q, not\ a\}$ and $\{not\ q, not\ b\}$.

Contradiction supports are sets of revisables true in the $WFSX_p$ of the program and involved in some support of contradiction (i.e. $\perp$)[17].

Having defined the sets of revisables that together support some literal, it is easy to produce sets of revisables such that, if all become undefined, the truth of that literal would necessarily become ungrounded. To coupe with indissociability, these sets are closed under indissociable literals.

Definition 8.3.16 (Removal set). *A pre-removal set of a literal L belonging to the $WFSX_p$ of a program P is a set of literals formed by the union of some nonempty subset from each $SS(L)$.*

A removal set (RS) of L is the closure under indissociable literals of a pre-removal set of L.

If the empty set is a $SS(L)$, then the only $RS(L)$ is, by definition, the empty set. Note that a literal not belonging to $WFSX_p(P)$ has no RSs defined for it.

In view of considering minimal changes to the WF Model, we next define those RSs which are minimal in the sense that there is no other RS contained in them.

Definition 8.3.17 (Minimal removal set). *In a program P, $RS_m(L)$ is minimal removal set iff there exists no $RS_i(L)$ in P such that*

$$RS_m(L) \supset RS_i(L).$$

We represent a minimal RS of L in P as $MRS_P(L)$.

Definition 8.3.18 (Contradiction removal set). *A contradiction removal set (CRS) of program P is a minimal removal set of the (reserved) literal $\perp$, i.e. a CRS of P is a $MRS_P(\perp)$.*

Example 8.3.16. Consider program P of Example 8.3.4. The only support of $\perp$ is $SS(\perp) = \{not\ a\}$. Thus the only pre-removal set of $\perp$ is also $\{not\ a\}$. Since

$$Ind(\{not\ a\}) = \{not\ b\},$$

the only contradiction removal set is $\{not\ a, not\ b\}$.

Example 8.3.17. The removal sets of $\perp$ in the program of Example 8.3.9 are:

$$RS_1 = \{not\ q\} \qquad RS_2 = \{not\ q, not\ a\}$$
$$RS_3 = \{not\ q, not\ b\} \qquad RS_4 = \{not\ a, not\ b\}$$

Thus RS_1 and RS_4 are contradiction removal sets. Note that these correspond exactly to the revisions of minimal noncontradictory submodels of figure 8.4.

---

[17] Note that there is a close relationship between the SSs of $\perp$ and the sets of nogoods of Truth Maintenance Systems.

Example 8.3.18. The only CRS of Example 8.3.7 is:

$$CRS = \{not\ p(i) \mid i > 0\}$$

It is important to guarantee that contradiction removal sets do indeed remove contradiction.

Lemma 8.3.1. *Let P be a contradictory program with contradiction removal set CRS. Then:*

$$P \cup IR(CRS)$$

is noncontradictory.

Proof. By construction of removal set of $\bot$,

$$P' = P \cup \{L \leftarrow not\ L \mid not\ L \in CRS\}$$

has no support of $\bot$. Thus, by proposition 8.3.10, $\bot \notin WFSX_p(P')$.

Now we prove that this process concurs with the intended revisions above. This is achieved by proving three theorems:

Theorem 8.3.2 (Soundness of CRSs). *Let R be a nonempty CRS of a contradictory program P. Then $\langle M, R \rangle$ is a MNS of P, where:*

$$M = WFSX(P \cup IR(R))$$

Proof. Since by definition R is closed under indissociables, it is clear that $\langle M, R \rangle$ is a submodel of P. By lemma 8.3.1, it is also a noncontradictory submodel of P.

Now, we prove, by contradiction, that there exists no noncontradictory submodel of P smaller than $\langle M, R \rangle$.

Let $\langle M', R' \rangle$ be a noncontradictory submodel, such that $R' \subset R$. If R' is not closed under indissociables, then $\langle M', R' \rangle$ is not a submodel of P. Otherwise, by construction of minimal removal sets $\bot$ has at least one support in the program obtained from P by introducing inhibition rules for elements of R'. Thus, by proposition 8.3.10, $\langle M', R' \rangle$ is a contradictory submodel.

Theorem 8.3.3 (Completeness of CRSs). *Let $\langle M, R \rangle$ be a MNS, with $R \neq \{\}$, of a contradictory program P. Then R is a CRS of P.*

Proof. By proposition 8.3.6 $R \subseteq WFSX_p(P)$. So, by proposition 8.3.10, every literal of R has at least one support in P.

We begin by proving, by contradiction, that:

$$\forall not\ L \in R,\ \exists SS(\bot) \mid not\ L \in Ind(SS(\bot))$$

Assume the contrary. Then there exists a $not\ L \in R$ not belonging to the indissociables of any support of $\bot$. Thus, by definition of support, the supports of $\bot$ do not change if $L \leftarrow not\ L$ is added to P. Consequently:

$$\langle WFSX(P \cup IR(R - \{not\ L\})), R - \{not\ L\}\rangle$$

is a noncontradictory submodel of P, and so $\langle M, R\rangle$ is not minimal.

The rest of the proof follows by construction of removal sets, and its closure under indissociables.

Theorem 8.3.4 (Unrevisable programs). *If* $\{\}$ *is a CRS of a program* P *then* P *is unrevisable.*

Proof. By definition, $\{\}$ can only be a CRS if it is a support of $\perp$. Note that in the calculus of $\{\}$ as a support of $\perp$, no rules for any of the revisables were taken into account. Thus if one adds inhibition rules for any combination of the revisables, $\{\}$ remains as a support of $\perp$ in any of the resulting programs. By proposition 8.3.10, $\perp$ belongs to the well-founded model of each of those programs, and so every submodel of P is contradictory.

Theorem 8.3.5 (Sceptical revised program). *Let* P *be a contradictory program with CRSs,* R_k *such that* $k \in K$. *The sceptical revised program of* P *is:*

$$P \cup \left\{ L \leftarrow not\ L \mid\ not\ L \in \bigcup_{k \in K} R_i \right\}$$

Proof. The proof follows directly from Theorems 8.3.2 and 8.3.3.

Thus in order to compute the minimal and sceptical submodels:

− One starts by computing all supports of $\perp$. Although the definition of support requires one to know a priori the paraconsistent $WFSX$, an alternative definition exists such that this is not required. This definition is based on a top-down derivation procedure for $WFSX_p$, similar to the one for $WFSX$ described in Chapter 10. Computing all supports of $\perp$ is like computing all the derivations for $\perp$ in $WFSX_p$.
− If $\{\}$ is a support of $\perp$ then the program is unrevisable.
− If there are no supports of $\perp$ then the program is noncontradictory.
− Otherwise, after having all supports of $\perp$, the rest follows by operations on these sets, and computing indissociables. For such operations on sets one can rely on efficient methods known from the literature. For example the method of [190] for finding minimal diagnosis can be herein applied for finding CRSs given the supports. Example 8.3.19 shows that the issue of indissociables is simplified when the approch of CRS is considered.
− Finally, a minimal revised program is obtained by adding to P one inhibition rule for each element of a CRS, and the sceptical revision is obtained as the union of all such minimal revised programs.

Example 8.3.19. Consider program P :

$$\perp \leftarrow not\ a$$
$$a \leftarrow b$$

with $Rev = \{not\ a, not\ b\}$.

The submodels of P are:

$$\langle\{not\ a, not\ b, \perp\}, \quad \{\} \quad \rangle$$
$$\langle \quad \{not\ b\} \quad , \quad \{not\ a\} \quad \rangle$$
$$\langle \quad \{\} \quad , \quad \{not\ a, not\ b\}\rangle$$

and thus its only MNS (and the sceptical submodel) is the second one.

Note that there exists no submodel with revision $\{not\ b\}$ because

$$Ind(\{not\ b\}) = \{not\ a\}.$$

If such a revision would be considered then the sceptical submodel would be the last one.

The only support of $\perp$ is $\{not\ a\}$, and coincides with the only CRS. Note how the issue of indissociables becomes simplified, since eventhough for submodel it is necessary to compute indissociables in order to find correctly the sceptical submodel, this is not the case for CRSs.

Example 8.3.20. Recall the *"birds fly"* example from the introduction where

$$Rev = \{not\ abnormal(X)\}.$$

The only support of $\perp$ is:

$$\{not\ abnormal(tweety)\}$$

and so, it coincides with the only CRS.

Thus the only MRP, and sceptical revised program, is the original program augmented with $abnormal(tweety) \leftarrow not\ abnormal(tweety)$, whose *WFSX* is:

$$\{bird(tweety), \neg fly(tweety), not\ fly(tweety), man(socrates)\}$$

as expected.

Example 8.3.21. Consider the hiking/swimming program (Example 8.2.9):

$$hiking \leftarrow not\ rain$$
$$swimming \leftarrow not\ rain$$
$$swimming \leftarrow not\ cold\_water$$

$$\perp \leftarrow hiking, swimming$$

and let $Rev = \{not\ rain, not\ cold\_water\}$.

The supports of $\perp$ are $\{not\ rain\}$ and $\{not\ rain, not\ cold\_water\}$. Thus its two removal sets are:

$$\{not\ rain\} \cup \{not\ rain\} = \{not\ rain\}$$
$$\{not\ rain\} \cup \{not\ rain, not\ cold\_water\} = \{not\ rain, not\ cold\_water\}.$$

The only CRS is $\{not\ rain\}$, so the only MRP of P, and its sceptical revised program is:

$$
\begin{array}{rcl rcl}
\bot & \leftarrow & hiking, swimming & rain & \leftarrow & not\ rain \\
hiking & \leftarrow & not\ rain & swimming & \leftarrow & not\ rain \\
& & & swimming & \leftarrow & not\ cold\_water
\end{array}
$$

whose $WFSX$ is:

$\{not\ cold\_water, swimming\}$

This results coincides with the WFS_{Opt} calculated in Example 8.2.9.

Example 8.3.22. Recall the program P of Example 8.3.11:

$$
\begin{array}{rcl rcl}
a & \leftarrow & not\ b & b & \leftarrow & not\ c \\
\neg a & & & c & &
\end{array}
$$

with revisables $Rev = \{not\ c\}$, whose paraconsistent $WFSX_p$ is:

$\{c, \neg a, not\ a, not\ b, a, not\ \neg a\}$

The supports of $\bot$ result from the union of supports of a and supports of $\neg a$. As the only rule for $\neg a$ is a fact, its only support is $\{\}$. Supports of a are the supports of $not\ b$, and supports of $not\ b$ are the supports of c. Again, as the only rule for c is a fact, its only support is $\{\}$.

Thus the only support of $\bot$ is $\{\}$, and so P is unrevisable.

8.4 Equivalence between avoidance and removal

In this section we discuss the equivalence between the approaches of contradiction avoidance and contradiction removal described in this chapter.

The need for semantics more sceptical than $WFSX$ can be seen as showing the inadequacy of the latter for certain problems. The equivalence results show that this is not case since, by providing a revision process, $WFSX$ can deal with the same problems as the more sceptical semantics $WFSX_{Opt}$, and gives the same results.

The advantages of using $WFSX$ plus the revision process reside mainly on its simplicity compared to the others, and its properties (studied in Section 9.1) that make it amenable for top-down and bottom-up computation procedures.

The revision procedure can be implemented as a preprocessor of programs, and the maintenace of noncontradiction might benefit from existing procedures for Truth Maintenance Systems.

In order to prove the main equivalence theorems, we begin by proving two important lemmas. These lemmas state that avoiding a hypothesis in contradiction avoidance is equivalent to adding an inhibition rule for that hypothesis in contradiction removal.

Lemma 8.4.1. *If $P \cup H$ is a complete scenario with respect to Opt of a program P with avoidance set S then $P' \cup H$ is a complete scenario of $P' = P \cup IR(S)$.*

Proof. Since the inhibition rules are only added for literals in the avoidance set (thus for literals that do not belong to H) it is clear that $P' \cup H$ is consistent, and every mandatory is in H. It remains to be proven that:

1. if *not* L is acceptable then *not* $L \in H$
2. if *not* $L \in H$ and is not mandatory then it is acceptable

For every hypotheses in S this is ensured because they do not belong to H, and none of them is acceptable once the inhibition rules are added[18]. For hypotheses not in S :

1. If *not* $L \notin S$ is acceptable in $P' \cup H$ then it is also acceptable in $P \cup H$, because the latter, having less rules, provides less evidence to the contrary. It's left to prove that:

   if *not* $L \in Acc(P \cup H)$ then *not* $L \in Acc_{Opt}(P \cup H)$.

   Assume the contrary, i.e.

   not $L \in Acc(P \cup H)$ and *not* $L \notin Acc_{Opt}(P \cup H)$.

   By definiton 8.2.4, this is the case where *not* L is acceptable with respect to $P \cup H \cup not\ S$. In this case *not* $L \notin Acc(P' \cup H)$ because, by having the inhibiton rules, some *not* $L' \in S$ provides evidence for L. Thus an hypotheses is contradicted.

2. If *not* $L \notin S$ is not mandatory and is in H then it must belong to $Acc_{Opt}(P \cup H)$, and thus, by definition of acceptable hypothesis with respect to Opt, it also belongs to $Acc(P \cup H)$. So it can only not belong to $Acc(P' \cup H)$ if some of the inhibition rules provide evidence to L, which can never happen because *not* $L \in Acc_{Opt}(P \cup H)$.

Lemma 8.4.2. *If $P' \cup H$ is a complete scenario of $P' = P \cup IR(R)$, and $R \subseteq Opt$, then $P \cup H$ is complete with respect to Opt.*

Proof. Similar to the proof of lemma 8.4.1.

Theorem 8.4.1 (Quasi-complete scenaria and MNSs).
$P \cup H$ is a quasi-complete scenario with respect to Opt of a program P with an avoidance set S iff $\langle M, S \rangle$ is a MNS of P with revisables Opt, where:

$$M = WFSX(P \cup IR(S))$$

---

[18] Note that for any program with the $L \leftarrow not\ L$ rule, *not* L constitutes evidence for L, and thus *not* L can never be acceptable.

Proof. $\Rightarrow$ By lemma 8.4.1, if $P \cup H$ is a quasi-complete scenario with respect to Opt of P with an avoidance set S then it is a complete scenario of

$$P' = P \cup \{L \leftarrow not\ L \mid not\ L \in S\}.$$

Moreover, given that $P \cup H$ is a base scenario, by definition of quasi-complete, it is the least complete scenario with respect to Opt with avoidance set S, and thus the $WFSX$ of P'. By definition of quasi-complete no smaller combination of Opt exists, i.e. no smaller set of inhibition rules closed under indissociables removes the contradiction. So $\langle M, S \rangle$ is a MNS of P with revisables Opt.

$\Leftarrow$ Since $\langle M, S \rangle$ is a MNS of P, M is the least complete scenario of $P \cup IR(S)$. Thus, by lemma 8.4.2, $P \cup H$ is complete with respect to Opt. Moreover, since S is by definition closed under indissociables, $P \cup H$ is the least complete scenario with respect to Opt with avoidance set S. Thus it is a base scenario. By definition of MNS, no smaller combination of Opt removes the contradiction, and there are no base scenaria with a smaller subset of Opt, i.e $P \cup H$ is quasi-complete.

This theorem states that assuming hypotheses maximally and avoiding the contradiction, corresponds to minimally introducing inhibition rules, and then computing the $WFSX$.

Theorem 8.4.2 (Sceptical revision and WFS_{Opt}). *$P \cup H$ is the WFS_{Opt} of a program P with an avoidance set S iff $\langle M, S \rangle$ is the sceptical submodel of P with revisables Opt.*

Proof. The proof follows directly from Theorem 8.4.1 and the fact that the sceptical submodels is the join of MNSs, and WFS_{Opt} is the meet of quasi-complete scenaria.

From these theorem it follows that the rôle of optatives in contradiction avoidance is the same as the rôle of revisables in contradiction removal. Thus the discussion about special criteria to automatically infer optatives from a program, applies directly in the issue of finding special criteria to infer revisables from the program.

9. Further properties and comparisons

Throughout the previous chapters, several properties of *WFSX* were studied, and many comparisons with other semantics were made. Special importance was given to epistemic properties, and to comparisons based on epistemic arguments.

In this chapter we present some additional properties of *WFSX*, and make further comparisons with other semantics based on these properties, which are essentially structural in nature.

9.1 Properties of *WFSX*

Although most of the properties of *WFSX* presented up to now are of an epistemic nature, some structural properties too were already presented:

In Section 4.3, it is shown that a least partial stable model – the well-founded model – always exists for noncontradictory programs (cf. Theorem 4.3.1), and that that model can be obtained by an iterative bottom-up construction (cf. Theorem 4.3.2 and Definition 4.3.1). Moreover, we produced an iterative process for finding if a program is contradictory (cf. Theorem 4.3.3). Also in that section, we prove that for normal programs the results of *WFSX* are equivalent to the results of the well-founded semantics of [76] (cf. Theorem 4.3.4).

In Section 5.1.3 some other properties of extended logic programs are brought out, namely: intrinsic consistency, coherence and supportedness. The proof that *WFSX* complies with the first two is trivial. The proof of the third is to be found below in Section 9.1.2.

In Section 6.3 some properties of Ω-default theories are exhibited and proven. Given the correspondence result of Theorem 6.6.1, all these properties are verified by *WFSX* as well. In particular, *WFSX* complies with the property of modularity.

In Section 6.7 an alternative definition of *WFSX* is given, and additional properties concerning it are supplied. Among these are several different iterative constructions for the well-founded model.

Via the equivalence result of Theorem 7.4.5, all the properties presented in Section 7.4 for complete scenaria semantics are also properties of *WFSX*. In particular, one such property points out that partial stable models under set inclusion are organized into a downward-complete semilattice (cf. point 1 of Theorem 7.4.1), its least element being the well-founded model (cf. point 2 of the same theorem).

In order to make more formal comparisons between the various semantics for normal programs, in [53, 57] the author submits some abstract properties a semantics should comply with. He begins by studying the application to normal logic program semantics of some structural properties defined for nonmonotonic reasoning formalisms in [108], and points out the importance, in normal programs, of properties such as *cumulativity* and *rationality*, that provide for a *cautious* form of nonmonotonicity.

More recently, in [54, 58], this author generalizes his previous work and presents an assortment of properties he claims must be obeyed by every *reasonable* semantics of normal programs. The motivation is to provide combinations of properties that guarantee a complete and unique characterization of a semantics via such properties. In this section we generalize some of the properties presented in [53, 57, 54, 58] for extended logic programs, and study whether *WFSX* complies with them.

Here too, we study the complexity of *WFSX*, and prove results needed for the proofs of previous theorems in this work.

The structure of this section is as follows: in Section 9.1.1 we study structural properties related to the form of nonmonotonicity used by the semantics; then, in Section 9.1.2, we study properties related to the form and transformations of programs; finally, in Section 9.1.3 we prove some complexity results for *WFSX*.

9.1.1 Cumulativity and rationality

It is well known that semantics for logic programs with negation by default are nonmonotonic. However, some weak forms of monotonicity can still be verified by such semantics. Here we point out the importance of two such weak forms of monotonicity – cumulativity and rationality – for extended logic programs semantics, and examine whether *WFSX* complies with them.

Monotonicity imposes that for every program P and every pair of objective literals A and B of P

$$B \in Sem(P) \quad \Rightarrow \quad B \in Sem(P \cup \{A\})$$

In semantics of logic programs this property is not verified, and not even desired, for every such pair of objective literals. However, for some pairs, this property can be verified by some semantics, and in fact it can be very computationally useful.

One such case is when A is itself a consequence of P under the semantics *Sem*. The imposition of such a restricted form of monotonicity expresses that the addition of consequences of the semantics does not interfere with other consequences or, in other words, the consequences of a program, or lemmas, can safely be added to it. This weak form of monotonicity is usually called cumulativity.

Before defining cumulativity for extended logic programming we make a preliminary remark:

Remark 9.1.1. The study of this kind of properties of logic programs is made in the sceptical version of a semantics (cf. [53, 57]), i.e. $L \in Sem(P)$ is understood as: L belongs to all models determined by the semantics Sem when applied to the program P. Here this study is simplified since, by Theorem 4.3.1, a literal belongs to all models of the semantics *WFSX* iff it belongs to the well-founded model. Thus, in the sequel we use $L \in WFSX(P)$ to denote that L belongs to the well-founded model of P or, equivalently, to all partial stable models of P.

The generalization of cumulativity for extended logic programs is straightforward: it is just a rephrasing of cumulativity for normal programs as it appears in [53, 57], with the additional proviso that the program be noncontradictory:

Definition 9.1.1 (Cumulativity). *A semantics Sem is cumulative[1] iff for every noncontradictory program P and any two objective literals A and B of P :*

  if $A \in Sem(P)$ and $B \in Sem(P)$ then $B \in Sem(P \cup \{A\})$

This properties states that whenever an objective literal A has been derived from P, A can be used as a lemma and does not affect the set of objective literals derivable from P alone. If this condition is not valid, intermediate lemmas are of no use. This indicates that noncumulative semantics may be computationally very expensive. As shown below, *WFSX* is a cumulative semantics, and so memoizing techniques can be used in its computation:

Theorem 9.1.1. *The WFSX semantics for extended logic programs is cumulative.*

Proof. We will prove that the complete scenaria semantics (Definition 7.3.3) is cumulative. Given the equivalence between this semantics and *WFSX* (cf.

---

[1] This property is usually dubed "cautious monotonicity"(CM). In rigour, cumulativity stands for CM plus *Cut*, where this last property is defined by:

  if $A \in Sem(P)$ and $B \in Sem(P \cup \{A\})$ then $B \in Sem(P)$

Since all known semantics for normal and extended programs trivially comply with Cut, it is equivalent to say that a semantics is cumulative, or that it complies with CM. Here, for the sake of generality, we use the term cumulativity.

Theorem 7.4.5) this proves cumulativity for the latter.

Let $P \cup H$ be the least complete scenario of the noncontradictory program P. To prove this theorem, it is enough to show that if $P \cup H \vdash A$ and $P \cup H \vdash B$ then:

$-\ P \cup H \cup \{A\} \vdash B;$
$-\ P \cup H \cup \{A\}$ is the least complete scenario of $P \cup \{A\}$.

The proof of the first point is trivial since in the scenaria framework a scenario is a set of Horn clauses, and thus its consequences comply with monotonicity.

The proof of the second point is made in two steps. First we prove that $P \cup H \cup \{A\}$ is a complete scenario of $P \cup \{A\}$. Then we prove that there is no smaller complete scenario of $P \cup \{A\}$.

1. First we have to guarantee that $P \cup H \cup \{A\}$ is noncontradictory, i.e. it does not derive an objective literal L and its complement $\neg L$. Since $P \cup H \vdash A$, and $P \cup H$ is a set of Horn clauses, it follows clearly that the consequences of $P \cup H$ are the same of those of $P \cup H \cup \{A\}$. Given that $P \cup H$ is by hypothesis a complete scenario, it is also noncontradictory, and so the same happens with $P \cup H \cup \{A\}$.

   Furthermore, we have to show that every hypothesis in H is either mandatory or acceptable, and that all mandatory and acceptable hypotheses are in H.

   Recall that both the definitions of mandatory and acceptable are solely based on the consequences of the scenario.

   Again given that $P \cup H \vdash A$ and $P \cup H$ is a set of Horn clauses, the consequences of $P \cup H$ are the same of those $P \cup H \cup \{A\}$. Thus mandatory and acceptable hypotheses are the same for both $P \cup H$ and $P \cup H \cup \{A\}$, and given that the former is a complete scenario, the latter is also one.

2. The proof that it is the least scenario follows easily using the same arguments as in 1.

In [53, 57], the author presents another property – rationality – also related to cautious forms of nonmonotonicity. For normal logic programs this property is stronger than cumulativity, in the sense that every rational semantics is cumulative, but not vice-versa [2]. The straightforward generalization of this property for extended programs, following the same lines of that of cumulativity, is:

Definition 9.1.2 (Strong rationality). *A semantics Sem is strongly rational iff for every noncontradictory program P and any two objective literals A and B of P:*

---

[2] For example the O-semantics of normal logic programs [149, 151, 8] is not rational but is cumulative (cf. [55]).

if $not\ A \notin Sem(P)$ and $B \in Sem(P)$ then $B \in Sem(P \cup \{A\})$

The example below shows that this definition might cause some confusion when applied to extended programs, because then $Sem(P\cup\{A\})$ is not always defined:

Example 9.1.1. Consider program P :

$$\neg b$$
$$b \ \leftarrow \ a$$
$$a \ \leftarrow \ not\ a$$

For this program $not\ a \notin WFSX(P)$ and $\neg b \in WFSX(P)$. However, the program $P \cup \{a\}$ is contradictory, i.e. $WFSX(P \cup \{a\})$ is not defined.

At this point we would like to recall the rationale behind rationality. While cumulativity expresses that the addition of some consequences of the semantics do not interfere with the other consequences, rationality expresses that the addition of literals that are *compatible* with the program does not interfere with its consequences.

For normal logic programs an atom A is compatible with a program P iff its negation *not* A is not in the semantics of P. Note that the same does not happen for extended programs. For instance, in the program of Example 9.1.1 *not a* is not a consequence of the semantics, but a is not compatible with the program.

In extended programs, and in order to guarantee that some objective literal L is compatible with a program P, we have not only to verify that *not* L is not a consequence of P, but also that the program obtained by adding L to P is noncontradictory, so that the semantics is defined. This suggests a more cautious version of the rationality for extended programs, that avoids the possible confusion arising from $Sem(P \cup \{A\})$ not being defined::

Definition 9.1.3 (Cautious rationality). *A semantics Sem is cautiously rational iff for every noncontradictory program P and any two objective literals A and B of P, if not $A \notin Sem(P)$, and $P \cup \{A\}$ is a noncontradictory program, and $B \in Sem(P)$, then:*

$$B \in Sem(P \cup \{A\})$$

Theorem 9.1.2. *The* WFSX *semantics for extended logic programs is cautiously rational.*

Proof. As in the proof of Theorem 9.1.1, here we also prove the property for *WFSX* via its equivalence to complete scenaria semantics.

For simplicity, and without loss of generality (cf. corollary 9.1.2), we assume that programs are in the semantic kernel form, i.e. no objective literal appears in the body of rules.

Let P be a noncontradictory program in that form, let $P \cup H$ be its least complete scenario, and let A and B be two objective literals of P such that:

(i) $not\ A \notin H$
(ii) $P \cup \{A\}$ is noncontradictory
(iii) $P \cup H \vdash B$

We begin by proving that:

1. if $not\ L$ is mandatory in $P \cup H$, it is also mandatory in $P \cup H \cup \{A\}$.

Given that $P \cup H$ is a complete scenario, it contains all its mandatories. Thus $not\ L$ is mandatory iff $P \cup H \vdash \neg L$. Given that scenaria are sets of Horn clauses, $P \cup H \cup \{A\} \vdash \neg L$, and so, by definition of mandatory, $not\ L$ is mandatory in $P \cup H \cup \{A\}$.

2. if $not\ L$ is acceptable in $P \cup H$ it is also acceptable in $P \cup H \cup \{A\}$.

By definition of acceptable hypothesis, $not\ L$ is acceptable in $P \cup H$ iff

$$\forall E, P \cup E \vdash L \Rightarrow \exists not\ L' \in E \mid P \cup H \vdash L'$$

Again given that a scenario is a set of Horn clauses, its consequences are monotonic, and so the above formula entails that:

$$\forall E, P \cup E \vdash L \Rightarrow \exists not\ L' \in E \mid P \cup H \cup \{A\} \vdash L'$$

By condition (i) it follows that $not\ A$ is not acceptable in $P \cup H$. Thus we can assume in the formula above that L is different from A. Given that by hypotheses the program is in the semantic kernel form, for every objective literal L different from A:

$$P \cup E \vdash L \quad \Leftrightarrow \quad P \cup E \cup \{A\} \vdash L$$

So, if $not\ L$ is acceptable in $P \cup H$ then:

$$\forall E, P \cup E \cup \{A\} \vdash L \Rightarrow \exists not\ L' \in E \mid P \cup H \cup \{A\} \vdash L'$$

i.e., by definition of acceptable, $not\ L$ is acceptable in $P \cup H \cup \{A\}$.

By condition (iii), and given that consequences of a scenario are monotonic, it follows that

$$P \cup H \cup \{A\} \vdash B$$

Since, by points 1 and 2 above, mandatory and acceptable hypotheses subsist in $P \cup H \cup \{A\}$, and consistency is guaranteed by condition (ii), it follows that the least complete scenario of $P \cup \{A\}$ is of the form:

$$P \cup H' \cup \{A\}$$

where $H' \supseteq H$.

Thus $P \cup H' \cup \{A\} \vdash B$, i.e. $B \in WFSX(P \cup \{A\})$.

9.1.2 Partial evaluation and relevance

Here we study properties related to the form of programs, and with the preservation of the semantics when some transformations are applied to programs.

One such important property is the so called *principle of partial evaluation* [54, 58]. This principles states that the semantics of every program should be preserved under unfolding of objective literals. The example below shows that *WFSX* is not preserved under the usual unfolding techniques[3] for normal programs:

Example 9.1.2. Recall program P of Example 4.2.8:

$$c \leftarrow a \qquad a \leftarrow b$$
$$\neg a \leftarrow \qquad b \leftarrow not\ b$$

whose *WFSX* is:

$$\{\neg a, not\ a, not\ c, not\ \neg b, not\ \neg c\}$$

By unfolding the objective literal a in the rule for c we obtain the program P':

$$c \leftarrow b \qquad a \leftarrow b$$
$$\neg a \leftarrow \qquad b \leftarrow not\ b$$

whose *WFSX* is:

$$\{\neg a, not\ a, not\ \neg b, not\ \neg c\}$$

Note that the truth value of c is not preserved.

This happens because the unfolding of a did not take into account the fact that $\neg a$ is a consequence of the program. In order to define an unfolding technique for extended logic programs care must be taken in such cases. One has to guarantee that the unfolding of some atom A does not interfere with the fact that $\neg A$ belongs to the consequences of the program.

We shall see that one way of guaranteeing this is by adjoining to objective literal L the default literal $not\ \neg L$, before using the usual techique for unfolding L. Note that program P'':

$$c \leftarrow not\ \neg a, b \qquad a \leftarrow b$$
$$\neg a \leftarrow \qquad b \leftarrow not\ b$$

has indeed the same *WFSX* of program P.

In order to define the unfolding technique for extended programs we first prove the theorem:

---

[3] In this work we do not give a formal definition of unfolding for normal programs, and assume that this is known to the reader.

Theorem 9.1.3. *Let P be any extended logic program, and let P' be the a program obtained from P by adding to the body of some rule:*

$$H \leftarrow B_1, \ldots, B_n, not\ C_1, \ldots, not\ C_m$$

the default literal $not\ \neg B_i$, where $1 \leq i \leq n$ and $\neg B_i$ denotes the objective complement of B_i.
    Then:

– *M is a PSM of P iff M is a PSM of P'.*
– *P is contradictory iff P' is contradictory.*

Proof. In appendix.

From this theorem there follows an important corollary, already used above in this work (e.g. in the definition of scenaria):

Corollary 9.1.1. *For every program P and its canonical program P'*

$$WFSX(P) = WFSX(P')$$

Proof. Follows directly from the theorem and the Definition 2.1.1 of canonical program.

Let us define now the principle of partial evaluation for extended programs:

Definition 9.1.4 (Principle of partial evaluation). *Let P be an extended logic program, and let:*

$$L \quad \leftarrow \quad BodyL_1$$
$$\vdots$$
$$L \quad \leftarrow \quad BodyL_n$$

be all rules of P with head L. Assume further that $BodyL_1, \ldots, BodyL_n$ do not contain L.
    We denote by $unfold(P, L)$ the program obtained from P by replacing each rule $H \leftarrow L, BodyH$ (i.e. each rule with L in the body) by:

$$H \quad \leftarrow \quad not\ \neg L, BodyL_1, BodyH$$
$$\vdots$$
$$H \quad \leftarrow \quad not\ \neg L, BodyL_n, BodyH$$

The principle of partial evaluation states that the semantics of P is equal to the semantics of $unfold(P, L)$.

Theorem 9.1.4. WFSX *complies with the principle of partial evaluation.*

Proof. Let $P' = unfold(P, L)$.

Recall that, according to Theorem 6.7.1, $T \cup not\ F$ is a PSM of a program P iff

$$T = \Gamma_P \Gamma_{P_s} T$$
$$T \subseteq \Gamma_{P_s} T$$
$$F = \{L \mid L \notin \Gamma_{P_s} T\}$$

and that $\Gamma_P S$ is the least Herbrand model of the positive program $\frac{P}{S}^{gl}$ obtained by deleting from P all rules with a literal $not\ A$ in the body such that $A \in S$, and then deleting all default literals from the body of the remaining rules.

We begin by proving that for any set of objective literals S :

$$\Gamma_{P_s} S = \Gamma_{P'_s} S \quad (*)$$

If $\neg L \notin S$ then the default literals $not\ \neg L$ introduced by the partial evaluation are deleted in $\frac{P'}{S}^{gl}$, and so this program is obtainable from $\frac{P}{S}^{gl}$ via unfolding of L. Given that unfolding preserves the least Herbrand model of a positive program, $\Gamma_{P_s} S = \Gamma_{P'_s} S$.

If $\neg L \in S$ then the only possible difference between the $\frac{P}{S}^{gl}$ and $\frac{P'}{S}^{gl}$ is that rules with $not\ \neg L$ in the body are deleted in the latter but not in the former. Given that the program is seminormal, by definition all rules with head L are deleted in both positive programs.

The rules that remain in $\frac{P}{S}^{gl}$ and are deleted in $\frac{P'}{S}^{gl}$, have in the former the objective literal L in their bodies. Thus, since no rules for L exist in $\frac{P}{S}^{gl}$, the remaining rules are useless to determine the least Herbrand model of that program, and so $\Gamma_{P_s} S = \Gamma_{P'_s} S$.

Now, let us assume that $T \cup not\ F$ is a PSM of P. Then $T = \Gamma_P \Gamma_{P_s} T$. By (*):

$$T = \Gamma_P \Gamma_{P'_s} T$$

If $\neg L \notin \Gamma_{P_s} T$ then the default literals $not\ \neg L$ introduced by the partial evaluation are deleted in $\frac{P'}{\Gamma_{P'_s} T}^{gl}$, and so this program is obtainable from $\frac{P}{\Gamma_{P_s} T}^{gl}$ via unfolding of L. Thus, for the same reasons as before, $\Gamma_P \Gamma_{P'_s} T = \Gamma_{P'} \Gamma_{P'_s} T$.

If $\neg L \in \Gamma_{P_s} T$ then $L \notin T$, since otherwise L would be true in the PSM and $\neg L$ undefined, which is impossible because every PSM complies with coherence. So the rules that are deleted in $\frac{P'}{\Gamma_{P_s} T}^{gl}$ but not in $\frac{P}{\Gamma_{P_s} T}^{gl}$ are useless to determine the least Herbrand model (for the same reasons as before) and thus $\Gamma_P \Gamma_{P'_s} T = \Gamma_{P'} \Gamma_{P'_s} T$.

So:

$$T = \Gamma_{P'} \Gamma_{P'_s} T$$

Directly from ($*$) it follows that:

$$T \subseteq \Gamma_{P'_s} T$$
$$F = \{L \mid L \notin \Gamma_{P'_s} T\}$$

Thus $T \cup not\ F$ is a PSM of P'.

The proof that if $T \cup not\ F$ is a PSM of P' then it is also a PSM of P, is quite similar to the one above and is omitted for brevity.

Another property presented in [54, 58] is equivalence. It is especially important in this work because, together with the partial evaluation principle, it allows us to prove a result that has been widely used to simplify the proofs of theorems throughout this work.

Definition 9.1.5 (Equivalence). *Let P' be the extended logic program obtained from P by deleting every rule:*

$$L \leftarrow L, Body$$

i.e. every rule whose head is contained in the body.

Equivalence states that the semantics of P' is equal to the semantics of P.

Theorem 9.1.5. WFSX *complies with equivalence.*

Proof. Given the equivalence between this semantics and *WFSX* (cf. Theorem 7.4.5), we prove that the complete scenaria semantics (Definition 7.3.3) complies with equivalence.

By definition, scenaria are sets of Horn clauses, and rules of the form $L \leftarrow L, Body$ result in tautologies in the scenaria framework. Thus for any program P, any set of hypotheses H and any objective literal A :

$$P \cup \{L \leftarrow L, Body\} \cup H \vdash A \quad \Leftrightarrow P \cup H \vdash A \quad (*)$$

So, by their respective definitions, it follows directly that for every hypothesis $not\ A$:

$-\ not\ A \in Mand(P \cup H)$ iff $not\ A \in Mand(P \cup \{L \leftarrow L, Body\} \cup H)$.
$-\ not\ A \in Acc(P \cup H)$ iff $not\ A \in Acc(P \cup \{L \leftarrow L, Body\} \cup H)$.

By definition of complete scenario:

$$P \cup H \text{ is a complete scenario } \Leftrightarrow H = Mand(P \cup H) \cup Acc(P \cup H)$$

By the results above, $H = Mand(P \cup H) \cup Acc(P \cup H)$ iff

$$H = Mand(P \cup \{L \leftarrow L, Body\} \cup H) \cup Acc(P \cup \{L \leftarrow L, Body\} \cup H)$$

Again, by definition of complete scenario:

$$H = Mand(P \cup \{L \leftarrow L, Body\} \cup H) \cup Acc(P \cup \{L \leftarrow L, Body\} \cup H)$$
$$\Leftrightarrow$$
$$P \cup \{L \leftarrow L, Body\} \cup H \text{ is a complete scenario of } P \cup \{L \leftarrow L, Body\}$$

Thus the complete scenaria of P are the same as the complete scenaria of $P \cup \{L \leftarrow L, Body\}$.

By $(*)$ it follows also that the consequences of those scenaria are the same in both programs.

Given the results of Theorems 9.1.4 and 9.1.5, we next define a bottom-up process that transforms every extended program into another with no objective literals in the body of rules, and with the same *WFSX*.

Intuitively, in order to obtain such a transformed program, we begin by recording all rules with no objective literals in the body (hereafter called rules in the desired form). Then we unfold all literals such that all of its rules are in the desired form. By performing this partial evaluation more rules become of that form. The process is iterated until a fixpoint is reached.

In order to formally define this process we begin with some preliminary definitions:

Definition 9.1.6. *Let P be an extended logic program. We define:*

- $sk\_lits(P)$ *is the set of objective literals L such that there is no rule in P with head L and with objective literals in the body.*
- $sk\_rules(P)$ *is the set of all rules in P such that their heads belong to $sk\_lits(P)$.*

Definition 9.1.7 (Semantic kernel transformation). *Let P and P' be two extended logic programs with the same Herbrand base, such that P' does not contain any objective literal in the body of its rules.*

Additionally, let $heads(P')$ be the set of all objective literals in the head of some rule of P', and let P_r be the program obtained from P by first deleting from it every rule whose head is in $heads(P')$, and then making the union of the result with P'.

We define:

$$SK_P(P') = P' \cup sk\_rules(unfold(P_r, heads(P')))$$

The semantic kernel transformation SK_P of program P is the least fixpoint of the sequence:

$$
\begin{aligned}
P_0 &= sk\_rules(P) \\
P_{\alpha+1} &= SK_P(P_\alpha)
\end{aligned}
$$

Theorem 9.1.6. *The semantic kernel transformation SK_P of an extended program P uniquely exists, and is in the semantic kernel form, i.e. it is a set of rules with no objective literal in their bodies.*

Moreover the WFSX of SK_P is equal to the WFSX of P.

Proof. The existence, uniqueness, and semantic kernel form of SK_P are guaranteed by its construction.

The *WFSX* equivalence with the program P follows easily from the fact that the transformation is solely based on partial evaluations, and that the rules that are never added are clearly those that for some partial evaluation their head is contained in the body. Thus Theorems 9.1.4 and 9.1.5 guarantee such an equivalence.

From this theorem it follows directly that:

Corollary 9.1.2. *For every program P there exists one program P' with no objective literals in the body of its rules, such that the WFSX of P is equal to the WFSX of P'.*

Example 9.1.3. Consider program P :

$$
\begin{array}{llll}
a & \leftarrow & \neg b, not\ c \qquad & p \leftarrow q \\
\neg b & \leftarrow & d, not\ e \qquad & q \leftarrow p, not\ c \\
\neg b & \leftarrow & not\ p \\
d & \leftarrow & f \\
f &
\end{array}
$$

and let us calculate SK_P.

– $sk\_rules(P) = \{f\}$, and so $P_0 = \{f\}$. Note that $\neg b \leftarrow not\ p$ does not belong to P_0. This is because there is another rule with head $\neg b$ and with an objective literal in its body.

– By unfolding f in P (cf. Definition 9.1.4) we obtain:

$$
\begin{array}{llll}
a & \leftarrow & \neg b, not\ c \qquad & p \leftarrow q \\
\neg b & \leftarrow & d, not\ e \qquad & q \leftarrow p, not\ c \\
\neg b & \leftarrow & not\ p \\
d & \leftarrow & not\ \neg f \\
f &
\end{array}
$$

and thus $P_1 = \{d \leftarrow not\ \neg f;\ f\}$.

– By unfolding both d and f in the program, using their rules in P_1 we obtain:

$$
\begin{array}{llll}
a & \leftarrow & \neg b, not\ c \qquad\qquad & p \leftarrow q \\
\neg b & \leftarrow & not\ \neg d, not\ \neg f, not\ e \qquad & q \leftarrow p, not\ c \\
\neg b & \leftarrow & not\ p \\
d & \leftarrow & not\ \neg f \\
f &
\end{array}
$$

So $P_2 = P_1 \cup \{\neg b \leftarrow not\ \neg d, not\ \neg f;\ \neg b \leftarrow not\ p\}$.

– By also unfolding $\neg b$ we get:

$$
\begin{aligned}
a &\leftarrow \ not\ b, not\ \neg d, not\ \neg f, not\ e, not\ c & p &\leftarrow q \\
a &\leftarrow \ not\ b, not\ p, not\ c & & \\
\neg b &\leftarrow \ not\ \neg d, not\ \neg f, not\ e & q &\leftarrow p, not\ c \\
\neg b &\leftarrow \ not\ p & & \\
d &\leftarrow \ not\ \neg f & & \\
f & & &
\end{aligned}
$$

and thus:

$$
P_3 = P_2 \cup \left\{ \begin{aligned}
a &\leftarrow \ not\ b, not\ \neg d, not\ \neg f, not\ e, not\ c \\
a &\leftarrow \ not\ b, not\ p, not\ c
\end{aligned} \right\}
$$

– It is easy to see that $P_4 = P_3$.

Thus SK_P is the program:

$$
\begin{aligned}
a &\leftarrow \ not\ b, not\ \neg d, not\ \neg f, not\ e, not\ c \\
a &\leftarrow \ not\ b, not\ p, not\ c \\
\neg b &\leftarrow \ not\ \neg d, not\ \neg f, not\ e \\
\neg b &\leftarrow \ not\ p \\
d &\leftarrow \ not\ \neg f \\
f &
\end{aligned}
$$

Note that in fact $WFSX(P) = WFSX(SK_P)$.

Relevance is another property of semantics, related with transformations over programs, and also studied in [54, 58] for comparing semantics of normal logic program. Intuitively, a semantics complies with relevance iff the truth value of any literal in it is determined by the rules on which that literal depends. In order to formalize this notion we first define the dependency relation:

Definition 9.1.8 (Dependency relation). *An objective literal A depends on a literal L in an extended logic program P iff $L = A$ or there is a rule in P with head A and L' in its body and L' depends on L.*

A default literal not A depends on a literal L in P iff $L = not\ A$, $L = \neg A$ or there is a rule in P with head A and not L' in the body and not L' depends on L. Here, by $\neg A$ (resp. not L') we mean the objective (resp. default) complement of A (resp. L').

By dep_on(A, P) we mean the set of all literals L such that A depends on L.

Example 9.1.4. Consider program P :

$$
\begin{aligned}
(1) \quad a &\leftarrow \ b, not\ c & c &\leftarrow \ d, not\ e \quad (3) \\
(2) \quad \neg c &\leftarrow \ not\ g & e &\leftarrow \ f \quad (4)
\end{aligned}
$$

The reader can check that, for example:

$$
\begin{aligned}
dep\_on(a, P) &= \{a, b, not\ c, \neg c, not\ g, \neg g, not\ d, \neg d, e, f\} \\
dep\_on(not\ a, P) &= \{not\ a, \neg a, not\ b, \neg b, c, d, not\ e, \neg e, not\ f, \neg f\} \\
dep\_on(b, P) &= \{b\} \\
dep\_on(not\ b, P) &= \{not\ b, \neg b\} \\
dep\_on(c, P) &= \{c, d, not\ e, not\ f\} \\
dep\_on(not\ c, P) &= \{not\ c, \neg c, not\ g, not\ d, \neg d, e, f\}
\end{aligned}
$$

Definition 9.1.9 (Relevant rules). *The set of relevant rules of program P for literal L,*

$$rel\_rul(P, L)$$

is the set of all rules with head H such that $H \in dep\_on(L, P)$ *or not* $H \in dep\_on(L, P)$.

Example 9.1.5. For program P of Example 9.1.4, the set of relevant rules for the literals whose dependencies were calculated there, are (where for brevity only their identifying numbers are presented):

$$
\begin{aligned}
rel\_rul(P, a) &= \{(1), (2), (3), (4)\} \\
rel\_rul(P, not\ a) &= \{(1), (3), (4)\} \\
rel\_rul(P, b) &= \{\} \\
rel\_rul(P, not\ b) &= \{\} \\
rel\_rul(P, c) &= \{(3), (4)\} \\
rel\_rul(P, not\ c) &= \{(2), (3), (4)\}
\end{aligned}
$$

Definition 9.1.10 (Relevance). *A semantics Sem complies with the principle of relevance iff for every noncontradictory program P and every literal L*

$$L \in Sem(P) \quad \Leftrightarrow \quad L \in Sem(rel\_rul(P, L))$$

The importance of this structural property is well recognizable if we think of top-down procedures for deciding the truth value of some literal. A semantics not complying with this principle cannot have a purely top-down procedure based on rewriting techiques.

Theorem 9.1.7. WFSX *complies with the principle of relevance.*

Proof. It is easy to see that for the definition of support (Definition 8.3.14) of some literal L in any program P, only rules of $rel\_rul(P, L)$ are used. Since the truth value of a literal can be determined from the existence or not or a support for it (cf. proposition 8.3.10), it follows easily that *WFSX* complies with relevance.

Another property mentioned above in this work (in Section 5.1.3) is supportedness. Recall that a semantics complies with supportedness if an objective literal L is true in the semantics of P iff there is rule in P with head L and whose body is also true in the semantics of P.

Theorem 9.1.8. WFSX *complies with supportedness.*

Proof. Trivial in the complete scenario semantics (which is equivalent to *WFSX* by Theorem 7.4.5).

9.1.3 Complexity results

Several times in this work we've said that we are interested in a computable semantics, and that computational cost is for us an important issue.

Unfortunately *WFSX* is not recursively enumerable (cf. Definition 4.3.1). This is a difficulty *WFSX* shares with most reasonable semantics for normal logic programs, including the well-founded semantics (WFS) of [76].

However, as proven in [76], the complexity of the decision problem in WFS for Datalog programs (i.e. programs without function symbols) is polynomial. In this section we show that the addition of explicit negation into WFS does not increase the complexity of the latter.

We begin by showing that if one knows a priori that some Datalog program P is noncontradictory then the decision problem[4] in *WFSX* of P is polynomial.

Theorem 9.1.9. *The decision problem for any noncontradictory Datalog program P under* WFSX *is polynomial in the size of the ground version of P.*

Proof. This proof follows closely the proof about the complexity of WFS in [76].

We show that the well-founded model can be constructed in polynomial time, after which any query can be answered immediately. We do this proof using the equivalent definition of *WFSX*, of Theorem 6.7.2.

According to that theorem, the positive part of the well-founded model T is the least fixpoint of the operator $\Gamma\Gamma_s$, the negative part F being the complement of the application of Γ_s to that least fixpoint.

At each stage T_α of the induction, until the fixpoint is reached, at least one element of the Herbrand base is added to $T_{\alpha+1}$, so the fixpoint must be reached in a number of steps polynomial in the size of the $\mathcal{H}$[5]. So we need only show that $\Gamma\Gamma_s T_\alpha$ can be found in polynomial time and that, given T, F can also be found in polynomial time.

It is clear that for these proofs it is enough to show that, for any set S of objective literals, the computation of both ΓS and $\Gamma_s S$ is polynomial. Since $\Gamma_s S$ is equal to ΓS applied to a seminormal version of the program, and clearly the seminormal version is computable in linear time, we only show that the computation of ΓS is polynomial.

---

[4] As usual, by decision problem we mean the problem of deciding whether some literal L belongs to the semantics of the program.

[5] This kind of argument is standard, viz. [37, 208, 85, 90, 76].

- The computation of ΓS starts by deleting all rules whose body contains a default *not* L such that $L \in S$. It is clear that this computation is $O(|S| * |P|)$.
- Then all default literals in the bodies of the remaining rules are deleted. This computation is $O(|P|)$.
- Finally, the T_P of the resulting positive program is computed. It is well known that the computation of T_P of a positive program is polynomial.

Thus the computation of ΓS is polynomial.

According to this theorem we can only say that if one knows that some program P is noncontradictory then it can be decided in polynomial time whether some literal is true in $WFSX(P)$. However the result can be generalized by withdrawing the a priori knowledge about the noncontradiction of P. This is so because:

Theorem 9.1.10. *The problem of determining whether a Datalog extended program P is contradictory under* WFSX *is polynomial in the size of the ground version of P.*

Proof. From the correspondence Theorem 6.6.1 and proposition 6.3.2 it follows directly that a Datalog program P is contradictory iff the least fixpoint of the sequence:

$$
\begin{aligned}
T_0 &= \{\} \\
T_{\alpha+1} &= \Gamma\Gamma_s(T_\alpha)
\end{aligned}
$$

contains some objective literal L and its complement $\neg L$.

Since the computation of that fixpoint is polynomial (cf. Theorem 9.1.9), it follows easily that to determine whether P is contradictory is also polynomial.

9.2 Comparisons

Throughout the text above, several comparisons were made between *WFSX* and other semantics for extended logic programs.

Comparisons with the semantics of [180] were made in Chapter 3 and Section 5.1 where we argued that this semantics does not impose any connection between the two types of negations. In fact, as mentioned in Chapter 3, our insatisfaction with the semantics of [180] in what concerns that desired connection was one of the main motivations for defining a new semantics for extended logic programs.

Also in Section 5.1, some comparisons were made with the semantics of [183]. There we point out that that semantics does not comply with supportedness. Epistemic comparisons with that semantics were made not only in that very section, where we argued that supportedness closely relates to the use of logic as a programming language, but also in Section 5.2 where we related the use of classical negation $\sim L$ of [183] with the epistemic reading *"L is not provenly true"*. In contradistinction, explicit negation $\neg L$ of *WFSX* has the reading *"L is provenly false"*. In Section 5.2 we compared these two readings and argued in favour of the latter.

Epistemic comparisons with answer-set semantics [80] were drawn indirectly in Section 5.2 (via the correspondence between answer-set semantics and Moore's autoepistemic logic), and in Chapter 6 (via the correspondence between answer-set semantics and Reiter's default logic).

However no detailed comparisons between *WFSX* and answer-set semantics concerning structural properties were made yet. The only structural properties pointed out for answer-sets were the ones studied in Section 5.1, where we found out that intrinsic consistency, coherence and supportedness are verified by both answer-sets and *WFSX*.

Recall that, as mentioned in Chapter 3, one of our main qualms with answer-set semantics was in what regards its structural and computational properties. In this section we make additional comparisons between *WFSX* and answer-sets. These comparisons are made either using the properties in the previous section, or via structural properties of nonmonotonic formalisms that correspond to answer-sets.

We start by comparing the complexity results of both semantics. In the previous section we have shown that for Datalog programs the complexity of both the decision problem and the problem of finding if some program is contradictory in *WFSX* is polynomial. In contrast, in [124] the authors show that, even for Datalog programs, the problem of finding if a program has answer-sets is NP-complete, and the decision problem for programs with answer-sets is co-NP-complete.

As proven above, *WFSX* enjoys some structural properties with regard to the organization of its models. In particular:

- partial stable models under set inclusion are organized into a downward-complete semilattice, its least element being the well-founded model;
- the intersection of all partial stable models is equal to the well-founded model, and can be computed by an iterative bottom-up process.

None of these properties is enjoyed by answer-set semantics. In fact, by its very definition, no answer-set is comparable (with respect to $\subseteq$) with other answer-sets. Thus, for deciding if some literal is a consequence of a program under the answer-set semantics one cannot rely on a single least model (as in *WFSX*) and, in contrast, have first to compute all answer-sets and then their intersection.

Given that answer-set semantics corresponds to Reiter's default logic (cf. [80]), this problem is related with the property of uniqueness of minimal extension studied in Section 6.2. There we point out more problems with

Reiter's default logic (and given the correspondence results of [80], also with answer-set semantics) that result from the inexistence of a unique minimal extension. In particular, we argue it is undesirable that the *cautious (or sceptical) version* of the semantics not be itself a model of it. Next we present some other undesirable properties of the sceptical version of answer-set semantics.

By the sceptical version of the answer-set semantics we mean (as usual) the semantics $AS(P)$ determined by:

$$L \in AS(P) \quad \text{iff} \quad L \text{ is in all answer-sets of } P$$
$$not\ L \in AS(P) \quad \text{iff} \quad \text{there is no answer-set of } P \text{ containing } L$$

where L is any objective literal of the extended program P.

Cumulativity is one structural property obeyed by *WFSX* (cf. Theorem 9.1.1) and not by the sceptical version of answer-sets. The example below shows this is indeed the case:

Example 9.2.1. Consider program P :

$$
\begin{array}{rcl}
a & \leftarrow & not\ b \\
b & \leftarrow & not\ a \\
c & \leftarrow & not\ a \\
c & \leftarrow & not\ c
\end{array}
$$

whose only answer-set is $\{c, b\}$. Thus $c \in AS(P)$, and $b \in AS(P)$. However

$$b \notin AS(P \cup \{c\}).$$

In fact $P \cup \{c\}$ has two answer-sets:

$$\{p, a\} \quad \text{and} \quad \{p, b\}$$

Since one of them does not contain b, $b \notin AS(P \cup \{c\})$.

This very same example also shows that answer-set semantics is neither strongly nor cautiously rational. In fact $not\ c \notin AS(P)$, $b \in AS(P)$, and $P \cup \{c\}$ is noncontradictory, but $b \notin AS(P \cup \{c\})$.

Being noncumulative, answer-set semantics not only gives in some cases very unintuitive results, but also some added problems in its computation accrue. In particular, even for propositional programs, the computation of answer-sets cannot be made by approximations[6]: once it is found that an objective literal is in every answer-set, that literal cannot be added as a fact to the program.

This also points out problems in finding an iterative bottom-up process for computing answer-set semantics, since usually such methods use already

---

[6] For nonpropositional programs, it was already shown (in Section 7.5) that the computation of an answer-set cannot in general be made by finite approximations.

computed results as lemmas.

Another structural property studied in the previous section and obeyed by *WFSX* is relevance. The example below shows that answer-set semantics does not comply with relevence.

Example 9.2.2. Consider program P :

$$
\begin{array}{rcl}
a & \leftarrow & not\ b \\
b & \leftarrow & not\ a \\
c & \leftarrow & not\ a \\
\neg c
\end{array}
$$

whose only answer-set is $\{\neg c, a\}$. The rules relevant for a are the first two. However a is not in the answer-set semantics of just those relevant rules.

In fact, $rel\_rul(P, a)$ has two answer-sets: $\{a\}$, and $\{b\}$. Since one of them does not contain a, $a \notin AS(rel\_rul(P, a))$.

This shows that, in contradistinction with *WFSX*, there can be no purely top-down procedure for determining if some literal is true under the answer-set semantics. Such a procedure would have to examine more rules than the ones on which the literal depends.

Another interesting result concerning comparisons between *WFSX* and answer-sets is:

Theorem 9.2.1. *If an extended logic program has at least one answer-set it has at least one partial stable model.*

Proof. Follows directly from Theorem 6.4.2, given the correspondence between Ω-extensions and PSMs (cf. Theorem 6.6.1), and the correspondence between Reiter's extensions and answer-sets (cf. [80]).

From this theorem it follows that *WFSX* gives semantics to at least the same programs answer-sets does. Examples in Section 7.5 show that some programs have partial stable models and no answer-set. Thus we say that *WFSX* generalizes answer-set semantics, in the sense that it assigns meaning to more programs.

For programs where both answer-set semantics and *WFSX* assign a meaning, the computational methods of the latter can be viewed as sound methods for the former:

Theorem 9.2.2 (Soundness wrt to answer-set semantics). *Let P be an extended logic program with at least one answer-set. Then* WFSX *is sound with respect to the answer-set semantics, i.e. for every literal L :*

$$
L \in WFSX(P) \quad \Rightarrow \quad L \in AS(P)
$$

Proof. Follows directly from Theorem 6.4.3, given the correspondence between Ω-extensions and PSMs (cf. Theorem 6.6.1), and the correspondence between Reiter's extensions and answer-sets (cf. [80]).

This theorem only guarantees soundness for programs with answer-sets. As stated above in this section, the problem of determining whether a program has answer-sets is NP-complete. Thus, even though the methods of *WFSX* seem to be good sound computational methods for answer-sets, they are not as good for that purpose because one first has to determine the existence of answer-sets.

One way to define good computational methods for the decision problem in answer-set semantics is to restrict the class of programs (based on some syntatic criteria, in the spirit of [64]) where those methods can be applied, and then use *WFSX*. The study of syntatic properties guaranteeing the existence of answer-sets and its equivalence to *WFSX*, i.e. guaranteeing that *WFSX* can be used to correctly compute answer-set semantics, is however beyond the scope of this work.

10. Top-down derivation procedures for *WFSX*

This chapter, which is not a pre-requisite for the understanding of the applications in Part III, concerns the definition of top-down derivation procedures for *WFSX*. Such procedures are indispensable in practice for the goal oriented querying of a program about the truth of literals, with no the need to compute the whole WFM beforehand. One can hardly overemphasize the importance of the structural properties enjoyed by *WFSX* for this purpose, that make the existance of such procedures possible, and which other competing semantics do not share. This was discussed at length in Section 9.1.

We begin the chapter by defining a sound and complete top-down semantic tree characterization of *WFSX*. Based on this characterization, we proceed with the definition of the SLX derivation procedure, and prove its soundness and (theoretical[1]) completeness with respect to *WFSX*.

To guarantee termination, (at least) for finite ground programs, we next introduce rules that prune the search space, and eliminate both cyclic positive recursion as well as cyclic recursion through negation by default.

The procedures and pruning rules described in this section are amenable to a simple implementation (in Appendix A) which, by its nature, readily allows pre-processing into Prolog, and has shown promise as an efficient basis for further development.

It is not the purpose of this chapter to resolve with full generality the issues and problems pertaining to the execution of nonground logic programs. A whole gamut of research in the last years exists, and is still underway, tackling just such issues. These are by no means easy, nor have generally accepted solutions. Accordingly, our stance is to keep to the ground case, with the expectancy that, in due course, it shall be shown how, and under what circumstances and restrictions, the generalizing move from the ground to the nonground case can be made. This generalization and implementation for the nonground case, involving tabulation and constructive negation, is ongoing work not reported in this book.

---

[1] In practice completeness cannot be achieved because in general the WFM is not computable [76]. However, in theory, and with the possible need of constructing more than ω derivations, completeness is obtained.

10.1 Semantic tree characterization of *WFSX*

In this section we define a top-down semantic tree characterization of *WFSX* which is sound and complete (and consequently also with respect to WFS when the program contains no explicit negation) for (possibly infinite) ground programs. It is not our aim in this section to address the problems of loops and of termination for programs without function symbols. These are dealt with further down, by means of pruning rules.

The top-down characterization relies on the construction of AND-trees (T-Trees), whose nodes are either assigned the status *successful* or *failed*. A successful (resp. failed) tree is one whose root is successful (resp. failed). If a literal L has a successful tree rooted in it then it belongs to the WFM; otherwise, i.e. when all trees for L are failed, L does not belong to the WFM. Unlike other top-down methods for WFS [40, 41, 27, 16], we deliberately do not assign the status *unknown* to nodes. We do not do so because this way the characterization is most similar to SLDNF, and to avoid the complications of other approaches, involved in returning three distinct truth values. Thus, in our approach, *failure does not mean falsity*, but simply failure to prove verity.

We start by examining the simpler case of programs without explicit negation. It is well known [155, 195, 40, 41, 27] that the main issues in defining top-down procedures for WFS are those of infinite positive recursion, and of infinite recursion through negation by default. The former results in the truth value false (so that the query L should fail and the query *not* L succeed, for some L involved in the recusion), and the latter results in the truth value undefined (so that verity proofs for both L and *not* L should fail).

Apart from these problems we mainly follow the ideas of SLDNF, where atoms with no rules fail, *true* succeeds[2], atoms resolve with program rules, and the negation as failure rule that *not* L succeeds if L fails, and fails if L succeeds.

In order to solve the problem of positive recursion we follow the same approach as in SLS-resolution [177], i.e. we consider a failure rule for not necessarily finite branches.

Example 10.1.1. Let $P = \{p \leftarrow p\}$. The only tree for p,

is infinite. So p fails and consequently *not* p succeeds.

---

[2] In the sequel we assume, without loss of generality, that the only fact of a program is *true*. Other facts of programs are translated into rules with *true* in the body.

For recursion through negation by default the solution is not so simple because, as noted above, in this case we want to fail both L and *not L*, which violates the negation as failure rule. To deal with this problem we introduce a new kind of tree, TU-Tree, that rather than proving verity, proves nonfalsity[3]. TU stands for true or undefined, i.e. non-false. Now, for any L, the verity proof of *not L* fails iff there is a nonfalsity proof of L.

TU-Trees are contructed similarly to T-Trees: atoms with no rules are failed leafs (as they fail to be true or undefined), *true* succeeds, atoms resolve with program rules (since a literal L is true or undefined if there is a rule for L whose body is true or undefined), and *not L* fails if L succeeds in a verity proof, and succeeds otherwise (note that *not L* is true or undefined iff L is true).

Having these two kinds of trees, it becomes easy to assign a status to an occurrence of a literal L involved in recursion through negation by default. Indeed, and this is the crux of our method, since in this case, L is undefined according to WFS, it must be assigned the status failed if it is in a T-Tree, and successful if it is in a TU-Tree.

Example 10.1.2. Let $P = \{p \leftarrow not\ p\}$. In order to prove the verity of p we build its T-Trees. In this case the only tree is

$$p$$
$$|$$
$$not\ p$$

The node labeled *not p* is failed if there is a successful TU-Tree for p, and successful otherwise.

The only TU-Tree for p is[4]:

and so there is a recursion in p through negation by default. So p in the TU-Tree is assigned the status successful, and consequently *not p* in the T-Tree is failed. Thus the proof of verity for p fails.

The formalization of these solutions, presented below, yields a correct characterization of WFS for normal programs (cf. Theorem 10.1.3). Now we show how to generalize the characterization to deal with explicit negation in *WFSX*.

In a lot of points, the treatment of extended programs is akin to that of normal ones, where instead of atoms we refer to objective literals, namely because, as expected, objective literals are treated exactly like atoms are in WFS.

---

[3] A similar idea, but in the context of bottom-up procedures, is expounded in [97].
[4] In the sequel, to better distinguish between T and TU-trees, the latter will be shown inside a box.

The main difference in the generalization to extended programs resides in the treatment of negation by default. In order to fulfill the coherence requirement there must be an additional way to succeed a proof of *not L*. In fact *not L* must succeed if ¬*L* does.

Example 10.1.3. Recall program P of Example 3.0.6:

$$
\begin{array}{rcl}
a & \leftarrow & not\ b \\
b & \leftarrow & not\ a \quad \cdot \\
\neg a & &
\end{array}
$$

whose *WFSX* is (cf. Example 4.2.5):

$$\{\neg a, b, not\ a, not\ \neg b\}$$

The only T-Tree for b is:

$$
\begin{array}{c}
b \\
| \\
not\ a
\end{array}
$$

According to the methods described for normal programs in order to prove *not a* we have to look at all possible TU-Trees for a. The only one is:

Since this is a case of recursion through negation by default, *not b* succeeds and consequently *not a* fails. However, since ¬*a* is true, by coherence *not a* (and thus also *b*) must succeed, by the additional required proof method for default literals.

Thus, for extended programs, in a T-Tree *not L* succeeds iff all TU-Trees for L fail or if there is a successful T-Tree for ¬*L*, and fails otherwise. Regarding TU-Trees, *not L* succeeds in the same cases of normal programs, plus the case when ¬*L* is true (i.e. there is a succesful T-Tree for ¬*L*). ¬*L* being undefined is irrelevant for the nonfalsity of *not L* (e.g. in Example 10.1.3 where the undefinedness of c does not prevent *not* ¬*c*).

Care must also be taken in nonfalsity proofs because the coherence requirement overrides undefinedness. The problem is akin to that of partial evaluation of objective literals within *WFSX*, discussed in Section 9.1.2:

Example 10.1.4. Recall program P of Example 4.2.8:

$$
\begin{array}{rclcrcl}
c & \leftarrow & a & \quad & a & \leftarrow & b \\
\neg a & \leftarrow & & & b & \leftarrow & not\ b
\end{array}
$$

whose *WFSX* is:

$$\{\neg a, not\ a, not\ c, not\ \neg b, not\ \neg c\}$$

As shown in Example 9.1.2, if a in the first rule is replaced by b (the body of the single existing rule for a), then the truth value of c is not preserved.

The problem of unfolding objective literals without changing the semantics was solved in Section 9.1.2, by adjoining to each objective literal L the default literal $not \neg L$, before using the usual technique for unfolding L. Similarly, in the semantic tree characterization, when expanding tree nodes there must be additional sucessors, corresponding to the negation by default of the complements of objective literals in the chosen rule, i.e. making the adjoining of $not \neg L$ implicit rather than explicit.

In this example, without the additional sucessors, the only T-Tree for $not\ c$ is one with the single node $not\ c$. Since there are no rules for $\neg c$, all T-Trees for $\neg c$ fail. Thus, in order to prove $not\ c$ we have to look at all possible TU-Trees for c. The only one is:

which succeeds because $not\ b$ in the TU-Tree is involved in a recursion through negation. So the T-Tree for $not\ c$ fails, which is an incorrect result since $not\ c$ belongs to the WFM. Note that the problem here is that a in the TU-Tree is expanded to b. Accordingly, the result for a becomes the same as the one for b. However b and a of different truth value in the WFM (b is undefined whilst a is false).

If the additional sucessors are added then the TU-Tree for c is:

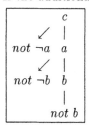

This tree is failed because $not \neg a$ fails. Thus $not\ c$ in the T-Tree succeds, as desired.

Summarizing, and formally:

Definition 10.1.1 (T-Tree, TU-Tree). *A T-Tree $\mathcal{T}(A)$ (resp. TU-Tree $\mathcal{TU}(A)$), for an arbitrary fixed ground extended logic program P, is an AND tree with root labeled A and nodes labeled by literals.*

T-Trees (resp. TU-Trees) are constructed top-down starting from the root by successively expanding new nodes using the following rules:

1. *For a node n labeled with an objective literal A: if there are no rules for A in P then n is a leaf; otherwise, select (non-deterministically) one rule:*

$$A \leftarrow B_1, \dots, B_j, not\ B_{j+1}, \dots, not\ B_k\ from\ P$$

where the B_is are objective literals. In a T-Tree the successors of n are

$$B_1, \dots, B_j, not\ B_{j+1}, \dots, not\ B_k.$$

In a TU-Tree there are, additionally, the successors

$$not\ \neg B_1, \dots, not\ \neg B_j.$$

2. *Nodes labeled with default literals are leaves.*

Definition 10.1.2 (Success and failure for *WFSX*). *Each node in a T-Tree (resp. TU-Tree) has an associated status that can be either failed or successful. All infinite trees are failed. A finite T-Tree (resp. TU-Tree) is successful if its root is successful and failed if its root is failed. The status of a node in a finite tree is determined according to the following rules:*

1. *A leaf node n labeled with* true *is successful;*
2. *A leaf node n labeled with an objective literal (distinct from* true*) is failed;*
3. *A leaf node n in a T-Tree (resp. TU-Tree) labeled with the literal* not A *is successful if all TU-Trees (resp. T-Trees) with root A (subsidiary trees of n) are failed or if there is a successful T-Tree with root $\neg A$ (the only other subsidiary tree of n);*
4. *A leaf node n in a T-Tree (resp. TU-Tree) labeled with the literal* not A *is failed if there is a successful TU-Tree (resp. T-Tree) with root A (the subsidiary trees of n);*
5. *An intermediate node n in a T-Tree (resp. TU-Tree) is successful if all its children are successful, and is failed if one of its children is failed.*

After applying the previous rules some nodes may still have their status undetermined due to infinite recursion through negation by default. To undetermined nodes in T-Trees the status failed is assigned, and in TU-Trees the status successful is assigned.

Theorem 10.1.1 (Correctness wrt *WFSX*). *Let P be a ground (possibly infinite) extended logic program, M its well-founded model according to WFSX, and let L be an arbitrary fixed literal. Then:*

– *if there is a successful T-Tree with root L then $L \in M$ (soundness);*
– *if $L \in M$ then there is a successful T-Tree with root L (completeness).*

Proof. The proof of this theorem follows easily from the correctness of SLX (Theorems 10.2.1 and 10.2.2).

This theorem only guarantees correctness for noncontradictory programs. However, it is possible to determine with the above characterization whether a program is contradictory:

Theorem 10.1.2 (Contradictory programs). *An extended program P is contradictory iff there exists some objective literal L of P such that there is a successful T-Tree for L and a successful T-Tree for ¬L.*

The above definition is directly presented for extended programs. But since extended programs are a generalization of normal ones, and in these *WFSX* coincides with WFS, the definitions also characterize the WFM of normal programs. However, for such programs some simplifications can be made. Namely, and since proofs of literals of the form ¬L fail in normal programs (and hence *not* ¬L literals succeed), point 3 can be simplified to:

> *A leaf node n in a T-Tree (resp. TU-Tree) labeled with the literal not A is successful if all TU-Trees (resp. T-Trees) with root A are failed;*

and, furthermore, in the construction of TU-Tree the additional sucessors are not needed.

Theorem 10.1.3 (Correctness wrt WFS). *The above method, even with the prescribed simplifications, is correct with respect to the well-founded semantics of normal programs.*

10.2 SLX – a derivation procedure for *WFSX*

Based on the above semantic tree characterization, we can easily proceed to define a top-down derivation for *WFSX*, SLX(where X stands for eXtended, and SL stands for Selected Linear). This is done in the usual way, where expansion of tree nodes is equated with replacement of a goal in a resolvent, success is equated with refutation, etc.

Given the similarities of the semantic tree characterization and SLX, we present the SLX definition directly, without any further considerations on the way it is defined. The rest of this section is devoted to the correctness proofs of SLX.

Definition 10.2.1 (SLX-T-derivation). *Let P be an extended program, and R an arbitrary but fixed computational rule. A SLX-T-derivation*

$$G_0, G_1, \ldots$$

for G in P via R is defined as follows: $G_0 = G$. Let G_i be

$$\leftarrow L_1, \ldots, L_n$$

and suppose that R selects the literal L_k $(1 \leq k \leq n)$. Then:

− if L_k is an objective literal, and the input rule is

$$L_k \leftarrow B_1, \ldots, B_m$$

the derived goal is

$$\leftarrow L_1, \ldots, L_{k-1}, B_1, \ldots, B_m, L_{k+1}, \ldots L_n.$$

- *if L_k is not A then, if there is a SLX-T-refutation for $\neg A$ in P or there is no SLX-TU-refutation for A in P, the derived goal is:*

$$\leftarrow L_1, \ldots, L_{k-1}, L_{k+1}, \ldots L_n$$

- *otherwise G_i is the last goal in the derivation.*

Definition 10.2.2 (SLX-TU-derivation). *Let P be an extended program, and R an arbitrary but fixed computational rule. A SLX-T-derivation*

$$G_0, G_1, \ldots$$

for G in P via R is defined as follows: $G_0 = G$. Let G_i be $\leftarrow L_1, \ldots, L_n$ and suppose that R selects the literal L_k $(1 \leq k \leq n)$. Then:

- *if L_k is an objective literal then*
  - *if there exists a SLX-T-refutation for $\neg L_k$ then G_i is the last goal in the derivation.*
  - *otherwise, if the input rule is*
      $$L_k \leftarrow B_1, \ldots, B_m$$
      the derived goal is
          $$\leftarrow L_1, \ldots, L_{k-1}, B_1, \ldots, B_m, L_{k+1}, \ldots L_n$$
  - *if there is no rule for L_k then G_i is the last goal in the derivation.*
- *if L_k is not A then:*
  - *if there is a SLX-T-refutation for $\leftarrow A$ in P then G_i is the last goal in the derivation.*
  - *if all SLX-T-derivations for $\leftarrow A$ are SLX-T-failures then the derived goal is*
      $$\leftarrow L_1, \ldots, L_{k-1}, L_{k+1}, \ldots L_n.$$
  - *due to infinite recursion through default negation, it might happen that the previous cases are not enough to determine the derived goal. In such a case, by definition, the derived goal is also*
      $$\leftarrow L_1, \ldots, L_{k-1}, L_{k+1}, \ldots L_n.$$

Definition 10.2.3 (SLX refutation and failure). *A SLX-T-refutation (resp. SLX-TU-refutation) for G in P is a finite SLX-T-derivation (resp. SLX-TU-derivation) which ends in the empty goal $(\leftarrow \Box)$.*

A SLX-T-derivation (resp. SLX-TU-derivation) for G in P is a SLX-T-failure iff it is not a refutation, i.e. it is infinite or it ends with a goal other than the empty goal.

10.2.1 Correctness of SLX

In order to prove the soundness, and theoretical completeness of the SLX derivation procedure, we assign ranks to derivations. The proofs of correctness essentially rely on two lemmas proven by transfinite induction on the rank of derivations. To trim the proof we begin by making some simplifications in the above definitions of derivations:

In Definition 10.2.1 of SLX-T-derivation one possible way of removing a selected default literal *not A* from a goal is to find a SLX-T-refutation for $\leftarrow \neg A$. However this case is redundant. Note that the other case for removing *not A* is when there is no SLX-TU-refutation for $\leftarrow A$. But Definition 10.2.2 states that in a SLX-TU-derivation, if there is a SLX-T-refutation for the explicit complement of a selected objective literal then the goal is the last in the derivation. Thus, if there is a SLX-T-refutation for $\leftarrow \neg A$, the only SLX-TU-derivation for $\leftarrow A$ is this single goal and is a failure, and so, even when not considering the first possibility, *not A* is nevertheless removed from the goal. Thus, in Definition 10.2.1 the case $L_k = not\ A$ can be simplified to: *if there is no SLX-TU-refutation for A in P then the derived goal is*

$$\leftarrow L_1, \ldots, L_{k-1}, L_{k+1}, \ldots L_n$$

Now let's look at the cases for a selected objective literal L_k in Definition 10.2.2. Clearly the first one corresponds to introducing $not\ \neg L_k$ in the derived goal. This is so because if there is a SLX-T-refutation for $\leftarrow \neg L$ the derivation will become a failure (and this is equivalent to the first case), and if there is no such refutation it is simply removed (and this is equivalent to the second case). Consequently, in Definition 10.2.2 we remove the first case for a selected objective literal, keep the third, and modify the second to: *if the input rule is* $L_k \leftarrow B_1, \ldots, B_m$ *the derived goal is*

$$\leftarrow L_1, \ldots, L_{k-1}, not\ \neg L_k, B_1, \ldots, B_m, L_{k+1}, \ldots L_n$$

Now we assign ranks to these simplified derivations. As the proofs shall show, we do not need to assign a rank neither to SLX-T-failures nor to SLX-TU-refutations. These do not contribute towards proving literals that belong to the WFM[5].

Intuitively, the rank of a SLX-T-refutation reflects the depth of "calls" of subsidiary derivations that are considered in the refutation. Its definition, below, can be seen as first assigning to each literal removed from a goal an associated rank. When removing an objective literal no subsidiary derivation is considered, and so the rank is not affected. The empty goal has rank 0. When removing a default literal, the depth of subsidiary derivations that has to be considered is the maximum (more precisely, the least upper bound for the infinite case) of the depth of all SLX-TU-failures[6]. The depth needed

---

[5] This is tantamount to having no need to assign a rank to indetermined nodes in [195].

[6] Note that for removing a default literal all SLX-TU-failures must be considered. This is the reason behind "maximum".

for finally removing all literals from a goal is the maximum of the ranks associated with each of the literals in the goal.

Definition 10.2.4 (Rank of a SLX-T-refutation). *The rank of a SLX-T-refutation is the rank of its first goal. Ranks of goals in the refutation are:*

- *The rank of* $\leftarrow \Box$ *is 0.*
- *Let* G_i *be a goal in a refutation whose next selected literal is objective. The rank of* G_i *is the rank of* G_{i+1}.
- *Let* G_i *be a goal in a refutation whose next selected literal is a default one, not* L, *and let* α *be the least ordinal upper bound (i.e. maximum in the finite case) of the ranks of the SLX-TU-failures for* $\leftarrow L$[7]. *The rank of* G_i *is the maximum of* α *and the rank of* G_{i+1}.

Ranks of SLX-TU-failures reflect the depth of "calls" that is needed to fail the subsidiary derivations. Note that the failure of a derivation is uniquely determined by the last goal in it, and more precisely by its selected literal. If that literal is objective then no subsidiary derivation is needed to fail it, and thus its rank is 0. For failing a default literal *not L* one has to find a SLX-T-refutation for $\leftarrow L$. Several might exist, but it is enough to consider the one with minimum depth. Moreover, in this case one has to increment the rank, since the default literal *not L* was failed, and caused an extra "call". Note that, for SLX-T-refutations this increment is not considered. The issue of incrementing the rank only for one kind of derivations is tantamount to that of considering the increment of levels of I_is in the sequence for constructing the WFM only after the application of the two operators, Γ and Γ_s, defined in Section 6.7.

Definition 10.2.5 (Rank of a SLX-TU-failure).
An infinite SLX-TU-failure has rank 0. The rank of a finite SLX-TU-failure is the rank of its last goal. Let G_n *be the last goal of the derivation, and* L_k *be its selected literal:*

- *if* L_k *is an objective literal then the rank is 0.*
- *if* L_k *is a default literal, not A, then the rank is* $\alpha + 1$, *where* α *is the minimum of the ranks of all SLX-T-refutations for* $\leftarrow A$.

The following lemma is used in the proofs of correctness. This lemma relates the existence of sequences where some default literals are removed to the Γ operator by which some default literals are removed from the body of rules:

Lemma 10.2.1. *Let* I *be an interpretation, and let* $(\leftarrow L), G_1, \ldots$ *be a sequence of goals constructed as per Definition 10.2.2 (resp. Definition 10.2.1), except that selected default literals not* L_k *such that* $L_k \notin I$ *are immediately removed from goals. Then:* $L \in \Gamma_s I$ *(resp.* $L \in \Gamma I$) *iff the sequence is finite and ends with the empty goal.*

---

[7] Since we are in a SLX-T-refutation, all SLX-TU-derivations for $\leftarrow L$ are failures.

Proof. Here we omit the proof for $L \in \Gamma I$ with Definition 10.2.1, which is similar. If $L \in \Gamma_s I$ then, as per the definition of Γ_s, there must exist a finite set of rules in $\frac{P_s}{I}$ such that L belongs to its least model. According to the definition of $\frac{P_s}{I}$ and of semi-normal program, there is a finite set of rules in P such that for each default literal *not L* in their bodies $L \notin I$, and for each such rule with head H, $\neg H \notin I$. Let P^* be the subset of P formed by those rules. The only default literals to be considered by Definition 10.2.2 will be those in the bodies, plus the default negations of $\neg$-complements of the heads of rules used in the derivation. So, given the completeness of SL-resolution[8] [118], and the fact that all these introduced literals are not in I (as shown above), a sequence of goals considering only the rules in the finite P^* exists and ends in $\leftarrow \square$. Thus the least model of $\frac{P^*}{I}$ contains L.

Lemma 10.2.2. *Let P be a noncontradictory extended logic program, L an objective literal, and $\{I_\alpha\}$ be the sequence constructed for the WFM of P, according to the WFSX definition in Section 6.7. In that case:*

1. *if there is a SLX-T-refutation for $\leftarrow L$ in P with rank $< i$ then $L \in I_i$.*
2. *if all SLX-TU-derivations for $\leftarrow L$ in P are failures with rank $\leq i$ then $L \notin \Gamma_s I_i$.*

Proof. For point 1, by transfinite induction on i(for point 2 the proof is similar, and omitted here for brevity):

i is a limit ordinal δ: Assume that there is a SLX-T-refutation for $\leftarrow L$ with rank $< \delta$. Thus, there is a $\alpha < \delta$ for which such a refutation exists with rank $< \alpha$. Then, $\exists_{\alpha < \delta} L \in I_\alpha$. Thus, $L \in \bigcup_{\alpha < \delta} I_\alpha$, i.e. $L \in I_\delta$.

Induction step: If there is a SLX-T-refutation for $\leftarrow L$ with rank $< i+1$ then, by definition of ranks for these refutations, all subsidiary derivations for default literals *not L_j* in the refutation are failed and of rank $< i + 1$ (and thus $\leq i$) and are simply removed. So, given point 2, $\forall j, L_j \notin \Gamma_s I_i$. From lemma 10.2.1, by tacking there the interpretation $I = \Gamma_s I_i$, and by removing all *not L_j* literals, it follows that $L \in \Gamma\Gamma_s I_i$, i.e. $L \in I_{i+1}$.

Theorem 10.2.1 (Soundness of SLX). *Let P be a noncontradictory extended logic program, L an arbitrary literal from P. If there is an SLX-T-refutation for $\leftarrow L$ in P then $L \in WFM(P)$.*

Proof. If L is an objective literal, then the result follows immediately from lemma 10.2.2, and the monotonicity of $\Gamma\Gamma_s$.

Let $L = not\ A$. If there is a SLX-T-refutation for $\leftarrow not\ A$ with rank i then, by definition of SLX-T-refutation, all SLX-TU-derivations for $\leftarrow A$ are failures of rank $\leq i$. By point 2 of lemma 10.2.2, $A \notin \Gamma_s I_i$.

Let M be the least fixpoint of $\Gamma\Gamma_s$. Given that $\Gamma\Gamma_s$ is monotonic, $I_i \subseteq M$, i.e. for any objective literal A, $A \in I_i \Rightarrow A \in M$. By antimonotonicity of Γ_s,

---

[8] For definite programs both T and TU derivations reduce to SL-derivation.

$A \in \Gamma_s M \Rightarrow A \in \Gamma_s I_i$. Thus, since $A \notin \Gamma_s I_i$, $A \notin \Gamma_s M$ i.e., by definition of the WFM, *not* $A \in WFM(P)$.

Given the soundness of *WFSX* with respect to the answer-sets semantics (Theorem 9.2.2) and the soundness of SLX with respect to *WFSX*, it follows easily that SLX can be used as a sound derivation procedure for the answer-sets semantics.

Corollary 10.2.1 (Soundness wrt answer-sets). *Let P be an extended logic program with at least one answer-set, and L an arbitrary objective literal from P. If there is an SLX-T-refutation for $\leftarrow L$ in P then L belongs to all answer-sets of P. If there is an SLX-T-refutation for $\leftarrow$ not L in P then there is no answer-set of P with L.*

Next we prove the theoretical completeness of SLX. To do so we begin by presenting a lemma that, like lemma 10.2.1 (and with a similar proof), relates sequences with the Γ operator. Then we prove completeness for objective literals by transfinite induction on the ranks for a particular class of selection rules. Finally we lift this restriction, and prove completeness also for default literals.

Lemma 10.2.3. *Let I be an interpretation, and L an objective literal. If $L \notin \Gamma_s I$ (resp. $L \notin \Gamma I$) then each possible sequence of goals starting with $\leftarrow L$ and constructed as per Definition 10.2.2 (resp. Definition 10.2.1), except that selected default literals not L_k such that $L_k \notin I$ are immediately removed from goals, is either: infinite; ends with a goal where the selected literal is objective; ends with a goal where the selected literal is not A and $A \in I$.*

Lemma 10.2.4. *Let P be an extended logic program, L an objective literal, and $\{I_\alpha\}$ be the sequence constructed for the WFM of P. Then, there exists a selection rule R such that:*

1. *if $L \in I_i$ then there is a SLX-T-refutation for $\leftarrow L$ in P with rank $< i$.*
2. *if $L \notin \Gamma_s I_i$ then all SLX-TU-derivations for $\leftarrow L$ in P are failures with rank $\leq i$.*

Proof. Let R be a selection rule that begins by selecting all objective literals, and then default ones subject to that it selects a *not L* before a *not L'* if there is a j in the sequence of the $\{I_\alpha\}$ such that $L \notin \Gamma_s I_j$ and $L' \in \Gamma_s I_j$.

By transfinite induction on i:

i is a limit ordinal δ: For point 1 the proof is similar to the one presented in lemma 10.2.2 when $i = \delta$.

For point 2 assume that $L \notin \Gamma_s I_\delta$. By lemma 10.2.3, making the I in that lemma equal to I_δ, each SLX-TU-derivation for $\leftarrow L$ is either: infinite, and in this case a failure of rank 0; ends with a goal where the selected literal is objective, i.e. a failure of rank 0; ends with a goal where the selected literal is *not A* and $A \in I_\delta$. In this case, and given that point 1 is already proven for $i = \delta$, there is a SLX-T-refutation for $\leftarrow A$ with rank $< \alpha$ such that $\alpha < \delta$. Thus, and according to the definition of ranks, the rank of this derivation is $\leq \delta$.

Note that, by considering the special selection rule R in the sequences mentioned in lemma 10.2.3, these become indeed equal to derivations, where the *not* L_k such that $L_k \not\in I_\delta$ are never selected.

Induction step: Assume points 1 and 2 of the lemma hold. We begin by proving that point 1 also holds for $i + 1$.

Assume that $L \in \Gamma\Gamma_s I_i$. By lemma 10.2.1, there exists a sequence ending with the empty goal, constructed as per Definition 10.2.1, except that selected default literals *not* L_k such that $L_k \not\in \Gamma_s I_i$ are immediately removed from goals. By point 2, for any L_k, all SLX-TU-derivations for $\leftarrow L_k$ are failures with rank $\leq i$. Therefore the sequence is a refutation. Moreover its rank is $\leq i$ and thus also $< i$. This proves point 1.

Now we prove that point 2 also holds for $i + 1$. Assume that $L \not\in \Gamma_s I_{i+1}$. By lemma 10.2.3, considering the I in that lemma equal to I_{i+1}, each SLX-TU-derivation for $\leftarrow L$ is either: infinite, and in this case a failure of rank 0; ends with a goal where the selected literal is objective, i.e. a failure of rank 0; ends with a goal where the selected literal is *not A* and $A \in I_{i+1}$. In this case, and given that point 1 is already proven, there is a SLX-T-refutation for $\leftarrow A$ with rank $< i + 1$. Thus, and according to the definition of ranks, the rank of this derivation is $< i + 2$, i.e. $\leq i + 1$. The argument for saying that the sequences of lemma 10.2.3 are derivation is similar to the one used above for limit ordinals.

Mark that, in the proof of point 1 above, we never use the special selection rule R. Thus, for SLX-T-derivations an arbitrary selection rule can be used.

Moreover, in point 2, the only usage of R is to guarantee that the rank of all SLX-TU-failures is indeed $\leq i$. This is needed for proving the lemma by induction. However, it is clear that if by using R all SLX-TU-derivations are failures, although with a possibly greater rank, the same happens with an arbitrary selection rule[9]. This is why there is no need to consider the special selection rule in the theorem below.

Theorem 10.2.2 (Theoretical completeness of SLX). *Let P be a non-contradictory extended program, and L an arbitrary literal from P. If $L \in WFM(P)$ then there exists a SLX-T-refutation for $\leftarrow L$ in P.*

Proof. If L is an objective literal the proof follows from lemma 10.2.4.

Let $L = not\ A$. By definition of WFM there exists an ordinal λ such that I_λ is the least fixpoint of $\Gamma\Gamma_s$. Thus, again by definition of WFM, $A \not\in \Gamma_s I_\lambda$, and by point 2 of lemma 10.2.4 all SLX-TU-derivations for $\leftarrow A$ in P are

---

[9] Literals involved in infinite recursion through negation do not give rise to SLX-TU-failures.

failures. Consequently, the SLX-T-derivation consisting of the single goal ←
not A is a refutation.

This theorem requires one to know "a priori" whether the program is
contradictory. However this is not problematic since SLX can detect contradictions:

Theorem 10.2.3 (Contradictory programs). *If P is contradictory, there
exists a* $L \in \mathcal{H}$ *for which there are SLX-T-refutations for both* ← *L and*
← ¬*L.*

10.3 On guaranteeing termination of SLX

Although sound and complete for *WFSX*, SLX is not effective (even for finite ground programs). In fact, and because it furnishes no mechanism for
detecting loops, termination is not guaranteed. Completeness here is only
ideal completeness. In order to provide an effective implementation of SLX
we have first to tackle the issue of guaranteeing termination.

As for the WFS of normal programs, *WFSX* too is in general not computable. Thus, it is not possible to guarantee termination in the general case.
In this section we modify SLX such that termination is guaranteed (at least)
for finite ground programs[10].

This modified SLX procedure can be easily implemented via a Prolog
meta-interpreter[11]. Due to its SLDNF-resemblance, it has also been rather
easy to implement a pre-processor that compiles *WFSX* programs into Prolog, using a format corresponding to the specialization of the interpreter rules,
plus a small number of general "built-in" predicates. The code of the preprocessor is available from the authors on request.

To guarantee termination (at least) for finite ground programs, we introduce rules that prune SLX-derivations, and eliminate both cyclic positive
recursion and cyclic recursion through negation by default (hereafter simply
called cyclic negative recursion).

To detect both kinds of cyclic recursions we use two kinds of derivation
ancestors:

– *Local ancestors* are assigned to literals in the goals of a derivation, and are
used for detecting cyclic positive recursion. For the purpose of including
local ancestors, we replace literals in goals by pairs $L_i : S_i$, where L_i is a
literal and S_i is the set of its local ancestors.

---

[10] The technique we're about to define also guarantees termination for allowed
bounded-term nonground programs. The discussion of guaranteeing termination
for these cases is, however, beyond the scope of this work.

[11] This can be simply done by mimicking the definition of SLX-derivations with
ancestors, considering a left-most selection rule, and is presented in Appendix
A.

– *Global ancestors* are assigned to derivations, and are used to detect cyclic negative recursion.

Intuitively, and if one thinks of a derivation as the expanding of an AND-tree, the local ancestors of a literal's occurrence are the literals appearing in the path from the root of the tree to that occurrence.

Global ancestors of a subsidiary derivation are the local ancestors of the literal L that invoked it, plus the ancestor goal of the derivation in which L appears. The top-goal derivation has no global ancestors. Moreover we divide global ancestors into two sets: global T-ancestors and global TU-ancestors. Global T-ancestors (resp. TU-ancestors) are those that were introduced in a SLX-T-derivation (resp. SLX-TU-derivation).

To deal with the non-termination problem of cyclic positive recursion it suffices to guarantee that no such infinite derivations are generated. This can be achieved if no selected literal belonging to its set of local ancestor is ever expanded. It leads to the following pruning rule:

1. Let G_i be a goal in a SLX-derivation (either T or TU), and let L_k be the literal selected by R. If L_k belongs to its local ancestors then G_i is the last goal in the derivation.

To treat cyclic negative recursion, tests over the global ancestors are necessary. It is easily shown that any form of this recursion reduces to one of four combination cases, depending on the cycle occurring between the two possible derivation types. In SLX-TU-derivations the selected literal is removed from the goal, and in SLX-T-derivations the goal is the last in the derivation. Moreover, all these combinations can be reduced to just one:

Lemma 10.3.1 (Reduction of negative cycles). *All cyclic negative recursions can be detected in SLX-T-derivations by looking only at its global T-ancestors.*

The same does not hold for any other combination case, i.e. there are cycles that are only detectable with the test of lemma 10.3.1:

Example 10.3.1. The negative cycle in P :

$$a \leftarrow not\ b$$
$$b \leftarrow not\ a$$

is not detectable by only testing if goals in a SLX-T-derivation belong to its global TU-ancestors, nor by only testing if literals in a SLX-TU-derivation belong to its global T-ancestors.

The following derivations are constructed:

SLX-T-der.	SLX-TU-der.	SLX-T-der.	SLX-TU-der.	
$\leftarrow a$	$\leftarrow b$	$\leftarrow a$	$\leftarrow b$	...
$\leftarrow not\ b$	$\leftarrow not\ a$	$\leftarrow not\ b$	$\leftarrow not\ a$	

and no ocurrence of the objective literal a in the SLX-T-derivations appears in the SLX-TU-derivations. The same is applicable to b but exchanging SLX-T-derivations with SLX-TU-derivations. Notice that all SLX-T-derivations for $\neg a$ are failed.

Only testing whether literals in SLX-TU-derivations belong to its global TU-ancestors does not detect the recursion in:

$$\neg a \quad \leftarrow \quad not\ a$$
$$\neg a$$

because successive SLX-T-derivations ($\leftarrow \neg a$, $\leftarrow not\ a$) are generated.

Lemma 10.3.1 yields pruning rule 2:

2. Let G_i be a goal in a SLX-T-derivation, and let L_k be the literal selected by R. If L_k belongs to the set of global T-ancestors then G_i is the last goal in the derivation.

Theorem 10.3.1 (Elimination of cyclic recursion for WFSX).
Pruning rules 1 and 2 are necessary and sufficient for guaranteeing that all positive and negative cyclic recursions are eliminated.

We now embed these two pruning rules in the definitions of SLX-derivation (refutations and failures remain as before). Note that the pruning rules do not make use of TU-ancestors. So they will not be considered in the definitions:

Definition 10.3.1 (SLX-T-derivation with ancestors).
Let P be an extended program, and R an arbitrary but fixed computational rule. A SLX-T-derivation $G_0, G_1, \ldots$ for G in P via R, with T-ancestors ST is defined as follows: $G_0 = G : \{\}$. Let G_i be $\leftarrow L_1 : S_1, \ldots, L_n : S_n$ and suppose that R selects $L_k : S_k$ ($1 \leq k \leq n$). Then:

– if L_k is an objective literal, $L_k \notin S_k \cup ST$, and the input rule is

$$L_k \leftarrow B_1, \ldots, B_m$$

the derived goal is

$$\leftarrow L_1 : S_1, \ldots, L_{k-1} : S_{k-1}, B_1 : S', \ldots, B_m : S',$$
$$L_{k+1} : S_{k+1}, \ldots L_n : S_n$$

where $S' = S_k \cup \{L_k\}$.

– if L_k is not A then, if there is a SLX-T-refutation for $\leftarrow \neg A : \{\}$ in P with T-ancestors $ST \cup S_k$, or there is no SLX-TU-refutation for $\leftarrow A : \{\}$ in P with the same ancestors, the derived goal is

$$\leftarrow L_1 : S_1, \ldots, L_{k-1} : S_{k-1}, L_{k+1} : S_{k+1}, \ldots L_n : S_n.$$

– otherwise G_i is the last goal in the derivation.

Definition 10.3.2 (SLX-TU-derivation with ancestors). *Let P be an extended program, and R an arbitrary but fixed computational rule. A SLX-TU-derivation $G_0, G_1, \ldots$ for G in Γ via R, with T-ancestors ST is defined as follows: $G_0 = G : \{\}$. Let G_i be $\leftarrow L_1, \ldots, L_n$ and suppose that R selects $L_k : S_k$ $(1 \leq k \leq n)$. Then:*

- *if L_k is an objective literal then*
    - *if $L_k \in S_k$ or there is no rule for L_k then G_i is the last goal in the derivation.*
    - *else if there exists a SLX-T-refutation for $\leftarrow \neg L_k : \{\}$ with T-ancestors ST then G_i is the last goal in the derivation.*
    - *otherwise, if the input rule is $L_k \leftarrow B_1, \ldots, B_m$ the derived goal is:*
        $$\leftarrow L_1 : S_1, \ldots, L_{k-1} : S_{k-1}, B_1 : S', \ldots, B_m : S',$$
        $$L_{k+1} : S_{k+1}, \ldots L_n : S_n$$
      where $S' = S_k \cup \{L_k\}$.
- *if L_k is not A then:*
    - *if there is a SLX-T-refutation for $\leftarrow A : \{\}$ in P with T-ancestors ST then G_i is the last goal in the derivation.*
    - *otherwise the derived goal is*

    $$\leftarrow L_1 : S_1, \ldots, L_{k-1} : S_{k-1}, L_{k+1} : S_{k+1}, \ldots L_n : S_n.$$

Theorem 10.3.2 (Correctness for SLX with ancestors). *Let P be a noncontradictory extended program. Then:*

- *If $L \in WFM(P)$ then there is a SLX-T-refutation for $\leftarrow L : \{\}$ with empty T-ancestors. Moreover, all the subsidiary derivations needed in the refutation are finite, and in finite number.*
- *If $L \notin WFM(P)$ then all SLX-T-derivations for $\leftarrow L : \{\}$ with empty T-ancestors are finite and end with a goal different from $\leftarrow \square$. Moreover, all the subsidiary derivations needed are finite, and in finite number.*

Proof. Follows from Theorems 10.3.1, 10.2.1, and 10.2.2.

10.4 Comparisons

To the best of our knowledge [205] is the only paper in the literature that addresses the topic of proof procedures for extended logic programs. The author uses the notion of conservative derivability [211] as the proof-theoretic semantics for extended programs. The paper provides a program transformation from such programs to normal ones. Then it is proved that Kunen semantics [109] applied to the transformed program is sound and complete with respect to conservative derivability. This approach has several problems mainly motivated by the interpretation of default negation as finite failure as recognized by the author. For instance, in the program $\{a \leftarrow a\}$ the literal $\neg a$ is false but a is undefined, contrary to the results obtained by answer sets and WFSX where *not a* is true. As a final remark, conservative derivability is not defined for programs with functor symbols. Therefore the approach is only applicable to extended programs without functor symbols. *WFSX* solves all these problems properly.

From now on we will restrict our comparisons to the scope of normal logic programs. We start by considering SLDNF-resolution [42, 118]. The non termination problems of SLDNF, even for finite ground programs, motivated the development of the semantics that correctly handles both types of infinite recursion (positive and negative). Przymusinski in [178] showed that SLDNF is sound with respect to WFS, i.e. it can be seen as a crude approximation to WFS. Our method can be seen as a generalization of SLDNF, because all recursion problems are reduced to and solved with the notions of failure and success of trees, interpreting *not L* true in SLX-T-derivations (resp. SLX-TU-derivations) when all possible SLX-TU-derivations for *L* (resp. SLX-T-derivations) fail. This (re-)understanding of *not* greatly simplifies the construction of meta-interpreters and enables the compilation of logic programs directly into Prolog code.

Przymusinski in [178] introduced SLS-resolution, which extends SLDNF to stratified programs. This is achieved by understanding negation by default as negation as (possibly infinite) failure, instead of finite failure. An extension of SLS for normal programs is defined in [177] but assumes the existence of the dynamic stratification. Przymusinski argues that the use of dynamic stratification made is effectively computable in some cases and reduces to avoiding negative recursion in the derivations. But the author doesn't show how this can be implemented in practice. Further extensions of this work [175, 185, 195] implicitly or explicitly assume a positivistic selection rule that selects negative literals in parallel as stated in [16]. For more details the reader is referred to [16]. The definition of SLX doesn't impose any order on the selection of the literals, i.e. it is independent of the selection rule.

Apt and Bol [16] present a definition of SLS that deals with all general programs and all selection rules. Their approach rests on the definition of oracle SLS-trees. But to build such trees it is necessary to know the WFM "a priori". Then they define a SLS-tree as the limit of a sequence of oracle SLS-trees. The authors argue that the use of the WFM to solve default literals will be justified "at the end" in the SLS-tree. We don't agree with this claim because in the SLS-tree undefined default literals will justify themselves, i.e. if there is recursion through negation then it is necessary to know the WFM in order to "determine" the WFM. However, as recognized by the authors, it is not at all clear how these trees could be constructed in a top-down way.

A top-down procedure for finite ground programs was presented in [155]. This procedure suffers from severe efficiency problems. When expanding a *not* goal an exponential number of resolvents in the size of the program can be generated, because all (minimal) combinations of literals are generated for failing all the rule bodies for the literal of a default goal, and so a procedure that has polynomial complexity turns out to be exponential. Also, the procedure is not easily extendable to handle infinite ground programs because infinite resolvents can be generated. Furthermore, simple extensions of this procedure to the nonground case introduce more floundering problems then SLX.

Another way of detecting loops is to use tabulation techniques. Several approaches use them to define query evaluation procedures for WFS. These methods are more general than ours in the case of function free nonground programs, but for important classes of normal programs the aforesaid techniques are unnecessary. Our main criticism is that they do not draw a clear border between their use of tabulation and the overall method incorporating it.

These techniques were first defined for stratified programs where only one table needs to be constructed to deal with positive recursions. For normal programs, subsequent methods introduce rather complicated mathematical structures to deal with negative recursion [24, 40].

Bol and Degerstedt's [27] method constructs only one table but the treatment of negation by default literals supposes them undefined at first, only to be forced to a complex filtering stage later.

For further and more extended comparisons, the reader is referred to [16] and [41] which defines SLG resolution. SLG relies on program transformations based on modular partial evaluation rewrite rules for top-down query evaluation under WFS; it focuses on positive goals, and delays nonground negative ones.

The notion of doubled program was first introduced in [97] but in the context of bottom-up evaluation. They showed that magic-sets transformations do not preserve well-founded semantics and described a technique in [98] applicable to the class of normal programs.

Eshgi and Kowalski's abductive procedure [70], corrected in [62], is sound with respect to preferred extensions. In spite of not treating positive recursion and non-cyclic negative recursion, it has several similarities with our method. The "abductive derivations" and "consistency derivations" resemble our SLX-T-derivations and SLX-TU-derivations. The big difference is in how negative cyclic recursion is treated: they succeed abductive derivations when the former kind of recursion is detected. Accordingly, they do not compute the WFM, but the preferred extensions of [62].

10.5 Further developments

In theory, SLX is only applicable to (infinite) ground programs. A natural required generalization of SLX is that for nonground programs.

A straightforward generalization method for nonground programs would be to proceed as usual in the expansion of goals with rule variants, and keeping the test for inclusion in the ancestors lists. However it has two problems: first, as shown in [17], this loop detection method does not guarantee termination in the nonground case, even for term-bounded programs; second, the procedure flounders on nonground default literals. Nevertheless, its correctness and termination are guaranteed for call-consistent term-bounded programs.

To guarantee termination for nonground term-bounded programs, we intend to introduce tabulation methods into SLX[12]. Another subject of future work is that of introducing in SLX constructive negation techniques for solving the floundering problem.

The present SLX implementation relies on a top-down left-to-right search strategy. However, and since our procedure imposes no restrictions on the way goals are selected from the resolvent, other search strategies can be used. In particular, we are keen on the application of sidetracking based search strategies.

The sidetracking principle is an instance of the principle of procrastination, advising postponement of the problematic until the inevitable has been dealt with. A sidetracking strategy for definite programs was first detailed in [165], where determinate calls (i.e. those that unify with at most one rule head) are executed first. The same approach can be applied in the context of SLX. Moreover, nonground default literals can be postponed, so that the floundering problem may be abated; notably there are cases of determinate nonground default literal calls, e.g. *not* $p(X)$ where $p(X)$ as no rules, that need not be postponed.

---

[12] Mark that by being cumulative, *WFSX* is amenable to such methods. In fact, tabulation requires the addition of intermidiate lemmas, i.e. it requires cumulativity.

Part III

Illustrative Examples of Application

11. Application to classical nonmonotonic reasoning problems

In this chapter we show how to cast in the language of extended logic programs different forms of nonmonotonic reasoning such as defeasible reasoning, abductive reasoning and hypothetical reasoning, and apply it to diverse domains of knowledge representation such as hierarchies and reasoning about actions.

Our main purpose in this chapter is to abstract out and exhibit a modular and systematic method of representing nonmonotonic reasoning problems with the above presented contradiction removal semantics. We argue that logic programming extended with the concept of undefinedness and a suitable form of explicit negation, is very rich to represent such problems.

This chapter is organized as follows: First we identify simple forms of commonsense reasoning (e.g. defeasible reasoning with exceptions, hypothetical reasoning) and show how they are represented by extended logic programs. Using the notion of defeasibility and exception rules we then show how to formalize hierarchical reasoning where exceptions are also present. Next we represent problems where hypothetical reasoning is used to capture brave reasoning.

Afterwards we use our approach to represent additional classical non-monotonic problems in reasoning about actions, arguing that it is sufficiently generic. Finally, we show how to cast counterfactual reasoning.

11.1 Summary of our representation method

In this section we summarize and systematize the representation method adopted in all examples in this chapter. The type of rules for which we propose a representation is, in our view, general enough to capture a wide domain of nonmonotonic problems. Each type of rule is described in a subsection by means of a schema in natural language and its corresponding representation rule.

- **Definite Rules** *If A then B.* The representation is: $B \leftarrow A$.
- **Definite Facts** *A is true.* The representation is: A. *A is false.*
  The representation is: $\neg A$.

- **Defeasible (or maximally applicable) Rules** *Normally if A then B.* The representation is:

$$B \quad \leftarrow \quad A, not\ ab.$$

where *not ab* is a new predicate symbol. As an example consider the rule "Normally birds fly". Its representation is:

$$fly(X) \quad \leftarrow \quad bird(X), not\ ab(X).$$

- *Defeasible Facts* are a special case of *Defeasible Rules* where A is absent.
- **Exceptions to Defeasible Rules** *Under certain conditions COND there are exceptions to the defeasible rule* $H_1 \leftarrow B_1, not\ ab_1$.

$$ab_1 \leftarrow COND.$$

As an example, the representation of the exception "Penguins are exceptions to the "normally birds fly" rule (i.e. rule $f \leftarrow b, not\ abb$)" is:

$$abb \leftarrow penguin.$$

Preference rules are a special kind of exception to defeasible rules:
- **Preference Rules** *Under conditions COND, prefer to apply the defeasible rule* $H_1 \leftarrow B_1, not\ ab_1$ *instead of the defeasible rule* $H_2 \leftarrow B_2, not\ ab_2$.

$$ab_1 \leftarrow COND, not\ ab_2.$$

As an example consider "For penguins, if the rule that says "normally penguins don't fly" is applicable then inhibit the "normally birds fly" rule". This is represented as:

$$ab\_b \leftarrow penguin(X), not\ ab\_penguin(X).$$

- **Unknown Possible Fact** *F might be true or not* (in other words, the possibility or otherwise of F should be considered).

$$F \quad \leftarrow \quad not\ \neg F.$$
$$\neg F \quad \leftarrow \quad not\ F.$$

- **Hypothetical (or possibly applicable) Rules** *Rule "If A then B" may or may not apply.* Its representation is:

$$B \quad \leftarrow \quad A, hyp$$
$$hyp \quad \leftarrow \quad not\ \neg hyp$$
$$\neg hyp \quad \leftarrow \quad not\ hyp$$

where *hyp* is a new predicate symbol. As an example consider the rule "Quakers might be pacifists". Its representation is:

$$pacifist(X) \leftarrow quaker(X), hypqp(X).$$

$$hypqp(X) \quad \leftarrow \quad not\ \neg hypqp(X).$$
$$\neg hypqp(X) \quad \leftarrow \quad not\ hypqp(X).$$

11.2 Defeasible Reasoning

In this section we show how to represent defeasible reasoning with logic programs extended with explicit negation. We want to express defeasible reasoning and give a meaning to sets of rules, (some of them being defeasible) when contradiction arises from the application of the defeasible rules. In this case we suggest how to explicitly represent exceptions and preference rules. We do not intend to address the problem of automatic generation of exception rules or preference rules[1] in order to restore consistency, but only to show how exceptions and preferences may be represented in the language. For instance, we want to represent defeasible rules such as *birds normally fly* and *penguins normally don't fly*. Given a penguin, which is a bird, we adopt the skeptical point of view and none of the conflicting rules applies. Later on we show how to express preference for one rule over another in case they conflict and both are applicable. Consider for the moment a simpler version of this problem:

Example 11.2.1. Consider the statements:

> (*i*) *Normally birds fly.*   (*ii*) *Penguins don't fly.*
> (*iii*) *Penguins are birds.*   (*iv*) a *is a penguin.*

represented by the program P (with obvious abbreviations, where ab stands for abnormal):

$$
\begin{aligned}
f(X) &\leftarrow b(X), not\ ab(X) \quad &\text{(i)} \\
\neg f(X) &\leftarrow p(X) \quad &\text{(ii)} \\
b(X) &\leftarrow p(X) \quad &\text{(iii)} \\
p(a) \quad &&\text{(iv)}
\end{aligned}
$$

Since there are no rules for $ab(a)$, $not\ ab(a)$ holds and $f(a)$ follows. On the other hand we have $p(a)$ and $\neg f(a)$ follows from rule (ii). Thus the program is contradictory. In this case we argue that the first rule gives rise to a contradiction depending on the assumption of $not\ ab(a)$ and so must not conclude $f(a)$. The intended meaning requires $\neg f(a)$ and $not\ f(a)$. We say that in this case a revision occurs in predicate instance $ab(a)$, which must turn to be undefined. $not\ f(a)$ follows from $\neg f(a)$ in the semantics.

In this case the contradiction removal semantics identifies, when the revisables are $Rev = \{not\ ab(X)\}$, one contradiction removal set $CRS = \{not\ ab(a)\}$.

The corresponding minimally revised program (which in this case coincides with the sceptical revision) is

$$P \cup \{ab(a) \leftarrow not\ ab(a)\}$$

whose *WFSX* is:

$$\{p(a), not\ \neg p(a), b(a), not\ \neg b(a), \neg f(a), not\ f(a), not\ \neg ab(a)\}$$

---

[1] See [107] where an implicit preference for negative information over positive information is introduced in the semantics of logic program

In the example above the revision process is simple and the information to be revised is clearly the assumption about the abnormality predicate, and something can be said about a flying. However this is not always the case, as shown in the following example:

Example 11.2.2. Consider the following statements:

(i) *Normally birds fly.*   (ii) *Normally penguins don't fly.*
(iii) *Penguins are birds.*   *There is a penguin a, a bird b,*
                          and a rabbit c which does not fly.

The program P corresponding to this description is:

$$
\begin{array}{rcll}
f(X) & \leftarrow & b(X), not\ ab_1(X) & \text{(i)} \\
\neg f(X) & \leftarrow & p(X), not\ ab_2(X) & \text{(ii)} \\
b(X) & \leftarrow & p(X) & \text{(iii)}
\end{array}
\qquad
\begin{array}{c}
p(a) \\
b(b) \\
r(c) \\
\neg f(c)
\end{array}
$$

Remark 11.2.1. In program P above the facts and rule (iii) play the rôle of non-defeasible information, and should hold whichever the world view one may choose for the interpretation of P together with those facts.

– About the bird b everything is well defined and we have:

$$
\left\{
\begin{array}{l}
not\ p(b), \quad\ b(b),\ not\ r(b),\ not\ ab_1(b),\ not\ ab_2(b), \quad f(b) \\
not\ \neg p(b), not\ \neg b(b), not\ \neg r(b), not\ \neg ab_1(b), not\ \neg ab_2(b), not\ \neg f(b)
\end{array}
\right\}
$$

which says that bird b flies, $f(b)$, and it can't be shown it is a penguin, $not\ p(b)$. This is the intuitive result, since we may believe that b flies (because it is a bird) and it is not proven to be a penguin, and so rules (i) and (ii) are noncontradictory w.r.t. bird b.

– About the penguin a, the use of rules (i) and (ii) leads to a contradiction: by rule (i) we have $f(a)$ and by rule (ii) we have $\neg f(a)$. Thus nothing can be said for sure about a flying or not, and the only non-ambiguous conclusions we may infer are:

$$
\left\{
\begin{array}{l}
p(a), \quad\ b(a),\ not\ r(a), \\
not\ \neg p(a), not\ \neg b(a), not\ \neg r(a), not\ \neg ab_1(a), not\ \neg ab_2(a)
\end{array}
\right\}
$$

Note that we are being skeptical w.r.t. $ab_1(a)$ and $ab_2(a)$ whose negation by default would rise a contradiction.

– About c rules (i) and (ii) are noncontradiction producing since $not\ p(c)$ and $not\ b(c)$ both hold, and we have:

$$
\left\{
\begin{array}{l}
not\ p(c),\ not\ b(c), \quad\ r(c),\ not\ ab_1(c),\ not\ ab_2(c), \quad \neg f(c) \\
not\ \neg p(c), not\ \neg b(c), not\ \neg r(c), not\ \neg ab_1(c), not\ \neg ab_2(c), not\ f(c)
\end{array}
\right\}
$$

The view of the world given by the paraconsistent *WFSX* is[2]:

---

[2] Note that the difference between the paraconsistent *WFSX* presented and the set of literals considered as the intuitive result in the previous remark differ precisely in the truth valuation of predicate instances $ab_1(a)$, $ab_2(a)$ and $f(a)$.

$$p(a), \quad b(a), \; not\; r(a), \; not\; ab_1(a), \; not\; ab_2(a), \quad f(a), \quad \neg f(a),$$
$$not\; \neg p(a), not\; \neg b(a), not\; \neg r(a), not\; \neg ab_1(a), not\; \neg ab_2(a), not\; \neg f(a), not\; f(a),$$
$$not\; p(b), \quad b(b), \; not\; r(b), \; not\; ab_1(b), \; not\; ab_2(b), \quad f(b),$$
$$not\; \neg p(b), not\; \neg b(b), not\; \neg r(b), not\; \neg ab_1(b), not\; \neg ab_2(b), not\; \neg f(b),$$
$$not\; p(c), \; not\; b(c), \quad r(c), \; not\; ab_1(c), \; not\; ab_2(c), \qquad \neg f(c),$$
$$not\; \neg p(c), not\; \neg b(c), not\; \neg r(c), not\; \neg ab_1(c), not\; \neg ab_2(c), \qquad not\; f(c)$$

A contradiction arises about penguin a ($f(a)$ and $\neg f(a)$ both hold) because of the assumptions on $ab_1(a)$ and $ab_2(a)$. The contradiction removal sets of this program, when $Rev = \{not\; ab_1(X), not\; ab_2(X)\}$, are:

$$CRS_1 = \{not\; ab_1(a)\}$$
$$CRS_2 = \{not\; ab_2(a)\}$$

The sceptical revised program is:

$$P \cup \{ab_1(a) \leftarrow not\; ab_1(a), ab_2(a) \leftarrow not\; ab_2(a)\}$$

and it makes preference about abnormalities involving a.

In fact, in the sceptical revised program a is a penguin and a bird, and it is undefined whether it flies.

11.2.1 Exceptions

In general we may want to say that a given element is an exception to a normality rule. The notion of exception may be expressed in two different ways.

Exceptions to predicates.

Example 11.2.3. We express that the rule $flies(X) \leftarrow bird(X)$ applies whenever possible but can be defeated by exceptions using the rule:

$$flies(X) \leftarrow bird(X), not\; ab(X)$$

If there is a bird b and a bird a which is known not to fly (and we don't know the reason why) we may express it by $\neg flies(a)$. In this case $\neg flies(a)$ establishes an *exception to the conclusion predicate* of the defeasible rule, and the meaning of the program[3] is:

$$\left\{ \begin{array}{l} bird(b), not\; ab(b), not\; \neg ab(b), not\; \neg bird(b), not\; \neg flies(b), \quad flies(b), \\ bird(a), \qquad\qquad not\; \neg ab(a), not\; \neg bird(a), \quad \neg flies(a), not\; flies(a) \end{array} \right\}$$

Note that nothing is said about $ab(a)$, i.e. the assumption *not* $ab(a)$ is avoided in the revised program, since it would give rise to a contradiction on $flies(a)$. This is the case where we know that bird a is an exception to the *normally birds fly* rule, by observation of the fact that it does not fly: $\neg flies(a)$.

---

[3] This is a simplified version of Example 11.2.1.

Exceptions to rules. A different way to express that a given animal is some exception is to say that a given rule must not be applicable to the animal. To state that an element is an exception to a specific rule rather than to its conclusion predicate (more than one rule may have the same conclusion), we state that the element is abnormal w.r.t. the rule, i.e. the rule is not applicable to the element:

> if element a is an exception to the flying birds rule we express it as $ab(a)$.

In general we may want to express that a given X is abnormal under certain conditions. This is the case where we want to express penguins are abnormal w.r.t. the flying birds rule above, as follows:

$$ab(X) \leftarrow penguin(X) \tag{11.1}$$

Remark 11.2.2. Rule (11.1) together with the non-defeasible rule $bird(X) \leftarrow penguin(X)$ add that *penguins are birds which are abnormal w.r.t. flying.*

Similarly of dead birds; i.e.

$$ab(X) \leftarrow bird(X), dead(X)$$

adding that *dead birds are abnormal w.r.t. flying.*

Remark 11.2.3. Alternatively, given $\neg flies(X) \leftarrow dead(X)$, the non-abnormality of dead bird a w.r.t. flying, i.e. *not* $ab(a)$, may not be consistently assumed since it leads to a contradiction regarding $flies(a)$ and $\neg flies(a)$.

Exceptions to exceptions. In general we may extend the notion of exceptioned rules to exception rules themselves, i.e. exception rules may be defeasible. This will allow us to express an exception to the exception rule for birds to fly, and hence the possibility that an exceptional penguin may fly, or that a dead bird may fly. In this case we want to say that the exception rule is itself a defeasible rule:

$$ab(X) \leftarrow bird(X), dead(X), not\ ab\_deadbird(X)$$

11.2.2 Preferences among rules

We may express now preference between two rules, stating that if one rule may be used, that constitutes an exception to the use of the other rule:

Example 11.2.4. Consider again the flying birds example:

$$
\begin{aligned}
f(X) &\leftarrow b(X), not\ ab_1(X) &\text{(i)}\\
\neg f(X) &\leftarrow p(X), not\ ab_2(X) &\text{(ii)}\\
b(X) &\leftarrow p(X) &\text{(iii)}
\end{aligned}
$$

In some cases we want to apply the most specific information; above, there should be (since a penguin is a specific kind of bird) an explicit preference of the non-flying penguins rule over the flying birds rule:

$$ab_1(X) \leftarrow p(X), not\ ab_2(X) \tag{11.2}$$

If we have also $penguin(a)$ and $bird(b)$ the unique model contains:

$$\left\{ \begin{array}{lll} p(a), b(a), & ab_1(a), not\ f(a), & not\ ab_2(a), \\ not\ p(b), b(b), not\ ab_1(b), & f(b), not\ \neg f(b), & not\ ab_2(b) \end{array} \right\}$$

Rule (11.2) says that if a given penguin is not abnormal w.r.t. non-flying then it must be considered abnormal w.r.t. flying. In this case we infer that b is a flying bird, and a is a penguin and also a bird, and there is no evidence (assume it is false) that it flies $not\ f(a)$.

11.3 Hierarchical taxonomies

Here we illustrate how to represent taxonomies with extended logic programs. In this representation we wish to express general absolute (i.e. non-defeasible) rules, defeasible rules, exceptions to defeasible rules and to exceptions, explicitly making preferences among defeasible rules. We also show how to express preference for one defeasible rule over another whenever they conflict. In taxonomic hierarchies we wish to express that in the presence of contradictory defeasible rules we prefer the one with most specific[4] information (e.g. for a penguin, which is a bird, we want to conclude that it doesn't fly).

Example 11.3.1. The statements about the domain are:

(1) Mammals are animals.	(6) Normally animals don't fly.
(2) Bats are mammals.	(7) Normally bats fly.
(3) Birds are animals.	(8) Normally birds fly.
(4) Penguins are birds.	(9) Normally penguins don't fly.
(5) Dead animals are animals.	(10) Normally dead animals don't fly.

and the following elements:

(11) Pluto is a mammal.	(12) Tweety is a bird.
(13) Joe is a penguin.	(14) Dracula is a bat.
(15) Dracula is a dead animal.	

depicted as in fig. 11.1, and the preferences:

(16) Dead bats do not fly though bats do.
(17) Dead birds do not fly though birds do.
(18) Dracula is an exception to the above preferences.

---

[4] In [137], the author suggests using this notion of more specific information to resolve conflicts between contradictory defeasible rules.

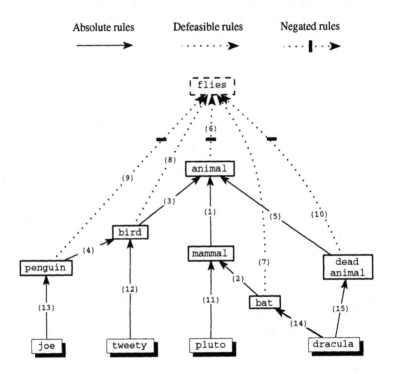

Fig. 11.1. A hierarchical taxonomy

The above hierarchy can be represented by the program:

$$animal(X) \leftarrow mammal(X) \qquad (1)$$
$$mammal(X) \leftarrow bat(X) \qquad (2)$$
$$animal(X) \leftarrow bird(X) \qquad (3)$$
$$bird(X) \leftarrow penguin(X) \qquad (4)$$
$$animal(X) \leftarrow dead\_animal(X) \qquad (5)$$
$$\neg flies(X) \leftarrow animal(X), not\ ab_1(X) \qquad (6)$$
$$flies(X) \leftarrow bat(X), not\ ab_2(X) \qquad (7)$$
$$flies(X) \leftarrow bird(X), not\ ab_3(X) \qquad (8)$$
$$\neg flies(X) \leftarrow penguin(X), not\ ab_4(X) \qquad (9)$$
$$\neg flies(X) \leftarrow dead\_animal(X), not\ ab_5(X) \qquad (10)$$
$$mammal(pluto) \qquad (11)$$
$$bird(tweety) \qquad (12)$$
$$penguin(joe) \qquad (13)$$
$$bat(dracula) \qquad (14)$$
$$dead\_animal(dracula) \qquad (15)$$

with the implicit hierarchical preference rules (not shown in fig. 11.1):

$$ab_1(X) \leftarrow bat(X), not\ ab_2(X)$$
$$ab_1(X) \leftarrow bird(X), not\ ab_3(X)$$
$$ab_3(X) \leftarrow penguin(X), not\ ab_4(X)$$

and the explicit problem statement preferences:

$$ab_2(X) \leftarrow dead\_animal(X), bat(X), not\ ab_5(X) \qquad (16)$$
$$ab_3(X) \leftarrow dead\_animal(X), bird(X), not\ ab_5(X) \qquad (17)$$
$$ab_5(dracula) \qquad (18)$$

As expected, this program has exactly one partial stable model (coinciding with its well founded model), no choice being possible and everything being defined in the hierarchy. The model is given by the table in figure 11.2 where $\sqrt{}$ means that the predicate (in the row entry) is true about the element (in the column entry), e.g. $penguin(joe)$ holds in the model.

Thus pluto doesn't fly, and isn't an exception to any of the rules; tweety flies because it's a bird and an exception to the "animals don't fly" rule; joe doesn't fly because it's a penguin and an exception to the "birds fly" rule.

Although dracula is a dead animal, which by default don't fly (cf. rule (10)) it is also considered an exception to this very same rule. Furthermore rule (16) saying that "dead bats normally do not fly" is also exceptioned by dracula and thus the "bats fly" rule applies and dracula flies.

Note that preferences rules must be present in order to prevent contradiction to arise, thus preference rules play the rôle of removing contradictions arising in the initial specification of the problem.

individ. predicat.	joe	dracula	pluto	tweety
dead_animal	not , not ¬	✓ , not ¬	not , not ¬	not , not ¬
bat	not , not ¬	✓ , not ¬	not , not ¬	not , not ¬
penguin	✓ , not ¬	not , not ¬	not , not ¬	not , not ¬
mammal	not , not ¬	✓ , not ¬	✓ , not ¬	not , not ¬
bird	✓ , not ¬	not , not ¬	not , not ¬	✓ , not ¬
animal	✓ , not ¬	✓ , not ¬	✓ , not ¬	✓ , not ¬
ab_4	not , not ¬	not , not ¬	not , not ¬	not , not ¬
ab_2	not , not ¬	not , not ¬	not , not ¬	not , not ¬
ab_3	✓ , not ¬	not , not ¬	not , not ¬	not , not ¬
ab_1	not , not ¬	✓ , not ¬	not , not ¬	✓ , not ¬
ab_5	not , not ¬	✓ , not ¬	not , not ¬	not , not ¬
flies	¬ , not	✓ , not ¬	¬ , not	✓ , not ¬

Fig. 11.2. The well founded model of the hierarchy

11.4 Hypothetical reasoning

In this section we capture hypothetical reasoning in extended programs and interpret the results under the *WFSX* and the contradiction removal. In hierarchies everything is defined as seen, leaving no choices available (a unique model is identified as the meaning of the program). This is not the case in hypothetical reasoning situations.

11.4.1 The birds world

In Example 11.2.1 we showed that the cautious or sceptical revision of defeasible rules gives a minimal model where no defeasible rule is used. There are however two other (non-minimal) models corresponding to alternative (non-cautious or hypothetical) meanings of the program (corresponding to alternative defeasible rules being applied or, equivalently, alternative revisions) when different assumptions are made.

Example 11.4.1. Consider the program:

$$
\begin{aligned}
f(X) &\leftarrow b(X), not\ ab_1(X) \quad \text{(i)} \\
\neg f(X) &\leftarrow p(X), not\ ab_2(X) \quad \text{(ii)} \\
b(X) &\leftarrow p(X) \\
p(a) &
\end{aligned}
$$

Here we may consider two alternative hypothetical worlds (note there is no preference rule present). In one of them (model M_1) we consider the hypothesis that a is not an abnormal bird, $not\ ab_1(a)$, and so it flies, $f(a)$. In this case we must also assume that $not\ ab_2(a)$ does not hold.

Another alternative (model M_2) suggests that a is not an abnormal penguin, $not\ ab_2(a)$, and thus it does not fly, $\neg f(a)$. Per force, $not\ ab_1(a)$ does not hold. A third model M_3 accounts for the case where no assumption is made.

The submodels lattice is shown in figure 11.3, where the shadowed submodel corresponds to the most sceptical view.

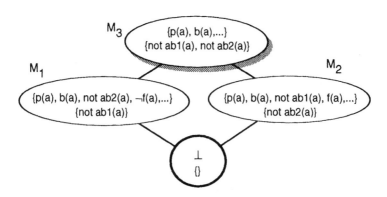

Fig. 11.3. The birds example submodels lattice

Remark 11.4.1. Note that every model with *not* $ab_1(a)$ is also a model with $f(a)$, that is,

$$P \models_{crs} not\ ab_1(a) \Rightarrow f(a)$$

The same holds for the other assumption, that is,

$$P \models not\ ab_2(a) \Rightarrow \neg f(a)$$

Another way of interpreting these rules is by saying that if we hypothesize that, say rule (ii) has an exception in a, in the sense that $ab_2(a) \leftarrow not\ ab_2(a)$ viz. *not* $ab_2(a)$ cannot hold, then $f(a)$ holds; i.e.

$$P \cup \{ab_2(a) \leftarrow not\ ab_2(a)\} \models_{WFSX} f(a)$$

Compare model M_2 above with the unique model where an explicit preference was made (c.f. Section 11.2.2 in page 214).

11.4.2 Hypothetical facts and rules

In some cases we want to be make a rule hypothetically applicable, in the sense that we may consider the case where the rule is used to reason with, as well as the case where the rule is not considered in force. The same is desired of some facts, i.e. we want to be able to explicitly represent that some unknown fact may be hypothesized true as well as false. If no hypothesis is made about the fact the information it conveys is unknown or undecided, just like the conclusion of a hypothetical rule which is not hypothesized.

Hypothetical facts. Similarly to rules about which we are undecided regarding their applicability, we might be unsure about some facts. Note that this is different from not having any knowledge at all about such a fact.

Consider this simple example:

John and Nixon are quakers.   John is a pacifist.

represented by the program P_1:

$$quaker(john). \quad pacifist(john). \quad quaker(nixon).$$

The *WFSX* well-founded model (which is the only partial stable model) is:

$$\left\{ \begin{array}{llll} & quaker(nixon) & & quaker(john) \\ not & pacifist(nixon) & & pacifist(john) \\ not \, \neg & quaker(nixon) & not \, \neg & quaker(john) \\ not \, \neg & pacifist(nixon) & not \, \neg & pacifist(john) \end{array} \right\}$$

and expresses exactly what is intended, i.e. John and Nixon are quakers, John is a pacifist and we don't have reason to believe Nixon is a pacifist, in this or any other model (there aren't any others in fact). Now suppose we want to add:

Nixon might *be a pacifist*   (11.3)

In our view we wouldn't want in this case to be so strong as to affirm $pacifist(nixon)$, thereby not allowing for the possibility of Nixon not being a pacifist. What we are prepared to say is that Nixon might be a pacifist if we don't have reason to believe he isn't and, vice-versa, that Nixon might be a non-pacifist if we don't have reason to believe he isn't one. Statement (11.3) is expressed as:

$$pacifist(nixon) \quad \leftarrow \quad not \, \neg pacifist(nixon) \tag{11.4}$$

$$\neg pacifist(nixon) \quad \leftarrow \quad not \, pacifist(nixon) \tag{11.5}$$

The first rule states that Nixon is a pacifist if there is no evidence against it. The second rule makes a symmetric statement. Let P_2 be the program P together with these rules. P_2 is noncontradictory, and its *WFSX* is:

$$\left\{ \begin{array}{llll} & quaker(nixon) & & quaker(john) \\ & & & pacifist(john) \\ not \, \neg & quaker(nixon) & not \, \neg & quaker(john) \\ & & not \, \neg & pacifist(john) \end{array} \right\}$$

P_2 has two more partial stable models:

$$PSM_1 = WFSX(P_2) \cup \{pacifist(nixon), not \, \neg pacifist(nixon)\}$$
$$PSM_2 = WFSX(P_2) \cup \{\neg pacifist(nixon), not \, pacifist(nixon)\}$$

which is the result we were seeking. Statements of the form of (11.3) we call *unknown possible facts*, and are expressed as by (11.4) and (11.5). They can be read as a fact and its negation, each of which can be assumed only if it is consistent to do so.

Hypothetical rules. Consider now the well known nixon-diamond example using now hypothetical rules instead of defeasible ones.

We represent these rules as named rules (in the fashion of [167]) where the rule name may be present in one model as true, and in others as false.

Normally quakers are pacifists.	Pacifists are non hawks.
Normally republicans are hawks.	Hawks are non pacifists.
Nixon is a quaker and a republican.	Pacifists are non hawks.
There are other republicans.	There are other quakers.

The corresponding logic program is:

$$
\begin{aligned}
pacifist(X) &\leftarrow quaker(X), hypqp(X) \\
hypqp(X) &\leftarrow not\ \neg hypqp(X) \\
hawk(X) &\leftarrow republican(X), hyprh(X) \\
hyprh(X) &\leftarrow not\ \neg hyprh(X) \\
\neg hawk(X) &\leftarrow pacifist(X) \\
\neg pacifist(X) &\leftarrow hawk(X) \\
quaker(nixon) & \\
republican(nixon) & \\
quaker(another\_quaker) & \\
republican(another\_republican) &
\end{aligned}
$$

where the following rules are also added making, each normality instance rule about Nixon hypothetical rather than defeasible (c.f. the representation of defeasible rules in Section 11.2):

$$
\begin{aligned}
hypqp(nixon) &\leftarrow not\ \neg hypqp(nixon) \\
\neg hypqp(nixon) &\leftarrow not\ hypqp(nixon)
\end{aligned}
$$

$$
\begin{aligned}
hyprh(nixon) &\leftarrow not\ \neg hyprh(nixon) \\
\neg hyprh(nixon) &\leftarrow not\ hyprh(nixon)
\end{aligned}
$$

which is represented as in fig. 11.4.

The minimal noncontradictory submodels, the sceptical revision M_1, and submodels between the formers and the latter are represented in figure 11.5, where edge labels represent the hypothesis being made when going from one model to another.

The submodels (with obvious abbreviations) are:

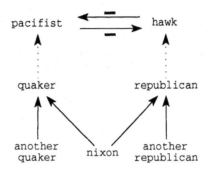

Fig. 11.4. The Nixon diamond

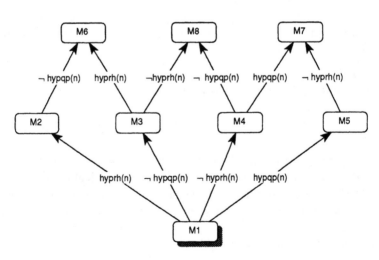

Fig. 11.5. Submodels of the nixon-diamond problem using hypothetical rules

$M_1 =$ { $qua(n), rep(n), not \ \neg qua(n), not \ \neg rep(n),$
        $qua(a\_qua), not \ \neg qua(a\_qua), not \ rep(a\_qua), not \ \neg rep(a\_qua),$
        $hypqp(a\_qua), not \ \neg hypqp(a\_qua), pac(a\_qua), not \ \neg pac(a\_qua),$
        $hyprh(a\_qua), not \ \neg hyprh(a\_qua), not \ \neg pac(a\_qua),$
        $not \ hawk(a\_qua), rep(a\_rep), not \ \neg rep(a\_rep), not \ qua(a\_rep),$
        $not \ \neg qua(a\_rep), hyprp(a\_rep), not \ \neg hyprp(a\_rep), rep(a\_rep),$
        $not \ \neg rep(a\_rep), hypqp(a\_rep), not \ \neg hypqp(a\_rep),$
        $not \ pac(a\_rep), not \ \neg hawk(a\_rep)$ }

$M_2 = M_1 \cup \{hyprh(n), not \ \neg hyprh(n), hawk(n), not \ \neg hawk(n),$
        $\neg pac(n), not \ pac(n)\}$

$M_3 = M_1 \cup \{\neg hypqp(n), not \ hypqp(n), not \ pac(n), not \ \neg hawk(n)\}$

$M_4 = M_1 \cup \{\neg hyprh(n), not \ hyprh(n), not \ hawk(n), not \ \neg pac(n)\}$

$M_5 = M_1 \cup \{hypqp(n), not \ \neg hypqp(n), pac(n), not \ \neg pac(n), \neg hawk(n),$
        $not \ hawk(n)\}$

$M_6 = M_2 \cup \{\neg hypqp(n), not \ hypqp(n), not \ pac(n), not \ \neg hawk(n)\}$

$M_7 = M_4 \cup \{hypqp(n), not \ \neg hypqp(n), pac(n), not \ \neg pac(n), not \ \neg hawk(n)\}$

$M_8 = M_3 \cup \{\neg hyprh(n), not \ hyprh(n), not \ hawk(n), not \ \neg pac(n)\}$

The models M_2 and M_6 consider the applicability of the *republicans are hawks* normality rule, whereas the models M_4, M_5, and M_8 explore not applying it. Model M_1, being the most skeptical one, remains undefined about the applicability of the rule. The rationale for this undefinedness is that since the application and the non-application of the rule are equally plausible, one should remain undecided about it.

Note here the distinction between "hypothetical rules" and "defeasible rules". While the latter are applied "whenever possible" unless their applications leads to contradiction, the former provide equally plausible alternative extensions.

Remark 11.4.2. Note that with this form of representation we might as well add *abqp* or *¬abqp*, and thus the treatment of explicit negative information becomes similar to that of positive information. In this case we may now hypothesize about the applicability and non-applicability of each normality rule. However, the most sceptical model (where no hypotheses are made) is still identical to the one where normality rules were interpreted as defeasible rules, the difference being that in this case revision is enforced since the program is noncontradictory.

In this form of representation of the nixon-diamond problem there is no need for revision since the program is noncontradictory.

11.5 Reasoning about actions

Here we study one classical problem of reasoning about actions using the situation calculus, and show how the major drawbacks of other representations can be easily solved by using *WFSX* with the contradiction removal procedures introduced.

Situation calculus has three kinds of entities: fluents, actions and situations. We use the predicate $h(F, S)$ to say that fluent F holds in situation S, and a term $r(A, S)$ represents the new situation obtained as the result of performing action A in situation S. It's also necessary to add a frame axiom which expresses the *"common sense law of inertia"* [126] stated in [115] as:

> *"In the absence of information to the contrary, properties of objects can be assumed to remain unchanged after an action is performed"*

which can be formalized as $[h(F, r(A, S)) \Leftrightarrow h(F, S)] \Leftarrow not\ ab(A, F, S)$ and will be represented by the four rules:

$$
\begin{aligned}
h(F, r(A, S)) &\leftarrow h(F, S), not\ ab(A, F, S) \\
\neg h(F, r(A, S)) &\leftarrow \neg h(F, S), not\ ab(A, F, S) \\
h(F, S) &\leftarrow h(F, r(A, S)), not\ ab(A, F, S) \\
\neg h(F, S) &\leftarrow \neg h(F, r(A, S)), not\ ab(A, F, S)
\end{aligned}
$$

As [81] explains, the first two rules are used to apply the law of inertia in reasoning from past to future and the other two from future to past.

If the negation of the abnormality predicate is interpreted as classical negation, as in McCarthy's original formulation, it becomes necessary to have the following two extra rules added to the program:

$$
\begin{aligned}
ab(A, F, S) &\leftarrow \neg h(F, S), h(F, r(A, S)) \\
ab(A, F, S) &\leftarrow h(F, S), \neg h(F, r(A, S))
\end{aligned}
$$

But as we shall see, our approach automatically infers the situations that are exceptions to the frame axiom. This is the essence of the frame problem: Having incomplete knowledge about the world, what properties of objects (fluents) are changed as a result of action A in situation S ?

11.5.1 The Yale shooting problem

This problem, supplied in [86], will be represented in a form nearer to the one suggested in [107].

Example 11.5.1. The problem and its formulation are as follows:

– Initially (in situation $s0$) a person is alive:

$holds(alive, s0)$

– After loading a gun the gun is loaded:

$holds(loaded, result(load, S))$

– If the gun is loaded then after shooting it the person will not be alive:

$\neg holds(alive, result(shoot, S)) \leftarrow holds(loaded, S)$

Consider the question *"What holds and what doesn't hold after the loading of a gun, a period of waiting, and a shooting ?"* represented as two queries:

$$\leftarrow holds(P, result(shoot, result(wait, result(load, s0))))$$
$$\leftarrow \neg holds(P, result(shoot, result(wait, result(load, s0))))$$

With this formulation the *WFSX* well-founded model is the only partial stable model. The subset of its elements that match with at least one of the queries is[5]:

$$\{ \quad holds(loaded, s3), not \neg holds(loaded, s3),$$
$$\neg holds(alive, s3), not \ holds(alive, s3) \quad \}$$

which means that in situation $s3$ the gun is loaded and the person is not alive. This result coincides with the one obtained in [104] for *holds*.

11.5.2 Multiple extensions

Example 11.5.2. To get the result given by circumscription [126] and default logic [188], we must reformulate the problem by adding the sentence:

– the *wait* event might not preserve the persistence of the *loaded* property; in other words, after a *wait* event the gun might (or might not) be loaded.

This clearly means an unknown but hypothetical application of (pp). So the rules to add are:

$$ab(loaded, wait, S) \quad \leftarrow not \quad \neg ab(loaded, wait, S)$$
$$\neg ab(loaded, wait, S) \quad \leftarrow \quad\quad not \ ab(loaded, wait, S)$$

Now the *WFSX* contains $not \neg holds(loaded, s3)$. This means that in it we have no proof that the gun is not loaded. This is acceptable because there is no evidence for it to be unloaded. All other properties are unknown in the *WFSX*.

The rules above state that it is equally possible for *load* to be abnormal with respect to the *wait* event, as well as to be non-abnormal. We have two partial stable models corresponding to the two extensions. One extension contains:

$$\{ \ holds(alive, s3), not \neg holds(alive, s3), not \neg holds(loaded, s3) \ \}$$

and the other contains:

$$\{ \quad \neg holds(alive, s3), not \ holds(alive, s3),$$
$$holds(loaded, s3), not \neg holds(loaded, s3) \quad \}$$

---

[5] Where $s3$ denotes the term $result(shoot, result(wait, result(load, s0)))$.

11.5.3 The Stolen car problem

Here we discuss a (new) version of the stolen car problem [95] showing how it is handled using contradiction removal with intuitive results. For sake of simplicity, we do not present other instances of this problem (c.f. [199]) that are also correctly handled and easily represented in extended logic programs with contradiction removal.

The formulation of the stolen car problem (SCP) is:

You leave your car parked, return after a while, and your car is gone.
How can you explain that ?

This problem is easily represented in situation calculus. In the initial situation, s_0, the car is parked. After a finite number of wait actions, for instance 4, the car has disappeared. Now suppose that after two wait actions the car was still seen parked by someone. This problem statement is represented by the logic program:

$$h(cp, s_0)$$
$$h(cp, r(w, r(w, s_0)))$$
$$\neg h(cp, r(w, r(w, r(w, r(w, s_0)))))$$

plus the above four frame axiom rules.

First we must determine what are the supports of contradiction. There are only two:

$$SS_1 = \{not\ ab(w, cp, s_2), not\ ab(w, cp, s_3)\}$$
$$SS_2 = \{not\ ab(w, cp, s_0), not\ ab(w, cp, s_1), not\ ab(w, cp, s_2),$$
$$not\ ab(w, cp, s_3)\}$$

with $s_i = r(w, s_{i-1}), i \geq 1$. Thus there are two $CRSs$:

$$CRS_1 = \{not\ ab(w, cp, s_2)\}$$
$$CRS_2 = \{not\ ab(w, cp, s_3)\}$$

corresponding to the intuitive result that something abnormal happened during either the third or fourth wait action.

11.5.4 Other reasoning about action problems

In this section we represent problems D2 and D6 of [114] which are classified as "Reasoning about Action - Temporal Projection" and "Reasoning about Action - Temporal Explanations with Actions of Unknown Kinds", respectively.

Example 11.5.3. The assumption of problem D2 and its representation are as follows:

– After an action is performed things normally remain as they were: represented with the four rules in the beginning of this section.
– When the robot grasps a block, the block will normally be in the hand:

$$holds(hand(B), result(grasp(B), S)) \leftarrow not\ ab(hand(B), grasp(B), S)$$

– When the robot moves a block onto the table, the block will normally be on the table:

$$
\begin{aligned}
holds(table(B), result(move(B), S)) \leftarrow & \\
& holds(hand(B), S), \\
& not\ ab(table(B), move(B), S)
\end{aligned}
$$

– Initially block A is not in the hand and not on the table.

$$\neg holds(table(a), s0) \qquad \neg holds(hand(a), s0)$$

The conclusion "After the robot grasps block a, waits, and then moves it onto the table, the block will be on the table" can be represented by:

$$\leftarrow holds(table(a), result(move(a), result(wait, result(grasp(a), s0))))$$

and belongs to the *WFSX* of the program.

Example 11.5.4. The assumptions of problem D6 are those of D2 plus "After the robot performed two actions, *a* was on the table". The conclusion is "The first action was grasping *a*, and the second was moving it onto the table". We reach this conclusion by verifying that

$$\leftarrow holds(table(a), result(move(a), result(grasp(a), s0)))$$

is the only goal of the form

$$\leftarrow holds(table(a), result(Action2, result(Action1, s0)))$$

which is in the *WFSX* of the program.

11.6 Counterfactual reasoning

In this section we present a semantics for counterfactual implication relative to definite extended programs with integrity constraints and protected rules (unrevisable), and show the adequacy of the contradiction removal semantics to define the notion of similarity needed for defining counterfactual truth. The concepts introduced in chaphter 8 are adequate to support the revision process required by contravening hypoteses [192] when evaluating counterfactuals.

11.6.1 Lewis's counterfactuals

Counterfactuals are usually defined based on a notion of possible (or alternative) worlds (or simply worlds), and the definition of the truth value of a counterfactual $p > q$ considers the possible worlds "maximally similar" to the world S, where the counterfactual is being evaluated. We don't need to quantify how similar two worlds S_1 and S_2 are, but only to define a partial order between worlds, enabling to determine whether S_1 is more similar than S_2 with respect to §.

Given a similarity relation $\geq_F$ that nests layers of similar worlds relative to F, obeying some reasonable precepts, Lewis [112] defines a counterfactual $p > q$ to be true in some world F only in either of two cases:

- (A) if there exists some world U such that:
  - (A1) p is true in U and
  - (A2) $p \rightarrow q$ is true in any world V with $V \geq_F U$ (i.e. if V is any world at least as similar to F as U is, q will hold in V if p does);
- (B) if there is no world U in which p holds $p > q$ is vacuously true.

Lewis uses $\square \rightarrow$ in place of $>$. Let p-world mean a world where p holds. He also provides a "might" counterfactual defined as $p \Diamond \rightarrow q =_{def} \neg(p \square \rightarrow \neg q)$, meaning "there is a nearest p-world where $p \rightarrow q$".

Counterfactual implication is also equivalently defined by Lewis [112] in a different way, which we adopt, directly based on a notion of maximally similar worlds. Let $f(p, w)$ stand for the set of nearest p-worlds from w.

$$p >_w q =_{def} f(p, w) \subset [\![q]\!]$$

where f is a selection function [112], $[\![q]\!]$ represents the set of worlds in which q is true, and meaning: "the counterfactual implication $p > q$ is true in world w iff in all the nearest p-worlds from w, q is also true"; in other words, if the set of the nearest p-worlds is a subset of the q-worlds (if the set of nearest p-worlds is empty then $p > q$ is vacuously true).

Definition 11.6.1 (Selection function). *A function f from sentences and worlds to sets of worlds is a selection function if and only if, for all sentences ϕ and ψ and for each world i, the following four conditions hold.*

i) If ϕ is true at i then $f(\phi, i)$ is the set $\{i\}$ having i as its only member.
ii) $f(\phi, i)$ is included in $[\![\phi]\!]$.
iii) If $[\![\phi]\!]$ is included in $[\![\psi]\!]$ and $f(\phi, i)$ is nonempty then $f(\psi, i)$ is also nonempty.
iv) If $[\![\phi]\!]$ is included in $[\![\psi]\!]$ and $[\![\phi]\!]$ overlaps $f(\psi, i)$ then $f(\phi, i)$ is the intersection of $[\![\phi]\!]$ and $f(\psi, i)$.

11.6.2 Counterfactual reasoning by revising assumptions

Definition 11.6.2 (Program Base). *A Program Base* $PB = \langle K; S; IC \rangle$, *where* K *is a definite extended program*[6] *(cf. Section 5.2.2),* S *is a set of protected rules, with* $S \subseteq K$, *and a set* IC *of definite integrity constraints.*

The semantics of a Program Base is defined by the $M = least(K \cup IC \cup NIC)$ where $least(P)$ is the least operator of Definition 4.2.2 and NIC is as definied in proposition 8.2.1.

Definition 11.6.3 (Contradictory PB). *A Program Base* PB *is contradictory iff*

$$\bot \in least(K \cup IC \cup NIC)$$

Definition 11.6.4 (Program associated with a Program Base).
The program P *associated with a Program Base* $PB = \langle K; S; IC \rangle$ *is an extended logic program obtained from* PB *as follows:*

− *for each unprotected rule*

$$H \leftarrow B_1, \ldots, B_n \ (n \geq 0)$$

in K, *P contains instead the rule*

$$H \leftarrow B_1, \ldots, B_n, not\ A$$

where A *is a new atom.*
− *P contains all the other rules in* K *and* IC.

This defines a transformation $\mathcal{T} : PB \rightarrow P$ from program bases to logic programs.

Example 11.6.1. Consider the "flying birds (and penguins)" Program Base, with K :

$$
\begin{array}{rcll}
f & \leftarrow & b & (i) \\
\neg f & \leftarrow & p & (ii) \\
b & & & (iii) \\
p & & & (iv)
\end{array}
$$

and facts b and p protected, i.e. $S = \{b, p\}$.

The associated logic program is $P_{PB} = \mathcal{T}(PB)$:

$$
\begin{array}{rcll}
f & \leftarrow & b, not\ bf & (i)' \\
\neg f & \leftarrow & p, not\ pnf & (i)' \\
b & & & (iii) \\
p & & & (iv)
\end{array}
$$

which is contradictory.

---

[6] This definition is not more general, i.e. applicable to general extended logic programs, because it can be shown that the properties Lewis's original selection function must obey are only guaranteed for this type of Program Base. A new type of selection function is needed to account for the presence of *not* .

The inverse transformation T^{-1} may be defined as follows:

Definition 11.6.5 (Inverse transformation-T^{-1}). *Given a logic program P associated with a Program Base $PB = \langle K, S, IC \rangle$ the latter may be obtained as follows:*

- *For each definite rule $H \leftarrow B_1, \ldots, B_n$ in P there is a similar rule both in K and in S.*
- *For each non definite rule $H \leftarrow B_1, \ldots, B_n, not\ A$ in P such that not $A \in WFM(P)$ there is instead the rule $H \leftarrow B_1, \ldots, B_n$ in K.*
- *IC is the set of all integrity constraints in P.*

Given a $PB = \langle K; S; IC \rangle$, by the **current world** i we mean the (possibly contradictory) $WFSX(T(PB))$ which may be contradictory.

Definition 11.6.6 (Counterfactual value). *Given a $PB = \langle K, S, IC \rangle$ and $P_{PB} = T(PB)$ we define a counterfactual implication $\phi > \psi$ to be true, iff ψ holds in all minimal noncontradictory submodels of $P_{PB} \cup \{\phi\}$, i.e.*

$$\psi \in \bigcap_i MNS_i(T(P_{PB} \cup \{\phi\}))$$

Definition 11.6.6 implicitly specifies the set of most similar ϕ-worlds as follows:

Definition 11.6.7 (Most similar ϕ-worlds). *Given a Program Base PB with associated program P_{PB}, the set of most similar ϕ-worlds $f(\phi, i)$ is defined as:*

$$f(\phi, i) = \{M | M = MNS_j(T(PB) \cup \{\phi\})\}$$

Given the results in Section 8.3.3, the selection function $f(\phi, i)$ in the above definition may also be equivalently defined as:

$$f(\phi, i) = \{M_j | M_j = WFSX(T(PB) \cup \{\phi\} \cup IR(CRS_j))\}$$

or, by definition:

$$f(\phi, i) = \{least(T^{-1}(S_j)) | S_j = T(PB) \cup \{\phi\} \cup IR(CRS_j)\}$$

Since $T(P_i \cup \{\phi\}) = T(P_{PB}) \cup \{\phi\}$[7]

$$f(\phi, i) = \{least(T^{-1}(S_j)) | S_j = P \cup \{\phi\} \cup IR(CRS_j)\}$$

This means that, given a Program Base PB, in order to obtain a counterfactual implication $\phi > \psi$, first obtain program P, then add $\{\phi\}$ and evaluate the minimal noncontradictory submodels of the new program. The counterfactual is true iff ψ holds in all such minimal noncontradictory submodels, which are the most similar ϕ-worlds of i.

---

[7] This follows easily from the definiton of T.

Remark 11.6.1. Note that the transformation result does not depend on any particular counterfactual antecedent, i.e. the associated logic program P is independent of the counterfactual being evaluated. This plays an important role if we consider the logic program as an implementation of the Program Base. Moreover, for any Program Base PB_1 and PB_2 we have $T(PB_1 \cup PB_2) = T(PB_1) \cup T(PB_2)$, a modular construction.

Example 11.6.2. Consider the counterfactual premise ww and

$$PB = \langle K, S, \{\} \rangle$$

where K :

$$
\begin{array}{rcll}
\neg ww & \leftarrow & \neg pt, \neg bs & (i) \\
\neg pt & & & (ii) \\
\neg bs & & & (iii)
\end{array}
$$

and $S = \{\neg ww \leftarrow \neg pt, \neg bs\}$. The associated logic program is $T(PB) = P_{PB}$:

$$
\begin{array}{rcll}
\neg ww & \leftarrow & \neg pt, \neg bs & (i) \\
\neg pt & \leftarrow & not\ pt' & (ii)' \\
\neg bs & \leftarrow & not\ bs' & (iii)'
\end{array}
$$

The submodels lattice of $P_{PB} \cup \{ww\}$ is depicted in figure 11.6. In this case the counterfactual $ww > bs$ is false, since bs does not belong to all MNSs of the program.

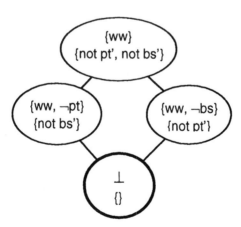

Fig. 11.6. Counterfactuals example

11.6.3 Lewis's similarity precepts obeyed

In this section we prove that the notion of similarity introduced in Definition 11.6.7 satisfies lewis precepts of similarity. To that purpose we begin by presenting some trivial to prove propositions:

Proposition 11.6.1. Let $PB = \langle K; IC; S \rangle$ be a Program Base and a an objective literal. Then

$$a \in least(K \cup IC) \equiv a \in WFSX_p(T(PB))$$

Corollary 11.6.1. A Program Base PB is contradictory iff $T(PB)$ is contradictory.

Proposition 11.6.2. Let P be a logic program, IC a set of integrity constraints and a an objective literal. Then:

$$a \in WFSX_p(P) \text{ iff } a \in least(T^{-1}(P)).$$

Corollary 11.6.2. A program P is contradictory w.r.t. a set of ICs iff $T^{-1}(P)$ is contradictory.

Proposition 11.6.3. Let $PB = \langle K; IC; S \rangle$ be a Program Base and a an objective literal. Then

$$T(PB) \cup \phi = T(\langle P \cup \{\phi\}; IC; S \cup \{\phi\}\rangle)$$

In the sequel we consider the current world (i.e. the $WFSX(P_{PB})$) to be noncontradictory.

Lewis's selection function properties.

i) If ϕ is true at i, then $f(\phi, i)$ is the set $\{i\}$ having i as its only member.

   Proof. As $i \models \phi$ then $least(i) = least(i \cup \{\phi\})$. So $i \cup \{\phi\}$ is noncontradictory. By proposition 11.6.1, the program $T(i \cup \{\phi\})$ is also noncontradictory. Thus:

   $$f(\phi, i) = \{least(T^{-1}(T(i \cup \{\phi\})))\}$$

   which by, proposition 11.6.2, is equal to $\{i\}$.

ii) $f(\phi, i)$ is included in $[\![\phi]\!]$.

   Proof. According to contradiction removal every fact of a program belongs to the *WFSX* of the sceptically revised program (and to all its *MNS*'s). As

   $$T(\phi \cup \{i\})$$

   has ϕ as a fact, ϕ belongs to ali its *MNS*s. By proposition 11.6.2 elements of $f(\phi, i)$ have ϕ, i.e. are ϕ-worlds.

iii) If $[\![\phi]\!]$ is included in $[\![\psi]\!]$ and $f(\phi,i)$ is nonempty, then $f(\psi,i)$ is also nonempty.

Proof.

(1) If $\phi \in least(i)$, i.e. $i \in [\![\phi]\!]$: by hypothesis $i \in [\![\psi]\!]$ and by proposition 11.6.1:
$$f(\psi,i) = \{\psi\} \neq \{\}$$

(2) If $\phi \notin least(i)$: by hypothesis $\exists S_r$ s.t. $T(i \cup \{\phi\}) \cup S_r$ is a noncontradictory program (where S_r is a set of inhibition rules). Then:

$\exists S_r \ |T(i) \cup \{\phi\} \cup S_r \qquad$ is noncontradictory.

$\exists S_r \ |T(i) \cup \{\psi\} \cup \{\phi\} \cup S_r \quad$ is noncontradictory by the 1st hyp

$\exists S_r \ |T(i \cup \{\psi\}) \cup \{\phi\} \cup S_r \quad$ is noncontradictory.

For $T(i \cup \{\psi\}) \cup S_r$ to be contradictory there should exist one $S = SS(\bot)$ such that:

$\qquad not \ \phi \in SS(\bot)$ in $T(i \cup \{\psi\}) \cup S_r$

By definition of inhibition rule none of the S_r literals belong to the *WFSX*. So for $not \ \phi$ to belong to S it must belong to $T(i \cup \{\psi\})$. By definition of T, the only literals negative in $WFSX(T(PB))$ that appears in a body of any rule in $T(PB)$ are new atoms. So $not \ \phi$ cannot be in any SS of any positive literal (in particular of $\bot$). Thus:

$\exists S_r \ | \ T(i \cup \{\psi\}) \cup S_r$ is noncontradictory

iv) If $[\![\phi]\!] \subseteq [\![\psi]\!]$ and $f(\psi,i) \cap [\![\phi]\!] \neq \{\}$ then $f(\phi,i) = f(\psi,i) \cap [\![\phi]\!]$.

Proof. If $f(\psi,i) \cap [\![\phi]\!]$ is non-empty then $f(\psi,i) \neq \{\}$ and:

$f(\psi,i) \cap [\![\phi]\!] =$

$\{least(T^{-1}(S_j))|S_j = T(i \cup \{\psi\}) \cup IR(CRS_j) \wedge \phi \in WFSX(S_j)\}$

$= \{least(T^{-1}(S_j))|S_j = T(i \cup \{\psi\}) \cup \{\phi\} \cup IR(CRS_j)\}$

$= \{least(T^{-1}(S_j))|S_j = T(i) \cup \{\psi\} \cup \{\phi\} \cup IR(CRS_j)\}$

$=^8 \{least(T^{-1}(S_j))|S_j = T(i) \cup \{\phi\} \cup IR(CRS_j)\}$

$= f(\phi,i)$ by definition

---

[8] By cumulativity.

12. Application to diagnosis and debugging

The aim of this chapter is to illustrate the usefulness of extended logic programming, and the semantics defined above, to diagnosis, to declarative debugging, and to knowledge base updates.

In Section 8.3 the contradiction removal is achieved by unassuming some default literal that lead to contradiction. This is enough to deal with diagnosis problems without fault mode, i.e. only with the description of the correct behaviour of the system to be diagnosed.

When rules describing (some) incorrect behaviours of the system are added to the description of the problem, i.e. some fault mode is introduced, unassuming default literals in order to remove the contradiction is not enough. This is so because, in order to both use the fault mode and explain the incorrect behaviour, faults must be assume.

Example 12.0.3. Consider the simple one-inverter circuit of figure 12.1, described by the program P:

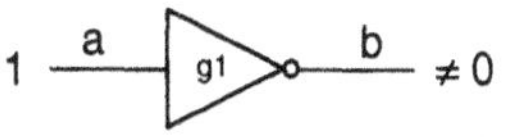

Fig. 12.1. Simple circuit

$$
\begin{aligned}
inv(G, I, 0) &\leftarrow node(I, 1), not\ ab(G) \\
inv(G, I, 1) &\leftarrow node(I, 0), not\ ab(G)
\end{aligned}
$$

$$
node(b, V) \leftarrow inv(g1, a, V)
$$

and the input and output observations:

$$
\begin{aligned}
&node(a, 1) \\
&\neg node(b, 0)
\end{aligned}
$$

The program together with these facts is contradictory and, by considering as revisables all literals of the form $not\ ab(G)$, has one minimal revisions:

$$P \cup \{ab(g1) \leftarrow not\ ab(g1)\}$$

This revision accords with the expect result for the circuit, i.e. since the output of the inverter is not 0 it can not be assumed that the gate is behaving normally.

Now assume that, additionally to the specification of the circuit, one adds that when an inverter gate is abnormal it returns as output the input value (fault model). This can be described by the rules:

$$inv(G, I, 0) \quad \leftarrow \quad node(I, 0), ab(G)$$
$$inv(G, I, 1) \quad \leftarrow \quad node(I, 1), ab(G)$$

The program obtained by adding these rules to P is contradictory, and it has a unique minimal revision, also obtained by adding $ab(g1) \leftarrow not\ ab(g1)$. Note that this revision does not capture the expected result since from it does not follow that the value of node b is 1, as suggested by the fault model. In fact, in well-founded model of the revised program assigns the value undefined to both $ab(g1)$ and $node(b, 1)$.

In order to make use of fault modes, and thus explain incorrect behaviours of systems, in this chapter we begin by generalizing the contradiction removal techniques defined in Section 8.3 to deal with two valued revisions. In two-valued revision, assumptions are changed into their complements instead of being undefined. In the example above this would provide for a single revision consisting of adding to the program the fact $ab(g1)$, thus deriving $node(b, 1)$.

Then we apply this theory to diagnosis. Because [46] unifies the abductive and consistency based approaches to diagnosis for generality we present a methodology that transforms any diagnostic problem of [46] into an extended logic program, and solve it with our contradiction removal methods. Another unifying approach to diagnosis with logic programming [169] uses Generalised Stable Models [94]. The criticisms they voice of Console and Torasso's approach do not carry over to our representation, ours having the advantage of a more expressive language: explicit negation as well as default negation[1].

In addition, we apply our theory to debugging, setting forth a method to debug normal Prolog programs, and showing that declarative debugging [119] can be envisaged as contradiction removal, and so providing a simple and clear solution to this problem. Furthermore, we show how diagnostic problems can be solved with contradiction removal applied to the artifact's representation in logic plus observations. Declarative debugging can thus be used to diagnose blueprint specifications of artifacts.

Our final application concerns the problems of updating knowledge bases expressed by logic programs. We compare with previous work and show, as

---

[1] In [48], we further extend the expressivity by introducing preferences and strategies in the diagnosis framework. This is, however, beyond the scope of this book

before, the superiority of the results obtained by our theoretical developments regarding the semantics of the extended logic programs and its attending contradiction removal techniques.

All the reported application examples were successfully run in our implementation available on request. A simplified implementation of our contradiction removal techniques is presented in Appendix B.

The structure of this chapter is as follows:

We begin by defining two-valued contradiction removal similarly to the contradiction removal defined in Section 8.3. Simultaneously, we provide algorithms that implement these techniques and all of soundness, completeness and termination properties are stated.

In Section 12.2 we illustrate the application of those techniques to solve general diagnosis problems. We start by reporting a major theorem that defines the contradiction removal applicability spectrum to diagnosis. In essence, we have shown that we can capture an unifying framework of the two main streams of model-based diagnosis: the consistency-based and abductive approaches. The proposed method defines a translation from this framework into the language of extended logic programming with integrity constraints. This section closes with several illustrative application examples of our approach to diagnosis.

Subsequently, in Section 12.3, we show how the debugging of normal logic programs can be fruitfully understood as a diagnosis/contradiction removal problem. We describe and analyse these two views, the main achievement being a program transformation that is able to identify all the possible minimal sets of bugs that can explain the abnormal behaviour of an erroneous program.

We conclude this chapter with a small section that exhibits how the above debugging transformation can be used for the view update problem in deductive databases, and compare to previous work.

12.1 Two-valued contradiction removal

In this section we define a two-valued contradiction removal procedure. Instead of revising assumptions from true to undefined we change their truthvalue to false. Contradiction removal is achieved by adding to the original program the complements of some revisable literals.

Definition 12.1.1 (Revision facts). *The revision fact for a default literal not L is: L*

By RF(S) where S is a set of default literals, we mean:

$$RF(S) = \{L \mid not\ L \in S\}$$

These facts allows, by adding them to a program, to force default literals in the paraconsistent *WFSX* to become false.

Definition 12.1.2 (Submodels of a program). *A submodel of a (contradictory) program P with ICs, and revisable literals Rev, is any pair $\langle M, R \rangle_2$ where R is a subset of Rev:*

$$M = WFSX_p(P \cup RF(R))$$

In a submodel $\langle M, R \rangle_2$ we dub R the submodel revision, and M are the consequences of the submodel revision. A submodel is contradictory iff M is contradictory (i.e. either contains $\perp$ or is not an interpretation).

As we are interested in revising contradiction in a minimal way, we care about those submodels that are noncontradictory and among these, about those that are minimal in the sense of set inclusion.

Definition 12.1.3 (Two-valued revision). *A submodel $\langle M, R \rangle_2$ is a two-valued revision of a program P iff it is noncontradictory.*

Definition 12.1.4 (Minimal two-valued revision).
A two-valued revision $\langle M, R \rangle_2$ is a two-valued minimal revision, of a program P iff there exists no other two-valued revision $\langle M', R' \rangle_2$, such that $R' \subset R$.

Example 12.1.1. Consider contradictory program P:

$$
\begin{array}{rclrcl}
a & \leftarrow & not\ b, not\ c & \perp & \leftarrow & a, \neg a \\
\neg a & \leftarrow & not\ d & \perp & \leftarrow & b \\
c & \leftarrow & e & \perp & \leftarrow & d, not\ f
\end{array}
$$

Intuitively literals *not b*, *not d* and *not e* are true, entailing a and $\neg a$, and thus $\perp$ via violation of the integrity rule $\perp \leftarrow a, \neg a$.

The revisions of the above program are $\{e\}$, $\{d, f\}$, $\{e, f\}$ and $\{d, e, f\}$. The minimal ones are $\{e\}$ and $\{d, f\}$.

Even for very simple programs it is possible to have three-valued revisions and no two-valued revision.

Example 12.1.2. Given the set of revisables $\{not\ a\}$, the program

$$
\begin{array}{rcl}
\perp & \leftarrow & not\ a \\
\perp & \leftarrow & a
\end{array}
$$

has the unique three-valued revision $< \{not\ \neg a\}, \{not\ a\} >_2$ and no two-valued revision.

Also a sceptical revision is no longer defined for the two-valued case: the join of two minimal revisions may be contradictory:

Example 12.1.3. Consider program

$$a \quad \leftarrow \quad not\ b, not\ c$$

$$\bot \quad \leftarrow \quad a$$
$$\bot \quad \leftarrow \quad b, c$$

If the revisables are $\{not\ b, not\ c\}$ the two-valued minimal revisions are:

$< \{not\ a, b, not\ c, \ldots\}, \{not\ b\} >_2$ and $< \{not\ a, c, not\ b, \ldots\}, \{not\ c\} >_2$

The submodel corresponding to the revision facts $\{b, c\}$ is contradictory.

12.1.1 Computing minimal two-valued revisions

Based on the above, we have devised an iterative algorithm to compute the minimal revisions of a program P with respect to to revisables R, and shown its soundness and completeness for finite R. The algorithm is a repeated application of an algorithm to compute contradiction removal sets.

The algorithm starts by finding out the $CRSs$ of the original program plus the empty set of revision facts (assuming the original program is revisable, otherwise the algorithm stops after the first step). To each CRS there corresponds a set of revision facts obtained by taking the complement of their elements. The algorithm then adds, non-deterministically and one at a time, each of these sets of assumptions to the original program. One of three cases occurs: (1) the program thus obtained is non-contradictory and we are in the presence of one minimal revising set of assumptions; (2) the new program is contradictory and non-revisable (and this fact is recorded by the algorithm to prune away other contradictory programs obtained by it); (3) the new program is contradictory but revisable, and this very same algorithm is iterated until we finitely attain one of the two other cases. For the formal description see algorithm 12.1.5.

The sets of revision facts employed to obtain the revised non-contradictory programs are the minimal revisions of the original program. The algorithm can terminate after executing only one step when the program is either non-contradictory, or contradictory but non-revisable. It can be shown this algorithm is NP-hard.

The algorithm tries to restore consistency by looking at each step to the set of integrity rules currently violated. After satisfying these constraints, by adding a set of revision facts to the original program, the algorithm tests if new integrity constraints are violated. If all the denials are satisfied then the algorithm reports a minimal revision. Mark that there is a non-deterministic step in the selection of revision facts to add to the program.

Definition 12.1.5 (Algorithm for Minimal revisions of a program).

Input: *A possibly contradictory program P and a set R of revisables.*

$SS_0 := \{\{\}\}$
$Cs := \{\}$
$i := 0$
repeat
    $SS_{i+1} := \{\}$
    for each $A \in SS_i$
      if $\neg \exists C \in Cs : C \subseteq A$
        if $Rev(P, A) \models \bot$
          if $Rev(P, A)$ *is revisable*
            for each $CRS_j(R)$ *of* $P \cup A$
              Let $NAs := A \cup not\ CRS_j(R)$
              $SS_{i+1} := SS_{i+1} \cup \{NAs\}$
            endfor
          else
            $Cs := MinimalSetsOf(Cs \cup \{A\})$
          endif
        else
          $SS_{i+1} := SS_{i+1} \cup \{A\}$
        endif
      endif
    endfor
    $SS_{i+1} := MinimalSetsOf(SS_{i+1})$
    $i := i + 1$
until $SS_i = SS_{i-1}$.

Output: *SS_i, the collection of all minimal revisions of P with respect to R.*

Example 12.1.4. In Example 12.1.1, the integrity rule $\bot \leftarrow a, \neg a$ is violated. By adding to P any of the sets of facts $\{b\}$, $\{d\}$, or $\{e\}$, this rule becomes satisfied.

Program $Rev(P, \{e\})$ is non-contradictory: thus $\{e\}$ is a revision of P. But $Rev(P, \{b\})$ and $Rev(P, \{d\})$ still entail $\bot$, respectively violating integrity rules $\bot \leftarrow b$ and $\bot \leftarrow d, not\ f$. In $Rev(P, \{b\})$ integrity rule $\bot \leftarrow b$ cannot be satisfied: $\{b\}$ is not a revision. In $Rev(P, \{d\})$ integrity rule can be satisfied by adding to $\{d\}$ the assumption f, to obtain also the revision $\{d, f\}$ (cf. Fig. 12.2).

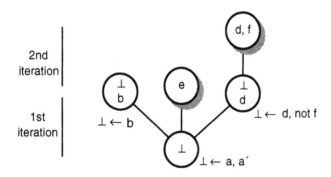

Fig. 12.2. Revision of Example 12.1.1.

Example 12.1.5. Detailed execution for contradictory program P:

$$p \leftarrow not\ a \qquad x$$
$$\neg p \leftarrow not\ c \qquad \neg x \leftarrow c, not\ a, not\ b$$

with set of revisables $R = \{not\ a, not\ \neg a, not\ b, not\ \neg b, not\ c, not\ \neg c\}$.

- $i = 0 : SS_0 = \{\{\}\}, Cs = \{\}$.
  The only A in SS_0 is $\{\}$. As $\bot \in SubM(\{\})$, with $CRS_1 = \{not\ a\}$ and $CRS_2 = \{not\ c\}$, $SS_1 = \{\{a\}, \{c\}\}$.
- $i = 1 : SS_1 = \{\{a\}, \{c\}\}, Cs = \{\}$.
  For $A = \{a\}$, $SubM(\{a\})$ is non-contradictory. The other option is $A = \{c\}$, with $\bot \in SubM(\{c\})$, so $CRS_1 = \{not\ a\}$ and $CRS_2 = \{not\ b\}$. Thus $SS_2 = \{\{a\}, \{b, c\}\}$ since $\{a\}$ is in $\{a, c\}$.
- $i = 2 : SS_1 = \{\{a\}, \{b, c\}\}, Cs = \{\}$.
  With $A = \{a\}$ and $A = \{b, c\}$ $SubM(A)$ is non-contradictory, which implies $SS_3 = SS_2$ and so the algorithm stops.

The sets of minimal two-valued revisions for this program with respect to R are $A_1 = \{a\}$ and $A_2 = \{b, c\}$. Note the need for retaining only minimal sets of revision facts to get the desired result without making useless computation.

We can guarantee soundness, completeness and termination when a finite number of revisables is employed.

Theorem 12.1.1 (Soundness). *If algorithm 12.1.5 terminates in iteration i, SS_i is the collection of all sets of minimal revising assumptions of P with respect to R.*

Theorem 12.1.2 (Completeness). *For finite R algorithm 12.1.5 stops.*

If the set of revisables is not finite two distinct situations may occur:

- The program has no $CRSs$ and the algorithm aborts;
- Some (partially) revised program has an infinite number of $CRSs$. The algorithm returns the minimal revisions after infinite time has elapsed.

12.2 Application to diagnosis

In this section we describe a general program transformation that translates diagnostic problems (**DP**), in the sense of [46], into logic programs with integrity rules. By revising this program we obtain the diagnostic problem's minimal solutions, i.e. the diagnoses. The unifying approach of abductive and consistency-based diagnosis presented by these authors enables us to represent easily and solve a major class of diagnostic problems using two-valued contradiction removal. Similar work has been done by [169] using Generalised Stable Models [94].

We start by making a short description of a diagnostic problem as defined in [46, 52]. A **DP** is a triple consisting of a system description, inputs and observations. The system is modelled by a Horn theory describing the devices, their behaviours and relationships. In this diagnosis setting, each component of the system to be diagnosed has a description of its possible behaviours with the additional restriction that a given device can only be in a single mode of a set of possible ones. There is a mandatory mode in each component modelled, the correct mode, that describes correct device behaviour; the other mutually exclusive behaviour modes represent possible faulty behaviours.

Having this static model of the system we can submit to it a given set of inputs (contextual data) and compare the results obtained with the observations predicted by our conceptualized model. Following [46] the contextual data and observation part of the diagnostic problem are sets of parameters of the form parameter(value) with the restriction that a given parameter can only have one observed valued.

From these introductory definitions [46] present a general diagnosis framework unifying the consistency-based and abductive approaches. These authors translate the diagnostic problem into abduction problems where the abducibles are the behaviour modes of the various system components. From the observations of the system two sets are constructed: Ψ^+, the subset of the observations that must be explained, and $\Psi^- = \{\neg f(X) : f(Y)$ is an observation, for each admissible value X of parameter f other than $Y\}$. A diagnosis is a minimal consistent set of abnormality hypotheses, with additional assumptions of correct behaviour of the other devices, that consistently explain some of the observed outputs: the program plus the hypotheses must derive (cover) all the observations in Ψ^+ consistent with Ψ^-. By varying the set Ψ^+ a spectrum of different types of diagnosis is obtained.

We show that it is always possible to compute the minimal solutions of a diagnostic problem by computing the minimal revising assumptions of a simple program transformation of the system model.

Example 12.2.1. Consider the following partial model of an engine, with only one component *oil_cup*, which has behaviour modes *correct* and *holed* [46]:

$$
\begin{aligned}
oil\_below\_car(present) &\leftarrow holed(oil\_cup) \\
oil\_level(low) &\leftarrow holed(oil\_cup) \\
oil\_level(normal) &\leftarrow correct(oil\_cup) \\
engine\_temperature(high) &\leftarrow oil\_level(low), engine(on) \\
engine\_temperature(normal) &\leftarrow oil\_level(normal), engine(on)
\end{aligned}
$$

An observation is made of the system, and it is known that the engine is on and that there is oil below the car. The authors study two abduction problems corresponding to this **DP** :

1. $\Psi^+ = \{oil\_below\_car(present)\}$ and $\Psi^- = \{\}$ (Poole's view of a diagnostic problem [168]) with minimal solution $W_1 = \{holed(oil\_cup)\}$.
2. $\Psi^+ = \Psi^- = \{\}$ (De Kleer's **DP** view [51]) with minimal solution $W_2 = \{\}$.

To solve abduction problem 1 it is necessary to add the following rules:

$$
\begin{aligned}
\bot &\leftarrow not\ oil\_below\_car(present) \\
correct(oil\_cup) &\leftarrow not\ ab(oil\_cup) \\
holed(oil\_cup) &\leftarrow ab(oil\_cup), fault\_mode(oil\_cup, holed)
\end{aligned}
$$

The above program has only one minimal revision

$$\{ab(oil\_cup), fault\_mode(oil\_cup, holed)\}$$

as wanted.

To solve the second problem, the transformed program has the same rules of the program for problem P, except the integrity constraint – it is not necessary to cover any set of observations. The program thus obtained is noncontradictory having minimal revision $\{\}$.

Next, we present the general program transformation which turns a diagnostic abduction problem into a contradiction removal problem.

Theorem 12.2.1. *Given an abduction problem (**AP**) corresponding to a diagnostic problem, the minimal solutions of **AP** are the minimal revising assumptions of the modelling program plus contextual data and the following rules:*

1. $\perp \leftarrow not\ obs(v)$, *for each* $obs(v) \in \Psi^+$.
2. $\neg obs(v)$, *for each* $\neg obs(v) \in \Psi^-$.

and for each component c_i with distinct abnormality behaviour modes b_j and b_k:

3. $correct(c_i) \leftarrow not\ ab(c_i)$.
4. $b_j(ci) \leftarrow ab(c_i), fault\_mode(c_i, b_j)$.
5. $\perp \leftarrow fault\_mode(c_i, b_j), fault\_mode(c_i, b_k)$ *for each* b_j, b_k.

with revisables $fault\_mode(c_i, b_j)$ and $ab(c_i)$.

We don't give a detailed proof of this result here but take into consideration the following direct mappings of problem specification:

- Rule 1 ensures that, for each consistent set of assumptions, $obs(v) \in \Psi^+$ must be entailed by the program.
- Rule 2 guarantees the consistency of the sets of assumptions with Ψ^-.
- Rules 4 and 5 deal and generate all the possible mutually exclusive behaviours of a given component.

Finally, in no revision there appears the literal $fault\_mode(c, correct)$, thus guaranteeing that minimal revising assumptions are indeed minimal solutions to the **DP**.

The concept of declarative debugging, see Section 12.3, can be used to aid in the development of logic programs and in particular to help the construction of behavioural models of devices. Firstly, a Prolog prototype or blueprint of the component is written and debugged using the methodology presented in that section. After the system is constructed, the diagnostic problems can be solved using contradiction removal as described above, in the correct blueprint.

In the rest of this section we'll present several examples of diagnosis problems. Whenever possible, we'll try to write the logic programs as close as possible to the ones obtained by the previous program transformation. We start by a very simple example which shows how difficult the modelization task can be.

Example 12.2.2. Consider the simple logic circuit of figure 12.3. We'll present two models of the circuit. Both are correct for predicting the behaviour of the circuit, but only one can be used to perform correctly the diagnosis task.

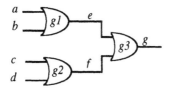

Fig. 12.3. The three or problem

The naïve solution would model an or gate with the following program:

$$or\_gate(G, 1, 1, 1) \leftarrow correct(G)$$
$$or\_gate(G, 0, 1, 1) \leftarrow correct(G)$$
$$or\_gate(G, 1, 0, 1) \leftarrow correct(G)$$
$$or\_gate(G, 0, 0, 0) \leftarrow correct(G)$$

$$correct(G) \leftarrow not\ ab(G)$$

The topology of the circuit is captured by:

$$node(e, E) \leftarrow node(a, A), node(b, B), or\_gate(g1, A, B, E)$$
$$node(f, F) \leftarrow node(c, C), node(d, D), or\_gate(g2, C, D, F)$$
$$node(g, G) \leftarrow node(e, E), node(f, F), or\_gate(g3, E, F, G)$$

Given the inputs, this program correctly predicts the outputs. But our main concern is diagnosis, and this program can not be used to do it !!! Suppose the situation where the value at nodes "a", "b", "c" and "d" is 1 and the output at node "g" is 0. Obviously, we cannot explain this wrong output because we have no description of the behaviour of an or gate when it is abnormal, i.e. there are no fault-models. So we only require the consistency with the observed output ($\Psi^+ = \{\}$ and $\Psi^- = \{\neg node(g, 1)\}$):

$$node(a, 1) \quad node(c, 1) \quad \neg node(g, 1)$$
$$node(b, 1) \quad node(d, 1)$$

If we apply the contradiction removal method, with the revisables being the ab literals, we obtain as minimal revisions:

$$\{ab(g_1)\} \quad \{ab(g_2)\} \quad \{ab(g_3)\}$$

Intuitively, the first two diagnoses are incorrect. For instance, consider the diagnosis $\{ab(g1)\}$. In this situation gate 3 still has an input node with logical value 1, therefore its output should be also 1. The problem is that in the program above an "or" gate to give its output must have both inputs determined, i.e. the absorption property of these gates is not correctly modeled. An alternative and correct description of this circuit is given below:

$$or\_gate(G, I1, I2, 1) \;\leftarrow\; node(I1, 1), correct(G)$$
$$or\_gate(G, I1, I2, 1) \;\leftarrow\; node(I2, 1), correct(G)$$
$$or\_gate(G, I1, I2, 0) \;\leftarrow\; node(I1, 0), node(I2, 0), correct(G)$$

$$correct(G) \;\leftarrow\; not\; ab(G)$$

The connection's representation part is slightly simplified:

$$node(e, E) \;\leftarrow\; or\_gate(g1, a, b, E)$$
$$node(f, F) \;\leftarrow\; or\_gate(g2, c, d, F)$$
$$node(g, G) \;\leftarrow\; or\_gate(g3, e, f, G)$$

Now, with the same set of inputs and constraints we obtain the expected diagnosis:

$$\{ab(g_1), ab(g_2)\} \quad \{ab(g_3)\}$$

Finally, notice that using this new model it is also not possible to explain the output of gate g3. If we set $\Psi^+ = \{node(g, 0)\}$ and $\Psi^- = \{\neg node(g, 1)\}$, translated according to Theorem 12.2.1 to:

$$\bot \;\leftarrow\; not\; node(g, 0)$$
$$\neg node(g, 1)$$

This new program (plus the input and circuit description) is contradictory, i.e. there is no two-valued revision.

Other solution is given to the previous problem is described in the next example: we mantain the wrong model of the gates an add a particular fault model to it. Besides, the example will exemplify in a concrete situation the distinction between three-valued revision and two-valued revision.

Example 12.2.3. Consider the circuit of figure 12.4, with inputs $a = 0$, $b = 1$,

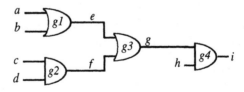

Fig. 12.4. Logic circuit of Example 12.2.3

$c = 1$, $d = 1$, $h = 1$ and (incorrect) output 0. Its behavioural model is:

% Normal behaviour of and gates

$and\_gate(G, 1, 1, 1) \quad \leftarrow \quad correct(G)$

$and\_gate(G, 0, 1, 0) \quad \leftarrow \quad correct(G)$

$and\_gate(G, 1, 0, 0) \quad \leftarrow \quad correct(G)$

$and\_gate(G, 0, 0, 0) \quad \leftarrow \quad correct(G)$

% Faulty behaviour

$and\_gate(G, 1, 1, 0) \quad \leftarrow \quad abnormal(G)$

$and\_gate(G, 0, 1, 1) \quad \leftarrow \quad abnormal(G)$

$and\_gate(G, 1, 0, 1) \quad \leftarrow \quad abnormal(G)$

$and\_gate(G, 0, 0, 1) \quad \leftarrow \quad abnormal(G)$

And a similar set of rules for *or* gates, as in Example 12.2.2. According to the program transformation two auxiliary rules are needed:

$correct(G) \quad \leftarrow \quad not\ ab(G)$

$abnormal(G) \quad \leftarrow \quad ab(G)$

and the description of the circuit and its connections:

$node(a, 0) \quad node(b, 1) \quad node(c, 1)$

$node(d, 1) \quad node(h, 1)$

Connections

$node(e, E) \quad \leftarrow \quad node(a, A), node(b, B), or\_gate(g1, A, B, E)$

$node(f, F) \quad \leftarrow \quad node(c, C), node(d, D), and\_gate(g2, C, D, F)$

$node(g, G) \quad \leftarrow \quad node(e, E), node(f, F), or\_gate(g3, E, F, G)$

$node(i, I) \quad \leftarrow \quad node(g, G), node(h, H), and\_gate(g4, G, H, I)$

Selecting a consistency-based approach, i.e $\Psi^+ = \{\}$:

$\neg node(i, 1)$

The minimal solutions to this problem are highlighted in figure 12.5. The two-valued minimal revisions , $ab(g3)$ and

$\{ab(g1), ab(g2)\} \quad \{ab(g3)\} \quad \{ab(g4)\}$

are the minimal solutions to the diagnosis problem. The above representation does not suffer from the problems of the Example 12.2.2. This is due to the fact that when an abnormality assumption is made the gate's fault-model become "active", an output value is produced which can be used by other gates in the circuit. Notice that this program is able to explain the outputs: if an integrity rule enforcing that the output at node "g" should be 0 is added to the program then the minimal revisions are the same as before.

If instead of two-valued contradiction removal the three-valued one is used four (with two intuitively incorrect) single-fault diagnoses are found:

$\{ab(g1)\} \quad \{ab(g2)\} \quad \{ab(g3)\} \quad \{ab(g4)\}$

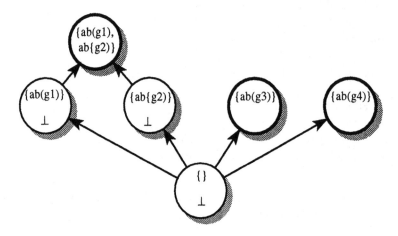

Fig. 12.5. Diagnoses of Example 12.2.3

Remember that these literals are revised to undefined, blocking the propagation of values from inputs to outputs. This short example shows again that the naïve model of logical gates is not adequate for diagnosis. More differences between three-valued and two-valued contradiction will be drawn in the next example.

In Example 12.2.4 we'll show how to represent and reason with fault-models in the diagnosis task.

Example 12.2.4. Consider the situation in figure 12.6, where two inverters are connected in series. This particular situation can be represented by the program below:

$$
\begin{array}{lll}
inv(T,G,I,1) & \leftarrow & node(T,I,0), not\ ab(G) \quad 1 \\
inv(T,G,I,0) & \leftarrow & node(T,I,1), not\ ab(G) \quad 2 \\
\\
node(T,b,B) & \leftarrow & inv(T,g1,a,B) \quad\quad\quad 3 \\
node(T,c,C) & \leftarrow & inv(T,g2,b,C) \quad\quad\quad 4 \\
\\
node(0,a,0) & & \quad\quad\quad\quad\quad\quad\quad\quad 5 \\
\neg node(0,c,0) & & \quad\quad\quad\quad\quad\quad\quad\quad 6
\end{array}
$$

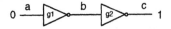

Fig. 12.6. Two inverters circuit

Rules 1-2 model normal inverter behaviour, where *correct* has been replaced by *not ab*. Rules 3-4 specify the circuit topology. Rule 5 establishes the input as 0. Rule 6 specifies the observed output should not be 0 (consistency-based approach). The extra parameter T in all rules is a time-stamp that let us encode multiple observations. For the time being suppose that the previous observation was made at time 0. The revisables are, as usual, the *ab* literals.

Revising this program, using either contradiction removal methods, these minimal revisions are obtained:

$$\{ab(g1)\} \quad \{ab(g2)\}$$

Now, trying to explain the output, via integrity rule $\bot \leftarrow not\ node(0, c, 1)$, the program is contradictory and non-revisable. It is necessary to add a fault-model to the program:

$$
\begin{array}{llll}
inv(T, G, I, 0) & \leftarrow & fault\_mode(G, s0) & 7 \\
inv(T, G, I, 1) & \leftarrow & fault\_mode(G, s1) & 8 \\
inv(T, G, I, V) & \leftarrow & node(T, I, V), fault\_mode(G, sh) & 9
\end{array}
$$

$$
\begin{array}{llr}
\bot & \leftarrow & fault\_mode(G, M1), fault\_mode(G, M2), \\
& & M1 \neq M2 \qquad\qquad\qquad\qquad\qquad 10
\end{array}
$$

Rules 7-9 model three fault modes: one expresses the output is stuck at 0, the other that it is stuck at 1, whatever the input may be, and the other that the output is shorted with the input. According to rule 10 the three fault modes are mutually exclusive. If a pure consistency-based diagnosis is performed the revisions are the same as before. Whereas, the observed output can be explained:

$$\bot \leftarrow not\ node(0, c, 1) \quad 11$$

The program consisting of rules 1-11 is revisable with minimal diagnosis (with either of the contradiction removal techniques):

$$\{ab(g1), fault\_mode(g1, sh)\} \quad \{ab(g1), fault\_mode(g1, s0)\}$$
$$\{ab(g2), fault\_mode(g2, s1)\} \quad \{ab(g2), fault\_mode(g2, sh)\}$$

Regardless of the minimal revisions being the same with both methods, they have different consequences. The two-valued approach really explains the output, i.e. $node(0, c, 1)$ is entailed by any of the revised programs. The three-valued method doesn't: it satisfies the constraints by (indirectly) undefining the literals $node(0, c, 0)$ and $node(0, c, 1)$. The distinct effects will be clear soon.

Suppose now that an additional experiment is made at time 1, by setting the input to 1 and observing output 1. This test is modeled by the rules:

$$
\begin{array}{lr}
node(1, a, 1) & 12 \\
\neg node(1, c, 0) & 13 \\
\bot \leftarrow not\ node(1, c, 1) & 14
\end{array}
$$

With the third-valued contradiction removal method the minimal diagnoses are the same as before, whereas with the two-valued one they are:

$$\{ab(g1), fault\_mode(g1, s0)\} \quad \{ab(g2), fault\_mode(g2, s1)\}$$
$$\{ab(g1), fault\_mode(g1, s1)ab(g2), fault\_mode(g2, sh)\}$$

Next, a typical and problematic problem is presented and correctly (and easily) solved.

Example 12.2.5. [203] Three bulbs are set in parallel with a source via connecting wires and a switch (cf. figure 12.7), as specified in the first three rules (where *ok* is used instead of *correct*). Normality is assumed by default in the rule for *ok*. The two integrity rules enforce that the switch is always either *open* or *closed*. Since both cannot be assumed simultaneously, this program has two minimal revisions, with *ab, open, closed* being the revisables: one obtained by revising the assumption of *not open* (i.e. adding *open*); the other by revising the assumption of *not closed* (i.e. adding *closed*). In the first *open, not on(b1), not on(b2), not on(b3)* are true in the model; in the second *closed, on(b1), on(b2), on(b3)* do.

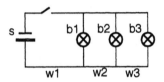

Fig. 12.7. Three bulbs circuit

$$
\begin{aligned}
on(b1) \;&\leftarrow\; closed, ok(s), ok(w1), ok(b1) \\
on(b2) \;&\leftarrow\; closed, ok(s), ok(w1), ok(w2), ok(b2) \\
on(b3) \;&\leftarrow\; closed, ok(s), ok(w1), ok(w2), ok(w3), ok(b3) \\
ok(X) \;&\leftarrow\; not\ ab(X)
\end{aligned}
$$

$$
\begin{aligned}
\bot \;&\leftarrow\; not\ open, not\ closed \\
\bot \;&\leftarrow\; open, closed
\end{aligned}
$$

Further integrity rules specify observed behaviour to be explained. For instance, to explain that bulb 1 is on it is only necessary to add $\bot \leftarrow not\ on(b1)$ to obtain the single, intuitive, minimal revision $\{closed\}$.

Suppose instead we wish to explain that bulb 2 is off (i.e. not on). Adding $\bot \leftarrow on(b2)$, five minimal revisions explain it, four of which express faults:

$$\{closed, not\ ab(s)\} \quad \{closed, not\ ab(w_1)\}$$
$$\{closed, not\ ab(b_2)\} \quad \{closed, not\ ab(w_2)\}$$
$$\{open\}$$

Adding now both integrity rules, only two of the previous revisions remain: both with the switch closed, but one stating that bulb 2 is abnormal and the other that wire 2 is.

Finally, we show a more extensive example due to [45].

Example 12.2.6. [45] Causal nets are a general representation schema used to describe possibly incomplete causal knowledge, in particular to represent the faulty behaviour of a system. Consider the (simple) causal model of a car engine in figure 12.8.

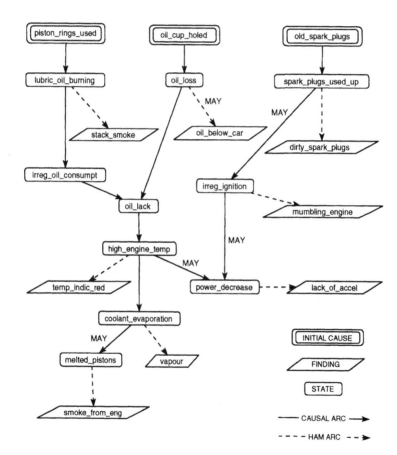

Fig. 12.8. Causal model in a mechanical domain

A causal net is formed by nodes and arcs connecting nodes. There are (at least) three types of nodes:

– *Initial Cause* nodes - represent the deep causes of the faulty behaviour. It is assumed that the initial perturbations are not directly observable;

– *State* nodes - describe partial states of the modeled system;
– *Finding* nodes - observable manifestations of the system.

There are two kinds of arcs: *causal arcs* that represent cause/effect relationships and *has manifestations* arcs connecting states with their observable manifestations. These arcs can be labeled by a MAY tag, stating some sort of incompleteness in the model.

This formalism can be easily translated to logic programming:

$$
\begin{aligned}
lubric\_oil\_burning &\leftarrow piston\_rings\_used \\
stack\_smoke &\leftarrow lubric\_oil\_burning \\
\\
irreg\_oil\_consumpt &\leftarrow lubric\_oil\_burning \\
oil\_loss &\leftarrow oil\_cup\_holed \\
oil\_below\_car &\leftarrow oil\_loss, may(oil\_below\_car, oil\_loss) \\
\\
oil\_lack &\leftarrow oil\_loss \\
oil\_lack &\leftarrow irreg\_oil\_consumpt \\
\\
high\_engine\_temp &\leftarrow oil\_lack \\
temp\_indic\_red &\leftarrow high\_engine\_temp \\
\\
coolant\_evaporation &\leftarrow high\_engine\_temp \\
vapour &\leftarrow coolant\_evaporation \\
\\
power\_decrease &\leftarrow high\_engine\_temp, \\
&\quad may(power\_dec, high\_eng\_temp) \\
lack\_of\_accel &\leftarrow power\_decrease \\
\\
melted\_pistons &\leftarrow coolant\_evaporation, \\
&\quad may(melted\_pistons, cool\_evap) \\
smoke\_from\_eng &\leftarrow melted\_pistons
\end{aligned}
$$

...

If the findings "dirty spark plugs", "lack of acceleration", "temperature indicator is red" and "vapour" are observed the following integrity rules are added to the program:

$$
\begin{aligned}
\bot &\leftarrow not\ dirty\_spark\_plugs & \bot &\leftarrow not\ vapour \\
\bot &\leftarrow not\ lack\_of\_accel & \bot &\leftarrow not\ temp\_indic\_red
\end{aligned}
$$

By revising the program, with the revisables being the *initial cause* nodes and *may* literals, the minimal revisions are:

$\{ \quad old\_spark\_plugs, may(irreg\_ignition, spark\_plugs\_used\_up)$

$piston\_rings\_used, may(power\_decrease, irreg\_ignition) \qquad \}$

$\{ \quad oil\_cup\_holed, may(irreg\_ignition, spark\_plugs\_used\_up),$

$old\_spark\_plugs, may(power\_decrease, irreg\_ignition) \qquad \}$

$\{ \quad oil\_cup\_holed, old\_spark\_plugs,$

$may(power\_decrease, high\_engine\_temp) \qquad \}$

$\{ \quad old\_spark\_plugs, piston\_rings\_used,$

$may(power\_decrease, high\_engine\_temp) \qquad \}$

12.3 Application to debugging

It is clear that fault-finding or diagnosis is akin to debugging. In the context of logic, both arise as a confrontation between theory and model. Whereas in debugging one confronts an erroneous theory, in the form of a set of clauses, with models in the form of input/output pairs, in diagnosis one confronts a perfect theory (a set of rules acting as a blueprint or specification for some artifact) with the imperfect input/output behaviour of the artifact (which, if it were not faulty, would behave in accordance with a theory model).

What is common to both is the mismatch. The same techniques used in debugging to pinpoint faulty rules can equally be used to find the causes, in a perfect blueprint, which are at odds with artifact behaviour. Then, by means of the correspondence from the blueprint's modelization to the artifact's subcomponents whose i/o behaviour they emulate, the faulty ones can be spotted.

Declarative debugging then is essentially a diagnosis task, but until now its relationship to diagnosis was unclear or inexistent. We present a novel and uniform technique for normal logic program declarative error diagnosis by laying down the foundations on a general approach to diagnosis using logic programming. In so doing the debugging activity becomes clarified, thereby gaining a more intuitive appeal and generality. This new view may beneficially enhance the cross-fertilization between the diagnosis and debugging fields. Additionally, we operationalize the debugging process via a contradiction removal (or abductive) approach to the problem. The ideas of this work extend in several ways the ones of [119].

A program can be thought of as a theory whose logical consequences engender its actual input/output behaviour. Whereas the program's intended input/output behaviour is postulated by the theory's purported models, i.e. the truths the theory supposedly accounts for.

The object of the debugging exercise is to pinpoint erroneous or missing axioms, from erroneous or missing derived truths, so as to account for each discrepancy between a theory and its models. The classical declarative debugging theory [119] assumes that these models are completely known via an omniscient entity or "oracle".

In a more general setting, that our theory accounts for, these models may be only partially known and the lacking information might not be (easily) obtainable. By hypothesizing the incorrect and missing axioms that are compatible with the given information, possible incorrections are diagnosed but not perfected, i.e. sufficient corrections are made to the program but only virtually. This process of performing sufficing virtual corrections is the crux of our method.

From the whole set of possible diagnoses we argue that the set of minimal ones is the expected and intuitive desired result of the debugging process. When the intended interpretation (model) is entirely known, then a unique minimal diagnosis exists which identifies the bugs in the program. Whenever in the presence of incomplete information, the set of minimal diagnoses corresponds to all conceivable minimal sets of bugs; these are exactly the ones compatible with the missing information; in other words, compatible with all the imaginable oracle answer sequences that would complete the information about the intended model. It is guaranteed one of these sets pinpoints bugs that justify the disparities observed between program behaviours and user expectations. Mark that if only one minimal diagnosis is obtained then at least part of the bugs in the program were sieved, but more may persist.

Diagnostic debugging can be enacted by the contradiction removal methods introduced in Section 12.1 [162]. Indeed, a simple program transformation affords a contradiction removal approach to debugging, on the basis of revising the assumptions about predicates' correctness and completeness, just for those predicates and goals that support buggy behaviour. We shall see this transformation has an effect similar to that of turning the program into an artifact specification with equivalent behaviour, whose predicates model the components, each with associated abnormality and fault-mode literals. When faced with the disparities between the expected and observed behaviour, the transformed program generates, by using contradiction removal methods, all possible virtual corrections of the original program This is due to a one-to-one mapping between the (minimal) diagnoses of the original program and the (minimal) revisions of the transformed one.

These very same methods can be applied to the updating of knowledge bases with integrity constraints represented as logic programs. By only partially transforming the program the user can express which predicates are liable to retraction of rules and addition of facts. The iterative contradiction removal algorithm of Section 12.1.1 ensures that the minimal transactions thus obtained do satisfy the integrity constraints.

These ideas on how debugging and fault-finding relate are new, the attractiveness of the approach being its basis on logic programs. In the same vein that one can obtain a general debugger for normal logic programs, irrespective of the program domain, one can aim at constructing a general fault-finding procedure, whatever the faulty artifact may be, just as long as it can be modelled by logic programs not confined to being normal logic programs, but including more expressive extensions such as explicit negation.

However we must still go some way until this ultimate goal can be achieved. The current method applies only to a particular class of normal logic programs where the well-founded model [76] and SLDNF-resolution [118] coincide in meaning. The debugging of programs under *WFSX* is also foreseen, where new and demanding problems are yet to be solved. On the positive side, the loop detection properties of well-founded semantics will allow for a declarative treatment of otherwise endless derivations.

We examine here the problem of declarative error diagnosis, or debugging, for the class of normal logic programs, where SLDNF-Resolution can be used to finitely compute *all* the logic consequences of these programs, i.e. SLDNF-Resolution gives the complete meaning of the program. In the sequel we designate this particular class of programs as source programs.

Well-founded semantics plays an important rôle in our approach to declarative debugging. By considering only source programs, we guarantee that the well-founded model is total and equivalent to the model computed by SLDNF-Resolution. In [177], Przymusinski showed that SLDNF-Resolution is sound with respect to well-founded semantics. Thus, for these programs it is indifferent to consider the WFM or Clark's completion semantics [42].

On the other hand, we intend to further develop this approach, and then deal with the issue of debugging of programs under WFS. By using WFS, loop problems are avoided. Conceivably, we could so debug symptoms in loop-free parts of a normal program under SLDNF, even if some other parts of it have loops.

Last, but not least, the basis of our declarative debugging proposal consists in applying the two-valued contradiction removal method defined in Section 12.1.

12.3.1 Declarative error diagnosis

Next we present the classical theory of declarative error diagnosis, following mainly [119], in order to proceed to a different view of the issue.

It would be desireable that a program gave all and only the correct answers to a user's queries. Usually a program contains some bugs that must be corrected before it can produce the required behaviour.

Let the meaning of a logic program P be given by the normal Herbrand models for $comp(P)$, Clark's completion of P [42]. Let the ultimate goal of a program be for its meaning to respect the user's intended interpretation of the program.

Definition 12.3.1 (Intended interpretation [119]). *Let P be a program. An intended interpretation for P is a normal Herbrand interpretation for $comp(P)$.*

Definition 12.3.2 (Program correct [119]). *A logic program P is correct with respect to an intended interpretation I_M iff I_M is a model for $comp(P)$.*

Errors in a terminating logic program manifest themselves through two kinds of symptoms (we deliberately ignore for now the question of loop detection).

Definition 12.3.3 (Symptoms). *Let P be a logic program, I_M its intended interpretation, and A an atom in the Herbrand base of P.*

- *if $P \vdash_{SLDNF} A$ and $A \notin I_M$ then A is a* wrong solution *for P with respect to I_M.*
- *if $P \nvdash_{SLDNF} A$ and $A \in I_M$ then A is a* missing solution *for P with respect to I_M.*

Of course, if there is a missing or a wrong solution then the program is not correct with respect to its intended interpretation, and therefore there exists in it some bug requiring correction. In [119] two kinds of errors are identified: uncovered atoms and incorrect clause instances. As we deal with ground programs only, we prefer to designate as incorrect rules the latter type of error.

Definition 12.3.4 (Uncovered atom). *Let P be a program and I_M its intended interpretation. An atom A is an uncovered atom for P with respect to I_M iff $A \in I_M$ but for no rule $A \leftarrow W$ in P, $I_M \models W$.*

Definition 12.3.5 (Incorrect rule). *Let P be a program and I_M its intended interpretation. A rule $A \leftarrow W$ is incorrect for P with respect to I_M iff $A \notin I_M$ and $I_M \models W$.*

Theorem 12.3.1 (Two types of bug only [119]). *Let P be a program and I_M its intended interpretation. P is incorrect with respect to I_M iff there is an uncovered atom for P with respect to I_M or there is an incorrect rule for P with respect to I_M.*

Thus, if there is a missing or a wrong solution there is, at least, an uncovered atom or an incorrect rule for P.

Example 12.3.1. Let P be the (source) program with model $\{not\ a, b, not\ c\}$:

$$a \leftarrow not\ b$$
$$b \leftarrow not\ c$$

Suppose the intended interpretation of P is

$$I_M = \{not\ a, not\ b, c\}$$

i.e. b is a wrong solution, and c a missing solution for P with respect to I_M. The reader can check, c is an uncovered atom for P with respect to I_M, and $a \leftarrow not\ b$ is an incorrect rule for P with respect to I_M.

12.3.2 What is diagnostic debugging?

We now know (cf. Theorem 12.3.1) that if there is a missing or a wrong solution then there is, at least, an uncovered atom or an incorrect rule for P. In classical declarative error diagnosis the complete intended interpretation is always known from the start. Next we characterize the situation where only partial knowledge of the intended interpretation is available but, if possible or wanted, extra information can be obtained. To formalise this debugging activity we introduce two entities: the user and the oracle.

Definition 12.3.6 (User and Oracle). *Let P be a source program and I_M the intended interpretation for P. The user is identified with the limited knowledge of the intended model that he has, i.e. a set $U \subseteq I_M$.*

The oracle is an entity that knows everything, that is, knows the whole intended interpretation I_M.

By definition, the user and the oracle share some knowledge and the user is not allowed to make mistakes nor the oracle to lie. The user has a diagnosis problem and poses the queries and the oracle helps the user: it knows the answers to all possible questions. The user may coincide with the oracle as a special case.

Our approach is mainly motivated by the following obvious theorem: if the incorrect rules of a program[2] are removed, and a fact A for each uncovered atom A is added to the program, then the model of the new transformed program is the intended interpretation of the original one.

Theorem 12.3.2. *Let P be a source program and I_M its intended interpretation.*
If $WFM(P) \neq I_M$, and

$$Unc = \{ \ A \ : \ A \text{ is an uncovered atom for } P \text{ wrt } I_M\}$$
$$InR = \{A \leftarrow B: \ A \leftarrow B \text{ is incorrect for } P \text{ wrt } I_M\}$$

then $WFM((P - InR) \cup Unc) = I_M$.

Example 12.3.2. Consider the source program P

$$a \ \leftarrow \ not \ b$$
$$b \ \leftarrow \ not \ c$$

The $WFM(P)$ is $\{not \ a, b, not \ c\}$. If $I_M = \{not \ a, not \ b, c\}$ is the intended interpretation, then c is an uncovered atom for P with respect to I_M, and $a \leftarrow not \ b$ is an incorrect rule for P with respect to I_M. The WFM of the new program,

$$b \ \leftarrow \ not \ c$$
$$c$$

obtained by applying the transformation above, is I_M.

---

[2] In this section program means source program, unless stated otherwise.

Definition 12.3.7 (Diagnosis). *Let P be a source program, U a set of literals of the language of P, and D the pair $\langle Unc, InR \rangle$ where $Unc \subseteq \mathcal{H}_P$, $InR \subseteq P$.*

D is a diagnosis for U with respect to P iff

$$U \subseteq WFM((P - InR) \cup Unc).$$

Example 12.3.3. In Example 12.3.2, the diagnoses for $U = \{not\ a, c\}$ with respect to P are:

$$
\begin{aligned}
D_1 &= \langle \{b, c\}, & \{\} & & \rangle \\
D_2 &= \langle \{b, c\}, & \{a \leftarrow not\ b\} & & \rangle \\
D_3 &= \langle \{b, c\}, & \{b \leftarrow not\ c\} & & \rangle \\
D_4 &= \langle \{b, c\}, \{a \leftarrow not\ b;\ b \leftarrow not\ c\} \rangle & D_5 &= \langle \{c\}, \{a \leftarrow not\ b\} \rangle \\
D_6 &= \langle \{c\}\ , \{a \leftarrow not\ b;\ b \leftarrow not\ c\} \rangle
\end{aligned}
$$

Each one of these diagnoses can be viewed as a virtual correction of the program. For example, D_1 can be viewed as stating that if the program is corrected so that b and c become true, by adding them as facts say, then the literals in U also become true. Another possibility is to set c true and correct the first rule of the original program. This possibility is reflected by D_5.

However some of these diagnoses are redundant: for instance in D_6 there is no reason to consider the second rule wrong; doing so is redundant.

This is even more serious in the case of D_3. There, the atom b is considered uncovered and all rules for b are considered wrong.

Definition 12.3.8 (Minimal Diagnosis). *Let P be a source program and U a set of literals. Given two diagnosis $D_1 = \langle Unc_1, InR_1 \rangle$ and $D_2 = \langle Unc_2, InR_2 \rangle$ for U with respect to P we say that $D_1 \preceq D_2$ iff $Unc_1 \cup InR_1 \subseteq Unc_2 \cup InR_2$.*

D is a minimal diagnosis for U with respect to P iff there is no diagnosis D_1 for U with respect to P such that $D_1 \preceq D$. $\langle \{\}, \{\} \rangle$ is called the empty diagnosis.

Example 12.3.4. The minimal diagnoses of Example 12.3.2 for $U = \{not\ a, c\}$ with respect to P are D_1 and D_5 above.

Obviously, if the subset of the intended interpretation given by the user is already a consequence of the program, we expect empty to be the only minimal diagnosis: i.e. based on that information no bug is found. This is stated by the following trivial theorem:

Theorem 12.3.3. *Let P be a source program, and U a set of literals. Then $U \subseteq WFM(P)$ iff the only minimal diagnosis for U with respect to P is empty.*

A property of source programs is that if the set U of user provided literals is the complete intended interpretation (the case when the user knowledge coincides with oracle's), a unique minimal diagnosis exists. In this case the minimal diagnosis uniquely identifies all the errors in the program and provides one correction to all the bugs.

Theorem 12.3.4. *Let P be a source program and I_M its intended interpretation. Then $D = \langle Unc, InR \rangle$, where*

$$Unc = \{\; A \; : \; A \text{ is an uncovered atom for } P \text{ wrt } I_M\}$$
$$InR = \{A \leftarrow B : \; A \leftarrow B \text{ is incorrect for } P \text{ wrt } I_M\}$$

is the unique minimal diagnosis for I_M with respect to P.

Proof. It is clear from Theorem 12.3.2 that D is a diagnosis. We prove that D is the unique minimal diagnosis in two steps: first we prove that it is minimal; then we prove that no other minimal diagnosis exists. The proof of both steps is made by contradiction.

D is minimal: Let $D' = \langle Unc', InR' \rangle$ be a diagnosis such that $D' \prec D$.
Since $D' \prec D$ then either there exists at least one $A \notin Unc'$ uncovered for P with respect to I_M or at there exists at least one rule $A \leftarrow B \notin InR'$ incorrect for P with respect to I_M. It is clear in both cases that:

$$I_M \not\subseteq WFM((P - InR') \cup Unc)$$

i.e. D' is not a diagnosis (contradiction).
There is no other minimal diagnosis: Let now $D' = \langle Unc', InR' \rangle$ be a minimal diagnosis such that $D' \neq D$.
Again, and since $D \not\subseteq D'$, then either there exists at least one $A \notin Unc'$ uncovered for P with respect to I_M or at there exists at least one rule $A \leftarrow B \notin InR'$ incorrect for P with respect to I_M. Thus D' is not a diagnosis (contradiction).

The next lemma helps us show important properties of minimal diagnosis:

Lemma 12.3.1. *Let P be a source program, and U_1 and U_2 sets of literals. If $U_1 \subseteq U_2$ and if there are minimal diagnosis for U_1 and U_2 with respect to P then there is a minimal diagnosis for U_1 with respect to P contained in a minimal diagnosis for U_2 with respect to P.*

Proof. To prove this lemma it is enough to prove that for all minimal diagnosis D for U_2 there exists a minimal diagnosis D' for U_1 such that $D' \preceq D$.
Let $D = \langle Unc, InR \rangle$ be any fixed minimal diagnosis for U_2. By definition of diagnosis:

$$U_2 \subseteq WFM((P - InR) \cup Unc)$$

Then, since $U_1 \subseteq U_2$, also $U_1 \subseteq WFM((P - InR) \cup Unc)$, i.e. D is a diagnosis for U_1.
So, clearly, there exists a minimal diagnosis D' for U_1 such that $D' \preceq D$.

Let us suppose the set U provided by the user is a proper subset of the intended interpretation. Then it is expectable that the errors are not imediately detected, in the sense that several minimal diagnoses may exist. The next theorem guarantees that at least one of the minimal diagnoses finds an error of the program.

Theorem 12.3.5. *Let P be a source program, I_M its intended interpretation, and U a set of literals. If $U \subseteq I_M$ and if there are minimal diagnosis for U with respect to P then there is a minimal diagnosis $\langle Unc, InR \rangle$ for U with respect to P such that for every $A \in Unc$, A is an uncovered atom for P with respect to I_M, and for every rule $A \leftarrow B \in InR$, $A \leftarrow B$ is incorrect for P with respect to I_M.*

Proof. Follow directly from lemma 12.3.5.

As a special case, even giving the complete intended interpretation, if one single minimal diagnosis exists then it identifies at least one error.

Corollary 12.3.1. *Let P be a source program, I_M its intended interpretation, and U a set of literals. If there is a unique minimal diagnosis $\langle Unc, InR \rangle$ for U with respect to P then for every $A \in Unc$, A is an uncovered atom for P with respect to I_M, and for every rule $A \leftarrow B \in InR$, $A \leftarrow B$ is incorrect for P with respect to I_M.*

In a process of debugging, when several minimal diagnoses exist, queries should be posed to the oracle in order to enlarge the subset of the intended interpretation provided, and thus refine the diagnoses. Such a process must be iterated until a single minimal diagnosis is found. This eventually happens, albeit when the whole intended interpretation is given (cf. Theorem 12.3.4).

Example 12.3.5. As mentioned above, minimal diagnoses, of Example 12.3.2, for $U = \{not\ a, c\}$ with respect to P are:

$$\begin{aligned} D_1 &= \langle \{b, c\}, \{\} \rangle \\ D_5 &= \langle \{c\}, \{a \leftarrow not\ b\} \rangle \end{aligned}$$

By Theorem 12.3.5, at least one of these diagnoses contains errors. In D_1, b and c are uncovered. Thus, if this is the error, not only literals in U are true but also b. In D_5, c is uncovered and rule $a \leftarrow not\ b$ is incorrect. Thus, if this is the error, b is false.

By asking about the truthfulness of b one can, in fact, identify the error: e.g. should the answer to such query be *yes* the set U is augmented with b and the only minimal diagnosis is D_1; should the answer be *no* U is augmented with *not* b and the only minimal diagnosis is D_5.

The issue of identifying disambiguating oracle queries is dealt with in the next section.

In all the results above we have assumed the existence of at least one minimal diagnosis. This is guaranteed because:

Theorem 12.3.6. *Let P be a source program, I_M its intended interpretation, and U a finite set of literals. If $U \subseteq I_M$ and $U \not\subseteq WFM(P)$ then there is a non-empty minimal diagnosis $\langle Unc, InR \rangle$ for U with respect to P such that, for every $A \in Unc$, A is an uncovered atom for P with respect to I_M, and for every rule $A \leftarrow B \in InR$, $A \leftarrow B$ is incorrect for P with respect to I_M.*

12.3.3 Diagnosis as revision of program assumptions

In this section we show that minimal diagnosis are minimal revisions of a simple transformed program obtained from the original source one. Let's start with the program transformation and some results regarding it.

Definition 12.3.9. *The transformation Υ that maps a source program P into a source program P' is obtained by applying to P the following two operations:*

− *Add to the body of each rule*

$$H \leftarrow B_1, \ldots, B_n, not\ C_1, \ldots, not\ C_m \quad \in P$$

the literal $not\ incorrect(H \leftarrow B_1, \ldots, B_n, not\ C_1, \ldots, not\ C_m)$.
− *Add the rule*

$$p(X_1, X_2, \ldots, X_n) \leftarrow uncovered(p(X_1, X_2, \ldots, X_n))$$

for each predicate p with arity n in the language of P.

It is assumed predicate symbols incorrect and uncovered don't belong to the language of P.

It can be easily shown that the above transformation preserves the truths of P: the literals $not\ incorrect(\ldots)$ and $uncovered(\ldots)$ are, respectively, true and false in the transformed program. The next theorem captures this intuitive result.

Theorem 12.3.7. *Let P be a source program. If L is a literal with predicate symbol distinct from incorrect and uncovered then $L \in WFM(P)$ iff $L \in WFM(\Upsilon(P))$.*

Proof. Trivial since there are no rules for predicates $incorrect$ and $uncovered$ in $WFM(\Upsilon(P))$.

Example 12.3.6. By applying transformation Υ to P of Example 12.3.2, we get:

$$
\begin{aligned}
a &\leftarrow not\ b, not\ incorrect(a \leftarrow not\ b)\\
b &\leftarrow not\ c, not\ incorrect(b \leftarrow not\ c)\\[2mm]
a &\leftarrow uncovered(a)\\
b &\leftarrow uncovered(b)\\
c &\leftarrow uncovered(c)
\end{aligned}
$$

The reader can check that the WFM of $\Upsilon(P)$ is

$$\{not\ a, b, not\ c, not\ uncovered(a), not\ uncovered(b), not\ uncovered(c),$$
$$not\ incorrect(a \leftarrow not\ b), not\ incorrect(b \leftarrow not\ c)\}$$

A user can employ this transformed program in the same way he did with the original source program, with no change in program behaviour. If he detects an abnormal behaviour of the program, in order to debug the program he then just explicitly states what answers he expects:

Definition 12.3.10 (Debugging transformation). *Let P be a source program and U a set of user provided literals. The debugging transformation $\Upsilon_{debug}(P, U)$ converts the source program P into an object program P'. P' is obtained by adding to $\Upsilon(P)$ the integrity rules $\perp \leftarrow not\ a$ for each atom $a \in U$, and $\perp \leftarrow a$ for each literal not $a \in U$.*

Our main result is the following theorem, which links minimal diagnosis for a given set of literals with respect to a source program with minimal revisions of the object program obtained by applying the debugging transformation.

Theorem 12.3.8. *Let P be a source program and U a set of literals from the language of P. The pair $\langle Unc, InR \rangle$ is a diagnosis for U with respect to P iff*

$$\{uncovered(A) : A \in Unc\} \cup \{incorrect(A \leftarrow B) : A \leftarrow B \in InR\}$$

is a revision of $\Upsilon_{debug}(P, U)$, where the revisables are all literals of the form not incorrect($\ldots$) or of the form not uncovered($\ldots$).

The proof is trivial and it is based on the facts that adding a positive assumption *incorrect* has an effect similar to removing the rule from the program, and adding a positive assumption *uncovered*(A) makes A true in the revised program. The integrity rules in $\Upsilon_{debug}(P, U)$ guarantee that the literals in U are "explained".

For finite U, algorithm 12.1.5 can be used to compute the minimal diagnosis for the buggy source program.

Theorem 12.3.9 (Correctness). *Let P be a source program, I_M its intended interpretation, and U a finite set of literals. Algorithm 12.1.5 is sound and complete with respect to the minimal revisions of $\Upsilon_{debug}(P, U)$, using as revisables all the not incorrect($\_$) and not uncovered($\_$) literals.*

Proof. Follows directly from Theorem 12.3.8 and the correctness of algorithm 12.1.5 (cf. Theorems 12.1.1 and 12.1.2).

Corollary 12.3.2. *Let P be a source program, I_M its intended interpretation, and U a finite set of literals. If $U \subseteq I_M$ and $U \not\subseteq WFM(P)$ then there is a non-empty minimal revision R of $\Upsilon_{debug}(P, U)$, using as revisables* *all the not incorrect(_) and not uncovered(_) literals, such that for every uncovered(A) $\in R$, A is an uncovered atom for P with respect to I_M, and for every incorrect($A \leftarrow B$) $\in R$, $A \leftarrow B$ is incorrect for P with respect to I_M.*

From all minimal revisions a set of questions of the form "What is the truth value of $< AN\ ATOM >$ in the intended interpretation ?" can be compiled. The oracle answers to these questions identify the errors in the program.

Definition 12.3.11 (Disambiguating queries). *Let $D = \langle Unc, InR \rangle$ be a diagnosis for finite set of literals U with respect to the source program P, I_M its intended interpretation, and let (the set of atoms)*

$$Query = (Unc \cup Atom_{InR}) - U$$

where $Atom_{InR}$ is the set of all atoms appearing in rules of InR.
The set of disambiguating queries of D is:

$$\{What\ is\ the\ truth\ value\ of\ A\ in\ I_M?\ |\ A \in Query\}$$

The set of disambiguating queries of a set of diagnoses is the union of that for each diagnosis.

Now the answers, given by the oracle, to the disambiguating questions to the set of all diagnoses can be added to the current knowledge of the user, i.e. atoms answered true are added to U, and for atoms answered false their complements are added instead. The minimal diagnoses of the debugging transformation with the new set U are then computed and finer information about the errors is produced. This process of generating minimal diagnoses, and of answering the disambiguating queries posed by these diagnoses, can be iterated until only one final minimal diagnosis is reached:

Definition 12.3.12 (Algorithm for debugging of a source program).

1. *Transformation $\Upsilon(P)$ is applied to the program.*
2. *The user detects the symptoms and their respective integrity rules are inserted.*
3. *The minimal diagnosis are computed. If there is only one, one error or more are found and reported. Stop[3].*
4. *The disambiguating queries are generated and the oracle consulted.*
5. *Its answers are added in the form of integrity rules.*
6. *Goto 3.*

---

[3] We conjecture that termination occurs, in the worst-case, after the first time the oracle is consulted, i.e. the algorithm stops either the first or second time it executes this step.

Example 12.3.7. After applying Υ to P of Example 12.3.2, the user detects that b is a wrong solution. He causes the integrity rule $\bot \leftarrow b$ be added to $\Upsilon(P)$ and provokes a program revision to compute the possible explanations of this bug. He obtains two minimal revisions: $\{uncovered(c)\}$ and $\{incorrect(b \leftarrow not\ c)\}$.

Now, if desired, the oracle is questioned:

– What is the truth value of c in the intended interpretation ? Answer: true.

Then the user (or the oracle...) adds to the program the integrity rule $\bot \leftarrow not\ c$ and revises the program. The unique minimal revision is $\{uncovered(c)\}$ and the bug is found.

The user now detects that solution a is wrong. Then he adds the integrity rule $\bot \leftarrow a$ too and obtains the only minimal revision, that detects all the errors.

$\{incorrect(a \leftarrow not\ b), uncovered(c)\}$

Example 12.3.8. Consider the slight variation of Example 12.2.4:

$inv(T,G,I,1) \leftarrow node(T,I,0), not\ ab(G)$	1
$inv(T,G,I,0) \leftarrow node(T,I,1), not\ ab(G)$	2
$node(T,b,B) \leftarrow inv(T,g1,a,B)$	3
$node(T,c,C) \leftarrow inv(T,g2,b,C)$	4
$node(0,a,0)$	5
$\neg node(0,c,0)$	6
$inv(T,G,I,0) \leftarrow fault\_mode(G,s0)$	7
$inv(T,G,I,V) \leftarrow node(T,I,\_), V \neq 0, missing(G,V)$	12
$\bot \leftarrow fault\_mode(G,M1), fault\_mode(G,M2),$	10
$\quad M1 \neq M2$	
$\bot \leftarrow not\ node(0,c,1)$	11

We made the fault model partial by, withdrawing rules 8 and 9. So that we can still explain all observations, we "complete" the fault model by introducing rule 12, which expresses that in the presence of input to the inverter, and if the value to be explained is not equal to 0 (since that is explained by rule 7), then there is a missing fault mode for value V. Of course, *missing* has to be considered a revisable too.

Now the following expected minimal revisions are produced:

$\{ab(g1), fault\_mode(g1,s0)\} \quad \{ab(g2), missing(g2,1)\}$

The above fault model "completion" is a general technique for explaining all observations, with the advantage, with respect to [100]'s lenient explanations, that missing fault modes are actually reported. In fact, we are simply debugging the fault model according to the methods of the previous section: we've added a rule that detects and provides desired solutions not found by the normal rules, just as in debugging. But also solutions not explained by other fault rules: hence the $V \neq 0$ condition. The debugging equivalent of the latter would be adding a rule to "explain" that a bug (i.e. fault mode) has already been detected (though not corrected). Furthermore, the reason $node(I, \_)$ is included in 12 is that there is a missing fault mode only if the inverter actually receives input. The analogous situation in debugging would be that of requiring that a predicate must actually ensure some predication about goals for it (eg. type checking) before it is deemed incomplete.

The analogy with debugging allows us to debug artifact specifications. Indeed, it suffices to employ the techniques of the previous section. By adding $not\ ab(G, R, HeadArguments)$ instead of $not\ ab(G)$ in rules, where R is the rule number, revisions will now inform us of which rules possibly produce wrong solutions that would explain bugs. Of course, we now need to add $not\ ab(G, R)$ to all other rules, but during diagnosis they will not interfere if we restrict the revisables to just those with the appropriate rule numbers. With regard to missing solutions, we've seen in the previous paragraph that it would be enough to add an extra rule for each predicate. Moreover the same rule numbering technique is also applicable.

We now come full circle and may rightly envisage a program as just another artifact, to which diagnostic problems, concepts, and solutions, can profitably apply:

Example 12.3.9. The (buggy) model of the inverter gate of figure 12.9 entails $node(b, 0)$, and also (wrongly) $node(b, 1)$, when its input is 1.

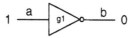

Fig. 12.9. One inverter circuit

$$
\begin{aligned}
inv(G, I, 0) &\leftarrow node(I, 1), not\ ab(G) \\
inv(G, I, 1) &\leftarrow node(I, 1), not\ ab(G) \ \% \ bug : node(I, 0) \\
node(b, V) &\leftarrow inv(g1, a, V) \\
node(a, 1)
\end{aligned}
$$

After the debugging transformation:

$$inv(G, I, 0) \leftarrow node(I, 1), not \ ab(G, 1, [G, I, 0])$$
$$inv(G, I, 1) \leftarrow node(I, 1), not \ ab(G, 2, [G, I, 1])$$

$$node(b, V) \leftarrow inv(g1, a, V), not \ ab(3, [b, V])$$
$$node(a, 1) \leftarrow not \ ab(4, [a, V])$$

Now, adding to it $\bot \leftarrow node(b, 1)$, and revising the now contradictory program the following minimal revisions are obtained:

$$\{ab(g1, 2, [g1, a, 1])\} \quad \{ab(3, [b, 1])\} \quad \{ab(4, [a, 1])\}$$

The minimal revision $\{ab(g1, 2, [g1, a, 1])\}$ states that either the inverter model is correct and therefore gate 1 is behaving abnormally or that rule 2 has a bug.

12.4 Updating Knowledge Bases

In this section we exhibit a program transformation to solve the problem of updating knowledge bases. Recall that a logic program stands for all its ground instances.

As stated in [83, 84] the problem of updating knowledge bases is a generalisation of the view update problem of relational databases. Given a knowledge base, represented by a logic program, an integrity constraint theory and a first order formula the updating problem consists in updating the program such that:

- It continues to satisfy the integrity constraint theory;
- When the existential closure of the first-order formula is not (resp., is) a logical consequence of the program then, after the update, it becomes (resp., no longer) so.

Here, we restrict the integrity constraint theory to sets of integrity rules and the first-order formula to a single ground literal. The method can be generalised as in [84], in order to cope with first-order formulae.

We assume there are just two primitive ways of updating a program: retracting a rule (or fact) from the program or asserting a fact. A transaction is a set of such retractions and assertions.

Next, we define a program transformation in all respects similar to the one used to perform declarative debugging:

Definition 12.4.1. *The transformation Υ that maps a logic program P into a logic program P' is obtained by applying to P the following two operations:*

- *Add to the body of each rule*

$$H \leftarrow B_1, \ldots, B_n, not \ C_1, \ldots, not \ C_m \quad \in P$$

the literal not retract_inst$((H \leftarrow B_1, \ldots, B_n, not \ C_1, \ldots, not \ C_m))$.

– Add the rule

$$p(X_1, X_2, \ldots, X_n) \leftarrow assert\_inst(p(X_1, X_2, \ldots, X_n))$$

for each predicate p with arity n in the language of P.

It is assumed that the predicate symbols retract_inst *and* assert_inst *don't belong to the language of P. The revisables of the program P' are the* retract_inst *and* assert_inst *literals.*

If an atom A is to be inserted in the database P, then the integrity rule $\bot \leftarrow not\ A$ is added to $\Upsilon(P)$. The minimal revisions of the latter program and integrity rule are the minimal transactions ensuring that A is a logical consequence of P. If an atom A is to be deleted, then add the integrity rule $\bot \leftarrow A$ instead. With this method the resulting transactions are more "intuitive" than the ones obtained by [84]:

Example 12.4.1. Consider the following program and the request to make

$$pleasant(fred)$$

a logical consequence of it *(insertion problem)*:

$$
\begin{aligned}
pleasant(X) &\leftarrow not\ old(X), likes\_fun(X) \\
pleasant(X) &\leftarrow sports\_person(X), loves\_nature(X) \\[6pt]
sports\_person(X) &\leftarrow swimmer(X) \\
sports\_person(X) &\leftarrow not\ sedentary(X) \\[6pt]
old(X) &\leftarrow age(X, Y), Y > 55 \\
swimmer(fred) & \\
age(fred, 60) &
\end{aligned}
$$

The transactions returned by Guessoum and Lloyd's method [84] are:

1. $\{assert(pleasant(fred))\}$
2. $\{assert(likes\_fun(fred)), retract((old(X) \leftarrow age(X, Y), Y > 55))\}$
3. $\{assert(likes\_fun(fred)), retract(age(fred, 60))\}$
4. $\{assert(sports\_person(fred)), assert(loves\_nature(fred))\}$
5. $\{assert(swimmer(fred)), assert(loves\_nature(fred))\}$
6. $\{assert(loves\_nature(fred))\}$

Notice that transactions 4 and 5 assert facts ($sports\_person(fred)$, respectively $swimmer(fred)$) that are already conclusions of the program. Also remark that in transaction 2 the whole rule is being retracted from the program, rather than just the appropriate instance. On the contrary, our method returns the transactions:

1. $\{assert\_inst(pleasant(fred))\}$

2. $\{assert\_inst(likes\_fun(fred)),$
   $\quad retract\_inst((old(fred) \leftarrow age(fred, 60), 60 > 55))\}$
3. $\{assert\_inst(likes\_fun(fred)), retract\_inst(age(fred, 60))\}$
4. $\{assert\_inst(loves\_nature(fred))\}$

If the second transaction is added to the program then it is not necessary to remove the rule

$$old(X) \leftarrow age(X, Y), Y > 55$$

from it. Only an instance of the rule is virtually retracted via assertion of the fact

$$retract\_inst(age(fred, 60))^4$$

Another advantage of our technique is that the user can express which predicates are liable to retraction of rules and addition of facts by only partially transforming the program, i.e. by selecting to which rules the *not retract_inst* is added, or to which predicates the second rule in the transformation is applied.

In [83] is argued that the updating procedures should desirably return minimal transactions, capturing the sense of making "least" changes to the program. These authors point out a situation where minimal transactions do not obey the integrity constraint theory:

Example 12.4.2. [83] Consider the definite logic program from where $r(a)$ must not be a logical consequence of it *(the deletion problem)*:

$$r(X) \quad \leftarrow \quad p(X)$$
$$r(X) \quad \leftarrow \quad p(X), q(X)$$
$$p(a)$$
$$q(a)$$

and the integrity constraint theory

$$\forall_X (p(x) \leftarrow q(x))$$

Two of the possible transactions that delete $r(a)$ are:

$$T_1 = \{retract\_inst(p(a))\}$$
$$T_2 = \{retract\_inst(p(a)), retract\_inst(q(a))\}$$

Transaction T_1 is minimal but the updated program does not satisfy the integrity contrainst theory. On the contrary, the updated program using T_2 does satisfy the integrity constraint theory.

---

[4] It may be argued that we obtain this result because we consider only ground instances. In fact, we have devised a sound implementation of the contradiction removal algorithm that is capable of dealing with non-ground logic programs such as this one. For the above example the transactions obtained are the ones listed.

With our method, we first apply Υ to the program, obtaining (notice how the integrity constraint theory is coded):

$$
\begin{aligned}
r(X) &\leftarrow p(X), not\ retract\_inst((r(X) \leftarrow p(X))) \\
r(X) &\leftarrow p(X), q(X), not\ retract\_inst((r(X) \leftarrow p(X), q(X))) \\
p(a) &\leftarrow not\ retract\_inst(p(a)) \\
q(a) &\leftarrow not\ retract\_inst(q(a))
\end{aligned}
$$

$$
\begin{aligned}
p(X) &\leftarrow assert\_inst(p(X)) \\
q(X) &\leftarrow assert\_inst(q(X)) \\
r(X) &\leftarrow assert\_inst(r(X))
\end{aligned}
$$

$$
\bot \leftarrow not\ p(X), q(X)
$$

The request to delete $r(a)$ is converted into the integrity rule $\bot \leftarrow r(a)$ which is added to the previous definition. As the reader can check, this program is contradictory. By computing its minimal revisions, the minimal transactions that *satisfy* the integrity theory are found:

1. $\{retract\_inst(p(a)), retract\_inst(q(a))\}$
2. $\{retract\_inst(r(a) \leftarrow p(a)), retract\_inst((r(a) \leftarrow p(a), q(a)))\}$
3. $\{retract\_inst(q(a)), retract\_inst((r(a) \leftarrow p(a)))\}$

Remark that transaction T_1 is not a minimal revision of the previous program.

Due to the uniformity of the method, i.e. both insert and delete requests are translated to integrity rules, the iterative contradiction removal algorithm ensures that the minimal transactions obtained, when enacted, do satisfy the integrity constraints.

References

1. J. J. Alferes, C. V. Damásio, and L. M. Pereira. SLX – A top-down derivation procedure for programs with explicit negation. In M. Bruynooghe, editor, *International Symposium on Logic programming*. MIT Press, 1994.
2. J. J. Alferes, C. V. Damásio, and L. M. Pereira. Top-down query evaluation for well-founded semantics with explicit negation. In A. Cohn, editor, *European Conference on Artificial Intelligence*, pages 140–144. Morgan Kaufmann, 1994.
3. J. J. Alferes, C. V. Damásio, and L. M. Pereira. A logic programming system for non-monotonic reasoning. *Journal of Automated Reasoning*, Special Issue on Implementation of NonMonotonic Reasoning(14):93–147, 1995.
4. J. J. Alferes, P. M. Dung, and L. M. Pereira. Scenario semantics of extended logic programs. In L. M. Pereira and A. Nerode, editors, *2nd Int. Ws. on LP & NMR*, pages 334–348. MIT Press, 1993.
5. J. J. Alferes and L. M. Pereira. On logic program semantics with two kinds of negation. In K. Apt, editor, *Int. Joint Conf. and Symp. on LP*, pages 574–588. MIT Press, 1992.
6. J. J. Alferes and L. M. Pereira. Belief, provability and logic programs. In D. Pearce and L. M. Pereira, editors, *International Workshop on Logics in Artificial Intelligence, JELIA'94*, volume 838 of *Lecture Notes in Artificial Intelligence*, pages 106–121. Springer–Verlag, 1994.
7. J. J. Alferes and L. M. Pereira. Contradiction: when avoidance equal removal. Part I. In R. Dyckhoff, editor, *4th Int. Ws. on Extensions of LP*, volume 798 of *LNAI*. Springer–Verlag, 1994.
8. J. J. Alferes and L. M. Pereira. An argumentation theoretic semantics based on non–refutable falsity (extended version). In J. Dix, L. M. Pereira, and T. Przymusinski, editors, *Nonmonotonic Extensions of Logic Programming*, volume 927 of *LNAI*, pages 3–22. Springer–Verlag, 1995.
9. J. J. Alferes and L. M. Pereira. Belief, provability and logic programs (extended version). *Journal of Applied Nonclassical Logics*, 5(1):31–50, 1995.
10. J. J. Alferes, L. M. Pereira, and T. Przymusinski. Belief revision in non-monotonic reasoning and logic programming. In N. Mamede and C. Pinto-Ferreira, editors, *Proceedings of the 7th Portuguese AI Conf.*, volume 990 of *Lecture Notes in Artificial Intelligence*, pages 41–56. Springer–Verlag, 1995.
11. J. J. Alferes, L. M. Pereira, and T. Przymusinski. "Classical" negation in non monotonic reasoning and logic programming. In H. Kautz and B. Selman, editors, *4th Int. Symposium on Artificial Intelligence and Mathematics*. Florida Atlantic University, January 1996.
12. José Júlio Alferes. *Semantics of Logic Programs with Explicit Negation*. PhD thesis, Universidade Nova de Lisboa, October 1993.
13. A. Almukdad and D. Nelson. Constructible falsity and inexact predicates. *JSL*, 49:231–233, 1984.

14. K. Apt and M. Bezem. Acyclic programs. *New Generation Computing*, 29(3):335–363, 1991.

15. K. Apt, H. Blair, and A. Walker. Towards a theory of declarative knowledge. In J. Minker, editor, *Foundations of Deductive Databases and Logic Programming*, pages 89–142. Morgan Kaufmann, 1988.

16. K. Apt and R. Bol. Logic programming and negation: a survey. *Journal of LP*, 20:9–71, 1994.

17. K. Apt, R. Bol, and J. Klop. On the safe termination of Prolog programs. In Levi and Marteli, editors, *Proc. ICLP'89*, pages 353–368. MIT Press, 1989.

18. C. Baral and M. Gelfond. Logic programming and knowledge representation. *Journal of LP*, 20:73–148, 1994.

19. C. Baral and V. S. Subrahmanian. Stable and extension class theory for logic programs and default logics. In *Int. Ws. on Nonmonotonic Reasoning*, 1990.

20. C. Baral and V. S. Subrahmanian. Dualities between alternative semantics for logic programming and nonmonotonic reasoning. In A. Nerode, W. Marek, and V. S. Subrahmanian, editors, *LP & NMR*, pages 69–86. MIT Press, 1991.

21. N. D. Belnap. A useful four-valued logic. In G. Epstein and J. M. Dunn, editors, *Modern Uses of Many-valued Logic*, pages 8–37. Reidel, 1977.

22. N. Bidoit and C. Froidevaux. Minimalism subsumes default logic and circumscription in stratified logic programming. In *Symp. on Principles of Database Systems*. ACM SIGACT-SIGMOD, 1987.

23. N. Bidoit and C. Froidevaux. General logic databases and programs: default logic semantics and stratification. *Journal of Information and Computation*, 1988.

24. N. Bidoit and P. Legay. Well!: An evaluation procedure for all logic programs. In *Int. Conf. on Database Technology*, pages 335–348, 1990.

25. L. Birnbaum, M. Flowers, and R. McGuire. Towards an AI model of argumentation. In *Proceedings of AAAI'80*, pages 313–315. Morgan Kaufmann, 1980.

26. H. A. Blair and V. S. Subrahmanian. Paraconsistent logic programming. *Theoretical Computer Science*, 68:135–154, 1989.

27. R. Bol and L. Degerstedt. Tabulated resolution for well founded semantics. In *Proc. ILPS'93*. MIT Press, 1993.

28. P. Bonatti. Autoepistemic logics as a unifying framework for the semantics of logic programs. In K. Apt, editor, *Int. Joint Conf. and Symp. on LP*, pages 417–430. MIT Press, 1992.

29. P. Bonatti. Autoepistemic logic programming. In L. M. Pereira and A. Nerode, editors, *2nd Int. Ws. on LP & NMR*, pages 151–167. MIT Press, 1993.

30. A. Bondarenko, F. Toni, and R. Kowalski. An assumption–based framework for nonmonotonic reasoning. In L. M. Pereira and A. Nerode, editors, *2nd Int. Ws. on LP & NMR*, pages 171–189. MIT Press, 1993.

31. Stefan Brass and Jürgen Dix. A disjunctive semantics based on unfolding and bottom-up evaluation. In Bernd Wolfinger, editor, *Innovationen bei Rechnen- und Kommunikationssystemen*, (IFIP '94-Congress, Workshop FG2: Disjunctive Logic Programming and Disjunctive Databases), pages 83–91, Berlin, 1994. Springer.

32. Stefan Brass and Jürgen Dix. A General Approach to Bottom-Up Computation of Disjunctive Semantics. In J. Dix, L. Pereira, and T. Przymusinski, editors, *Nonmonotonic Extensions of Logic Programming*, LNAI 927, pages 127–155. Springer, Berlin, 1995.

33. Stefan Brass and Jürgen Dix. Disjunctive Semantics based upon Partial and Bottom-Up Evaluation. In Leon Sterling, editor, *Proceedings of the 12th Int. Conf. on Logic Programming, Tokyo*. MIT Press, June 1995.

34. G. Brewka and K. Konolige. An abductive framework for generalized logic programs and other nonmonotonic systems. In *Int. Joint Conf. on AI*. Morgan Kaufmann, 1993.

35. A. Brogi, E. Lamma, P. Mancarella, and P. Mello. Normal logic programs as open positive programs. In K. Apt, editor, *Int. Joint Conf. and Symp. on LP*, pages 783–797. MIT Press, 1992.

36. F. Bry. Logic programming as constructivism: a formalization and its applications to databases. In *Symp. on Priciples of Database Systems*, pages 34–50. ACM SIGACT–SIGMOD, 1989.

37. A. Chandra and D. Harel. Structure and complexity of relational queries. *JCSS*, 25(1):99–128, 1982.

38. B. Chellas. *Modal Logic: An introduction*. Cambridge Univ. Press, 1980.

39. J. Chen. Minimal knowledge + negation as failure = only knowing (sometimes). In L. M. Pereira and A. Nerode, editors, *2nd Int. Ws. on LP & NMR*, pages 132–150. MIT Press, 1993.

40. W. Chen and D. S. Warren. A goal–oriented approach to computing well–founded semantics. In K. Apt, editor, *Int. Joint Conf. and Symp. on LP*, pages 589–603. MIT Press, 1992.

41. W. Chen and D. S. Warren. Query evaluation under the well founded semantics. In *PODS'93*, 1993.

42. K. Clark. Negation as failure. In H. Gallaire and J. Minker, editors, *Logic and Data Bases*, pages 293–322. Plenum Press, 1978.

43. R. Cohen. Analyzing the structure of argumentative discourse. *Computational Linguistics*, 13:11–24, 1987.

44. A. Colmerauer, H. Kanoui, P. Roussel, and R. Pasero. Un systéme de communication homme–machine en français. Technical report, Groupe de Recherche en Intelligence Artificielle, Université d'Aix–Marseille II, 1973.

45. L. Console, D. Dupré, and P. Torasso. A theory of diagnosis for incomplete causal models. In *11th Int. Joint Conf. on Artificial Intelligence*, pages 1311–1317, 1989.

46. L. Console and P. Torasso. A spectrum of logical definitions of model-based diagnosis. *Computational Intelligence*, 7:133–141, 1991.

47. N. Costa. On the theory of inconsistency formal system. *Notre Dame Journal of Formal Logic*, 15:497–510, 1974.

48. C. V. Damásio, W. Nejdl, L. M. Pereira, and M. Schroeder. Model-based diagnosis preferences and strategies representation with logic meta-programming. In K. Apt and F.Turini, editors, *Meta-logics and Logic Programming*, pages 311–338. MIT Press, 1995.

49. C. V. Damásio and L. M. Pereira. A survey on paraconsistent semantics for extended logic programs. Technical report, UNL, 1995.

50. Carlos Viegas Damásio. *Logic programming at work (provisional title)*. PhD thesis, Universidade Nova de Lisboa, 1995. In preparation.

51. J. de Kleer and B.C. Williams. Diagnosing multiple faults. *AI*, 32:97–130, 1987.

52. J. de Kleer and B.C. Williams. Diagnosis with behavioral modes. In *Proc. IJCAI'89*, pages 1329–1330. Morgan Kaufmann, 1989.

53. J. Dix. Classifying semantics of logic programs. In A. Nerode, W. Marek, and V. S. Subrahmanian, editors, *LP & NMR*, pages 166–180. MIT Press, 1991.

54. J. Dix. A framework for representing and characterizing semantics of logic programs. In B. Nebel, C. Rich, and W. Swartout, editors, *3rd Int. Conf. on Principles of Knowledge Representation and Reasoning*. Morgan Kaufmann, 1992.

55. J. Dix. A framework for representing and characterizing semantics of logic programs (extended version). Technical report, Institute for Logic, Complexity and Deduction Systems. Univ. of Karlsruhe, December 1992.

56. Jürgen Dix. Default Theories of Poole-Type and a Method for Constructing Cumulative Versions of Default Logic. In Bernd Neumann, editor, *Proceedings ECAI*, pages 289–293. John Wiley & Sons, 1992.

57. Jürgen Dix. A Classification-Theory of Semantics of Normal Logic Programs: I. Strong Properties. *Fundamenta Informaticae*, XXII(3):227–255, 1995.

58. Jürgen Dix. A Classification-Theory of Semantics of Normal Logic Programs: II. Weak Properties. *Fundamenta Informaticae*, XXII(3):257–288, 1995.

59. Jürgen Dix. Semantics of Logic Programs: Their Intuitions and Formal Properties. An Overview. In Andre Fuhrmann and Hans Rott, editors, *Logic, Action and Information. Proceedings of the Konstanz Colloquium in Logic and Information (LogIn '92)*, pages 241–329. DeGruyter, 1995.

60. Jürgen Dix and Martin Müller. Partial Evaluation and Relevance for Approximations of the Stable Semantics. In Z.W. Ras and M. Zemankova, editors, *Proceedings of the 8th Int. Symp. on Methodologies for Intelligent Systems, Charlotte, NC, 1994*, LNAI 869, pages 511–520, Berlin, 1994. Springer.

61. Jürgen Dix and Martin Müller. The Stable Semantics and its Variants: A Comparison of Recent Approaches. In L. Dreschler-Fischer and B. Nebel, editors, *Proceedings of the 18th German Annual Conference on Artificial Intelligence (KI '94), Saarbrücken, Germany*, LNAI 861, pages 82–93, Berlin, 1994. Springer.

62. P. M. Dung. Negation as hypotheses: An abductive framework for logic programming. In K. Furukawa, editor, *8th Int. Conf. on LP*, pages 3–17. MIT Press, 1991.

63. P. M. Dung. Logic programming as dialog–games. Technical report, Division of Computer Science, Asian Institute of Technology, December 1992.

64. P. M. Dung. On the relations between stable and well–founded models. *Theoretical Computer Science*, 105:7–25, 1992.

65. P. M. Dung. An argumentation semantics for logic programming with explicit negation. In D. S. Warren, editor, *10th Int. Conf. on LP*, pages 616–630. MIT Press, 1993.

66. P. M. Dung. On the acceptability of arguments and its fundamental role in nonmonotonic reasoning and logic programming. In *Int. Joint Conf. on AI*. Morgan Kaufmann, 1993.

67. P. M. Dung, A. C. Kakas, and P. Mancarella. Negation as failure revisited. Technical report, Asian Institute of Technology, Univ. of Cyprus, and Univ. of Pisa, 1992. Preliminary Report.

68. P. M. Dung and P. Ruamviboonsuk. Well founded reasoning with classical negation. In A. Nerode, W. Marek, and V. S. Subrahmanian, editors, *LP & NMR*, pages 120–132. MIT Press, 1991.

69. M. Van Emden and R. Kowalski. The semantics of predicate logic as a programming language. *Journal of ACM*, 4(23):733–742, 1976.

70. K. Eshghi and R. Kowalski. Abduction compared with negation by failure. In *6th Int. Conf. on LP*. MIT Press, 1989.

71. D. Etherington, R. Mercer, and R. Reiter. On the adequacy of predicate circumscription for closed–world reasoning. *Journal of Computational Intelligence*, 1:11–15, 1985.

72. M. Fitting. A Kripke-Kleene semantics for logic programs. *Journal of LP*, 2(4):295–312, 1985.

73. H. Gallaire, J. Minker, and J. Nicolas. Logic and databases: a deductive approach. *ACM Computing Surveys*, 16:153–185, 1984.

74. P. Geerts and D. Vermeir. A nonmonotonic reasoning formalism using implicit specificity information. In L. M. Pereira and A. Nerode, editors, *2nd Int. Ws. on LP & NMR*, pages 380–396. MIT Press, 1993.

75. A. Van Gelder. Negation as failure using tight derivations for general logic programs. *Journal of LP*, 6(1):109–133, 1989.

76. A. Van Gelder, K. A. Ross, and J. S. Schlipf. The well-founded semantics for general logic programs. *Journal of the ACM*, 38(3):620–650, 1991.

77. M. Gelfond. On stratified autoepistemic theories. In *AAAI'87*, pages 207–211. Morgan Kaufmann, 1987.

78. M. Gelfond and V. Lifschitz. The stable model semantics for logic programming. In R. Kowalski and K. A. Bowen, editors, *5th Int. Conf. on LP*, pages 1070–1080. MIT Press, 1988.

79. M. Gelfond and V. Lifschitz. Compiling circumscriptive theories into logic programs. In M. Reinfrank, J. de Kleer, M. Ginsberg, and E. Sandewall, editors, *Non-Monotonic Reasoning: 2nd Int. Ws.*, pages 74–99. LNAI 346, Springer–Verlag, 1989.

80. M. Gelfond and V. Lifschitz. Logic programs with classical negation. In Warren and Szeredi, editors, *7th Int. Conf. on LP*, pages 579–597. MIT Press, 1990.

81. M. Gelfond and V. Lifschitz. Representing actions in extended logic programs. In K. Apt, editor, *Int. Joint Conf. and Symp. on LP*, pages 559–573. MIT Press, 1992.

82. M. Gelfond, H. Przymusinska, and T. Przymusinski. On the relationship between circumscription and negation as failure. *Artificial Intelligence*, 38:75–94, 1989.

83. A. Guessoum and J. W. Lloyd. Updating knowledge bases. *New Generation Computing*, 8(1):71–89, 1990.

84. A. Guessoum and J. W. Lloyd. Updating knowledge bases II. *New Generation Computing*, 10(1):73–100, 1991.

85. Y. Gurevich and S. Shelah. Fixed–point extensions of first order logic. *Annals of Pure and Applied Logic*, 32:265–280, 1986.

86. S. Hanks and D. McDermott. Default reasoning, non-monotonic logics and the frame problem. In *AAAI*, pages 328–333, 1986.

87. J. Hintikka. *The Game of Language*. Reidel Publishing Company, 1983.

88. HMSO. *British Nationality Act*. Her Majesty's Stationery Office, 1981.

89. G. Hughes and M. Cresswell. *A companion to modal logic*. Methuen, 1984.

90. N. Immerman. Relational queries computable in polynomial time. *Information and Control*, 68(1):86–104, 1986.

91. K. Inoue. Extended logic programs with default assumptions. In Koichi Furukawa, editor, *8th Int. Conf. on LP*, pages 490–504. MIT Press, 1991.

92. K. Jonker. On the semantics of conflict resolution in truth maintenance systems. Technical report, Univ. of Utrecht, 1991.

93. A. Kakas, R. Kowalski, and F. Toni. Abductive logic programming. *Journal of Logic and Computation*, 2:719–770, 1993.

94. A. C. Kakas and P. Mancarella. Generalised stable models: A semantics for abduction. In *Proc. ECAI'90*, pages 401–405, 1990.

95. H. Kautz. The logic of persistence. In *AAAI'86*, pages 401–405. Morgan Kaufmann, 1986.

96. H. A. Kautz and B. Selman. Hard problems for simple default logics. In R. Brachman, H. Levesque, and R. Reiter, editors, *1st Int. Conf. on Principles of Knowledge Representation and Reasoning*, pages 189–197. Morgan Kaufmann, 1989.

97. D. B. Kemp, P. J. Stuckey, and D. Srivastava. Magic sets and bottom-up evaluation of well–founded models. In *Proc. ILPS'91*, pages 337–351. MIT Press, 1991.

98. D. B. Kemp, P. J. Stuckey, and D. Srivastava. Query Restricted Bottom–up Evaluation of Normal Logic Programs. In *Proc. JICSLP'92*, pages 288–302. MIT Press, 1992.

99. M. Kifer and E. L. Lozinskii. A logic for reasoning with inconsistency. In *4th IEEE Symp. on Logic in Computer Science*, pages 253–262, 1989.

100. K. Konolige. Using default and causal reasoning in diagnosis. In B. Nebel, C. Rich, and W. Swartout, editors, *3rd Int. Conf. on Principles of Knowledge Representation and Reasoning*. Morgan Kaufmann, 1992.

101. R. Kowalski. Predicate logic as a programming language. In *Proceedings of IFIP'74*, pages 569–574, 1974.

102. R. Kowalski. Algorithm = logic + control. *Communications of the ACM*, 22:424–436, 1979.

103. R. Kowalski. The treatment of negation in logic programs for representing legislation. In *2nd Int. Conf. on AI and Law*, pages 11–15, 1989.

104. R. Kowalski. Problems and promises of computational logic. In John Lloyd, editor, *Computational Logic*, pages 1–36. Basic Research Series, Springer–Verlag, 1990.

105. R. Kowalski. Legislation as logic programs. In *Logic Programming in Action*, pages 203–230. Springer–Verlag, 1992.

106. R. Kowalski and D. Khuener. Linear resolution with selection function. *Artificial Intelligence*, 5:227–260, 1971.

107. R. Kowalski and F. Sadri. Logic programs with exceptions. In Warren and Szeredi, editors, *7th Int. Conf. on LP*. MIT Press, 1990.

108. S. Kraus, D. Lehmann, and M. Magidor. Nonmonotonic reasoning, preferential models and cumulative logics. *Artificial Intelligence*, 44:167–207, 1990.

109. K. Kunen. Negation in logic programming. *Journal of LP*, 4:289–308, 1987.

110. K. Kunen. Some remarks on the completed database. In R. Kowalski and K. A. Bowen, editors, *5th Int. Conf. on LP*, pages 978–992. MIT Press, 1988.

111. P. Lamarre and Y. Shoham. On knowledge, certainty, and belief (draft). Personal communication of the second author, Stanford Univ., 1993.

112. D. Lewis. *Counterfactuals*. Harvard, 2nd edition, 1973.

113. V. Lifschitz. Computing circumscription. In *Int. Joint Conf. on AI*, pages 121–127. Morgan Kaufmann, 1985.

114. V. Lifschitz. Benchmarks problems for formal non–monotonic reasoning. In M. Reinfrank, J. d. Kleer, M. Ginsberg, and E. Sandewall, editors, *Non Monotonic Reasoning: 2nd International Workshop*, pages 202–219. Springer–Verlag, 1988.

115. V. Lifschitz. Logic and actions. In *5th Portuguese AI Conf.*, 1991. Invited talk.

116. V. Lifschitz. Minimal belief and negation as failure. Technical report, Dep. of Computer Science and Dep. of Philisophy, Univ. of Texas at Austin, 1992.

117. V. Lifschitz and G. Schwarz. Extended logic programs as autoepistemic theories. In L. M. Pereira and A. Nerode, editors, *2nd Int. Ws. on LP & NMR*, pages 101–114. MIT Press, 1993.

118. J. Lloyd. *Foundations of Logic Programming*. Springer–Verlag, 1984.

119. J. Lloyd. Declarative error diagnosis. *New Generation Computing*, 5(2), 1987.

120. J. Lloyd and R. Topor. A basis for deductive database systems. *Journal of LP*, 2:93–109, 1985.

121. J. Lloyd and R. Topor. A basis for deductive database systems II. *Journal of LP*, 3:55–67, 1986.

122. V. Marek and M. Truczczinski, editors. *Logic Programming and Non-monotonic Reasoning: Proceedings of the Int. Conf.*, Lexington, USA, 1995. Springer-Verlag.

123. V. Marek and M. Truszczynski. Reflexive autoepistemic logic and logic programming. In L. M. Pereira and A. Nerode, editors, *2nd Int. Ws. on LP & NMR*, pages 115–131. MIT Press, 1993.

124. W. Marek and M. Truszczynski. Autoepistemic logics. *Journal of the ACM*, 38(3):588–619, 1991.

125. J. McCarthy. Circumscription - a form of non–monotonic reasoning. *Artificial Intelligence*, 13:27–39, 1980.

126. J. McCarthy. Applications of circumscription to formalizing common sense knowledge. *Artificial Intelligence*, 26:89–116, 1986.

127. D. McDermott. Non–monotonic logic II. *Journal of the ACM*, 29(1):33–57, 1982.

128. R. McGuire, L. Birnbaum, and M. Flowers. Towards an AI model of argumentation. In *Int. Joint Conf. on AI*, pages 58–60. Morgan Kaufmann, 1981.

129. J. Minker. On indefinite databases and the closed world assumption. In M. Ginsberg, editor, *Readings in Nonmonotonic Reasoning*, pages 326–333. Morgan Kaufmann, 1987.

130. J. Minker. *Foundations of Deductive Databases and Logic Programming*. Morgan Kaufmann, 1988.

131. L. Monteiro. Notes on the negation in logic programs. Technical report, Dep. of Computer Science, Univerdade Nova de Lisboa, 1992. Course Notes, 3rd Advanced School on AI, Azores, Portugal, 1992.

132. R. Moore. Semantics considerations on nonmonotonic logic. *Artificial Intelligence*, 25:75–94, 1985.

133. P. H. Morris. Autoepistemic stable clousure and contradiction resolution. In *2nd Ws. on Nonmonotonic Reasoning*, pages 60–73, 1988.

134. W. Nejdl, G. Brewka, L. Consolle, P. Mancarella, and L. M. Pereira. *LAP – Logic Agents Programming*. ESPRIT BRA proposal (no. 8099), April 1993.

135. D. Nelson. Constructible falsity. *JSL*, 14:16–26, 1949.

136. A. Nerode, W. Marek, and V. S. Subrahmanian, editors. *Logic Programming and Non–monotonic Reasoning: Proceedings of the First Int. Ws.*, Washington D.C., USA, 1991. The MIT Press.

137. D. Nute. Ldr : A logic for defeasible reasoning. Technical report, Advanced Computational Center, Univ. of Georgia, 1986.

138. D. Pearce. Reasoning with Negative Information, II: hard negation, strong negation and logic programs. In D. Pearce and H. Wansing, editors, *Nonclassical logic and information processing*, LNAI 619, pages 63–79. Springer-Verlag, 1992.

139. D. Pearce. Answer sets and constructive logic, II: Extended logic programs and related nonmonotonic formalisms. In L.M. Pereira and A. Nerode, editors, *2nd Int. Ws. on LP & NMR*, pages 457–475. MIT Press, 1993.

140. D. Pearce. Safety, stability and deductive basis. Technical report, German Research Center for Artificial Intelligence (DFKI), 1994.

141. D. Pearce and G. Wagner. Reasoning with negative information I: Strong negation in logic programs. In L. Haaparanta, M. Kusch, and I. Niiniluoto, editors, *Language, Knowledge and Intentionality*, pages 430–453. Acta Philosophica Fennica 49, 1990.

142. D. Pearce and G. Wagner. Logic programming with strong negation. In P. Schroeder-Heister, editor, *Extensions of LP*, pages 311–326. LNAI 475, Springer-Verlag, 1991.

143. L. M. Pereira and J. J. Alferes. Well founded semantics for logic programs with explicit negation. In B. Neumann, editor, *European Conf. on AI*, pages 102–106. John Wiley & Sons, 1992.

144. L. M. Pereira and J. J. Alferes. Optative reasoning with scenario semantics. In D. S. Warren, editor, *10th Int. Conf. on LP*, pages 601–615. MIT Press, 1993.

145. L. M. Pereira and J. J. Alferes. Contradiction: when avoidance equal removal. Part II. In R. Dyckhoff, editor, *4th Int. Ws. on Extensions of LP*, volume 798 of *LNAI*. Springer-Verlag, 1994.

146. L. M. Pereira, J. J. Alferes, and J. N. Aparício. Contradiction Removal within Well Founded Semantics. In A. Nerode, W. Marek, and V. S. Subrahmanian, editors, *LP & NMR*, pages 105–119. MIT Press, 1991.

147. L. M. Pereira, J. J. Alferes, and J. N. Aparício. The extended stable models of contradiction removal semantics. In P. Barahona, L. M. Pereira, and A. Porto, editors, *5th Portuguese AI Conf.*, pages 105–119. LNAI 541, Springer–Verlag, 1991.

148. L. M. Pereira, J. J. Alferes, and J. N. Aparício. A practical introduction to well founded semantics. In B. Mayoh, editor, *Scandinavian Conf. on AI*. IOS Press, 1991.

149. L. M. Pereira, J. J. Alferes, and J. N. Aparício. Adding closed world assumptions to well founded semantics. In *Fifth Generation Computer Systems*, pages 562–569. ICOT, 1992.

150. L. M. Pereira, J. J. Alferes, and J. N. Aparício. Default theory for well founded semantics with explicit negation. In D. Pearce and G. Wagner, editors, *Logics in AI. Proceedings of the European Ws. JELIA '92*, pages 339–356. LNAI 633, Springer–Verlag, 1992.

151. L. M. Pereira, J. J. Alferes, and J. N. Aparício. Adding closed world assumptions to well founded semantics (extended improved version). *Theoretical Computer Science. Special issue on selected papers from FGCS'92*, 122:49–68, 1993.

152. L. M. Pereira, J. J. Alferes, and J. N. Aparício. Contradiction removal semantics with explicit negation. In M. Masuch and L. Pólos, editors, *Knowledge Representation and Reasoning Under Uncertainty*, volume 808 of *LNAI*, pages 91–106. Springer-Verlag, 1994.

153. L. M. Pereira, J. J. Alferes, and C. Damásio. The sidetracking meta principle. In *Simpósio Brasileiro de Inteligência Artificial*, pages 229–242, 1992.

154. L. M. Pereira, J. N. Aparício, and J. J. Alferes. Counterfactual reasoning based on revising assumptions. In Ueda and Saraswat, editors, *Int. LP Symp.*, pages 566–577. MIT Press, 1991.

155. L. M. Pereira, J. N. Aparício, and J. J. Alferes. A derivation procedure for extended stable models. In *Int. Joint Conf. on AI*. Morgan Kaufmann, 1991.

156. L. M. Pereira, J. N. Aparício, and J. J. Alferes. Hypothetical reasoning with well founded semantics. In B. Mayoh, editor, *Scandinavian Conf. on AI*. IOS Press, 1991.

157. L. M. Pereira, J. N. Aparício, and J. J. Alferes. Nonmonotonic reasoning with well founded semantics. In Koichi Furukawa, editor, *8th Int. Conf. on LP*, pages 475–489. MIT Press, 1991.

158. L. M. Pereira, J. N. Aparício, and J. J. Alferes. Non–monotonic reasoning with logic programming. *Journal of Logic Programming. Special issue on Nonmonotonic reasoning*, 17(2, 3 & 4):227–263, 1993.

159. L. M. Pereira, J. N. Aparício, and J. J. Alferes. Logic programming for non-monotonic reasoning. In M. Masuch and L. Pólos, editors, *Knowledge Rep-*

resentation and Reasoning Under Uncertainty, volume 808 of *LNAI*, pages 107–122. Springer-Verlag, 1994.

160. L. M. Pereira and M. Calejo. A framework for Prolog debugging. In R. Kowalski, editor, *5th Int. Conf. on LP*. MIT Press, 1988.

161. L. M. Pereira, C. Damásio, and J. J. Alferes. Debugging by diagnosing assumptions. In P. A. Fritzson, editor, *Automatic Algorithmic Debugging, AADEBUG'93*, volume 749 of *Lecture Notes in Computer Science*, pages 58–74. Springer–Verlag, 1993.

162. L. M. Pereira, C. Damásio, and J. J. Alferes. Diagnosis and debugging as contradiction removal. In L. M. Pereira and A. Nerode, editors, *2nd Int. Ws. on LP & NMR*, pages 316–330. MIT Press, 1993.

163. L. M. Pereira, C. Damásio, and J. J. Alferes. Diagnosis and debugging as contradiction removal in logic programs. In L. Damas and M. Filgueiras, editors, *6th Portuguese AI Conf.* Springer–Verlag, 1993.

164. L. M. Pereira and A. Nerode, editors. *Logic Programming and Non-monotonic Reasoning: Proceedings of the Second Int. Ws.*, Lisboa, Portugal, 1993. The MIT Press.

165. L. M. Pereira and A. Porto. Intelligent backtracking and sidetracking in Horn clause programs - the theory. Technical report, DI/UNL, 1979.

166. J. L. Pollock. How to reason defeasibly. *Artificial Intelligence*, 57:1–42, 1992.

167. D. Poole. A logical framework for default reasoning. *Artificial Intelligence*, 36(1):27–47, 1988.

168. D. Poole. Normality and faults in logic-based diagnosis. In *Proc. IJCAI-89*, pages 1304–1310. Morgan Kaufmann, 1989.

169. C. Preist and K. Eshghi. Consistency-based and abductive diagnoses as generalised stable models. In *Proc. FGCS'92*. ICOT, Omsha 1992.

170. G. Priest, R. Routley, and J. Norman. *Paraconsistent logics*. Philosophia Verlag, 1988.

171. H. Przymusinska and T. Przymusinski. Weakly perfect model semantics. In R. Kowalski and K. A. Bowen, editors, *5th Int. Conf. on LP*, pages 1106–1122. MIT Press, 1988.

172. H. Przymusinska and T. Przymusinski. Semantic issues in deductive databases and logic programs. In R. Banerji, editor, *Formal Techniques in AI, a Sourcebook*, pages 321–367. North Holland, 1990.

173. H. Przymusinska and T. Przymusinski. Nonmonotonic reasoning and logic programming - Advanced Tutorial. Technical report, Dep. of Computer Science, California State Polytechnic and Dep. of Computer Science, Univ. of California at Riverside, 1991.

174. H. Przymusinska and T. Przymusinski. Stationary default extensions. Technical report, Dep. of Computer Science, California State Polytechnic and Dep. of Computer Science, Univ. of California at Riverside, 1993.

175. H. Przymusinska, T. C. Przymusinski, and H. Seki. Soundness and completeness of partial deductions for well–founded semantics. In A. Voronkov, editor, *Proc. of the Int. Conf. on Automated Reasoning*. LNAI 624, 1992.

176. T. Przymusinski. On the declarative semantics of stratified deductive databases. In J. Minker, editor, *Foundations of Deductive Databases and Logic Programming*, pages 193–216. Morgan Kaufmann, 1988.

177. T. Przymusinski. Every logic program has a natural stratification and an iterated fixed point model. In *8th Symp. on Principles of Database Systems*. ACM SIGACT-SIGMOD, 1989.

178. T. Przymusinski. On the declarative and procedural semantics of logic programs. *Journal of Automated Reasoning*, 5:167–205, 1989.

179. T. Przymusinski. Three–valued non–monotonic formalisms and logic programming. In R. Brachman, H. Levesque, and R. Reiter, editors, *1st Int. Conf. on Principles of Knowledge Representation and Reasoning*, pages 341–348. Morgan Kaufmann, 1989.

180. T. Przymusinski. Extended stable semantics for normal and disjunctive programs. In Warren and Szeredi, editors, *7th Int. Conf. on LP*, pages 459–477. MIT Press, 1990.

181. T. Przymusinski. Stationary semantics for disjunctive logic programs and deductive databases. In Debray and Hermenegildo, editors, *North American Conf. on LP*, pages 40–57. MIT Press, 1990.

182. T. Przymusinski. Autoepistemic logic of closed beliefs and logic programming. In A. Nerode, W. Marek, and V. S. Subrahmanian, editors, *LP & NMR*, pages 3–20. MIT Press, 1991.

183. T. Przymusinski. A semantics for disjunctive logic programs. In Loveland, Lobo, and Rajasekar, editors, *ILPS'91 Ws. in Disjunctive Logic Programs*, 1991.

184. T. Przymusinski. Static semantics for normal and disjunctive programs. *Annals of Mathematics and Artificial Intelligence*, 1994.

185. T. Przymusinski and D.S. Warren. Well–founded semantics: Theory and implementation. Draft, 1992.

186. A. Rajasekar, J. Lobo, and J. Minker. Weak generalized closed world assumptions. *Automated Reasoning*, 5:293–307, 1989.

187. R. Reiter. On closed–world data bases. In H. Gallaire and J. Minker, editors, *Logic and DataBases*, pages 55–76. Plenum Press, 1978.

188. R. Reiter. A logic for default reasoning. *Artificial Intelligence*, 13:68–93, 1980.

189. R. Reiter. Towards a logical reconstruction of relational database theory. In M. Brodie and J. Mylopoulos, editors, *On Conceptual Modelling*, pages 191–233. Springer–Verlag, 1984.

190. R. Reiter. A theory of diagnosis from first principles. *Artificial Intelligence*, 32:57–96, 1987.

191. R. Reiter. On asking what a database knows. In John Lloyd, editor, *Computational Logic*, pages 96–113. Basic Research Series, Springer–Verlag, 1990.

192. N. Rescher. *Hypothetical Reasoning*. North–Holland, 1964.

193. N. Rescher and R. Brandom. *The logic of inconsistency*. Basil Blackwell, 1980.

194. K. Ross and R. Topor. Inferring negative information from disjunctive databases. *Automated Reasoning*, 4:397–424, 1988.

195. K. A. Ross. A procedural semantics for well-founded negation in logic programs. *Journal of Logic Programming*, 13:1–22, 1992.

196. C. Sakama. Extended well-founded semantics for paraconsistent logic programs. In *Fifth Generation Computer Systems*, pages 592–599. ICOT, 1992.

197. C. Sakama and K. Inoue. Paraconsistent Stable Semantics for extended disjunctive programs. *Journal of Logic and Computation*, 5(3):265–285, 1995.

198. G. Schwarz. Autoepistemic logic of knowledge. In A. Nerode, W. Marek, and V. S. Subrahmanian, editors, *LP & NMR*, pages 260–274. MIT Press, 1991.

199. M. Shanahan. Explanations in the situation calculus. Technical report, Dep. of Computing, Imperial College of Science, Technology and Medicine, 1992.

200. J. Shepherdson. Negation in logic programming for general logic programs. In J. Minker, editor, *Foundations of Deductive Databases and LP*. Morgan Kaufmann, 1988.

201. J. Shepherdson. Negation as failure, completion and stratification. In *Handbook of AI and LP*, 1990.

202. L. J. Stein. Skeptical inheritance: computing the intersection of credulous extensions. In *Int. Joint Conf. on AI*, pages 1153–1158. Morgan Kaufmann Publishers, 1989.

203. P. Struss and O. Dressler. Physical negation: Integrating fault models into the general diagnostic engine. In *11th Int. Joint Conf. on Artificial Intelligence*, pages 1318–1323, 1989.

204. A. Tarski. A lattice–theoretic fixpoint theorem and its applications. *Pacific Journal of Mathematics*, 5:285–309, 1955.

205. F. Teusink. A proof procedure for extended logic programs. In *Proc. ILPS'93*. MIT Press, 1993.

206. S. Toulmin. *The uses of arguments*. Cambridge Univ. Press, 1958.

207. D. S. Touretzky, J. F. Horty, and R. H. Thomason. A clash of intuitions: the current state of nonmonotonic multiple inheritance systems. In *Int. Joint Conf. on AI*. Morgan Kaufmann Publishers, 1987.

208. M. Vardi. The complexity of relational query languages. In *14th ACM Symp. on Theory of Computing*, pages 137–145, 1982.

209. G. Wagner. A database needs two kinds of negation. In B. Thalheim, J. Demetrovics, and H-D. Gerhardt, editors, *Mathematical Foundations of Database Systems*, pages 357–371. LNCS 495, Springer–Verlag, 1991.

210. G. Wagner. Ex contradictione nihil sequitur. In *Int. Joint Conf. on AI*. Morgan Kaufmann, 1991.

211. G. Wagner. Neutralization and preeemption in extended logic programs. Technical report, Freien Universitat Berlin, 1993.

212. G. Wagner. Reasoning with inconsistency in extended deductive databases. In L. M. Pereira and A. Nerode, editors, *2nd Int. Ws. on LP & NMR*, pages 300–315. MIT Press, 1993.

213. G. Wagner. Vivid logic: Knowledge-based reasoning with two kinds of negation. *Lecture Notes on Artificial Intelligence*, 764, 1994.

214. D. H. Warren, L. M. Pereira, and F. Pereira. Prolog: The language and its implementation compared with Lisp. In *Symp. on AI and Programming Languages*, pages 109–115. ACM SIGPLAN–SIGART, 1977.

215. D.S. Warren. The XWAM: A machine that integrates Prolog and deductive databases. Technical report, SUNY at Stony Brook, 1989.

Part IV

Appendices

A. Prolog top-down interpreter for *WFSX*

Here, for the sake of completeness, we present a Prolog top-down interpreter for *WFSX*.

This interpreter is based on the SLXderivation procedure, and its correctness for propositional programs follows directly from the results in Chapter 10.

For this interpreter, programs are sets of rules of the form:

```
H <- B1, ..., Bn, not C1, ..., not Cm.
```

where H, B1, ..., Bn, C1, ..., and Cm are predicates or terms of the form -P where P is a predicate. -P stands for the explicit negation of P.

The goal demo(G) succeeds if the literal G is true in the well-founded model of the program, and fails otherwise.

```
% Operators definition
:- op(950,fy , '-' ).          % Explicit negation
:- op(950,fy , not ).          % Negation as failure
:- op(1110,xfy, '<-' ).        % Rule symbol

% demo( Goal, Ancestors for Loop Ckecking, Global Ans, Mode)
% If Mode=t then tests if Goal is true,
%           otherwise tests if Goal is true or undef

demo(G)  :- demo(G,[],[],t).

demo( true, _, _, _ ) :- !.
demo( (G,Cont), AnsL, AnsG, M ) :-
        !, demo(G, AnsL, AnsG,M), demo(Cont, AnsL, AnsG,M).
demo( not G, _, AnsG, _ ) :-
        compl_neg( G, CG ), demo( CG, AnsG, AnsG, t ).
demo( not G, _, AnsG, t ) :-
        !, \+ demo( G, [], AnsG, tu ).
demo( not G, _, AnsG, tu ) :-
        !, \+ demo( G, AnsG, AnsG, t ).
demo( G, Ans, _, _ ) :-
        loop_detect( G, Ans ), !, fail.
```

```
demo( G, AnsL, AnsG, t ) :-
      (G <- Body), demo( Body, [G|AnsL], [G|AnsG], t ).
demo( G, AnsL, AnsG, tu ) :-
      compl_neg(G, NG), \+ demo(NG, AnsG, AnsG, t),
      (G <- Body), demo( Body, [G|AnsL], [G|AnsG], tu ).

% Loop Detection
loop_detect(X,[Y|_]) :- X == Y, !.
loop_detect(X,[_|T]) :- loop_detect(X,T).

% Auxiliary predicates
compl_neg( - G, G ) :- !.
compl_neg( G, - G ).
```

B. A Prolog pre-processor for contradiction removal

Here we present a Prolog pre-processor for contradictory programs, and the implementation of a Prolog predicate that returns either 2 or 3-valued revisions of the pre-processed program.

Programs are sets of rules of the form:

```
H <- B1, ..., Bn, not C1, ..., not Cm.
```

where H, B1, ..., Bn, C1, ..., and Cm are predicates or terms of the form -P where P is a predicate. -P stands for the explicit negation of P. Rules with empty body can simply be represented by one of the two forms:

```
H.
H <- true.
```

Integrity constraints are rules of the form:

```
<- B1, ..., Bn, not C1, ..., not Cm.
```

By default, no literal is revisable. To declare revisable the predicate say $p/2$, add to the program the fact:

```
rev(p(_,_)).
```

The user predicates are:

readfile(File) - Reads and pre-processes the program in the file File

revise(M,Rev) - Returns in Rev the program revisions. Revision are 2-valued if M=2, and 3-valued otherwise.

```
% Operators declaration
:- op(950,fy , '-' ).              % Explicit negation
:- op(950,fy , not ).             % Negation as failure
:- op(1110,xfy, '<-' ).           % Rule symbol
:- op(1110,yf , '<-' ).           % Rule symbol
:- op(1110,fy , '<-' ).           % Rule symbol


% Dynamic predicates (for Sictus only)
:- dynamic '<-'/2.
:- dynamic '$revisable'/1.
:- dynamic '$indissoc'/2.



%%%%%%%%%%%%%%%%%%%%%%%%%%%%%%%%%%%%%%%%%%%%%%%%
%      Reading program clauses               %
%%%%%%%%%%%%%%%%%%%%%%%%%%%%%%%%%%%%%%%%%%%%%%%%

% readfile( FileName) reads a program from a file, and
% adds the implicit integrity rules of the form <- L, -L
% for literals L and -L appearing in the heads of rules
readfile(File) :-
    clean_database,
    see( File ), read_clauses, seen,
    write( 'File: ' ),
    write( File ), write( ' reconsulted.' ),
    add_implicit_ir.

% clean_database clears all the global information of the
% previous loaded program.
clean_database :-
    remove_clauses, clean_rev_data,
    retractall( '$revisable'( _ ) ),
    retractall( '$indissoc'( _, _ ) ).

remove_clauses :-
    recorded( _, (_ <- _), Ref ),
    erase( Ref ),
    fail.
remove_clauses.

clean_rev_data :-
    recorded( '$rev_rule', _, R2 ),
    erase( R2 ),
    fail.
clean_rev_data.

% read_clauses reads a term at a time and asserts it to
% the database.
read_clauses :-
    repeat,
    read( Term ),
    assert_term( Term, End ),
```

```
    End, !.

% assert_term( Term, End ) does the job. End is set to
% fail if there are more terms to read, otherwise is set
% to true. Term is the new term to assert to the
% database.

% End of File reached.
assert_term( end_of_file, true ) :- !.

% Revisables declaration
assert_term( rev( X ), fail ) :-
    functor( X, _, _ ), !,
    assert( '$revisable'( not X ) ).

% Asserts program rules to the program.
assert_term( ( <- Body ), fail ) :- !,
    assert_clause( false, Body ).
assert_term( ( Head <- Body ), fail ) :- !,
    assert_clause( Head, Body ).
assert_term( Fact, fail ) :-
    assert_clause( Fact, true ).

% Assert the program clauses
assert_clause( H, B ) :-
    recordz( H, (H <- B), _ ).
assert_clause( H, B, Ref ) :-
    recordz( H, (H <- B), Ref ).

% add_implicit_ir adds the implicit integrity rules of
% the current program to the database.
add_implicit_ir :-
    \+ get_clause( _, _ ), !.
add_implicit_ir :-
    get_heads(PH,NH), !,
    nl, write( 'Adding constraints...' ),
    assert_cons(PH,NH).

% get_clause unifies an head and a body with an existent
% clause.
get_clause( H, B ) :-
    recorded( H, (H <- B), _ ).

% get_heads( PosHeads, NegHeads ) gets all the heads of
% the current program in memory and splits them in
% positive and negative heads
get_heads(PosHeads,NegHeads) :-
    findall(HF,
        (get_clause(HF,_), \+ ( HF = -( _ ) ) ),
            PosHeads ),
    findall(HF,get_clause( - HF, _ ), NegHeads).

% The predicate assert_cons( PosHeads, NegHeads )
```

```
% generates all the possible implicit integrity rules
% obtained by combination of a positive literal with its
% explicit complement appearing in the heads of
% some rule in the current program.This predicate
% only traverses the list of positive literals.
% The rest of the job is done by assert_cons_lit.
assert_cons( [], _ ) :- !.
assert_cons( [L|P], N ) :-
    assert_cons_lit( N, L ),
    assert_cons( P, N ).
assert_cons( [_|P], N ) :- assert_cons( P, N ).


% assert_cons_lit( NegHeads, PosLit ) for each literal in
% NegHeads that unifies with PosLit a new integrity rule
% is added to the program.
assert_cons_lit( [], _ ) :- !.
assert_cons_lit( [L|_], L ) :-
    assert_clause( false, (L, -L) ),
    fail.
assert_cons_lit( [_|RestNeg], L ) :-
    assert_cons_lit( RestNeg, L ).



%%%%%%%%%%%%%%%%%%%%%%%%%%%%%%%%%%%%%%%%%%%%
%            Program revision            %
%%%%%%%%%%%%%%%%%%%%%%%%%%%%%%%%%%%%%%%%%%%%

% revise(R,L) returns the list of all revisions of the
% loaded program. Two valued revisions are obtained by
% making R=2.
revise(2,L) :- !,
    two_valued_revision( [[]], [], [], L ), !.
revise(_,L) :-
    three_valued_revision( L ), !.



%%%%%%%%%%%%%%%%%%%%%%%%%%%%%%%%%%%%%%%%%%%%%%
%      3-valued Program revision          %
%%%%%%%%%%%%%%%%%%%%%%%%%%%%%%%%%%%%%%%%%%%%%%

three_valued_revision( CRSs ) :-
    dss_rev_ind( DerInfo ),
    \+ DerInfo = [],
    assumption_support_sets( DerInfo, ASs, Contr ),
    compute_crs( Contr, ASs, CRSs ).
three_valued_revision( [[]] ).

% compute_crs computes the minimal hitting sets of the
% assumption sets, and their closure w.r.t. the
% indissociables.
compute_crs( false, ASs, CloCRSs ) :-
    find_mhs( ASs, CRSs ),
    ind_closure( CRSs, CloCRSs ).
```

```
compute_crs( true, _, [] ).


%%%%%%%%%%%%%%%%%%%%%%%%%%%%%%%%%%%%%%%%%%%%
%       2-valued Program revision         %
%%%%%%%%%%%%%%%%%%%%%%%%%%%%%%%%%%%%%%%%%%%%

two_valued_revision( ASi, Cs, Rev, MinRev ) :-
    revision_step( ASi, Cs, Rev, AuxASi, NewCs, NewRev ),
    remove_redundant( AuxASi, NewASi ),
    ( \+ NewASi = [] ->
        !,
      two_valued_revision( NewASi, NewCs, NewRev, MinRev )
    ;
        MinRev = NewRev
    ).


% revision_step(Assump,CSs,CurrRevs,
%                   NewAssump,NewContrSets,NewRevs )
%
% This predicate expands one complete level in the
% search-tree. If there is no element remaining to be
% expanded then the predicate ends, returning the new set
% of contradictory assumptions and the new set of minimal
% revisions. If the set of assumptions to be expanded
% contains a contradictory set of assumptions or a
% minimal revision, then it is not expanded. Otherwise,
% the revisions of the program plus the current set of
% assumptions are computed. If the revised program is
% non-contradictory then we are in the presence of a
% minimal revision. This minimal revision is added to the
% other ones ( last rule in the definition of
% revision_step ).
%
% If the program is contradictory and non-revisable then
% the current set of assumptions is added to the list of
% minimal sets contradictory of assumptions. If it is
% revisable then the current set of assumptions is added
% to each CRS of the revised program( expansion of a set
% of assumptions ). All the expansions are collected
% together and returned at the end in the fourth argument
% of revision_step.
revision_step( [], Cs, Rev, [], Cs, Rev ).
revision_step( [A|R], Cs, Rev, NewAS, NewCs, NewRev ) :-
    ( non_minimal( Cs, A ) ; non_minimal( Rev, A ) ), !,
    revision_step( R, Cs, Rev, NewAS, NewCs, NewRev ).
revision_step( [A|R], Cs, Rev, NewAS, NewCs, NewRev ) :-
    compute_revisions( A, Contr, CRSs ), !,
    ( Contr = false ->
        add_assumptions( CRSs, A, NewAS-DNewAs), !,
        revision_step( R, Cs, Rev, DNewAs, NewCs, NewRev )
    ;
        minimal_insertion( A, Cs, AuxCs ), !,
```

```
                revision_step(R, AuxCs, Rev, NewAS, NewCs, NewRev)
        ).
revision_step( [A|R], Cs, Rev, NewAS, NewCs, [A|NR] ) :-
        !, revision_step( R, Cs, Rev, NewAS, NewCs, NR ).


% compute_revisions( A, Contr, CloCRSs )  finds the
% contradiction removal sets of the program plus the set
% of assumptions A. If the current assumptions are
% contradictory and non-revisable then Contr is set to
% true, otherwise is set to false. The CRSs are returned
% on the last argument. This predicate fails if the
% program plus assumptions is non-contradictory.
compute_revisions( A, Contr, CloCRSs ) :-
        get_derivations( A, Info ),
        \+ Info = [],
        assumption_support_sets( Info, ASs, Contr ),
        ( Contr = false ->
            find_mhs( ASs, CRSs ),
            ind_closure( CRSs, CloCRSs )
        ;
            CloCRSs = []
        ).


% get_derivations( Assumptions, Info ) returns all the
% derivation for bottom.
get_derivations( Assumptions, Info )  :-
        add_revision_facts( Assumptions ),
        dss_rev_ind( Info ),
        remove_revision_rules.


% add_assumptions( CRSs, CurrentAssump, NewAssump )
%
% add_assumptions adds to each CRS in the list the set of
% current assumptions. A difference list is returned in
% order to be possible to add new CRSs of other sets of
% assumptions at the same level.
add_assumptions( [], _, X-X ).
add_assumptions( [CRS|RestCRSs], A, [NewA|NewAS]-DAs ) :-
        union_set( CRS, A, NewA ), !,
        add_assumptions( RestCRSs, A, NewAS-DAs ).


% add_revision_facts( Assumpt ) adds to the database the
% assumptions.
add_revision_facts( [] ).
add_revision_facts( [Lit|RestLits] ) :-
        add_revision_fact( Lit ), !,
        add_revision_facts( RestLits ).


% add_revision_fact( Lit ) turns Lit to true, by adding a
% fact to the program. The fact added is recorded in the
% database '$rev_rule'.
add_revision_fact( not Lit ) :-
        assert_clause( Lit, true, Ref1 ),
```

```
    recordz( '$rev_rule', Ref1, _ ).
```

```
% remove_revision_rules removes from the (extended)
% program all the revision facts.
remove_revision_rules :-
    recorded( '$rev_rule', R1, R2 ),
    erase( R1 ), erase( R2 ), fail.
remove_revision_rules.
```

```
%%%%%%%%%%%%%%%%%%%%%%%%%%%%%%%%%%%%%%%%%%%
%         Assumption Support Sets         %
%%%%%%%%%%%%%%%%%%%%%%%%%%%%%%%%%%%%%%%%%%%
```

```
% dss_rev_ind( Der ) returns for each possible derivation
% of false a 2-element list containing the dependency
% sets, and partial indissociables. These pairs are all
% collected together in the list Der.
dss_rev_ind( Der ) :-
    findall([DSs,Ind], demo_crsx(false, DSs, Ind), Der).
```

```
% assumption_support_sets( DerRevInd, ASs ) computes the
% assumption sets of a given program.
assumption_support_sets( DerInd, ASs, Contr ) :-
    compute_ind( DerInd, [], SSs ),
    compute_as( SSs, ASs, Contr ), !.
```

```
% compute_rev_ind( DerInfo, CurrInd, SupportSets ) :
%
% compute_rev_ind computes the indissociables.
% It also returns the support sets of false. In order to
% compute the indissociables it uses predicate
% indissociables/3. Given the current partition of
% literals (indissociables ) it updates the list with the
% self-supported sets returned by the derivation
% procedures on arguments Ind. This process is iterated
% until the list of derivation data is exhausted ( =
% number of ways of deriving false ). In the end the
% indissociables are added to the database
compute_ind( [], Ind, [] ) :- !,
    assert_indissociables( Ind ).
compute_ind( [[ SS,Ind]|Ds], ClassInd, [SS|SSs] ) :-
    indissociables( Ind, ClassInd, NewClassInd ),
    compute_ind( Ds, NewClassInd, SSs ).
```

```
% compute_as( DSs, ASs, Contr ) :
% For each dependency set given a correspondent
% assumption set is computed. The work is done by
% predicate compute_one_ass. If there is one empty
% assumption set the program is contradictory and
% non-revisable. In this case the flag Contr is set to
% true, otherwise it is set to false.
compute_as( [], [], false ).
```

```
compute_as( [DS|DSs], [AS|ASs], Contr ) :-
    compute_one_as( DS, AS ),
    ( AS = [] ->
        Contr = true
    ;
        compute_as( DSs, ASs, Contr )
    ).
```

```
% compute_one_as( DS, AS ) traverses the dependency set
% until the first revisable literal on each and-branch is
% reached (computed and declared by the user). The
% assumption set is obtained by collection these
% literals.
```

```
compute_one_as( [], [] ).
compute_one_as( [not Lit|_], [not Lit] ) :-
    '$revisable'( not Lit ), !.
compute_one_as( [and( Conj1, Conj2 )], ASAnd ) :- !,
    compute_one_as( Conj1, ASAnd1 ),
    compute_one_as( Conj2, ASAnd2 ),
    union_set( ASAnd1, ASAnd2, ASAnd ).
compute_one_as( [_|RestDSs], AS ) :-
    compute_one_as( RestDSs, AS ).
```

```
% demo_crsx( Lit, DSs, Ind ) does some initializations,
% and calls the meta-interpreter.
demo_crsx( Lit, DSs, Ind ) :-
    initial_cx( CxIn ),
    demo( Lit, CxIn, DSs, rev( _, _, Ind-[]) ).
```

```
% If the goal is true then the meta-interpreter succeeds
% with an empty dependency set, loops, partial support
% set, and partial indissociables.
demo(true, _, [], rev( Loop-Loop, SS-SS, Ind-Ind) ) :- !.
```

```
% Literal not true = false always fails.
demo( not true, _, _, _ ) :-
    !, fail.
```

```
% To prove a conjunction it is necessary to prove both
% conjuncts. All the auxiliary sets are merged together.
demo( (A,B), Cx, [and(DSsL, DSsR)],
    rev( LoopC-DLoop, SSC-DSS, IndC-DInd ) ) :- !,
    demo( A, Cx, DSsL,
        rev( LoopC-LoopR, SSC-SSR, IndC-IndR ) ),
    demo( B, Cx, DSsR,
        rev( LoopR-DLoop, SSR-DSS, IndR-DInd ) ).
```

```
demo( [A], Cx, DSs, Revs ) :- !,
    demo( A, Cx, DSs, Revs ).
demo( [A|B], Cx, [and(DSsL, DSsR)],
    rev( LoopC-DLoop, SSC-DSS, IndC-DInd ) ) :- !,
    demo( A, Cx, DSsL,
```

```
        rev( LoopC-LoopR, SSC-SSR, IndC-IndR ) ),
    demo( B, Cx, DSsR,
        rev( LoopR-DLoop, SSR-DSS, IndR-DInd ) ) ).


% Rewriting of the negation of a conjunction:
% To prove the negation of a conjunction it is enough to
% prove that one of the conjuncts is false.
demo( not (A,_), CxIn, DSs, Revs ) :-
    compl( A, NegA ),
    demo( NegA, CxIn, DSs, Revs ).
demo( not (_,B), CxIn, DSs, Revs ) :- !,
    compl( B, NegB ),
    demo( NegB, CxIn, DSs, Revs ).


%% Default Literals
% Fails if a negative non-direct loop is found.
demo( not Lit, cx([_|OtherLevels],_), _, _ ) :-
    loop( not Lit, OtherLevels ), !, fail.


% Succeeds if a negative direct loop is found .
% The literal is put in the dependency set and the
% literals in the loop are collected and it is returned
% in the rev argument.
demo( not Lit, cx([Level0|_],_), [not Lit],
        rev([loop(not Lit,Loop)|L]-L, SS-SS, Ind-Ind ) ) :-
    same_sign( not Lit, Level0),
    dir_loop( not Lit, Level0, Loop ), !.

% WFSX's Coherence Principle:   - Lit => not Lit.
demo( not Lit, CxIn, DSs, Revs ) :-
    complx( Lit, NotLit ),
    add_to_cx( not Lit, CxIn, NewCx ),
    demo( NotLit, NewCx, DSs, Revs ).


% not Lit   succeeds if there are no rules for Lit
demo( not Lit,cx(_,_),[not Lit],
        rev( L-L, SS-SS, [[not Lit]|Ind]-Ind ) ) :-
    \+ get_clause( Lit, _ ), !.


% There are rule for Lit. Collect all the Lit rule
% bodies, complement them and make its conjunctions. To
% prove not Lit this conjunction must be proved.
demo( not Lit, CxIn, [not Lit|DSs], Revs ) :-
    add_to_cx( not Lit, CxIn, NewCx ),
    collect_negbodies( Lit, NegBodies ),
    demo( NegBodies, NewCx, DSs, RevNeg ),
    pindiss( not Lit, RevNeg, Revs ).


%% Objective Literals
% Fails if a positive loop is found
demo( Lit, CxIn, _, _ ) :-
    \+ ( Lit = not(_) ),
    loop( Lit, CxIn ), !, fail.
```

```
% For each rule head that unifies with the goal, expand
% the goal to the body of this rule. A test for positive
% loops is made after the unification. The literal is
% added to the dependency set. The revisable information
% is simply passed back.
demo( Lit, CxIn, [Lit|DSs], Revs ) :-
    \+ ( Lit = not(_) ),
    add_to_cx( Lit, CxIn, NewCx ),
    get_clause( Lit, BodyLit ),
    positive_loop( Lit, CxIn ),
    demo( BodyLit, NewCx, DSs, Revs ).


% pindiss/3 updates partial sets of indissociables.
pindiss( Lit, rev( L, S-Aux, I ), NewRev ) :-
    del_loops( L, Lit, Loops, Aux-DS ),
    rev_ind( Loops, S-DS, I, Lit, NewRev ).


% Separates the loops in partial revisables and
% indissociables.
rev_ind( Loops, SS, Ind, _, rev( Loops, SS, Ind ) ) :-
    \+ empty_dl( Loops ), !.
rev_ind( Loops, SS, I-DI, Goal,
        rev( Loops, SS, [[Goal]|I]-DI ) ) :-
    empty_dl( SS ), !.
rev_ind( Loops, SS-[], I-DI, _,
        rev( Loops, S-S, [NewSS|I]-DI ) ) :-
    list2set( SS, NewSS ).


% del_loops( OldLoops, Lit, RestOfLoops, ListOnLit )
%
% From the list of loops OldLoops the literals on Lit are
% returned on the last argument and the rest of them on
% RestOfLoops. All the lists are difference lists for
% efficiency.
del_loops( L, _, NL-NL, ExpL-ExpL ) :-
    empty_dl( L ), !.
del_loops( [loop(Goal,Loop-DLoop)|L]-DL, G, NewL,
        Loop-ExpL ) :- !,
    del_loops( L-DL, G, NewL, DLoop-ExpL ).
del_loops( [Loop|L]-DL, G, [Loop|NewL]-DNL, ExpL ) :- !,
    del_loops(L-DL, G, NewL-DNL, ExpL ).


% Empty context and initial level 1
initial_cx( cx([[]],1) ).


% add_to_cx( Lit, OldCx, NewCx )
%
% A context is formed by a level and by a list of sets of
% literals. All the literals in each one of these sets of
% have the same sign. When a new literal is added to a
% context the level is incremented by one. If the literal
% has the same sign of the first set then the literal is
```

```
% added to this list, otherwise a new singleton set with
% the literal in it is added to the list.
add_to_cx(G,cx(Cx,Level),cx(NewCx,NextLevel)) :-
    NextLevel is Level+1,
    add2cx(G,Cx,NewCx).

add2cx(G,[[]],[[G]]) :- !.
add2cx(G,[[L|RI]|Others], [[G,L|RI]|Others]) :-
    same_sign( G, [L|RI] ), !.
add2cx(G,Cx,[[G]|Cx] ).

% in_other_cx( Lit, Cx )
%
% tests if Lit occurs in Cx. The implementation
% automatically skips the contexts of opposite signs.
in_other_cx(G,[[G1|_]|_]) :- G == G1, !.
in_other_cx(G,[[H|T]|Cx]) :-
    \+ same_sign(G,[H|T]), !,
    in_other_cx(G,Cx).
in_other_cx(G,[[_|S]|Cx]):-!,
    in_other_cx(G,[S|Cx]).
in_other_cx(G,[[]|Cx]) :-
    in_other_cx(G,Cx).

% same_sign( Lit, Cx ) tests if the literal and the
% context have the same sign
same_sign(not _,[not _|_]) :- !.
same_sign(G,[C|_]) :-
    \+ functor(G, not, 1),
    \+ functor(C, not, 1).

% loop( Lit, Cx ) tests if Lit belongs to Cx. Uses
% predicate in_other_cx
loop( Lit, cx(Context,_) ) :-
    in_other_cx( Lit, Context ), !.
loop( Lit, Context ) :-
    in_other_cx( Lit, Context ).

% dir_loop( Lit, SignInter, Loop )
% Succeeds if a direct loop is found and returns the
% loop.
dir_loop( X, [Y|_], [Y|DL]-DL ) :-
    X == Y.
dir_loop( X, [H|T], [H|NT]-DL ) :-
    dir_loop( X, T, NT-DL ).

% collect_negbodies( Lit, NegBodies ) collects all the
% bodies of rules with Lit in their head.
collect_negbodies( Lit, NegBodies ) :-
    findall( NegBody,
             (get_clause(Lit, Body), compl(Body,NegBody)),
             NegBodies ).
```

```
% If a positive loop is detected the goal fails
positive_loop( Lit, CxIn ) :-
    loop( Lit, CxIn ),
    !, fail.
positive_loop( _, _ ).


%%%%%%%%%%%%%%%%%%%%%%%%%%%%%%%%%%%%%%%%%
%          Indissociable literals      %
%%%%%%%%%%%%%%%%%%%%%%%%%%%%%%%%%%%%%%%%%

% ind_closure closes a given set of CRSs with the
% indissociables. Predicate crss_closures does the job
% and then the redundant sets of CRSs are removed.
ind_closure( CRSs, CloCRSs ) :-
    crss_closures( CRSs, ClosedCRSs ),
    remove_redundant( ClosedCRSs, CloCRSs ).

% crss_closures calls close_ind for each CRS in its first
% argument, the closure is returned on the second
% argument.
crss_closures( [], [] ).
crss_closures( [CRS|RestCRSs], [ClCRS|RestClCRSs] ) :-
    close_ind( CRS, ClCRS ),
    crss_closures( RestCRSs, RestClCRSs ).

% close_ind for each literal in its first argument picks
% from the database the previously computed
% indissociables.
close_ind( [], [] ).
close_ind( [Lit|RestCRS], CloCRS ) :-
    close_ind( RestCRS, CloRest ),
    indissociables( Lit, Ind ),
    union_set( Ind, CloRest, CloCRS ).

% indissociables/2 returns the set of indissociables of a
% given literal (maximal indissociable set where it
% belongs). This set is a class of equivalence of an
% intuitive binary relation between default literals.
indissociables( Lit, Ind ) :-
    '$indissoc'( Lit, Ind ), !.
indissociables( Lit, [Lit] ).

% indissociables( Loops, OldInd, NewInd ) adds a loop one
% at a time to the indissociable partition. After adding
% all the loops the new partition is returned.
indissociables( [], NewInd, NewInd ) :- !.
indissociables( [Loop|RestLoops], Ind, NewInd ) :-
    add_new_loop( Ind, Loop, Loop, Loop, AuxInd ),
    indissociables( RestLoops,  AuxInd, NewInd ).

% add_new_loop(OldInd,Loop,CurrInter,CurrUnion,NewInd)
% combines a new loop with the existing indissociable
```

```
% partition. This partition is organized in pairs
% [Inter,Union] where Union containssets of literals in
% loops that can access each other (closure of the loops)
% and Inter the literals common to these loops (possible
% indissociables).
% To add a new loop the set of pairs [Inter,Union] such
% that Union intersected with the Loop is non-empty.
% These pairs are removed and a new one introduced in the
% list with NewInter the intersection of all the
% collected Inters with the given loop and NewUnion the
% union of the loop with all the collected Unions.
add_new_loop( [], _, Inters, Union, [[Inters,Union]] ).
add_new_loop([[IndI,IndU]|RestInd],Loop,Int,Uni,
             [[IndI,IndU]|NewInd]) :-
    inter_set( Loop, IndU, [] ), !,
    add_new_loop( RestInd, Loop, Int, Uni, NewInd ).
add_new_loop( [[IndI,IndU]|RestInd], Loop, Int, Uni,
              NewInd ) :-
    inter_set( Int, IndI, NewInters ),
    union_set( IndU, Uni, NewUnion ),
    add_new_loop( RestInd, Loop, NewInters, NewUnion,
                  NewInd ).

% assert_indissociables( Ind ) adds to the database the
% diverse maximal sets of indissociable literals. The
% predicate add_indissociable is used to add a class one
% at a time. This predicate asserts to the database a
% fact of the form$indissoc( Lit, Class ) where Lit
% belongs to Class.
assert_indissociables( [] ).
assert_indissociables( [[[_],_]|RestInd] ) :- !,
    assert_indissociables( RestInd ).
assert_indissociables( [[Ind,_]|RestInd] ) :- !,
    add_indissociable( Ind ),
    assert_indissociables( RestInd ).

% add_indissociable( Ind ) records information of a set
% of indissociables.  It adds to the database facts of
% the form$indissoc( Lit, Ind ),where Lit is a literal
% belonging to Ind, in order to optimize search of
% indissociable sets.
add_indissociable( Ind ) :-
    member( Lit, Ind ),
    assert( '$indissoc'( Lit, Ind ) ),
    fail.
add_indissociable( _ ).


%%%%%%%%%%%%%%%%%%%%%%%%%%%%%%%%%%%%%%%%%%%%%%
%            Minimal Hitting Sets           %
%%%%%%%%%%%%%%%%%%%%%%%%%%%%%%%%%%%%%%%%%%%%%%

% find_mhs( Cs, HSs ) has two arguments. This predicate
```

```
% returns in the second argument the list of minimal
% hitting sets of the collection of sets given in its
% first argument, Cs.
find_mhs( Cs, HSs ) :-
    remove_redundant( Cs, MinimalCs ),
    pruned_hs_tree( [[]|DL]-DL, [], HSs, MinimalCs ).


% remove_redundant( Cs, MinimalCs ) removes from set
% collection Cs the non-minimal sets, returning in
% its second argument only
% the mininal sets of Cs. The order used is set
% inclusion.
remove_redundant( [], [] ).
remove_redundant( [Set|RestSets], MinimalSets ) :-
  check_minimality( RestSets, Set, NewRestSets, IsMin ),
  new_minimal_sets(IsMin, Set, NewRestSets, MinimalSets).


% new_minimal_sets( IsMin, Set, RestSets, MinimalSets )
% is an auxiliary predicate to predicate
% remove_redundant/2. If Set is not a minimal
% (IsMin=false), this predicates computes the minimal
% sets of collection RestSets and returns them in its
% last argument. Otherwise, Set is a minimal set
% (IsMin=true) and it is added to the previously
% collection of minimal sets.
new_minimal_sets(false, _, RestSets, MinimalSets) :-
    remove_redundant( RestSets, MinimalSets ).
new_minimal_sets(true,Set RestSets,[Set|MinimalSets]) :-
    remove_redundant( RestSets, MinimalSets ).


% check_minimality( Set, Cs, NewCs, IsMin ) tests if Set
% is contained in other set of Cs. Simultaneously it
% deletes from the collection Cs all the sets in which
% Set is contained, returning this new collection in
% argument NewCs. IsMin is true if the given set is
% minimal, false otherwise.
check_minimality( [], _, [], true ).
check_minimality( [Set1|RestOfSets], Set,
                  [Set1|RestOfSets], false ) :-
    in_set( Set1, Set ), !.
check_minimality([Set1|RestOfSets], Set, NewCs, IsMin) :-
    in_set( Set, Set1 ), !,
    check_minimality( RestOfSets, Set, NewCs, IsMin ).
check_minimality( [Set1|RestOfSets], Set, [Set1|NewRest],
                  IsMin ) :-
    check_minimality( RestOfSets, Set, NewRest, IsMin ).


% pruned_hs_tree( ToExpand, Leaves, MHS, Cs ) creates a
% pruned HS-tree.
% It has 4 arguments :
%
%    - The first one is the (difference) list of nodes
% remaining to be expanded which is generated
```

```
% breadth-first.
%    - The second argument is the current list of leaf
% nodes.
%    - In the third argument are returned the minimal
% hitting sets.
%    - The last argument contains the collection of sets
% Cs.
%
% If the list of labels to expand is empty, then the
% algorithm stops, with MHS being the current set of
% leaves. If the list of labels remaining to expand is
% non-empty then the head label is selected to be
% expanded. If it is a leaf, it is added to the current
% set of leaves (expanded labels), where only minimal
% leaves are retained, and the tree is pruned by removing
% labels to be expanded that are"bigger" than this new
% leaf. If the selected label is not a leaf, then it is
% expanded and the HS-tree is pruned. This algoritm is
% iterated until we have no more labels to expand.
%
% Notice that this implementation doesn't reuse node
% labels (step 2 of Reiter's algorithm) because the set
% collection is kwnown from the start. Tree pruning's
% step (iii) is not necessary, because the non-minimal
% sets of the collection are removed "a priori".
pruned_hs_tree( L-DL, Closed, Closed, _ ) :-
    L == DL, !.
pruned_hs_tree([Label|ToExpand]-DL, Expanded, MHS, Cs) :-
    new_labels( Label, Cs, ExpNodes, IsLeaf ),
    ( IsLeaf ->
        !,
        prune_non_minimal( ToExpand-DL, Label,
                          MinimalLabels ),
        pruned_hs_tree( MinimalLabels, [Label|Expanded],
                       MHS, Cs )
    ;
        !,
        prune_tree( ExpNodes, Expanded, ToExpand-DL,
                   Exp-DExp ),
        DL = Exp,
        pruned_hs_tree(ToExpand-DExp, Expanded, MHS, Cs)
    ).


% new_labels( Label, Cs, ExpNodes, IsLeaf ) expands Label
% by finding a set in Cs such that the label and this set
% are disjoint. If it can't find this set the node is
% closed (IsLeaf=true), otherwise IsLeaf is set to fail
% and the label is expanded using the previously set,
% returning the new nodes in argument ExpNodes.
new_labels( Label, Cs, ExpLabels, fail ) :-
    member( Set, Cs ),
    inter_set( Label, Set, [] ), !,
    expand_label( Set, Label, ExpLabels ).
```

```
new_labels( _, _, _, true ).

% expand_label( Set, Label, ExpNodes ) expands Label. One
% particular label expansion is obtained by adding to
% Label one element belonging to Set. All these new
% labels are returned in ExpLabels.
expand_label( [], _, [] ).
expand_label( Set, Label, [NewLabel|ExpLabels] ) :-
    del_set( Nd, Set, NewSet ),
    ins_set( Nd, Label, NewLabel ), !,
    expand_label( NewSet, Label, ExpLabels ).

% prune_non_minimal( Labels, ExpLabel, NewLabels )
% applies pruning rule 3i to the hs_tree removing from
% Labels all the labels containing Label, giving
% NewLabels. Labels and NewLabels are difference lists.
prune_non_minimal( L-DL, _, X-X ) :-
    L == DL, !.
prune_non_minimal( [Label|RestLabels]-DR, ExpLabel,
                   NewLabels ) :-
    in_set( ExpLabel, Label ), !,
    prune_non_minimal(RestLabels-DR, ExpLabel, NewLabels).
prune_non_minimal( [Label|RestLabels]-DR, ExpLabel,
                   [Label|NewLabels]-DNL ) :-
    prune_non_minimal( RestLabels-DR, ExpLabel,
                       NewLabels-DNL ).

% prune_tree( NewExpLabels, ExpLabels, ToExpand,
%             NewToExpand ), applies
% pruning rules 3i and 3ii to the new generated labels
% (NewExpLabels), the remaining ones are returned in the
% difference list NewToExpand.
prune_tree( [], _, _, L-L ).
prune_tree( [Hn|RestOfHn], Expanded, ToExpand, DL ) :-
    member( ExpHn, Expanded ),
    in_set( ExpHn, Hn ), !,
    prune_tree( RestOfHn, Expanded, ToExpand, DL ).
prune_tree( [Hn|RestOfHn], Expanded, ToExpand, DL ) :-
    member_dl( Hn, ToExpand ), !,
    prune_tree( RestOfHn, Expanded, ToExpand, DL ).
prune_tree( [Hn|RestOfHn], Exp, ToExpand, [Hn|L]-DL ) :-
    !, prune_tree( RestOfHn, Exp, ToExpand, L-DL ).


%%%%%%%%%%%%%%%%%%%%%%%%%%%%%%%%%%%%%%%%%%%%%%%%%
%              Set Operations                  %
%%%%%%%%%%%%%%%%%%%%%%%%%%%%%%%%%%%%%%%%%%%%%%%%%

% list2set( List, Set ) casts a list to a set
list2set( [X], [X] ) :- !.
list2set( List, Set ) :-
    sort( List, Set ).
```

```
% ins_set( El, Set, NewSet ) inserts El in Set giving
% NewSet. It's the auxiliary predicate $ins_set( Set, El,
% NewSet )that does the job...
ins_set( El, Set, NewSet ) :-
    '$ins_set'( Set, El, NewSet ).


'$ins_set'( [], El, [El] ) :- !.
'$ins_set'( [ES|RestOfSet], El, [El,ES|RestOfSet] ) :-
    El @< ES, !.
'$ins_set'( [ES|RestOfSet], El, [ES|RestOfSet] ) :-
    El == ES, !.
'$ins_set'( [ES|RestOfSet], El, [ES|NewRest] ) :-
    !, '$ins_set'( RestOfSet, El, NewRest ).


% del_set( El, Set, NewSet ) removes (one ocurrence) of
% El from Set giving NewSet.
del_set( El, [El|RestOfSet], RestOfSet ).
del_set( El, [ES|RestOfSet], [ES|NewRest] ) :-
  \+ \+ ( El = ES ), !, del_set( El, RestOfSet, NewRest).
del_set( El, [ES|RestOfSet], [ES|NewRest] ) :-
    ES @< El, !, del_set( El, RestOfSet, NewRest ).


% in_set( Set1, Set2 ) tests if Set1 is contained in Set2
in_set( [], _ ).
in_set( [El|RestOfSet1], [El|RestOfSet2] ) :-
    in_set( RestOfSet1, RestOfSet2 ).
in_set( [El|RestOfSet1], [_|RestOfSet2] ) :-
    var( El ), !, in_set( [El|RestOfSet1], RestOfSet2 ).
in_set( [El1|RestOfSet1], [El2|RestOfSet2] ) :-
    El2 @< El1, !, in_set([El1|RestOfSet1], RestOfSet2 ).


% union_set( Set1, Set2, NewSet ) NewSet is the union of
% Set1 with Set2
union_set( [], X, X ) :- !.
union_set( X, [], X ) :- !.
union_set( [X|RestOfSet1], [Y|RestOfSet2], [X|NewSet]) :-
    X @< Y, !,
    union_set( RestOfSet1, [Y|RestOfSet2], NewSet ).
union_set( [X|RestOfSet1], [Y|RestOfSet2], [Y|NewSet]) :-
    Y @< X, !,
    union_set( [X|RestOfSet1], RestOfSet2, NewSet ).
union_set( [X|RestOfSet1], [Y|RestOfSet2], [X|NewSet]) :-
    Y = X, !,
    union_set( RestOfSet1, RestOfSet2, NewSet ).


% inter_set( Set1, Set2, NewSet ) NewSet is the
% intersection of Set1 with Set2.
inter_set( [], _, [] ) :- !.
inter_set( _, [], [] ) :- !.
inter_set( [X|RestOfSet1], [Y|RestOfSet2], NewSet ) :-
    X @< Y, !,
    inter_set( RestOfSet1, [Y|RestOfSet2], NewSet ).
inter_set( [X|RestOfSet1], [Y|RestOfSet2], NewSet ) :-
```

```
        Y @< X, !,
        inter_set( [X|RestOfSet1], RestOfSet2, NewSet ).
inter_set( [X|RestOfSet1], [Y|RestOfSet2], [X|NewSet]) :-
        Y = X, !,
        inter_set( RestOfSet1, RestOfSet2, NewSet ).


%%%%%%%%%%%%%%%%%%%%%%%%%%%%%%%%%%%%%%%%%%%
%           Auxiliary predicates         %
%%%%%%%%%%%%%%%%%%%%%%%%%%%%%%%%%%%%%%%%%%%

% member_dl( X, DL ) tests if X is a member of difference
% list DL.
member_dl( _, L-DL ) :-
        L == DL, !, fail.
member_dl( X, [X|_]-_ ).
member_dl( X, [_|T]-DL ) :-
        member_dl( X, T-DL ).

% Default complement of a literal
compl(not (G),G) :- !.
compl(G, not (G)).

% Classical complement of a literal
complx(- G,G) :- !.
complx(G,- G).


% Non-deterministic member
member( X, [X|_] ).
member( X, [_|Y] ) :-
        member( X, Y ).

% Tests if the (difference) list is empty
empty_dl( X-Y ) :-
        X == Y.

% non_minimal( Sets, Set ) tests if there is a set in
% Sets smaller than Set(in the sense of set inclusion).
non_minimal( [X|_], Y ) :-
        in_set( X, Y ), !.
non_minimal( [_|Xs], Y ) :-
        non_minimal( Xs, Y ).

% minimal_insertion( ContrAssumpt, ContrSets,
% NewContrSets ) adds a new set of contradictory
% assumptions and retains only the minimal ones.
minimal_insertion( A, Cs, [A|AuxCs] ) :-
        check_minimality( Cs, A, AuxCs, true ), !.
minimal_insertion( _, Cs, Cs ).
```

C. Proofs of theorems

Proof of Theorem 5.1.1: We prove this theorem here only for the case of a stationary semantics. The proof for stable semantics is quite similar and is omitted.

$\Rightarrow$ If a stationary semantics is coherent then for any P^* every model M of P^* having $\neg\_A$ also has not_A. By proposition 5.1.1:

$$not\_A \in M \Leftrightarrow \sim A \in M.$$

Similarly we conclude that for every M :

$$A \in M \text{ iff } \sim\neg\_A \in M.$$

Thus, given that models of clausal programs are always total, every model containing A does not contains $\neg\_A$, and every model containing $\neg\_A$ does not contain A, which is the consistency requirement.

$\Leftarrow$ If a stationary semantics is consistent then for any P^* every model M of P^* having $\neg\_A$ does not have A, and vice-versa. By proposition 5.1.1:

$$A \notin M \Leftrightarrow \sim A \in M \Leftrightarrow not\_A \in M.$$

Similarly we conclude that for every M :

$$\neg\_A \notin M \Leftrightarrow \sim\neg\_A \in M \Leftrightarrow not\_\neg\_A \in M.$$

Thus:

$$\neg\_A \in M \Rightarrow A \notin M \Rightarrow not\_A \in M$$

and

$$A \in M \Rightarrow \neg\_A \notin M \Rightarrow not\_\neg\_A \in M$$

which, by definition of $AX_\neg$ model, is equivalent to coherence.

Proof of Theorem 5.1.4: Consider the fixpoint equation:

$$P^* = \neg\_P \cup AX_\neg \cup \left\{ not\_L \mid P^* \models_{CIRC} \sim L \right\} \cup \left\{ \sim not\_L \mid P^* \models_{CIRC} L \right\}.$$

By definition, the expansions of the stationary semantics with classical negation are the fixpoints of the equation obtained from the one above by deleting the set of axioms $AX_\neg$ and replacing in $\neg\_P$ every occurence of an objective literal $\neg\_L$ by $\sim L$. Hereafter we denote such programs by $\sim\_P$.

Let $P_1^* = \neg\_P \cup AX_\neg \cup S$ be a stationary $AX_\neg$ expansion of P, and let $P_2^* = \sim\_P \cup S$. We prove that P_2^* is an expansion of the stationary semantics with classical negation.

For every objective proposition L, by the axioms in $AX_\neg$, $\neg\_L \Leftrightarrow \sim L$. So, it is clear that the models of P_1^* are the models of P_2^* modulo propositions of the form $\neg\_L$. Thus for every atom A :

$$P_1^* \models A \Leftrightarrow P_2^* \models A \quad (+)$$

We now prove that for every atom A:

$$P_1^* \models_{CIRC} \sim A \Leftrightarrow P_2^* \models_{CIRC} \sim A \quad (\&)$$

($\Rightarrow$) Let $M_1', \ldots, M_n'$ be all the minimal models of P_1^*, and let M_i'' be the model obtained from M_i' by removing all propositions of the form $\neg\_L$. As we've seen above, all such M_i'' are models of P_2^* and, as only positive propositions are removed, they are also the minimal models of P_2^*. Thus, if $\sim A$ is a consequence of all minimal models of P_1^* it is also a consequence of all minimal models of P_2^*.

($\Leftarrow$) Let $M_1'', \ldots, M_n''$ be all the minimal models of P_2^*, and let

$$M_i' = M_i'' \cup \{\neg\_L \mid L \notin M_i''\}.$$

All such M_i' are models of P_1^*.
Let us assume that one M_i' is not a minimal models of P_1^*, i.e. there exists a model N of P_1^* such that $N \leq M_i'$, and $N \neq M$. In such a case, by definition of $\leq$:

$$N_{pos} \subsetneq M_i'' \vee (N_{pos} = M_i'' \wedge N \subseteq M_i')$$

where N_{pos} is the subset of N obtained by deleting from it all literals of the form $\neg\_L$.
Clearly N_{pos} is a model of P_2^*. Thus, if the first disjunct holds, M_i'' is not a minimal model of P_2^*, which contradicts one of our hypotheses.
If $N_{pos} = M_i''$ then for N to be a model of P_1^*, by the axioms in $AX_\neg$, for every atom A :

$$A \notin N_{pos} \Rightarrow \neg\_A \in N$$

So, by definition of M_i'' :

$$M_i'' \supseteq N$$

which also contradicts our hypotheses.

With the results above we now finalize the proof that P_2^* is an expansion. Since P_1^* is an expansion:

$$S = \left\{ not\_L \mid P_1^* \models_{CIRC} \sim L \right\} \cup \left\{ \sim not\_L \mid P_1^* \models_{CIRC} L \right\}$$

By (&) :

$$P_1^* \models_{CIRC} \sim L \Leftrightarrow P_1^* \models_{CIRC} \sim L$$

As already mentioned in page 54, it is known (cf. [113, 71, 82]) that for any proposition A of any theory T :

$$T \models_{CIRC} A \equiv T \models A$$

Thus:

$$P_1^* \models_{CIRC} L \Leftrightarrow P_1^* \models L \overset{by\ (+)}{\Leftrightarrow} P_2^* \models L \Leftrightarrow P_2^* \models_{CIRC} L$$

Replacing in S these equivalence results:

$$S = \left\{ not\_L \mid P_2^* \models_{CIRC} \sim L \right\} \cup \left\{ \sim not\_L \mid P_2^* \models_{CIRC} L \right\}$$

Recall that by definition $P_2^* = \sim\_P \cup S$ so, replacing S by its value:

$$P_2^* = \sim\_P \cup \left\{ not\_L \mid P_2^* \models_{CIRC} \sim L \right\} \cup \left\{ \sim not\_L \mid P_2^* \models_{CIRC} L \right\}$$

i.e. P_2^* is an expansion of the stationary semantics with classical negation.

The proof that every expansion of the stationary semantics with classical negation corresponds to a stationary $AX_\neg$ expansion is similar to the one above, and is omitted.

Proof of Theorem 5.1.6:
Proving the equivalence between the two alternative definitions is trivial. Thus we only prove the equivalence between *WFSX* and the second definition presented in the theorem.

Without loss of generality (cf. Theorem 9.1.2) we assume that programs are in the semantic kernel form, i.e. a program is a set of rules of the form:

$$L \leftarrow not\ A_1, \ldots, not\ A_n \quad n \geq 0$$

We begin by proving a lemma:

Lemma C.0.1. *Let $\neg\_P$ be a clausal program and let P^+ be:*

$$P^+ = \neg\_P \cup S_n \cup S_p$$

where S_n is a set of default literals of the form not_L, and S_p is a set of default literals of the form $\sim not\_L$.
For every clause with L in $\neg\_P$, i.e. of the form:

$$L \vee \sim\!not\_A_1 \vee \ldots \vee \sim\!not\_A_n \in \neg\_P$$

there exists $\sim\!not\_A_i \in S_p$, *iff*

$$P^+ \models_{CIRC} \sim\!L$$

Proof. ($\Rightarrow$) Let $\sim\!not\_A_j$ be one literal in the j-th clause with L such that $\sim\!not\_A_j \in S_p{}^1$.
Then all models of P^+ contain a set of such $\sim\!not\_A_j$:

$$\{\sim\!not\_A_1, \ldots, \sim\!not\_A_m\}$$

where m is the number of clauses with literal L.
Thus every clause with L is satisfied by all models of P^+ independently of the truth value of L, and thus:

$$P^+ \models_{CIRC} \sim\!L$$

($\Leftarrow$) Assume the contrary, i.e. there exists a clause:

$$L \vee \sim\!not\_A_1 \vee \ldots \vee \sim\!not\_A_n \in \neg\_P$$

such that $\{\sim\!not\_A_1, \ldots, \sim\!not\_A_n\} \cap S_p = \{\}$, and $P^+ \models_{CIRC} \sim\!L$.
Then, given that, by the form of programs, literals of the form $\sim\!not\,L$ can only be a consequence of P^+ if they belong to S_p, there exists a model M of the circumscription such that

$$\{not\_A_1, \ldots, not\_A_n\} \subseteq M$$

and thus L belongs to that model. So $P^+ \not\models_{CIRC} \sim\!L$.

Given that complete scenaria (Definition 7.3.1 in Section 7) correspond to partial stable models (cf. Theorem 7.4.5), it is enough to prove that there is a one to one correspondence between the fixpoints of:

$$P^* = \neg\_P \cup \left\{ not\_L \mid P^* \models_{CIRC} \sim\!L \text{ or } P^* \models \neg\_L \right\} \cup \{\sim\!not\,L \mid P^* \models L\}^2$$

and complete scenaria.
This correspondence is proven in two parts:

– first we prove that if $P \cup H$ is a complete scenario then

$$P^* = \neg\_P \cup H \cup \{\sim\!not\_L \mid P \cup H \vdash L\}$$

is an expansion.
– then we prove that if P^* is an expansion then

$$P \cup \left\{ not\,L \mid P^* \models_{CIRC} \sim\!L \text{ or } P^* \models \neg\_L \right\}$$

is a complete scenario.

---

[1] By hypothesis such a literal always exists.
[2] Within this proof we designate expansions as such fixpoints

Let us assume that $P \cup H$ is a complete scenario. i.e.

(i) $not\ L \in H \Rightarrow not\ L \in Mand(H)$ or $not\ L \in Acc(H)$
(ii) $not\ L \in Mand(H) \Rightarrow not\ L \in H$
(iii) $not\ L \in Acc(H) \Rightarrow not\ L \in H$

We show that

$$P^* = \neg\_P \cup H \cup \{\sim not\_L \mid P \cup H \vdash L\}$$

is an expansion of the clausal program $\neg\_P$ of P, i.e.

$$H \cup \{\sim not\_L \mid P \cup H \vdash L\} =$$
$$\left\{ not\_L \mid P^* \models_{CIRC} \sim L \text{ or } P^* \models \neg\_L \right\} \cup \{\sim not\ L \mid P^* \models L\}$$

We'll do that by separately proving the two equalities:

$$\{\sim not\_L \mid P \cup H \vdash L\} = \{\sim not\ L \mid P^* \models L\} \qquad (eq1)$$
$$H = \left\{ not\_L \mid P^* \models_{CIRC} \sim L \text{ or } P^* \models \neg\_L \right\} \qquad (eq2)$$

To prove the first equality we have to show that

$$P \cup H \vdash L \Leftrightarrow P^* \models L$$

By definition of $\vdash$, $P \cup H \vdash L$ iff there exists a rule

$$L \leftarrow not\ A_1, \ldots, not\ A_n \in P$$

such that

$$\{not\ A_1, \ldots, not\ A_n\} \subseteq H$$

By definition of clausal program $\neg\_P$ of a program P, such a rule exists iff

$$L \vee \sim not\_A_1 \vee \ldots \vee \sim not\_A_n \in \neg\_P$$

And, by construction of P^*,

$$\{not\ A_1, \ldots, not\ A_n\} \subseteq H \ \Leftrightarrow \ \{not\ A_1, \ldots, not\ A_n\} \subseteq P^*$$

Thus, clearly $P^* \models L$.

For the equality $(eq2)$, we have to prove that:

1. $P^* \models \neg\_L \Rightarrow not\ L \in H$
2. $P^* \models_{CIRC} \sim L \Rightarrow not\ L \in H$
3. $not\ L \in H \Rightarrow P^* \models_{CIRC} \sim L$ or $P^* \models \neg\_L$

1. By equality $(eq1)$:

$$P^* \models \neg\_L \Leftrightarrow P \cup H \vdash \neg L$$

and by definition of $Mand(H)$:

$$P \cup H \vdash \neg L \Rightarrow not\ L \in Mand(H) \overset{by\ (ii)}{\Rightarrow} not\ L \in H$$

2. By lemma C.0.1, $P^* \models_{CIRC} \sim L$ iff

$$\forall LV \sim not\_A_1 \vee \ldots \vee \sim not\_A_n \in \neg\_P \mid \exists \sim not\_A_i \in P^*$$

By construction of P^*, $\sim not\_A_i \in P^* \Leftrightarrow P \cup H \vdash A_i$.
By definition of clausal program $\neg\_P$ of a program P :

$$LV \sim not\_A_1 \vee \ldots \vee \sim not\_A_n \in \neg\_P$$
$$\Leftrightarrow$$
$$L \leftarrow not\ A_1, \ldots, not\ A_n \in P$$

By definition of acceptable hypotheses, if for every rule

$$L \leftarrow not\ A_1, \ldots, not\ A_n \in P$$

there exists an A_i such that $P \cup H \vdash A_i$, then $not\ L \in Acc(H)$.
Thus:

$$P^* \models_{CIRC} \sim L \Rightarrow not\ L \in Acc(H) \overset{by\ (iii)}{\Rightarrow} not\ L \in H$$

3. By (i) :

$$not\ L \in H \Rightarrow not\ L \in Mand(H)\ or\ not\ L \in Acc(H)$$

If $not\ L \in Mand(H)$ then, by definition of $Mand(H)$:

$$P \cup H \vdash \neg L$$

and, by equality $(eq1)$, $P^* \models \neg\_L$.

If $not\ L \in Acc(H)$ then, by definition of $Acc(H)$, for every rule of the form

$$L \leftarrow not\ A_1, \ldots, not\ A_n \in P$$

there exists an A_i such that $P \cup H \vdash A_i$.
By construction of P^*, if $P \cup H \vdash A_i$ then $\sim not\_A_i \in P^*$. Thus, for every clause

$$LV \sim not\_A_1 \vee \ldots \vee \sim not\_A_n \in \neg\_P$$

there exists $\sim not\_A_i \in P^*$, and by lemma C.0.1, $P^* \models_{CIRC} \sim L$.

- Let us assume that P^* is an expansion, i.e.

$$P^* = \neg\_P \cup \left\{ not\_L \mid P^* \models_{CIRC} \sim L\ or\ P^* \models \neg\_L \right\} \cup \{ \sim not\ L \mid P^* \models L \}$$

We prove now that

$$P \cup \left\{ not\ L \mid P^* \models_{CIRC} \sim L\ or\ P^* \models \neg\_L \right\}$$

is a complete scenario, i.e. by making

$$H = \left\{ not\ L \mid P^* \models_{CIRC} \sim L\ or\ P^* \models \neg\_L \right\}$$

the above conditions (i), (ii), and (iii) hold.

(i) By definition of H :

$$not\ L \in H \Rightarrow P^* \models_{CIRC} \sim L\ or\ P^* \models \neg\_L$$

Similarly to the proof in point 2 above, it is easy to prove that if $P^* \models_{CIRC} \sim L$ then $not\ L \in Acc(H)$, and that if $P^* \models \neg\_L$ then $not\ L \in Mand(H)$. So:

$$not\ L \in H \Rightarrow not\ L \in Mand(H)\ or\ not\ L \in Acc(H)$$

(ii) By definition of $Mand(H)$:

$$not\ L \in Mand(H) \Rightarrow P \cup H \vdash \neg L$$

Thus there exists a rule in P of the form

$$\neg L \leftarrow not\ A_1, \ldots, not\ A_n$$

such that

$$\{not\ A_1, \ldots, not\ A_n\} \subseteq H$$

So, by definition of H and given that P^* is an expansion, there is a clause in $\neg\_P$ of the form

$$\neg\_L \vee \sim not\_A_1 \vee \ldots \vee \sim not\_A_n$$

such that

$$\{not\_A_1, \ldots, not\_A_n\} \subseteq P^*$$

and clearly $P^* \models \neg\_L$. Thus, by definition of H, $not\ L \in H$.

(iii) If $not\ L \in Acc(H)$ then, by definition of $Acc(H)$, for every rule of the form

$$L \leftarrow not\ A_1, \ldots, not\ A_n \in P$$

there exists an A_i such that $P \cup H \vdash A_i$.

If $P \cup H \vdash A_i$ for some A_i, then there is a rule in P of the form

$$A_i \leftarrow not\ B_1, \ldots, not\ B_m$$

such that

$$\{not\ B_1, \ldots, not\ B_m\} \subseteq H$$

Thus, by definition of H and given that P^* is an expansion, there is a clause in $\neg\_P$ of the form

$$A_i \vee \sim not\_B_1 \vee \ldots \vee \sim not\_B_m$$

such that

$$\{not\_B_1, \ldots, not\_B_m\} \subseteq P^*$$

So $P^* \models A_i$ and, because it is an expansion, $\sim not\_A_i \in P^*$.
According to lemma C.0.1, $P^* \models_{CIRC} \sim L$ and, by definition of H, $not\ L \in H$.

Proof of proposition 6.4.1: We begin by proving a lemma:

Lemma C.0.2. *For every noncontradictory default theory Δ, and any context E of Δ:*

$$\Gamma'_{\Delta^s}(E) \subseteq \Gamma'_\Delta(E)$$

Proof. In Δ^s every default rule has more literals in the justifications than the corresponding rule in Δ. Thus for every context E, in Δ^s less rules are applicable, and so $\Gamma'_{\Delta^s}(E) \subseteq \Gamma'_\Delta(E)$.

Now we prove separately each of the points in the proposition:

1. Let S be the least fixpoint of $\Gamma'_{\Delta^s}\Gamma'_\Delta$.
   By lemma C.0.2:

   $$\Gamma'_\Delta(S) \supseteq \Gamma'_{\Delta^s}(S)$$

   By the antimonotonicity of Γ'_{Δ^s} (lemma 6.3.2):

   $$\Gamma'_{\Delta^s}(\Gamma'_\Delta(S)) \subseteq \Gamma'_{\Delta^s}(\Gamma'_{\Delta^s}(S))$$

   i.e., given that S is by its definition a fixpoint of $\Gamma'_{\Delta^s}\Gamma'_\Delta$:

   $$S \subseteq \Gamma'^2_{\Delta^s}(S)$$

   So:

   $$lfp(\Gamma'_{\Delta^s}\Gamma'_\Delta) \subseteq \Gamma'^2_{\Delta^s}(lfp(\Gamma'_{\Delta^s}\Gamma'_\Delta))$$

   i.e. the least fixpoint of $\Gamma'_{\Delta^s}\Gamma'_\Delta$ is a pre-fixpoint of $\Gamma'^2_{\Delta^s}$, and thus by the properties of monotonic operators:

   $$lfp(\Gamma'_{\Delta^s}\Gamma'_\Delta) \subseteq lfp(\Gamma'^2_{\Delta^s})$$

2. Again let S be the least fixpoint of $\Gamma'_{\Delta^s}\Gamma'_\Delta$, and let $GS = \Gamma'_\Delta(S)$.
   By lemma C.0.2:

   $$\Gamma'_{\Delta^s}(GS) \subseteq \Gamma'_\Delta(GS)$$

   i.e., by the definition of GS :

   $$\Gamma'_{\Delta^s}(\Gamma'_\Delta(S)) \subseteq \Gamma'_\Delta(\Gamma'_\Delta(S))$$

   So:

   $$lfp(\Gamma'_{\Delta^s}\Gamma'_\Delta) \subseteq \Gamma'^2_\Delta(lfp(\Gamma'_{\Delta^s}\Gamma'_\Delta))$$

   i.e. the least fixpoint of $\Gamma'_{\Delta^s}\Gamma'_\Delta$ is a pre-fixpoint of Γ'^2_Δ.
3. Now let S be the least fixpoint of $\Gamma'^2_{\Delta^s}$, and let $GS = \Gamma'_{\Delta^s}(S)$.
   By lemma C.0.2:

   $$\Gamma'_{\Delta^s}(GS) \subseteq \Gamma'_\Delta(GS)$$

   i.e., by the definition of GS :

   $$\Gamma'_{\Delta^s}(\Gamma'_{\Delta^s}(S)) \subseteq \Gamma'_\Delta(\Gamma'_{\Delta^s}(S))$$

So:

$$lfp(\Gamma_{\Delta^s}'^2) \subseteq \Omega(lfp(\Gamma_{\Delta^s}'^2))$$

i.e. the least fixpoint of $\Gamma_{\Delta^s}'^2$ is a pre-fixpoint of Ω.

4. Finally, let S be the least fixpoint of $\Gamma_{\Delta}'^2$.
   By lemma C.0.2:

$$\Gamma_{\Delta}'(S) \supseteq \Gamma_{\Delta^s}'(S)$$

By the antimonotonicity of Γ_{Δ}' (lemma 6.3.2):

$$\Gamma_{\Delta}'(\Gamma_{\Delta}'(S)) \subseteq \Gamma_{\Delta}'(\Gamma_{\Delta^s}'(S))$$

i.e., given that S is by its definition a fixpoint of $\Gamma_{\Delta}'^2$:

$$S \subseteq \Omega(S)$$

So:

$$lfp(\Gamma_{\Delta}'^2) \subseteq \Omega(lfp(\Gamma_{\Delta}'^2))$$

i.e. the least fixpoint of $\Gamma_{\Delta}'^2$ is a pre-fixpoint of Ω.

Proof of Theorem 6.6.1: We begin by stating some propositions useful in the sequel.

Proposition C.0.1. *Let $\Delta = (D, \{\})$ be a default theory and E a context such that $\Gamma_{\Delta}'(E)$ is noncontradictory. Then:*

$$L \in \Gamma_{\Delta}'(E) \Leftrightarrow \exists \frac{\{b_1, \ldots, b_n\} : \{c_1, \ldots, c_m\}}{L} \in D, \ \forall i, j \ b_i \in \Gamma_{\Delta}'(E) \wedge \neg c_j \notin E$$

Proof. It is easy to see that under these conditions $\Gamma_{\Delta}'(E) = \Gamma_{\Delta}(E)$. Thus the proof follows from properties of the Γ_{Δ} operator.

Proposition C.0.2. *Let E be an extension of a default theory $\Delta = (D, \{\})$. Then:*

$$L \in \Omega(E) \Leftrightarrow \exists \frac{\{b_1, \ldots, b_n\} : \{\neg c_1, \ldots, \neg c_m\}}{L} \in D \text{ such that}$$
$$\forall i, j, \ b_i \in E \wedge b_i \in \Gamma_{\Delta^s}'(E) \wedge c_j \notin \Gamma_{\Delta^s}'(E).$$

Proof. By definition of Γ_{Δ}', and given that $W = \{\}$, it follows from proposition C.0.1 that for $L \in \Omega(E)$ there must exist at least one default in D applied in the second step, i.e. with all prerequesites in $\Omega(E)$ and all negations of justifications not in $\Gamma_{\Delta^s}'(E)$. By hypothesis E is an extension; thus $E = \Omega(E)$ and $E \subseteq \Gamma_{\Delta^s}'(E)$; so for such a rule all prerequesites are in E and in $\Gamma_{\Delta^s}'(E)$, and all negations of justifications are not in $\Gamma_{\Delta^s}'(E)$.

Proposition C.0.3. *Let E be an extension of a default theory $\Delta = (D, \{\})$. Then:*

$$L \notin E \Rightarrow \forall \frac{\{b_1,...,b_n\} \;:\; \{\neg c_1,...,\neg c_m\}}{L} \in D, \; \exists i,j, \; b_i \notin E \lor c_j \in \Gamma'_{\Delta^s}(E)$$

Proof. If $L \notin E$ then, given that E is an extension, $L \notin \Omega_\Delta(E)$. Thus no default rule for L is applicable in the second step, i.e. given that $W = \{\}$, and by proposition C.0.1, no rule with conclusion L is such that all its prerequisites are in $\Omega_\Delta(E)$ and no negation of a justification is in $\Gamma'_{\Delta^s}(E)$.

Proposition C.0.4. *Let E be an extension of a default theory $\Delta = (D, \{\})$. Then:*

$$L \notin \Gamma'_{\Delta^s}(E) \Leftrightarrow \forall \frac{\{b_1,...,b_n\} \;:\; \{\neg c_1,...,\neg c_m\}}{L} \in D,$$

$$\exists i,j, \; b_i \notin \Gamma'_{\Delta^s}(E) \lor c_j \in E \lor \neg L \in E$$

Proof. Similar to the proof of C.0.3 but now applied to the first step, which imposes the use of seminormal defaults. Thus the need for $\neg L \in E$.

We now prove the main theorem:

($\Rightarrow$) E is a Ω-extension of $\Delta \Rightarrow I$ is a PSM of P.

Here we must prove that for any (objective and default) literal F, $F \in I \Leftrightarrow F \in \Phi(I)$. We do this in three parts: for any objective literal L :

1. $L \in I \Rightarrow L \in \Phi(I)$;
2. $L \notin I \Rightarrow L \notin \Phi(I)$;
3. *not* $L \in I \Leftrightarrow$ *not* $L \in \Phi(I)$.

Each of these proofs proceeds by: translating conditions in I into conditions in E via correspondence; finding conditions in Δ given the conditions in E, and the fact that E is an extension; translating conditions in Δ into conditions in P via correspondence; using those conditions in P to determine the result of operator Φ.

1. Since I corresponds to E and E is a Ω-extension:
$$L \in I \Leftrightarrow I(L) = 1 \Rightarrow L \in E \Leftrightarrow L \in \Omega_\Delta(E)$$
By proposition C.0.2:
$$L \in \Omega_\Delta(E) \Leftrightarrow \exists \frac{\{b_1,...,b_n\} \;:\; \{\neg c_1,...,\neg c_m\}}{L} \in D,$$
$$\forall i, b_i \in E \land b_i \in \Gamma'_{\Delta^s}(E) \text{ and}$$
$$\forall j, c_j \notin \Gamma'_{\Delta^s}(E).$$
By translating, via the correspondence definitions, the default and the conditions on E into a rule and conditions on I:
$$L \in E \Rightarrow \exists L \leftarrow b_1,...,b_n, \text{not } c_1,...,c_m \in P,$$
$$\forall i, I(b_i) = 1 \text{ and } \forall j, I(c_j) = 0$$
$$\Rightarrow L \in least\left(\frac{P}{I}\right)$$
by properties of $least\left(\frac{P}{I}\right)$.
Given that the operator Coh does not delete literals from I :
$$L \in I \Rightarrow L \in \Phi(I).$$

2. Since I corresponds to E :
$$L \notin I \Leftrightarrow L \notin E.$$
By proposition C.0.3:
$$L \notin E \Rightarrow \forall \frac{\{b_1, \ldots, b_n\} \; : \; \{\neg c_1, \ldots, \neg c_m\}}{L} \in D$$
where either a $b_i \notin E$ or a $c_j \in \Gamma'_{\Delta^s}(E)$, .
Translating, via the correspondence definitions, the default and the conditions on E into a rule and conditions on I :
$$\begin{aligned} L \notin E \quad &\Rightarrow \quad \forall L \leftarrow b_1, \ldots, b_n, not\ c_1, \ldots, c_m \in P, \\ &\qquad \exists i, j \; I(b_i) \neq 1 \lor I(c_j) \neq 0 \\ &\Rightarrow \quad L \notin least\left(\frac{P}{I}\right) \end{aligned}$$
by properties of $least\left(\frac{P}{I}\right)$.
Given that the operator Coh does not add objective literals to I :
$$L \notin I \Rightarrow L \notin \Phi(I).$$
3. Given that E corresponds to I :
$$not\ L \in I \Leftrightarrow L \notin \Gamma'_{\Delta^s}(E)$$
By proposition C.0.4:
$$L \notin \Gamma'_{\Delta^s}(E) \quad \Leftrightarrow \quad \begin{aligned}&\forall \frac{\{b_1, \ldots, b_n\} \; : \; \{\neg c_1, \ldots, \neg c_m\}}{L} \in D, \\ &\exists i, j \; b_i \notin \Gamma'_{\Delta^s}(E) \lor c_j \in E \lor \neg L \in E\end{aligned}$$
Translating into logic programs:
$$L \notin \Gamma'_{\Delta^s}(E) \quad \Leftrightarrow \quad \begin{aligned}&\forall L \leftarrow b_1, \ldots, b_n, not\ c_1, \ldots, c_m \in P, \\ &(\exists i, j \; I(b_i) = 0 \lor I(c_j) = 1) \lor \neg L \in E.\end{aligned}$$
By properties of the least operator.
$$not\ L \in I \Leftrightarrow not\ L \in least\left(\frac{P}{I}\right) \lor \neg L \in E \quad (*)$$
It was proven before that:
$$\begin{aligned}\neg L \in E \quad &\Leftrightarrow \quad \exists \neg L \leftarrow b_1, \ldots, b_n, not\ c_1, \ldots, not\ c_m \in P, \\ &\qquad \exists i, j \; I(b_i) = 1 \lor I(c_j) = 0.\end{aligned}$$
By properties of $least\frac{P}{I}$:
$$\neg L \in E \Leftrightarrow \neg L \in least\left(\frac{P}{I}\right)$$
Using correspondence, we can simplify the equivalence $(*)$ to:
$$\begin{aligned}not\ L \in I \quad &\Leftrightarrow \quad not\ L \in least\left(\tfrac{P}{I}\right) \lor \neg L \in least\left(\tfrac{P}{I}\right) \Leftrightarrow \\ &\Leftrightarrow \quad not\ L \in \Phi(I)\end{aligned}$$
this last equivalence being due to the definitions of operators Coh and Φ.

$(\Leftarrow)$ I is a PSM of $P \Rightarrow E$ is a Ω-extension of T.

By definition of correspondence between interpretations and contexts, it is easy to see that E is consistent and $E \subseteq \Gamma'_{\Delta^s}(E)$. So we only have to prove that $E = \Omega_\Delta(E)$. We do this by proving that:

$$\forall L \; L \in E \Leftrightarrow L \in \Omega_\Delta(E).$$

By definition of corresponding context:

$$L \in E \Leftrightarrow I(L) = 1$$

Since I is a PSM of P :

$$I(L) = 1 \quad \Leftrightarrow \quad \exists L \leftarrow b_1, \ldots, b_n, not\ c_1, \ldots, not\ c_m \in P,$$
$$\forall i\ I(b_i) = 1\ and\ \forall j\ I(c_j) = 0$$

where $n, m \geq 0$.

By translating, via the correspondence definitions, the rule and the conditions on I into a default and conditions on E:

$$I(L) = 1 \quad \Leftrightarrow \quad \exists \frac{\{b_1, \ldots, b_n\} : \{\neg c_1, \ldots, \neg c_m\}}{L} \in D,$$
$$\forall i\ b_i \in E \wedge b_i \in \Gamma'_{\Delta^s}(E)\ and$$
$$\forall j\ c_j \notin E \wedge c_j \notin \Gamma'_{\Delta^s}(E)$$

Given that such a rule exists under such conditions, it follows easily from proposition C.0.1 that:

$$L \in E \Leftrightarrow L \in \Omega_\Delta(E)$$

Proof of Theorem 7.4.1:

1. Let C be a (possibly infinite) set of complete scenaria, i.e.

$$C \subseteq CS_P \quad \text{and} \quad C \neq \{\}.$$

   Let $C_{\downarrow}$ be the set of all admissible scenaria contained in all scenaria of C, and let S_0 be the union of all elements in $C_{\downarrow}$.
   Since that:

$$\forall S \in C \mid S_0 \subseteq S$$

   it is clear that S_0 is admissible. It remains to prove that S_0 is also complete.
   Let $not\ L$ be a literal acceptable with respect to S_0. Then $S' = S_0 \cup \{not\ L\}$ is again admissible and so, by definition, $S' \in C_{\downarrow}$. Thus $not\ L \in S_0$.
   If $not\ L$ is mandatory with respect to S_0 then, since S_0 is admissible, $not\ L \in S_0$. Thus S_0 is complete.
2. The proof of this point is obvious given the previous one.
3. The program in Example 7.4.1 shows that in general a maximal element might not exist.

Proof of lemma 7.4.3: Without loss of generality (by Theorem 9.1.2) we consider that P is in semantic kernel form, i.e. P is a set of rules of the form:

$$L \leftarrow not\ A_1, \ldots, not\ A_n \quad n \geq 0$$

Let $S = T \cup not\ F$ be a PSM of P, i.e. (according to the equivalent definition of $PSMs$ (Theorem 6.7.1) in Section 6.7):

(i) $T = \Gamma\Gamma_s T$
(ii) $T \subseteq \Gamma_s T$
(iii) $\not\exists L \mid \{L, \neg L\} \subseteq T$

and additionally $F = \{L \mid L \notin \Gamma_s T\}$.
   Let $H = \{not\ L \mid L \notin \Gamma_s T\}$[3]. We prove that $P \cup H$ is a complete scenario, i.e. for all $not\ L$:

1. $not\ L \in H \Rightarrow P \cup H \not\vdash L$
2. $not\ L \in H \Rightarrow not\ L \in Mand(H) \vee not\ L \in Acc(H)$
3. $not\ L \in Mand(H) \Rightarrow not\ L \in H$
4. $not\ L \in Acc(H) \Rightarrow not\ L \in H$

   This proof is accomplished by proving separately each of the conditions above.

---

[3] I.e. $H \equiv not\ F$.

1. By definition of H :

   $not\ L \in H \Leftrightarrow L \notin \Gamma_s T.$

   Given that the P is in the semantic kernel form:

   $L \notin \Gamma_s T \Rightarrow \neg L \in T \vee \forall L \leftarrow not\ A_1, \ldots, not\ A_n \mid \exists A_i \in T$

   Let us assume the first disjunct:

   $\neg L \in T \overset{by\ (iii)}{\Rightarrow} L \notin T \overset{by\ (i)}{\Rightarrow} L \notin \Gamma\Gamma_s T$

   Again because P is in semantic kernel form:

   1st disjunct $\Rightarrow \forall L \leftarrow not\ A_1, \ldots, not\ A_n \mid \exists A_i \in \Gamma_s T$

   By definition of H :

   1st disjunct $\Rightarrow \forall L \leftarrow not\ A_1, \ldots, not\ A_n \mid \exists not\ A_i \notin H$
   $\overset{trivial}{\Rightarrow} P \cup H \not\vdash L$

   Now let us assume the second disjunct. Then:

   $A_i \in T \overset{by\ (ii)}{\Rightarrow} A_i \in \Gamma_s T \overset{by\ def\ of\ H}{\Rightarrow} not\ A_i \notin H$

   Thus:

   2nd disjunct $\Rightarrow \forall L \leftarrow not\ A_1, \ldots, not\ A_n \mid \exists not\ A_i \notin H$
   $\overset{trivial}{\Rightarrow} P \cup H \not\vdash L$

2. As proven at the begining of 1 above:

   $not\ L \in H \Rightarrow \neg L \in T \vee \forall L \leftarrow not\ A_1, \ldots, not\ A_n \mid \exists A_i \in T$

   Let us assume the first disjunct:

   $\neg L \in T \overset{by\ (i)}{\Rightarrow} \neg L \in \Gamma\Gamma_s T$
   $\Rightarrow \exists \neg L \leftarrow not\ B_1, \ldots, not\ B_m \mid \forall B_i,\ B_i \notin \Gamma_s T$

   By definition of H, $B_i \notin \Gamma_s T \Rightarrow not\ B_i \in H$. Thus trivially:

   1st disjunct $\Rightarrow P \cup H \vdash \neg L \overset{by\ def\ of\ Mand(H)}{\Rightarrow} not\ L \in Mand(H)$

   Now let us assume the second disjunct:

   $A_i \in T \overset{by\ (i)}{\Rightarrow} A_i \in \Gamma\Gamma_s T$

   2nd disjunct $\Rightarrow \exists A_i \leftarrow not\ C_1, \ldots, not\ C_k \mid$
   $\forall C_j,\ C_j \notin \Gamma_s T \Rightarrow P \cup H \vdash A_i$

   Thus the second disjunct implies:

   $\forall L \leftarrow not\ A_1, \ldots, not\ A_n \mid \exists A_i,\ P \cup H \vdash A_i$
   $\overset{by\ def\ of\ Acc(H)}{\Rightarrow} not\ L \in Acc(H)$

3. By definition of $Mand(H)$:

$$not\ L \in Mand(H) \Rightarrow$$
$$\Rightarrow \exists\neg L \leftarrow not\ A_1,\ldots, not\ A_n \mid \forall not\ A_i,\ not\ A_i \in H$$

By definition of H, $not\ A_i \in H \Leftrightarrow A_i \notin \Gamma_s T$. Thus:

$$\text{hyp.} \quad \Rightarrow \quad \neg L \in \Gamma\Gamma_s T \overset{by\ (i)}{\Rightarrow} \neg L \in T$$
$$\underset{\text{by seminormallity}}{\Rightarrow} \quad L \notin \Gamma_s T \Leftrightarrow not\ L \in H$$

4. By definition of $Acc(H)$:

$$not\ L \in Acc(H) \Rightarrow \forall L \leftarrow not\ A_1,\ldots, not\ A_n \mid \exists A_i,\ P \cup H \vdash A_i.$$

Now:

$$P \cup H \vdash A_i \Rightarrow \exists A_i \leftarrow not\ B_1,\ldots, not\ B_m \mid \forall not\ B_j,\ not\ B_j \in H$$

By definition of H :

$$not\ B_j \in H \Rightarrow B_j \in \Gamma_s T$$

Thus $A_i \in \Gamma\Gamma_s T$, and by (i) $A_i \in T$. So:

$$not\ L \in Acc(H) \Rightarrow \forall l \leftarrow not\ A_1,\ldots, not\ A_n \mid \exists not\ A_i,\ A_i \in T \Rightarrow$$
$$\Rightarrow L \notin \Gamma_s T \Rightarrow not\ L \in H$$

Proof of lemma 7.4.4: Given that $P \cup H$ is a complete scenario then, for all $not\ L$:

(i) $not\ L \in H \Rightarrow P \cup H \nvdash \neg L$
(ii) $not\ L \in H \Rightarrow not\ L \in Mand(H) \vee not\ L \in Acc(H)$
(iii) $not\ L \in Mand(H) \Rightarrow not\ L \in H$
(iv) $not\ L \in Acc(H) \Rightarrow not\ L \in H$

Let $S = \{L \mid P \cup H \vdash L\}$. According to Theorem 6.7.1 we must prove that:

1. $\forall L \mid L \in S \Rightarrow \neg L \notin S$
2. $S \subseteq \Gamma_s S$
3. $S = \Gamma\Gamma_s S$
4. $H = \{not\ L \mid L \notin \Gamma_s S\}$

In order to prove this lemma we begin by proving that

$$\Gamma_s S = \{L \mid not\ L \notin H\} \tag{C.1}$$

This is achieved by proving (where $U = \{L \mid not\ L \notin H\}$):

(a) $\forall L \mid L \notin \Gamma_s S \Rightarrow L \notin U$
(b) $\forall L \mid L \notin U \Rightarrow L \notin \Gamma_s S$

(a) By definition of Γ_s :

$$L \notin \Gamma_s S \Rightarrow \neg L \in S \vee \forall L \leftarrow not\ A_1, \ldots, not\ A_n \mid \exists A_i \in S$$

We prove that both disjuncts imply $L \notin U$:

$$\neg L \in S \overset{def\ of\ S}{\Rightarrow} P \cup H \vdash \neg L \overset{def\ of\ Mand(H)}{\Rightarrow} not\ L \in Mand(H)$$

Since $P \cup H$ is a complete scenario:

$$not\ L \in Mand(H) \Rightarrow not\ L \in H \overset{def\ of\ U}{\Rightarrow} L \notin U$$

Since:

$$A_i \in S \overset{def\ of\ S}{\Rightarrow} P \cup H \vdash A_i$$

the second disjunct implies:

$$\forall L \leftarrow not\ A_1, \ldots, not\ A_n \mid \exists A_i,\ P \cup H \vdash A_i$$
$$\overset{def\ of\ Acc(H)}{\Rightarrow} not\ L \in Acc(H)$$

Given that $P \cup H$ is a complete scenario:

$$not\ L \in Acc(H) \Rightarrow not\ L \in H \Leftrightarrow L \notin H$$

(b) By definition of U :

$$L \notin U \Leftrightarrow not\ L \in H$$

Since H is complete scenario then by (ii):

$$L \notin U \Rightarrow P \cup H \vdash \neg L \vee$$
$$\forall L \leftarrow not\ A_1, \ldots, not\ A_n \mid \exists A_i,\ P \cup H \vdash A_i$$

Both disjuncts lead to the conclusion that $L \notin \Gamma_s S$:

$$-\ P \cup H \vdash \neg L \overset{def\ of\ S}{\Rightarrow} \neg L \in S \overset{by\ seminormallity}{\Rightarrow} L \notin \Gamma_s S$$
$$-\ P \cup H \vdash A_i \overset{def\ of\ S}{\Rightarrow} A_i \in S \Rightarrow L \notin \Gamma_s S$$

Now we prove the four points above:

1. Trivial because $P \cup H$ is a consistent scenario.
2. Since $\Gamma_s S = U$, we have to prove that:

$$S = \{L \mid P \cup H \vdash L\} \subseteq \{L \mid not\ L \notin H\} = \Gamma_s S$$

which is also trivial because $P \cup H$ is a consistent scenario.
3. The proof of this point is divided into two parts.
   a) $\forall L \mid L \notin \Gamma\Gamma_s S \Rightarrow L \notin S$, i.e. $S \subseteq \Gamma\Gamma_s S$.
$$L \notin \Gamma\Gamma_s S \Rightarrow \forall L \leftarrow not\ A_1, \ldots, not\ A_n \mid \exists A_i \in \Gamma_s S$$
   If $A_i \in \Gamma_s S$ then by equivalence (C.1) above $not\ A_i \notin H$. Thus:
$$\forall L \leftarrow not\ A_1, \ldots, not\ A_n \mid \exists not\ A_i \notin H \Rightarrow P \cup H \not\vdash L$$
$$\overset{def\ of\ S}{\Rightarrow} L \notin S$$

b) $\forall L \mid L \in \Gamma\Gamma_s S \Rightarrow L \in S$, i.e. $S \supseteq \Gamma\Gamma_s S$. Thus:
$$L \in \Gamma\Gamma_s S \Rightarrow \exists L \leftarrow not\ A_1, \dots, not\ A_n \mid \forall A_i\ A_i \notin \Gamma_s S$$
If $A_i \notin \Gamma_s S$ then by equivalence (C.1) above $not\ A_i \in H$. Thus:
$$\exists L \leftarrow not\ A_1, \dots, not\ A_n \mid \forall not\ A_i,\ not\ A_i \in H$$
$$\Rightarrow P \cup H \vdash L \overset{\text{def of S}}{\Rightarrow} L \in S$$

4. From equation C.1, for every objective literal L :

$$L \in \Gamma_s S \Leftrightarrow not\ L \notin H$$

or equivalently:

$$L \notin \Gamma_s S \Leftrightarrow not\ L \in H$$

i.e.

$$H = \{not\ L \mid L \notin \Gamma_s S\}$$

Proof of Theorem 9.1.3:

Let P be an extended logic program and let P' be the program obtain from P by replacing the rule r of P

$$H \leftarrow B_1, \ldots, B_n, not\ C_1, \ldots, not\ C_m$$

by the rule r' :

$$H \leftarrow not\ \neg B_1, B_1, \ldots, B_n, not\ C_1, \ldots, not\ C_m$$

We begin by proving that if M is a PSM of P, and B_1 and $\neg B_1$ are not both undefined in M^4 then $\frac{P}{M} = \frac{P'}{M}{}^5$. Since the modulo transformation is made rule by rule, and $P - r = P' - r'$, to prove that it is enough to show that $\frac{r}{M} = \frac{r'}{M}$.

Assume that M is a PSM of P. Then:

- If $B_1 \in M$ then, since M is a PSM and thus also an interpretation, $not\ \neg B_1 \in M$, and so the default literal $not\ \neg B_1$ is deleted from r' in $\frac{r'}{M}$. Thus, trivially, $\frac{r'}{M} = \frac{r}{M}$.
- If $\neg B_1 \in M$, then it is clear that the rule is deleted in both cases, and so $\frac{r}{M} = \frac{r'}{M} = \{\}$.
- If $not\ B_1 \in M$ then both rules again are deleted.
- If $not\ \neg B_1 \in M$ then the literal is deleted from r', and so $\frac{r'}{M} = \frac{r}{M}$.
- Since we are assuming that B_1 and $\neg B_1$ are not both undefined in M, no other case can occur.

So for these cases:

$$M = Coh\left(least\left(\frac{P}{M}\right)\right) \quad \Rightarrow \quad M = Coh\left(least\left(\frac{P'}{M}\right)\right)$$

i.e. M is a PSM of P'.

Now let M be a PSM of P', such that:

$$M \cap \{B_1, \neg B_1, not\ B_1, not\ \neg B_1\} = \{\}$$

If the rule r is deleted in $\frac{P}{M}$, then it is clear that r' is also deleted in $\frac{P'}{M}$, and so $\frac{P}{M} = \frac{P'}{M}$. Thus we are in a similar situation as the one before, and M is a PSM of P.

Otherwise let:

$$\frac{r}{M} = H \leftarrow B_1, \ldots, B_n, not\ C_i, \ldots, not\ C_j$$

where $\{not\ C_i, \ldots, not\ C_j\} \subseteq \{not\ C_1, \ldots, not\ C_m\}$. Then:

$$\frac{r'}{M} = H \leftarrow \mathbf{u}, B_1, \ldots, B_n, not\ C_i, \ldots, not\ C_j$$

---

[4] I.e. $M \cap \{B_1, \neg B_1, not\ B_1, not\ \neg B_1\} \neq \{\}$.

[5] Where $\frac{P}{M}$ is as in Definition 4.2.1.

From the definition of the *least* operator, and the hypothesis that B_1 is undefined in M, it is clear that the rule $\frac{r}{M}$ does not provide a way of proving H in $\frac{P}{M}$ and *not* H does not belong to $least\left(\frac{P}{M}\right)$.

Since **u** is in the body of $\frac{r'}{M}$ the same happens in $\frac{P'}{M}$.

From this result it follows trivially that also in this case M is a PSM of P'. So in every case, if M is a PSM of P it is also a PSM of P'.

The proof that if M is a PSM of P' it is also a PSM of P, is quite similar and is omitted for brevity.

The proof that "P is contradictory iff P' is contradictory" follows directly from the proof above. Note that the statement is equivalent to "P is noncontradictory iff P' is noncontradictory".

If P is noncontradictory then it has at least one PSM. Let M be one PSM of P. Then, as proven above, M is also a PSM of P', i.e. P' is noncontradictory. Similarly, if P' is noncontradictory P is also noncontradictory.

Proof of Theorem 12.1.1: In order to prove the soudness theorem of the two-valued contradiction removal algorithm we need to state and prove four lemmas.

Lemma C.0.3. *Let A be a set of assumptions. If $SubM(A)$ is contradictory and $P \cup A$ is not revisable then for any set of assumptions B such that $A \subseteq B$, B is not a revision.*

Proof. If $P \cup A$ is not revisable then contradiction is not supported in any assumption. So, adding any other assumption can not remove it.

Lemma C.0.4. *Let P be a program and C a proper subset of a contradiction removal set of P. Then $P \cup C \vdash \perp$.*

Proof. This lemma is a direct result of the properties of contradiction removal sets.

Lemma C.0.5. *Let A and B be two sets of assumptions with $A \subseteq B$ of a program P. If $SubM(A)$ is contradictory and $SubM(B)$ is noncontradictory then there exists a non-empty contradiction removal set C of $P \cup A$ such that:*

$$A \cup not\ C \subseteq B$$

Proof. If A is contradictory then it must be revisable because, otherwise, since $A \subseteq B$, lemma C.0.3 would be contradicted. So $P \cup A$ has contradiction removal sets.

The contradiction removal sets are minimal sets of default literals which must not be false in order for $P \cup A$ to be noncontradictory, by lemma C.0.4. These sets, if the program is revisable, are non-empty.

The $CRSs$ of a program are used in three-valued contradiction removal semantics to eliminate the support of contradiction by making these literals undefined by adding for each such literal L the inhibition rule $L \leftarrow not\ L$.

The set B is obtained by adding to A sets of assumptions. Since B is noncontradictory it must contain at least the literals in a contradiction removal set in order to be able to remove the contradiction of $P \cup A$.

Lemma C.0.6. *Let B be a revision of a program P. Then:*

$$\forall_i : i \geq 0, \exists_A \mid A \in SS_i \text{ and } A \subseteq B$$

with SS_i the value of the variable with the same name in algorithm 12.1.5.

Proof. The proof is by induction on i.

$- i = 0$

$SS_0 = \{\{\}\}$ then the only A that can verify the condition is the empty set. Then, if B is a revision

$$\{\} \subseteq B \Rightarrow A \subseteq B$$

- **Induction step:** $P(i) \Rightarrow P(i+1)$

  With $P(i) = [B$ is a revision $\Rightarrow \exists_A : A \in SS_i$ and $A \subseteq B]$.

  Assume that $P(i)$ is true. Let A be a set belonging to SS_i such that $A \subseteq B$. This set exists by hypothesis. There are only two cases:

  1. If A is a revision algorithm 12.1.5 adds A to SS_{i+1}, therefore $P(i+1)$ is true.

  2. If A is not a revision then by lemma C.0.5 there exists a CRS such that $A \cup not\ C \subseteq B$. The algorithm adds to SS_{i+1} the union of A with each of the $CRSs$ of $P \cup A$ so, by lemma C.0.4, $\exists_{A'} : A' \in SS_{i+1}$ and $A' \subseteq B$, i.e. $P(i+1)$ is true.

Now, if we retain only the minimal sets of SS_{i+1} property $P(i+1)$ continues to hold.

Next we prove the soundness of algorithm 12.1.5.

First case, SS_i is non-empty. In this case in iteration i the algorithm didn't add or remove any set of assumptions from SS_i. This means that all the sets of assumptions with respect to R belonging to SS_i are revisions (if one of these sets is not a revision the algorithm either adds new sets of assumptions or it removes the set from SS_{i-1}). But if all the sets of assumptions SS_i are revisions they must be minimal by lemma C.0.6.

To complete the proof of this case we must guarantee that AS_i contains all the minimal revisions. Suppose that A is a minimal revision that doesn't belong to SS_i. By lemma C.0.6,

$$\exists_{A'} \mid A' \in AS_i \text{ and } A' \subseteq A \text{ and } A' \neq A$$

But then A is not minimal. Contradiction, thus A must be in SS_i.

Second case, SS_i is empty. We are going to prove that SS_i is empty iff P has no revisions. It's necessary to show that if SS_i is empty then P has no revisions and vice-versa.

The first implication is equivalent to

"if P has a revision then AS_i is not empty".

This was already proven because if there are revisions then there are minimal revisions.

Now we must prove that if P has no revisions then SS_i is empty. If P has no revisions then, for all A which is a set of assumptions of P, $SubM(A)$ is contradictory. In each step of algorithm 12.1.5 only sets of assumptions are kept for which $P \cup A$ is either noncontradictory or has three-valued revisions. By hypothesis, the algorithm has terminated, therefore $SS_i = SS_{i-1}$. But this is only possible if:

$$SS_i = SS_{i-1} = \{\}$$

Suppose that SS_{i-1} is non-empty, then let A be a set of assumptions such that $A \in SS_{i-1}$, implying that $A \in SS_i$. But if $A \in SS_{i-1}$ it cannot belong to SS_i because $P \cup A$ either has non-empty $CRSs$ and the algorithm adds to SS_{i-1} the new sets of assumptions $A \cup not\ C$ for each CRS of $P \cup A$, which are different from A, or removes A from SS_i because $P \cup A$ is not revisable.

Proof of Theorem 12.1.2: If the set of revisables is finite then the set of possible revisions is also finite.

Notice that in each step of algorithm 12.1.5, either at least a new assumption is added to each contradictory set of assumptions belonging to SS_i or the set of assumptions is removed from SS_i or kept there because it is noncontradictory.

The only case of interest is the first one, when new sets of assumptions are added to SS_i. Now, if there is a finite number of revisions the algorithm can add new assumptions to the existing sets only a finite number of times. Thus, algorithm 12.1.5 must terminate after a finite number of steps, in the worst-case after n iterations, with n being the number of possible assumptions.

Springer-Verlag
and the Environment

We at Springer-Verlag firmly believe that an international science publisher has a special obligation to the environment, and our corporate policies consistently reflect this conviction.

We also expect our business partners – paper mills, printers, packaging manufacturers, etc. – to commit themselves to using environmentally friendly materials and production processes.

The paper in this book is made from low- or no-chlorine pulp and is acid free, in conformance with international standards for paper permanency.

Lecture Notes in Artificial Intelligence, Vol. 1111

J.J. Alferes, L. Moniz Pereira
Reasoning with Logic Programming
ISBN 3-540-61488-5

Errata

- *Page 22, Example 2.2.1:*

$$eligible(X) \leftarrow minority(X), = highGPA(X)$$

should be

$$eligible(X) \leftarrow minority(X), fairGPA(X).$$

= The ground version of the program, in page 23, should be modified = accordingly.

- *Page 136, Example 8.2.5: not bs* is missing in both = avoidance sets.

- *Page 153:* $M = 3D\{\neg a, not\ a, not\ p(0)\}$ should be $M == 3D\{\neg a, not\ a\}$.

- *Page 160, Example 8.3.16: Ind(\{not\ a\})* should be $\{not\ = a, not\ b\}$.

- *Page 160, Example 8.3.17: not b* is missing in RS_2.

Lecture Notes in Artificial Intelligence (LNAI)

.Vol. 957: C. Castelfranchi, J.-P. Müller (Eds.), From Reaction to Cognition. Proceedings, 1993. VI, 252 pages. 1995.

Vol. 961: K.P. Jantke. S. Lange (Eds.), Algorithmic Learning for Knowledge-Based Systems. X, 511 pages. 1995.

Vol. 981: I. Wachsmuth, C.-R. Rollinger, W. Brauer (Eds.), KI-95: Advances in Artificial Intelligence. Proceedings, 1995. XII, 269 pages. 1995.

Vol. 984: J.-M. Haton, M. Keane, M. Manago (Eds.), Advances in Case-Based Reasoning. Proceedings, 1994. VIII, 307 pages. 1995.

Vol. 990: C. Pinto-Ferreira, N.J. Mamede (Eds.), Progress in Artificial Intelligence. Proceedings, 1995. XIV, 487 pages. 1995.

Vol. 991: J. Wainer, A. Carvalho (Eds.), Advances in Artificial Intelligence. Proceedings, 1995. XII, 342 pages. 1995.

Vol. 992: M. Gori, G. Soda (Eds.), Topics in Artificial Intelligence. Proceedings, 1995. XII, 451 pages. 1995.

Vol. 997: K. P. Jantke, T. Shinohara, T. Zeugmann (Eds.), Algorithmic Learning Theory. Proceedings, 1995. XV, 319 pages. 1995.

Vol. 1003: P. Pandurang Nayak, Automated Modeling of Physical Systems. XXI, 232 pages. 1995.

Vol. 1010: M. Veloso, A. Aamodt (Eds.), Case-Based Reasoning Research and Development. Proceedings, 1995. X, 576 pages. 1995.

Vol. 1011: T. Furuhashi (Ed.), Advances in Fuzzy Logic, Neural Networks and Genetic Algorithms. Proceedings, 1994. VIII, 223 pages. 1995.

Vol. 1020: I. D. Watson (Ed.), Progress in Case-Based Reasoning. Proceedings, 1995. VIII, 209 pages. 1995.

Vol. 1036: G. Adorni, M. Zock (Eds.), Trends in Natural Language Generation. Proceedings, 1993. IX, 382 pages. 1996.

Vol. 1037: M. Wooldridge, J.P. Müller, M. Tambe (Eds.), Intelligent Agents II. Proceedings, 1995. XVI, 437 pages, 1996.

Vol. 1038: W. Van de Velde, J.W. Perram (Eds.), Agents Breaking Away. Proceedings, 1996. XIV, 232 pages, 1996.

Vol. 1040: S. Wermter, E. Riloff, G. Scheler (Eds.), Connectionist, Statistical, and Symbolic Approaches to Learning for Natural Language Processing. IX, 468 pages. 1996.

Vol. 1042: G. Weiß, S. Sen (Eds.), Adaption and Learning in Multi-Agent Systems. Proceedings, 1995. X, 238 pages. 1996.

Vol. 1047: E. Hajnicz, Time Structures. IX, 244 pages. 1996.

Vol. 1050: R. Dyckhoff, H. Herre, P. Schroeder-Heister (Eds.), Extensions of Logic Programming. Proceedings, 1996. VIII, 318 pages. 1996.

Vol. 1053: P. Graf, Term Indexing. XVI, 284 pages. 1996.

Vol. 1056: A. Haddadi, Communication and Cooperation in Agent Systems. XIII, 148 pages. 1996.

Vol. 1069: J.W. Perram, J.-P. Müller (Eds.), Distributed Software Agents and Applications. Proceedings, 1994. VIII, 219 pages. 1996.

Vol. 1071: P. Miglioli, U. Moscato, D. Mundici, M. Ornaghi (Eds.), Theorem Proving with Analytic Tableaux and Related Methods. Proceedings, 1996. X, 330 pages. 1996.

Vol. 1076: N. Shadbolt, K. O'Hara, G. Schreiber (Eds.), Advances in Knowledge Acquisition. Proceedings, 1996. XII, 371 pages. 1996.

Vol. 1079: Z. W. Raś, M. Michalewicz (Eds.), Foundations of Intelligent Systems. Proceedings, 1996. XI, 664 pages. 1996.

Vol. 1081: G. McCalla (Ed.), Advances in Artificial Intelligence. Proceedings, 1996. XII, 459 pages. 1996.

Vol. 1082: N.R. Adam, B.K. Bhargava, M. Halem, Y. Yesha (Eds.), Digital Libraries. Proceedings, 1995. Approx. 310 pages. 1996.

Vol. 1083: K. Sparck Jones, J.R. Galliers, Evaluating Natural Language Processing Systems. XV, 228 pages. 1996.

Vol. 1085: D.M. Gabbay, H.J. Ohlbach (Eds.), Practical Reasoning. Proceedings, 1996. XV, 721 pages. 1996.

Vol. 1087: C. Zhang, D. Lukose (Eds.), Distributed Artificial Intelligence. Proceedings, 1995. VIII, 232 pages. 1996.

Vol. 1093: L. Dorst, M. van Lambalgen, F. Voorbraak (Eds.), Reasoning with Uncertainty in Robotics. Proceedings, 1995. VIII, 387 pages. 1996.

Vol. 1095: W. McCune, R. Padmanabhan, Automated Deduction in Equational Logic and Cubic Curves. X, 231 pages. 1996.

Vol. 1104: M.A. McRobbie, J.K. Slaney (Eds.), Automated Deduction – Cade-13. Proceedings, 1996. XV, 764 pages. 1996.

Vol. 1111: J. J. Alferes, L. Moniz Pereira, Reasoning with Logic Programming. XXI, 326 pages. 1996.

Vol. 1114: N. Foo, R. Goebel (Eds.), PRICAI'96: Topics in Artificial Intelligence. Proceedings, 1996. XXI, 658 pages. 1996.

Vol. 1115: P.W. Eklund, G. Ellis, G. Mann (Eds.), Conceptual Structures: Knowledge Representation as Interlingua. Proceedings, 1996. XIII, 321 pages. 1996.

Lecture Notes in Computer Science

Vol. 1083: K. Sparck Jones, J.R. Galliers, Evaluating Natural Language Processing Systems. XV, 228 pages. 1996. (Subseries LNAI).

Vol. 1084: W.H. Cunningham, S.T. McCormick, M. Queyranne (Eds.), Integer Programming and Combinatorial Optimization. Proceedings, 1996. X, 505 pages. 1996.

Vol. 1085: D.M. Gabbay, H.J. Ohlbach (Eds.), Practical Reasoning. Proceedings, 1996. XV, 721 pages. 1996. (Subseries LNAI).

Vol. 1086: C. Frasson, G. Gauthier, A. Lesgold (Eds.), Intelligent Tutoring Systems. Proceedings, 1996. XVII, 688 pages. 1996.

Vol. 1087: C. Zhang, D. Lukose (Eds.), Distributed Artificial Intelliegence. Proceedings, 1995. VIII, 232 pages. 1996. (Subseries LNAI).

Vol. 1088: A. Strohmeier (Ed.), Reliable Software Technologies – Ada-Europe '96. Proceedings, 1996. XI, 513 pages. 1996.

Vol. 1089: G. Ramalingam, Bounded Incremental Computation. XI, 190 pages. 1996.

Vol. 1090: J.-Y. Cai, C.K. Wong (Eds.), Computing and Combinatorics. Proceedings, 1996. X, 421 pages. 1996.

Vol. 1091: J. Billington, W. Reisig (Eds.), Application and Theory of Petri Nets 1996. Proceedings, 1996. VIII, 549 pages. 1996.

Vol. 1092: H. Kleine Büning (Ed.), Computer Science Logic. Proceedings, 1995. VIII, 487 pages. 1996.

Vol. 1093: L. Dorst, M. van Lambalgen, F. Voorbraak (Eds.), Reasoning with Uncertainty in Robotics. Proceedings, 1995. VIII, 387 pages. 1996. (Subseries LNAI).

Vol. 1095: W. McCune, R. Padmanabhan, Automated Deduction in Equational Logic and Cubic Curves. X, 231 pages. 1996. (Subseries LNAI).

Vol. 1096: T. Schäl, Workflow Management Systems for Process Organisations. XII, 200 pages. 1996.

Vol. 1097: R. Karlsson, A. Lingas (Eds.), Algorithm Theory – SWAT '96. Proceedings, 1996. IX, 453 pages. 1996.

Vol. 1098: P. Cointe (Ed.), ECOOP '96 – Object-Oriented Programming. Proceedings, 1996. XI, 502 pages. 1996.

Vol. 1099: F. Meyer auf der Heide, B. Monien (Eds.), Automata, Languages and Programming. Proceedings, 1996. XII, 681 pages. 1996.

Vol. 1100: B. Pfitzmann, Digital Signature Schemes. XVI, 396 pages. 1996.

Vol. 1101: M. Wirsing, M. Nivat (Eds.), Algebraic Methodology and Software Technology. Proceedings, 1996. XII, 641 pages. 1996.

Vol. 1102: R. Alur, T.A. Henzinger (Eds.), Computer Aided Verification. Proceedings, 1996. XII, 472 pages. 1996.

Vol. 1103: H. Ganzinger (Ed.), Rewriting Techniques and Applications. Proceedings, 1996. XI, 437 pages. 1996.

Vol. 1104: M.A. McRobbie, J.K. Slaney (Eds.), Automated Deduction – CADE-13. Proceedings, 1996. XV, 764 pages. 1996. (Subseries LNAI).

Vol. 1105: T.I. Ören, G.J. Klir (Eds.), Computer Aided Systems Theory – CAST '94. Proceedings, 1994. IX, 439 pages. 1996.

Vol. 1106: M. Jampel, E. Freuder, M. Maher (Eds.), Over-Constrained Systems. X, 309 pages. 1996.

Vol. 1107: J.-P. Briot, J.-M. Geib, A. Yonezawa (Eds.), Object-Based Parallel and Distributed Computation. Proceedings, 1995. X, 349 pages. 1996.

Vol. 1108: A. Díaz de Ilarraza Sánchez, I. Fernández de Castro (Eds.), Computer Aided Learning and Instruction in Science and Engineering. Proceedings, 1996. XIV, 480 pages. 1996.

Vol. 1109: N. Koblitz (Ed.), Advances in Cryptology – Crypto '96. Proceedings, 1996. XII, 417 pages. 1996.

Vol. 1111: J.J. Alferes, L. Moniz Pereira, Reasoning with Logic Programming. XXI, 326 pages. 1996. (Subseries LNAI).

Vol. 1112: C. von der Malsburg, W. von Seelen, J.C. Vorbrüggen, B. Sendhoff (Eds.), Artificial Neural Networks – ICANN 96. Proceedings, 1996. XXV, 922 pages. 1996.

Vol. 1113: W. Penczek, A. Szałas (Eds.), Mathematical Foundations of Computer Science 1996. Proceedings, 1996. X, 592 pages. 1996.

Vol. 1114: N. Foo, R. Goebel (Eds.), PRICAI'96: Topics in Artificial Intelligence. Proceedings, 1996. XXI, 658 pages. 1996. (Subseries LNAI).

Vol. 1115: P.W. Eklund, G. Ellis, G. Mann (Eds.), Conceptual Structures: Knowledge REpresentation as Interlingua. Proceedings, 1996. XIII, 321 pages. 1996. (Subseries LNAI):

Vol. 1117: A. Ferreira, J. Rolim, Y. Saad, T. Yang (Eds.), Parallel Algorithms for Irregularly Structured Problems. Proceedings, 1996. IX, 358 pages. 1996.

Vol. 1120: M. Deza, R. Euler, I. Manoussakis (Eds.), Combinatorics and Computer Science. Proceedings, 1995. IX, 415 pages. 1996.